Babygirl, You've Got This!

Babygirl, You've Got This!

Experiences of Black Girls and Women in the English Education System

April-Louise M. Pennant

BLOOMSBURY ACADEMIC
LONDON • NEW YORK • OXFORD • NEW DELHI • SYDNEY

BLOOMSBURY ACADEMIC
Bloomsbury Publishing Plc
50 Bedford Square, London, WC1B 3DP, UK
1385 Broadway, New York, NY 10018, USA
29 Earlsfort Terrace, Dublin 2, Ireland

BLOOMSBURY, BLOOMSBURY ACADEMIC and the Diana logo
are trademarks of Bloomsbury Publishing Plc

First published in Great Britain 2024

Cover design: Adriana Brioso

A catalogue record for this book is available from the British Library.

Library of Congress Cataloging-in-Publication Data

ISBN: HB: 978-1-3502-7900-1
PB: 978-1-3502-7899-8
ePDF: 978-1-3502-7902-5
eBook: 978-1-3502-7901-8

Series: Blackness in Britain

Typeset by Integra Software Services Pvt. Ltd.
Printed and bound in Great Britain

To find out more about our authors and books visit www.bloomsbury.com
and sign up for our newsletters.

Contents

List of Illustrations

Illustrations (Figures 1–8) by Jason Lee, www.jasonmation.co.uk.

List of Tables

Dedication

Baba God, all the glory & honour belongs to you! I will always be grateful for the path you created just for me. My life is a testimony to your greatness.

The stone the builders rejected
has become the cornerstone;
the Lord has done this,
and it is marvellous in our eyes. (Psalm 118.22-23)

For my mummy, Dupe, a.k.a. my motivation and my inspiration. Thank you for your love, protection, patience, sacrifice, wisdom, strength, resilience, empowerment, investment, support, audacity, courage, determination, vision and faith. Thank you for always believing in me, and never abandoning or giving up on me.

For my ancestors who paved the way for me and who walk before, behind and by my side.

For my future babies, may this world be easier and safer for you to navigate when you arrive. *Àṣẹ*.

For every Black girl and woman, I *see* you, I *hear* you, I *feel* you, I *am* you and I cherish *all* of you!

Acknowledgements

My deepest thanks to everyone who supported and encouraged me during the two-year process of writing this book.

A special thank you to the forty-two Black women who participated in my research, Daddy, Felicia, Oluwatobiloba, Sarah, Vanessa, Dr Marilyn Benjamin, Aunty Yana, Whitney, Sara, Samiya, the Economic and Social Research Council (ESRC), Professor Kehinde Andrews, Professor Heidi Safia Mirza, the Bloomsbury Publishing Team, the Anonymous Reviewers, Professor Sin Yi Cheung, Dr Sara Delamont, Dr Dan Burrows, Professor Paul Atkinson, Professor Matt Williams, the School of Social Sciences at Cardiff University, and finally, all the 'builders' who rejected me.

Glossary

Abacha and Ugba Cassava-based dish also known as African salad which originated from the Igbo tribe in Eastern Nigeria

Adinkra 'Adinkra are visual symbols with historical and philosophical significance originally printed on cloth which royals wore to important ceremonies. Originating from the Gyaman people of Ghana and la Côte d'Ivoire, the symbols have assumed global importance and are now found in logos, clothes, furniture, sculpture, earthenware pots, and many others' (See more: https://www.adinkrasymbols.org/)

Bakes Traditional fried snack from Barbados made with flour, sugar, and water, similar to doughnuts

Bariis Traditional Somali rice dish seasoned with various spices and ingredients like raisins, peas, etc.

Cornrows Also known as 'canerows', these are 'a braiding technique where small sections of hair are braided closely against the scalp' (See more: https://www.hairthoughts.net/what-are-cornrows/)

Educational steeplechase Originally a 3,000-metre obstacle race in athletics. In this book, it has been extended and used as an analogy and metaphor- in comparison to other groups who I argue are running a 26-mile marathon with fewer or no barriers. For Black girls and women, they are competing in a 26-mile steeplechase to empahsise the often difficult journeys, marked by the additional obstacles and barriers (anti-Black racism, sexism and classism) they endure. Not to be confused with the steeplechase in horse racing

Elélé/moin moin Black-eyed beans peeled, seasoned and steamed/boiled with other ingredients eaten across Nigeria

Fulani braids 'This look is essentially braids with beads, but the braid patterns used are inspired by the Fulani people – a primarily Muslim, traditionally pastoral ethnic group in Africa that's scattered throughout West Africa and parts of East Africa' (See more: https://un-ruly.com/fulani-braids-with-beads-styles-how-to-everything-need-know/)

Grilled tilapia with shito Type of fish with traditional Ghanaian hot pepper sauce

Halal Means 'permissible' in Arabic and is prepared in line with Islamic law as stated in the Koran

Hilib ari Somali dish which typically contains pieces of seasoned goat meat, boiled and simmered

Hot comb Metal comb which is heated (usually on a stove) and used to straighten kinky, afro-textured hair from the roots to the tip

Jollof Seasoned, tomato based sauce cooked to coat rice, cous-cous, etc. Originates from West Africa

Loc Hairstyle in which afro-textured hair is sectioned and formulated into 'rope-like strands' in various sizes and techniques which eventually 'loc' and grow together (Sandeen 2022)

Plantain A staple side dish in West African, Caribbean and Latin American cuisine, part of the banana family but with different taste. Cannot be eaten raw so often fried, boiled, baked, etc.

Roti Seasoned curried or stewed meat, vegetable or seafood fillings inside a wrap style flatbread eaten across Caribbean but with roots in Trinidad

Saltfish fritters Seasoned saltfish mixed with dough and fried

Single-plaits with extensions Also known as 'box braids' where natural hair is sectioned into small square parts and plaited individually. They 'may be of any width or length, but most women add synthetic or natural hair to the braid for length as well as thickness and fullness'
(See more: https://www.lovetoknow.com/life/style/what-are-box-braids#:~:text=Box%20braids%20are%20individual%20plaits%20that%20are%20usually,for%20length%20as%20well%20as%20thickness%20and%20fullness)

Smiley piercing A piercing on the skin between the upper lip and upper gum

Weave A weave is an artificial or natural hair extension that's fixed into human hair by sewing, gluing or clipping
(See more: https://un-ruly.com/weaves-101-everything-need-know-weaves/)

Abbreviations

BFE Black Feminist Epistemology

BTP Bourdieu's Theory of Practice

CRT Critical Race Theory

GM Global Majority

PW Predominantly White

PGM Predominantly Global Majority

Introduction

Babygirl, You've Got This! is first and foremost an ode to Black girls and women 'who are born into a society of entrenched loathing and contempt for whatever is Black and female', where 'we are strong and enduring [and] we are deeply scarred' (Lorde 1984: 151). It is a book-length 'Letter To My siStars', borrowing from Misha B's empowering song. While I am aware of the many connotations that 'babygirl' has, I use it as an insider, friendly term of endearment, in the same way I use it to address my girlfriends – with love, light, care and excitement! It's also what I call myself at the start of my many self-directed pep talks. Secondly, this book is for those who believe and are proactive in advancing social justice in education and beyond. It will provide alternative narratives, insights and wisdom about a distinct, diverse and powerful group – Black girls and women – and their educational journeys and experiences – which are often largely ignored. The content of this book was researched and written out of a labour of love, determination, discontent, curiosity and deep Overstanding. It centres and makes visible some of our experiences and journeys as Black British girls and women in the English education system. It is a reminder that when no one else sees us – I do, we do – we always have and we always will.

Who's checkin' for Black girls and women?

In 2021, I wrote a paper reflecting on how the intersection of the global Black Lives Matter movement and the global Covid-19 pandemic diminished the plight of Black girls and women – both here and in the US (Pennant 2022). I asked the question, which became part of the title, 'who's checkin' for Black girls and women?' – using Black, street vernacular which, in other words, asked 'who is looking out for Black girls and women?' and 'who cares about Black girls and women?' – apart from ourselves? This question was borne out of frustration, pain and passion as I witnessed, along with the world, the anti-Black state-sanctioned murders of unarmed Black people, and the justified, sustained outrage that was rightly shown when Black boys and men were the victims. On the other hand, I cried when seeing the unjustified, fleeting concern shown to Black girls and women when they were murdered as well. Around the same time, I had also seen several news items rightly raising the initial and disproportionate rates of Black men who were dying from Covid-19, but when I looked closer at the emerging data, I found that Black women were also dying disproportionately too. Once again, I had yet to see any coverage of this fact. This then got me reflecting back to my Ph.D. research where many of the Black British women graduates that I interviewed expressed that throughout their education they often felt like they were carrying what I termed an 'unfair burden of care' (2022: 543) alongside trying to 'succeed'. This, of course is not a novel finding as Black girls and women have been doing this since the beginning of time! Based on all of these observations, statistics and reflections, my paper brought this together in the context of what this means for Black girls and women within the education system, highlighting that these events both illustrate and will only exacerbate their unique, existing experiences as a result of the deeply entrenched anti-Black gendered racism and classism they endure leading them to suffer in silence as argued by Showumni (2017).

My focus on Black[1] *British* girls and women in particular is due to the long absences I found about their experiences, journeys and outcomes in British educational research, particularly in the last twenty-five-plus years. This is despite evidence that consistently shows that, even though as a group they invest heavily in education, this investment is not reflected in their outcomes at different stages when compared to their female peers of other races and ethnicities (Mirza 1992, 2006a, 2006b, 2008; AdvanceHE 2018, 2019, 2020, 2021; Gov.uk 2022a). I am indebted to the US's established body of work about Black girls' and women's educational experiences that I often refer to when looking for current and comprehensive research. However, although the US's Black girls' and women's educational literature shed some collective, relatable experiences – there was always something missing, namely the specificity of the English and wider British context and its legacies that continue to shape and influence the lived experiences of Black British communities, especially Black girls and women.

Additionally, I found that the existing British educational research about Black girls and women, mostly from the 1980s, 1990s and early 2000s, shared themes that were still familiar and I wanted to explore what, if anything, had changed. I was especially inspired by Mirza's 1992 groundbreaking book *Young, Female and Black* which was one of the few substantial studies in England that centred the educational experiences of young, second-generation, Black British Caribbean women at the end of their compulsory schooling. I wanted to build on this study and expand it to include Black British *African* girls,[2] diverse educational experiences and institutions and consider the full educational trajectory – from primary school to (undergraduate) university. In this way, my research explores and seeks to represent the next generation of young Black British women who continue to find ingenious ways to navigate through a complex and unequal education system. The main research question that guided this study was:

What are the educational journeys and experiences of Black British women graduates?

More specifically, my research sought to explore and have a clearer understanding about:

1. The characteristics of the educational journeys of Black British women graduates.
2. The key decisions and choices that have shaped their journeys.
3. The role of the family and extended networks in shaping these educational journeys and experiences.
4. The role of ethnicity, cultural background and social class, along with race and gender in mediating the aspirations, strategies and decision-making of Black British women graduates throughout their educational journeys.

While I interviewed the forty-two Black British women participants between 2016 and 2017 as part of my masters and Ph.D. research, my findings are timely now, as the experiences of Black girls and young women within educational settings have been publicly scrutinized. Such examples of public scrutiny include the case of Child Q – the young Black schoolgirl who was strip-searched in her English secondary school by police officers 'without an Appropriate Adult present and with the knowledge that Child Q was menstruating' (Child Safeguarding Commissioner 2022: 2). This connects to the exploration in Chapter 5 where Black girls and women discuss being positioned as 'unruly' in educational settings. Another example is the case of Ruby Williams – a mixed heritage (Black Caribbean and white) schoolgirl who was excluded from her English school for wearing her hair in an afro, which is the natural way it grows from her head (Virk 2020). The role of hair is an important theme that is discussed in Chapters 1, 3, 4, 5 and 6. I can also point to the statistics that show that Black Caribbean girls in England are twice as likely to be excluded from schools as white girls (Mohdin 2021; Gov.uk 2022c) and that mixed heritage – white and Black Caribbean girls – 'were excluded at three times the rate for white British female pupils during the school year 2020/21' (Agenda Alliance 2022). Notably, the previous examples should be viewed against the backdrop of the 'adultification bias' of Black children in the UK as a whole (and in the US) where they endure 'a persistent and ongoing act of dehumanisation, which explicitly impacts

… and influences how they are safeguarded and protected' (Davis 2022: 5). As I was finalizing this book, the racist incident involving Ngozi Fulani at Buckingham palace in 2022 (Sherine 2022), and the viral video of a fifteen-year-old Black schoolgirl being viciously attacked by a white girl gang outside her Surrey school in 2023 (White 2023) with no one coming to her aid, reminded me why a wider understanding of Black girls and women in England and wider Britain is urgently needed!

So in answer to my question, 'who's checkin' for Black girls and women?' – **I AM!**

However, now, more than ever, we all need to be checkin' for Black girls and women.

Theorizing Black girls' and women's anti-Black gendered racism and classism in the English education system

I should say at the outset that my focus on the English education system reflects the devolved powers and therefore different education systems across the four United Kingdom nations of England, Wales, Scotland and Northern Ireland (Civil Service 2022). Additionally, my focus on Black British[3] girls and women in education should not disregard the experiences of Black British boys or men who have worse educational outcomes and are also subjected to anti-Black gendered racism and classism in the English education system. Rather, this book highlights the ways in which anti-Black gendered racism and classism manifest in Black girl/woman experiences of the English education system, as well as the high costs it takes for some of this group to become 'successful' graduates. In addition, the 'Black woman graduate' focus of this book is not suggesting that every other Global Majority (GM), white working-class or marginalized community in England fully shares in the privileges of upper- and middle-class whiteness. Instead, as will become clearer over the course of this book, I argue that the specificity of anti-Black racism and classism creates uniquely different educational experiences and journeys for Black students as a whole, and, as is the main focus of this book, Black British girls and women. To make sense of Black British women's experiences in my research, I framed them in the following ways.

An intersectional approach

The concept of intersectionality was coined by Crenshaw (1989, 1991) to articulate how Black women experience both racism and sexism. Therefore, their experiences cannot be viewed separately around just race or gender as they both overlap and result in Black women being disadvantaged and excluded from anti-discrimination movements and laws where Feminism advances the interests of white women, and anti-racist movements focus on the needs of Black men. As she argues:

> These problems of exclusion cannot be solved simply by including Black women within an already established analytical structure. Because the intersectional experience is greater than the sum of racism and sexism, any analysis that does not take intersectionality into account cannot sufficiently address the particular manner in which Black women are subordinated.
>
> (Crenshaw 1989: 140)

While it is recognized that intersectionality is not exclusive to Black women, the intersections of anti-Black gendered racism and classism, as will be explained further in Chapter 2, are. In addition, Crenshaw's intersectionality has expanded to include other facets of identity such as class, sexuality, etc. alongside the intersections of race and gender (Davis-Yuval 2015). When doing research about Black women, intersectionality is necessary; as Berger and Guidroz (2010: 1) state, such an approach aids in explaining the 'race-class-gender matrix' in research to 'socially locate' individuals in the context of their lived experiences to 'examine how both formal and informal systems of power are deployed, maintained, and reinforced through axes of race, class and gender'. This helps in exploring the holistic identities of Black British women to understand their individual and collective educational journeys and experiences.

I have drawn on academic work to write this book where I employed an intersectional approach and selected three frameworks to aid in understanding Black women's educational experiences and journeys. These are Black Feminist Epistemology (BFE), Critical Race Theory (CRT), BlackCrit and Bourdieu's Theory of Practice (BTP) which I will briefly explain next. Those interested in the frameworks can look at the Methodological Appendix at the end of this book for more details.

Black Feminist Epistemology[4]

Black Feminist Epistemology (BFE) seeks to centre the lived experiences of Black women by facilitating the production of what is deemed to be specialized knowledge (Collins 1986, 2000; Reynolds 2002). In this way, it disrupts the master narrative defining which knowledge is valued and who is able to produce it (Nadar 2014). When concentrating on the educational journeys and experiences of Black British women, it is important to ground such research within an epistemology which 'reflects the interests and standpoints of its creators', as well as those that are under study (Collins 2000: 251). It is through the use of BFE when studying Black British women that a detailed representation of their lived experiences and journeys within the education system will be illustrated, centring their lived experiences of navigating it.

Critical Race Theory[5]

Critical Race Theory (CRT) originates from Critical Legal Studies which developed in the US from the 1970s. However, it has since expanded both geographically and academically and is currently employed in UK-based research in disciplines such as education, sociology and social policy. Its main focus is on the operation of racism in society and how racial inequalities are perpetuated. More specifically within educational contexts, CRT as a framework 'can be used to deepen understanding of the educational barriers for people of colour, as well as exploring how these barriers are resisted and overcome' (Taylor 2009: 9).

CRT enables the educational journeys and experiences of the Black women to be understood and viewed in ways that centre their racial identities and the role of racism within these. It provides an articulation of how the centrality of racism in society is upheld as well as the unequal power relations based on perceived racial differences that reproduce unequal lived experiences by privileging whiteness. Moreover, as CRT includes the intersections of other forms of subordination in its analysis, this is especially useful when exploring the roles of social class, gender and ethnicity alongside race in the Black women's experiences and journeys. BFE and CRT work hand in hand to centre Black women voices, especially as both challenge Eurocentric epistemologies and instead aim to 'offer a liberatory pedagogy that encourages inquiry, dialogue, and participation from a wide variety of stakeholders' (Taylor 2009: 10).

BlackCrit

When focusing on the distinct nature of anti-Black racism, I also employ literature from the emerging field of BlackCrit – an offshoot of CRT. For scholars in this area, BlackCrit helps to explain precisely 'how Black bodies become marginalised, disregarded, and disdained, even in their highly visible place in celebratory discourses on race and diversity' (Dumas and Ross 2016: 417). Again, while it originates from the US, it aids in articulating the anti-Black racism also experienced by Black British communities in the English education system which is characterized as 'fluid and relentless' and 'as both a structural characteristic of educational systems and an individual element in the ways that people present themselves and their arguments in relation to the dominant tropes of race/racism that are generally accepted at a particular point in time and space' (Gillborn 2018: 67).

Bourdieu's Theory of Practice

Bourdieu's Theory of Practice (BTP) provides a commentary about the operation of whiteness through social class formations and its exclusionary nature while highlighting the tensions between structure and agency as groups and individuals compete for social positions. BTP comprises the concepts of field, habitus and capital.

Field

The distinguished French theorist Bourdieu used the metaphor of field as a way for us all to think about social space. There are different fields which include political, religious, artistic, economic, education, etc. His theory of practice shows how groups and individuals engage in interactions in these fields as they actively compete for positions within predetermined structures. Each field has its own rules which maintain the social arrangement and power relations of individuals and groups operating within them (Bourdieu 1977). These rules allow the powerful groups to classify and name, as well as to conceal the unequal power relations that keep them at an advantage (Bourdieu and Wacquant 2004). In the field of the education system, it results in upper- and middle-class white individuals and groups being able to operate and navigate with ease.

Habitus

As individuals and groups compete in the field, they utilize 'trump cards' in the form of habitus. The habitus is intangible and attributed to the way in which individuals and groups behave, speak as well as their style, knowledge and understandings of the world. In essence, it can also equate to the established ways of 'feeling and thinking' (Bourdieu 1990a: 70). One type of habitus is generated from family socialization where behaviour, knowledge and speech are passed down. Educational institutions also have their own institutional habitus which reflect upper- and middle-class ways of being and where it operates within 'myriad, subtle, yet pervasive ways to invalidate working-class identities' (Reay 1998: 12), along with Black and other racially minoritized identities and, at times, gender.

One's habitus is closely connected to the field because it either does or does not align with the 'rules' of it and influences how individuals operate within it as the habitus is 'a structured body, a body which has incorporated the immanent structures of a world or of a particular sector of that world – a field – and which structures the perception of that world as well as action in that world' (Bourdieu 1998: 81). Due to the structure of the education system then, it is the habitus of upper- and middle-class white groups that are valued and seen as legitimate within the field of education and thus gives students who are racialized as white within those social class groups, an advantage.

Capitals

In terms of capitals, for Bourdieu these can be seen as powerful resources or additional 'trump cards' (Bourdieu and Wacquant 1992). The rules of the particular field controls capital in terms of what forms are valued and by whom (Anderson 2016: 694). Bourdieu's capitals are different to economic capital; they are intangible, additional resources employed within different fields by individuals and groups. It is closely associated with habitus which can determine both the volume of capitals and how they are deployed within the field (Brooker 2002; Rollock et al. 2015).

For Bourdieu, capitals come in the form of cultural (forms of knowledge, communication and values), social (connections and resources which are accrued from membership into certain social networks) and symbolic (power and status) (Bourdieu 1986). These capitals are interrelated, can be converted into each other as well as be accessed through and with economic capital. They are significant because capitals give meaning to the field and for instance, depending on the field, they are utilized in many ways as tools to advance successfully.

Black British women live and move in a world dominated by white, western ideologies which also shape its institutions. Therefore, the theoretical frameworks of CRT and BTP are drawn upon and placed within the overarching context of BFE. It is through CRT and BTP that a sociological perspective is provided to articulate specific elements of the Black women's educational experiences and journeys, namely how race, racism and social class are embedded into the institutional structures of the education system. With the incorporation of intersectionality, it weaves through, as well as brings together, the triad of BFE, CRT and BTP, with the recognition of the holistic identities of Black British women.

Inside the worlds of Black British women graduates: storytelling and composite characters

In the chapters that follow and to complement the frameworks explained above, the reader will find the book uses storytelling to present the women's educational narratives. CRT scholars advocate the importance of using 'voice' or 'naming your reality' in CRT research and storytelling facilitates this by linking 'form and substance in scholarship' (Ladson-Billings 1998: 14). Storytelling is also an important tool in Black Feminist research as it enables Black women 'to comprehend, resist, transform, and heal from patriarchies, racism, and various oppressions to explore uncharted journeys' (Hua 2013: 31). By using every day, imaginary settings like a Black-woman-owned nail shop in Chapter 1 or a hair salon in Chapter 4, I centre and honour the importance of such spaces as sites where Black women, over generations, have spent a great deal of time. These are rare, 'safe' spaces for women, especially Black women, used to converse, express, practice self-care and beautify themselves while exchanging stories. I also include prominent songs by Black women artists from across the diaspora that encouraged me on my own educational journey. These songs resonate with the overall theme of the chapters, further setting the scene and providing additional insights into Black women's lived experiences (see Resources at the end of the book for the full playlist).

These stories are narrated by the composite characters of *Shamari, Eve, Chika, Nia-Elise, Yaa, Hamda* and *Hodan* who are a blend of the forty-two Black British women interviewed over the course of my masters and Ph.D. research (see the Methodological Appendix on p.240 for more details). Creating and using composite characters assists in bringing the stories of Black women graduates to life by embodying and weaving together collective themes of anti-Black gendered racism and classism, resilience, wisdom, pain and power, but also individual educational stories of the participants 'to render visible the structures, mechanisms, and ideologies in systems that maintain white domination and oppression' (Cook and Bryan 2021: 252). The end result is composite counter-storytelling – a CRT methodology that 'aims to cast doubt on the validity of accepted premises or myths, especially ones held by the majority' (Delgado and Stefancic 2001: 144). In line with BFE, composite counter-storytelling centres lived experience, dialogue and emotions as well as the ability of Black women to be their own knowledge creators. It also demonstrates how race, gender, class, culture and ethnicity are key parts of one's habitus, the capitals that Black women create, have available and share with each other and how this operates and interacts within the field of the education system.

Book structure

In the chapter that follows, I employ 'Blackgirl autoethnography' (Boylorn 2016: 46) to provide context of the education system, through my own educational journey, to illustrate the different types of institutions I attended, and how this shaped my experiences, alongside the important role of my intersecting raced, classed, religious and gendered identities, my cultural background and ethnicity. I also reflect upon the important role played by my family and networks to navigate all the complexities and challenges I encountered, as well as my choices, aspirations, strategies and decision-making.

In Chapter 2, *Shamari* assists in conceptually situating Black girls and women in school and higher education to provide a broader context about the conditions within which they navigate. *Shamari* invites readers into the anti-Black world that fails to respect or protect Black peoples' humanity and how this manifests over and over in events like the Windrush Scandal in 2018 and the reemergence of the global Black Lives Matter movement in 2020. This chapter will also illustrate the depictions and positioning of Black women who are erased and invisible in British contexts, in contrast to being hypervisible and negatively stereotyped in America. The intersection of Black women's raced and gendered identities is considered in relation to social class which again highlights the prominence of anti-Black racism and how it influences their status, regardless of the resources they may or may not have access to.

Chapter 3 delves deep into what an anti-Black, sexist and classist education system looks like as operationalized by my metaphor of *educational steeplechase. Eve* assists in presenting the argument that meritocracy is outdated, abstract and was never created for an equal society, yet alone education system. *Eve* then talks us through what many Black British girls and women endure when having to merge opposing cultures and how they encounter the abrupt process of 'othering' in the education system – which happens via an awareness of the differences in ways of being, the Eurocentric and whitewashed curricula and the limiting beliefs and negative stereotyping that ultimately leaves Black British girls and women being misunderstood within educational spaces and places.

Chika is the voice of Chapter 4, detailing what it is like being the only Black girl or woman within predominantly white (PW) educational places and spaces. Such educational places and spaces include schools outside of inner cities in suburban or rural areas, as well as grammar or private schools and sixth form colleges within those, and elite or pre-1992 universities. This also extends to educational experiences and journeys characterized as 'being the only one' in certain university subject areas and undergraduate courses. She articulates the ways that whiteness in particular manifests within these spaces, specifically focusing on elite whiteness that shrouds private schools and the knowledge, preparation and financial resources needed in order to circumvent the restricted access. Once inside these PW educational settings, many Black girls and women are left feeling like what Collins (1986, 1999) defines as 'outsiders within' – that is, not truly ever fitting in or being accepted. However, on the flipside, they also experience becoming disconnected from themselves, others and their wider community as their educational experiences and journeys begin to socialize them into and closer to the norms and values of whiteness. While these experiences and journeys can be painful, they may have some advantages like becoming an expert in elite whiteness and acquiring different types of resources, encouragement and support – all of which cannot be gained anywhere else and provides benefits when for example, they enter into certain workplace settings.

The experiences of 'being the only one' are contrasted in Chapter 5 when *Nia-Elise* shares what it is like 'being one of many' Black girls or women within Predominantly Global Majority (PGM) educational spaces and places. These educational spaces and places have higher numbers of GM or in other words, pupils and students from African, Caribbean, Asian and other racially minoritized backgrounds in English contexts and are typically found in inner-city state schools and sixth form/further education colleges, as well as post-1992 universities. *Nia-Elise* illustrates the positives gained from such spaces and places like the appreciation and understanding of self and cultural diversity, as well as the strength in numbers which can provide valuable connections, solidarity and affirmation. On the flipside, she also reveals how PGM educational places and spaces are still largely controlled by white authority and how Black girls and women are positioned and treated as 'unruly' within them. She also questions whether PGM educational spaces and places limit educational opportunities due to the racialized, classed access and the inequality of resources which stunt the growth and exposure of GM students, specifically Black girls and women.

Against this backdrop, in Chapter 6, *Yaa* questions whether educational journeys and experiences culminate in educational 'success' or unnecessary stress. *Yaa* explores how society defines educational 'success' and what it takes to achieve in order to become a Black British woman graduate. She also highlights the unnecessary stresses such as working twice as hard to go half as far that characterizes the experiences of many Black girls and women in their pursuit to gain educational 'success'. These reflections lead to Black women graduates considering alternative options with the aim of illustrating the need to redefine educational 'success', especially when it pertains to Black girls and women.

In Chapter 7, the introduction of *Hamda* and *Hodan* alongside the other composite characters brings them all together in conversation to pay homage to the strength, resilience and power that assisted them to the end of the *educational steeplechase*. The sharing of strategies employed to cultivate strength, resilience and power include having a positive but determined mindset and drawing from their cultures, ethnicities, religions and spirituality. The important role of older Black women – their mothers and Black women lecturers and teachers – who can provide vital support, recognition and affirmation on their educational journeys and experiences is also discussed. Lastly, they impart the crucial wisdom they learn from their educational journeys and experiences to their younger selves and future generations of Black girls and women about how they believe the education system could be better navigated and challenged.

Finally, in Chapter 8, the book concludes by bringing everything together to make sense of the educational journeys and experiences of Black British women graduates in the hope that it will lead to Overstanding, moving forward in different ways and healing from a system that was not made in the best interests of most of us. This chapter ends by introducing my composite characters.

SHAMARI

Shamari is the youngest of five siblings. Born in England, she was raised in a lively, loving, Jamaican household. Much of her educational experiences have been a journey of following in her siblings' footsteps whilst trying to create a new pathway for herself. She attended local, state-funded schools – first a co-educational, PGM primary and then an all-girls, PGM secondary school where she completed a combination of GCSEs and BTECs. As her secondary school didn't offer A-Levels, she enrolled and completed them at another local, PGM, state-funded sixth form college. Deciding to move away from home, she studied a business degree at a reputable, PW, pre-1992 university in the south-east of England where she was awarded upper-second class honours. *Shamari* is now twenty-four years old and has put her business degree to good use as the co-founder and co-owner of a Black-woman-run nail shop, *BBYGRL Nails*.

Figure 2 *Shamari*

EVE

Figure 3 *Eve*

Eve, short for Genevieve, is twenty-three and of Ghanaian and Jamaican heritage. She studied at state-funded educational institutions – a local, co-educational, PGM primary and then a PW secondary school before deciding to attend a further education college far from her home to complete her A-Levels. She describes her university experience at a PW, elite university in the Midlands as "the biggest trial" due to issues around internalized pressure, mental health and friendships which negatively impacted upon her studies. Feeling close to dropping out several times, she pushed through, knowing that she was the first in her family to go to university and that she was a role model to her younger sister. This paid off and she gained a first-class English degree. As she figures out her next steps, she does temporary work such as private tutoring and has become a strong advocate of self-love, mental health and wellbeing, investing heavily in therapy to achieve healing, personal growth and authenticity.

CHIKA

Chika is the only child of Nigerian parents who emigrated to England in the 1980s to begin what they believed was a 'better life' for themselves and their future family. Growing up in a PW, middle-class area, she was used to being one of the only or very few Black students and faced her fair share of challenges when it came to race, culture, identity and a sense of belonging. Often visiting her extended family in the inner-city that she moved away from, her educational journey began at a small, PW, private school in a rural area where she excelled academically and with the support of her parents went on to attend a PW, top girls' private school where she remained to achieve excellent A-Level results. She went on to read law at a PW, elite university in up north earning a first-class degree, and at twenty-three years of age, she now works in the human rights, international relations and development sector.

Figure 4 *Chika*

NIA-ELISE

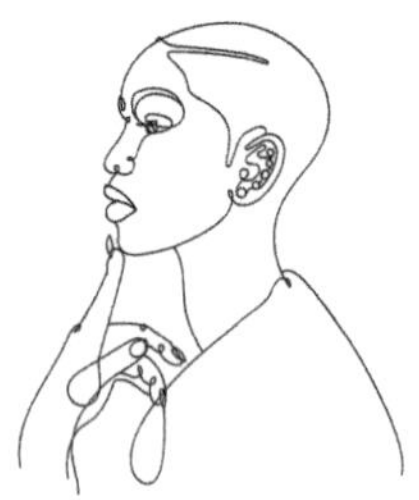

Figure 5 *Nia-Elise*

Nia-Elise hails from a large, blended, British Trinidadian and Grenadian family where she is the fourth of six children. Born in the south-east of England, she moved to the Midlands with her family at a young age where she completed most of her schooling. The local primary she studied at was mostly comprised of students from GM backgrounds with white students the minority. Her secondary school, which was close to her home, was also PGM and had a reputation of being 'rough'. Nia-Elise decided to attend a further education sixth form college where she gained a BTEC in creative arts. Despite getting top marks in her college course, she found it difficult to secure a place at a top university and instead completed a fashion degree in a PGM, post-1992 university away from home. Now twenty-five years old and unsuccessful in securing a graduate-level job in her field – despite graduating with a first – she works part time in retail while focusing on building her own art, design and fashion business and sells her creations on Etsy. She is currently working on pieces for her upcoming exhibition, *Babygirls inna, but not of, Babylon* collection which centres Black British women's experiences through a range of artistic mediums.

YAA

Figure 6 *Yaa*

Yaa is a second-generation British Ghanaian woman who was raised by her aunt after the passing of her mother when she was a baby. At her PGM, state-funded, inner-city primary school, she was 'one of many' Black pupils before becoming 'the only one' at her PW, state-funded secondary school in the surrounding areas of a big city. She then moved to a PW, suburban state-funded, grammar school for sixth form and completed the International Baccalaureate (IB) programme which was challenging but helped her to become a well-rounded intellectual. Though she got good grades, she didn't get to go to her first-choice university and so she went through Clearing and gained a place at a PW, pre-1992 university where she struggled with her mental health. Luckily, she had counselling which assisted in the completion of her sociology and criminology degree and she achieved upper-second-class joint honours. Opting to take some time out to rest and recover, and not knowing what she truly wanted to do after university, she landed a temporary role at an education charity and is enjoying being a dedicated plant mum and a natural-haired twenty-two-year-old babygirl.

HAMDA and HODAN

Figure 7 *Hamda and Hodan*

Hodan and Hamda are identical twin sisters of Somali descent. At twenty-one years old, they are fresh out of university and enjoying the achievement of 'successfully' completing their degrees. They have always enjoyed supporting, interacting and connecting with others, which resulted in the creation of their *Choppin' & Chattin' Babygirlz* podcast to bring together, discuss and learn from other Black women graduates about their educational experiences and journeys. Their own educational journeys included a primary school with a PGM and Muslim student demographic which was within walking distance of their home. Again, they were 'one of many' Black students within their local PGM, co-educational, state-funded secondary school where *Hamda* fell in love with science. They both achieved excellent GCSE results which secured their places at a top-performing, state-funded grammar school where they became two of the only Black, Muslim students there. Despite this, they finished their A-Levels and went on to study physiology and anthropology, respectively, at the same PW, pre-1992 university, graduating with an upper-second and first-class honours.

1

Becoming Dr April-Louise

Figure 1 *Babygirl*

Before I share the educational journeys and experiences of my research participants, it is only fitting to retell my own. This is because, as Nadar (2014: 20) states, 'the identity of the researcher is as important as the participants in the research'. In this chapter, I use 'Blackgirl autoethnography' as defined by Boylorn (2016: 46) 'to discuss and situate a way of being in and seeing/experiencing the world through a raced and gendered lens. I offer Blackgirl autoethnography as a way to talk about embodied, critical, and culturally situated research that begins and/or ends at home, in the bodies we live in, the people we live with, and the social circumstances we live through'. To do this, I share my foundations as I reflect upon who I am and where I come from. I summarize how it was to be April-Louise in different educational settings, revealing how powerful the influences of the education system can be, from primary school to Ph.D. level. I frame these personal experiences by focusing on how I often navigated at the intersections, and how this all came together in the end, providing the inspiration for research to explore and document alternative educational narratives of Black British women graduates as amplified in the following chapters.

The Foundations

The song 'Beautiful Flower' by India Arie plays in the background as I sip from my glass of Ribena. Until this day, since I first discovered the song in my teens, it stops me from giving up and reminds me of the power of my mind which has often unlocked different educational opportunities and experiences. A perfect accompaniment which helps me to conjure up memories, complementing this chapter's focus.

* * *

As a Black girl, who is now a woman, I have always been, and will always be, positioned and navigate life at the intersections. Here, Crenshaw's (1989, 1991) concept of intersectionality is key to understanding as it expresses how and why multiple, interlinking and devalued identities simultaneously come together to greatly influence the lived experiences of people that look like me, and how we often 'fall through the cracks' (Jones 2006) because society and its institutions are not tailored by or for us. This is discussed further, with examples, in Chapter 2. As a Black British woman, my Blackness is often the most prominent, relegating my Britishness and my womanhood as secondary. But I am also aware that my British nationality, my Christian faith, my educational history and achieved status as an academic researcher at a university provide a degree of relative privilege. While identities are social constructs and therefore should not be fixed, due to the way society is structured and how individuals interact with one another, they have real implications on everyday lives and futures. These considerations of identity are ones that the other Black women featured in this book also grapple with.

Becoming Black British

I am the product of 'Great' Britain and her vast empire, the grandchild of two couples born in two separate continents with connected pasts and ties to the 'Mother Country'. Both of the women – my grandmothers – were devout Catholics and, along with my grandfathers, they made the decision, took the risk, and answered the call to 'rebuild the country' after the Second World War, doing their part as British subjects. They came with hopes of gaining better opportunities by making England their home. One of the couples first set foot on these isles from Jamaica in 1952 as part of the so-called 'Windrush generation'. The other couple arrived from Nigeria at the start of the 1960s. Both settled in different parts of London, adding children to their newly laid foundations. My father, Gil, was born in South London, to his Jamaican parents nearly a decade after they arrived – the last of the seven children they would have together. My mother, Dupe, was 'sent for' by her own parents at least a decade after they had settled here. She left her own grandparents behind to be reunited with her parents, beginning life in East London as the first of their three children.

My parents grew up in England as the second generation of their families, reconciling their Jamaican and Nigerian culture with their English one, creating and navigating a path which they would merge when they met, fell in love and married each other. A path which was quite unusual of the time because, though they were both Black and living in England, they were from distinct ethnicities and cultures that were often placed, by the colonial legacy of their histories and as internalized by their communities, in opposition to one another via diaspora wars. So much so that both of their families were not too fond of my parents' cross-cultural union or the seeds, me and my sister, Felicia that bloomed from it. This was apparent as we grew, via our extended family's treatment, disinterest, inconsistent support and participation in our lives.

Like many of the other Black British women in this study, I am the third generation in England. I was born in April 1993 in South West London, eight days before the racist and brutal murder of an innocent young man, Stephen Lawrence. I entered the world as a poorly baby and my mother, who was still in the hospital having not yet been discharged so that the doctors could run tests on me, would have heard the news of the ending of one young Black life as her second daughter's own Black life was just starting. Stephen's historic murder marked the end of his life, but the beginnings of a critical period in British history as well as my own. Stephen's Blackness had also relegated his Britishness and he was not seen to truly belong by the racist, white thugs who murdered him, or the criminal justice system who failed to provide the justice he deserved. Stephen's family's battle for justice became the backdrop to a big chunk of my life – partly as it took so long to convict (some of) his killers. It also let me know from a young age that I was a Black British girl in a white British society and this could be dangerous. Yet, as a consequence of Stephen's family's quest for justice, monumental changes were made which shaped the collective consciousness of Britain in terms of legislation and how race and racism were thought of and talked about. The establishment of the Stephen Lawrence Day Foundation exemplifies the lasting legacy of how, ultimately, these efforts created a slightly safer Britain for me and subsequent generations of Black Britons to grow up in.

While I have always been British like my parents and grandparents, it has always been in a hyphenated capacity, marked by precarity and constant othering by the whiteness which underpins society. In many ways, my Blackness – with its own internal layers – is my buffer, shield and anchor. I was born at the intersection of the empire, encapsulating Nigerian, Jamaican, British and English cultures, ethnicities and nationalities. My parents made it their duty to familiarize, expose and root me and my sister within the vibrant, rich and powerful national, cultural and ethnic identities of Nigeria and Jamaica, infused with English-British-ness via, for example, food, music, history and traditions. Looking back, I now understand that they consciously chose to root us, me and my sister, in our English-British-ness alongside our Jamaican-ness and Nigerian-ness so that we would be affirmed in who we are. They wanted us to know that we belonged in these isles – just as much as anyone else – and perhaps they wanted to prepare us to be able to boldly respond, when we were asked the infamous question 'where are you really from?' or positioned as being the 'other', 'foreign', 'just arrived' and ultimately like we didn't belong here. To that end, I have always been a proud Black, English-British-Nigerian-Jamaican or English-British-Jamaican-Nigerian (British Nijam or Jamgerian for short) (young) woman. My Blackness comes first as I see it as enclosing the other identities and it is a reflection of its prominence in my life; then English as that is where I was born; British next as that is the wider context in which England and its empire sits; Nigeria or Jamaica (it alternates) after to honour my heritage and, lastly, my womanhood which I see as the outward form from which the previous identities are expressed. None of these identities can be separated as they are inextricably connected – not just through me, but historically. Therefore, I have always honoured my intersectionality – a blend of multiple, diverse, identities – all of which are valuable and contribute to my essence. I only became aware of social class identity and the part it played later on in my life, particularly when in different educational settings, and I will illustrate how in more detail shortly. My names also exemplify my identities – my first and last name are in the English language and represent the colonial legacies of my Jamaican and British heritage and sandwich my carefully selected Yoruba middle names. Apart from my surname, they are all feminine to identify my girl/womanhood. As you will see from the rest of this chapter, just as my identity has evolved and developed, parts of my British identity have also evolved and now includes Wales through my ancestral connections and living and working there via my postdoctoral fellowship.

My conscious and aspirational parents

To quote the great Toni Morrison, 'long before I was a success, my parents made me feel like I could be one'. However, my sister and I were taught by our parents that beyond our home, we had to work 'twice as hard' to be 'successful'. While I am not saying that this teaching is exclusive to

Black girls, in a similar way that an American study by Leath and Mims (2021: 3) highlights that 'Black girls and women are socialised to adhere to dominant cultural gender norms', I argue that this teaching was a key part of our own socialization as Black girls. We were also taught that despite doing so, we might receive 'half as much' and/or get 'half as far' as we deserved in return, but that we should never limit our aspirations because, in the words of my father, 'the world is your oyster'. The awareness and consequences of 'working twice as hard to get half as far' or 'half as much' are considered in Chapters 3, 6 and 8. In some ways, my parents aligned themselves with the notion of 'education-based meritocracy' – 'the assumption that the more one is educated, the more likely he/she is to enter the group of higher earning labour force regardless of their original social class position' (Themelis 2008: 432). In other words, anyone can, based on talent, ability and hard work, achieve 'success' within both the education system and wider society. However, my parents were also aware of the myth of meritocracy which failed to acknowledge the operations of anti-Black gendered racism and the other 'isms' that contribute to the limited returns of our hard work and which could unfortunately hinder our educational experiences, opportunities and outcomes. This has also been previously highlighted by Mitchell (2013: 352) in her paper about race, difference, meritocracy and English in schools, where she defines meritocracy as part of the majoritarian, or dominant, white, story which 'overlooks many issues of inequity that fundamentally undermine any actualisation of equality when it comes to schooling'. Meritocracy is discussed further in Chapter 3 and the notion of educational 'success' is considered in Chapter 6.

To counter the anti-Black gendered racism in society, my parents were active during my sister's and my early years, by embracing and celebrating our natural afro-textured hair which we mostly wore in cornrows with the occasional *hot comb*, familiarizing us with a range of different activities, places and people in order to develop our natural talents and to instil self-confidence, and a mindset that I and my sister belonged anywhere we wished to be. This meant for example, that on many weekends, during the holidays and after school, we would go on family trips – sometimes joined by my eldest sister, Sarah, from my dad's side – to museums, family friendly festivals as well as participating in cultural and educational events and activities like swimming classes, as members of the girl guides, a local athletics club, a Black supplementary school, performing arts school and learning to play instruments. This has been identified by Lareau (2002: 748) as 'concerted cultivation' and is a key attribute and distinction between both Black and white middle-class and working-class parents' child rearing which 'results in a wider range of experiences for children but also creates a frenetic pace for parents, a cult of individualism within the family, and an emphasis on children's performance'. Looking back, they were only able to do this as they both had knowledge and access to resources that I believe distinguishes them from the so-called working class. Yet, they were precariously in the so-called middle class, as, certainly for my mother, they had just made it there, hence the prefix of lower in this middle-class categorization. It can be said that through immersing myself and my sister within these different environments with a diverse range of people, my parents were also embarking on a strategic plan to 'arm … [us] against racism to resist the often subtle, but insidious positioning of Black children as inferior in a white-dominated society' (Vincent et al. 2012a: 436), as well as to prepare us to compete in the educational market.

My parents have brilliant minds but were not the most academically inclined people and had differing educational experiences and journeys. For instance, where my father had never experienced anything other than the English education system, my mother entered the English education system after completing her primary schooling in Nigeria. I might also add that my parents were schooled in the 1960s and 1970s – a time when Black children in English schools were branded as 'educationally subnormal' (Coard 1971), and their outcomes were limited. Yet, they were able to experience upward social mobility into lower-middle-class positions, according to both objective and subjective social class categorization, signified by being the second generation in both their families to own their home, higher qualifications, professional occupations and the knowledge and connections that provide additional resources, as defined by Bourdieu (1986) as cultural and social capital. The limits of social class classifications and where Black communities in England fit (or do not) are discussed later in Chapter 2.

Unfortunately, when I was about six years old, my parents divorced and this meant that my mother became the main provider for my sister and me. For the next decade or so, we spent time with my father on weekends and during school holidays, but the day-to-day decisions and actions fell to my mother – although my father reappears in my educational story more prominently later on. For my mother, her educational experiences and career journey cemented her views about the importance of understanding the education system and the need to utilize appropriate resources to navigate the education system effectively. Her own educational experiences and journey also contributed to a determination and passion that would be reflected in the educational trajectories of her children. As will become evident shortly, in many ways, my mother can be likened to what is described as an 'academic chooser' who:

privilege what they see as high-quality education that will give their children future opportunities and advantages. They view this as a price worth paying (financially and in social terms), partly because they view high achievement as a means of avoiding or at least minimising racial disadvantages in the future.

(Rollock et al 2015: 49)

This was also evident in how my mother raised myself and my sister in addition to being an academic chooser. Abbas (2007: 75) asserts how 'certain working-class South Asian parents possess strong middle-class attitudes towards selective education, irrespective of their ability to facilitate it as a function of their financial, cultural, or social capital'. I assert that my mother is similar – as although she *did* possess cultural and social capital, which will be illustrated shortly, due to being a single parent on a single income, she did not have as much disposable income.

The importance of having conscious and aspirational parents are shared by many of the other Black women in this study, particularly the role of mothers, as illustrated in Chapter 7. Due to having my own conscious and aspirational parents who believed in the transformative power of education, in all its many forms, I entered the education system with a strong sense of self-worth, pride in my heritage and confidence in my abilities. Next, I will speak to my educational experiences and journey at two primary schools, *Eaton Hill* and *St Clara;* three secondary schools, *Bluebird House*, *Holyway High* and *St Bernadine's* and, as an A-Level, undergraduate and postgraduate student at *Mountain Peak College* and the *Universities of Beddington* and *Zodiac* respectively – all key influences that contributed to becoming Dr April-Louise.

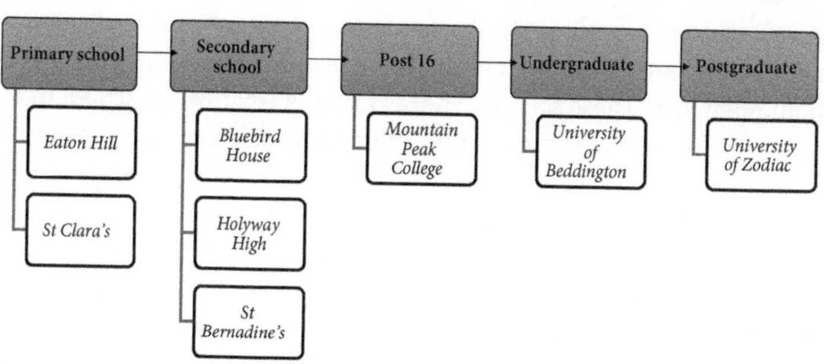

Figure 9 Map of the educational institutions in April-Louise's educational journey

Navigating at the intersections in different educational institutions

My educational experiences and journey within the English education system can be characterized as navigating at the intersections with the prominence of my Blackness being a defining feature, intersecting with and shaping my gender, social class and how I engaged with educational institutions and others sharing the space with me. My culture and ethnicity – which I see as part and parcel of my Blackness – also played a significant role. This is because, as I went to different schools in both the state and private sectors, at first, my sense of self-worth, particularly in relation to my Blackness, how it was perceived and how I responded manifested at *Eaton Hill* and *St Clara's*. At times, during my secondary school experiences, being a lower-middle class, Black girl meant that I became too posh but not posh enough at *Bluebird House*, Black but not Black enough at *Holyway High* and Blackity Black at *St Bernadine's*. In particular, the differing ways in which my Blackness was perceived and positioned by myself and others provides interesting reflections.

Developing a sense of self-worth beyond the home

As mentioned previously, my parents instilled a strong sense of self-worth which, for the most part, I was able to continue to develop in my primary school experiences. I initially began my primary schooling in reception at a co-educational, PW, private school named *Eaton Hill*. I can remember the small classes, ballet lessons and fun school outings. However, this was one of the first times I experienced racism at school. I went home crying as I had been excluded from playing a game by another child because he had told me that 'no "darkies" are allowed'. My mother consoled me and explained in a child-friendly way that, unfortunately, some people wouldn't like me and that I should play with those that do. She also swiftly went to the school to talk with my teacher *and* the boy's mother, to prevent this from happening again. Though this was a negative experience, it led to a heightened sense of being Black in a white space but, instead of shying away from it, I wanted to assert it more. This was exemplified shortly after, when, at the age of four, I told my mother that I wanted to dress up as a *Black* Barbie for a friend's costume party. My mother agreed, doing her best to interpret what that meant and helped to get my costume ready. At the party, I remember proudly beaming as I made it very clear by letting everyone know that I had not just come dressed up as Barbie, I had come as a *Black* Barbie. This incident showed that from an early age, I had a strong sense of identity and self-worth which I was bringing out beyond the home, and in response to being negatively singled out by others in the space because of it. While I was using Barbie as my muse, I was tailoring her to be more inclusive and to better represent me. These experiences of being the only Black girl or woman in an educational setting will be explored further in Chapter 4. While my parents' plan was for my elder sister, Felicia (two school years older) to join me at *Eaton Hill*, instead, I ended up joining my sister at the state-funded, GM primary school, *St Clara's*, which she had been attending, at the start of year one.

At *St Clara's* primary school, in contrast to *Eaton Hill*, I was one of many Black children and I had classmates from a range of other racial and ethnic backgrounds. In Chapter 5, the experiences of being one of many Black girls or women will be illustrated. It was a co-educational, Catholic school connected to a church that bore the same name and aligned with our religious affiliation as influenced and passed down by my grandmothers. *St Clara's* was great at building a sense of community and it was highly respected by the local community and beyond, boasting excellent academic results year after year, as reflected in pupil outcomes and the Office for Standards in Education (Ofsted) reports.

One defining feature in this school was the high standard and regard given to musical education. I had the pleasure of being taught by a passionate music teacher, *Ms O'Brien*, who engaged us with a diverse musical curriculum. For instance, all the pupils were exposed to and learned music and songs from other cultures as well as in other languages. Here I was a proud member of the school choir and we often performed at national school events and notably, at the Royal Albert Hall *three times* throughout my time there. I also had recorder and violin lessons. Though I was an above-average pupil, I remember additional tutoring playing a crucial role in the latter part of my primary schooling experiences, preparing me for secondary school entrance examinations. In particular, these tutoring sessions focused on verbal and non-verbal reasoning which were prerequisites for the types of secondary schools that I was going to apply to, namely academically selective and private schools. These skills were not taught in the curriculum at *St Clara's*. This preparation into what I term elite, PW educational institutions is a theme considered further in Chapter 4. This may have also been where I started to align my sense of self-worth according to my educational 'success', a theme shared by some of the other Black women as explored in Chapter 6.

As *St Clara's* was multicultural and ethnically diverse, the mainly white staff would encourage us to celebrate our cultural backgrounds, as well as making us aware of others as evidenced with the musical education.

I remember when a cultural day was organized, and all of the pupils were invited to wear traditional clothing from their family's cultures. The school was immersed in clothes representing Dominica, Eritrea, Ethiopia, Ghana, Nigeria, Trinidad, Spain, Columbia, Jamaica, Ireland, Mauritius, Italy, Peru, Greece, Scotland, Portugal, Malta, etc. I remember proudly parading around with my Nigerian and Jamaican attire. Events like this made me feel very comfortable to be myself in a school setting and encouraged me to bring my whole self into the space. It also highlighted the importance of sharing and celebrating different cultures alongside my own and the (white) Britishness that underpinned the rest of the curriculum. It was only when I left that I realized that this school and its staff were one of a kind, as I would soon find out that it was not 'normal' to be around, celebrate and centre other cultures in educational environments.

Being posh but not posh enough

When it was time to apply for secondary schools, my mother was dissatisfied with the quality of the options in the local area. Based on her own educational experiences, she desired for my sister and I to be educated at academically selective institutions such as private schools. She would always tell us that 'those are the types of schools where the future leaders, managers and entrepreneurs go' and clearly that is what she envisioned us being. She was not wrong, as a report jointly by the Sutton Trust and the Social Mobility Commission titled 'Elitist-Britain, 2019: The educational backgrounds of Britain's leading people' confirmed that parliament, senior judges, civil servant permanent secretaries, the House of Lords, the media and foreign and commonwealth office diplomats are disproportionately dominated by private school alumni. Using her understanding of the education system, her resources and experience from applying for my elder sister's schooling where she went through twelve applications for different selective secondary schools, and only successfully gained a place at one, when it came to my time, my mother decided to reduce the number of schools she applied to for me. The reduced number of secondary school choices was also because my mother was certain that I would gain a place at my sister's school due to the extra tuition that I had received to prepare me, as well as relying on the 'sibling link' which often strengthened your application. She applied to two schools – one Catholic, state-funded, all-girls' school and my older sister's Church of England, co-educational, private boarding school. Unfortunately, I was unsuccessful in gaining a place at either of the two schools. I was rejected by the first because I was told that I was not 'Catholic enough' – a seemingly subjective decision seeing as I had been baptized as a Catholic, was attending a Catholic primary school, going to mass regularly and I had received my first Holy Communion. I was rejected by the second school as I did not pass the newly introduced additional test, due to the school's increased popularity, which was required to be taken before sitting the school's entrance exam. According to the Sutton Trust (2008: 22) they evidence how selective education systems and the failure that pupils feel from being unsuccessful in passing school entrance exams is harmful as 'rejected pupils may see themselves as failures and intrinsically worth less than those who succeeded'. I agree with this finding as I remember feeling awful, and that I was not as smart as my big sister, along with believing that I had let myself and my mother down. My mother tried to hide her disappointment as she had invested so much in trying to support me to gain a school place, but she was determined to find somewhere better suited to me and continued to search and encourage me.

After my previous secondary school rejections, my mother discovered a 'sister school' to my sister's private, boarding school, *Bluebird House*, with a similar Church of England religious foundation. Though it was academically selective, it prided itself on *not* being a '"hothouse" … gaug(ing) people on their potential'. I sat *Bluebird House's* entrance exam, attended an interview and I was delighted to receive the news that I passed and had secured a place. To accept the place, I had to participate in a traditional initiation process as part of the enrolment at the school and I was invited, along with all the other new students in my year, to take it in turns to stand individually, at a carefully selected, prestigious location, before the governors to repeat an oath. It was at this point that the intersection of my race and social class as Black, lower-middle class became evident to me as I was entering into this new world when I started the school. I was now mixing with my privileged peers – some of whom were the fifth generation to be studying at the school. As Rollock (2014: 446) writes when reflecting on her own private schooling experiences, 'these *class signifiers* facilitate access to, and a *certain* acceptance within, mainly white (middle class) spaces but crucially, they also disturb and disrupt the fixed, stereotypical perceptions that many whites hold about Blacks' [emphasis in original]. On entrance into the school, I became exposed to more class signifiers during the social activities like afternoon tea with my boarding house on our weekend trips to the local village. I had entered a new, privileged world which only '6.5% of the total number of school children in the UK (and over 7% of the total number of school children in England)' had access to (Independent Schools Council 2021).

Bluebird House was PW and, as described on its website, situated in the 'glorious [name of county] countryside', and it differed slightly from my big sister's school because it had fewer pupils, was not exclusively boarding (it had day students that attended from the local area), with more expensive school fees. Additionally, in this PW and elite space, I was one of the very few Black British students from a lower social class as evidenced by my bursary, and therefore both my racial and class identity characterized my experiences. My mother reluctantly let me style my hair in *single-plaits with extensions* as they would last for longer periods and be less time-consuming to care for if they were in *cornrows* or left out and I was so excited. I remember, possibly for comfort, sticking closely to and creating a friendship with the only two other Black girls – one in my year and the other in the year above. Another close friend of mine was a white working-class girl who came from an area near to where I was from in London. We formed a small, tight-knit, core group until I left.

The benefits that came with attending a school like *Bluebird House* were undeniable. These included being in a class with a maximum of twelve students meaning we got more teacher encouragement and attention. I also continued my love of music by having one-to-one singing lessons alongside simultaneously learning three different languages – Latin, German and French. Classes took place on Saturday until midday which was advantageous to our learning, and Sundays were filled with a service at the school chapel and we were all given a bible when we started. I had access to advanced and high-quality facilities such as a swimming pool on the grounds, dance studios, a climbing wall, several sports fields and tennis courts that we were expected to utilize on Wednesday afternoons which were dedicated to sports. I was introduced to the sport of hockey here and I became a good player, representing the school on the girls' team and playing tournaments at other equally privileged schools with beautifully resourced playing fields and grounds. I excelled both academically and in the extra-curricular elements of study and although I initially felt like a 'fish out of water' (Bourdieu and Passeron 1979), I was able to adapt well to this new, privileged educational environment.

However, due to a lack of disposable income compared to my peers, there were many times when I became aware of my social class and income, which intersected with my racial identity, and highlighted my position as an 'outsider within' – this position in PW, elite spaces is explored further in Chapter 4. Additionally, Proweller's 1998 book *Constructing Female Identities: Meaning Making in an Upper Middle Class Youth Culture* examines some of these experiences when exploring the lives of thirty-four teenage girls at a historically elite, private, all-girls' high school. For instance, I remember the matron making comments about my toiletries as she didn't recognize the sponge I used and thought it was 'strange', or that my mother could not afford to pay for the annual ski trip or buy me the designer clothes that my eleven-year-old peers were casually wearing. Moreover, after two terms at *Bluebird House*, my mother had a change in circumstances and could no longer afford to pay my fees, despite the 50 per cent bursary I was awarded. When she relayed this to the school, they were unsympathetic and told her that if I did not return with a cheque after the Easter holidays then I would not be allowed to continue. She did, through her social capital, manage to acquire some financial assistance for me, but it was a small, one-off payment which wasn't sufficient to cover the rest of my school fees. I remember my mother frantically trying to find other ways and I remember her crying at the dinner table as she realized she could not. She exhausted her contacts and managed to get an educational charity to consider providing funding on the condition that they were able to 'assess' our circumstances. A woman from the charity turned up at our home to inspect it and, unfortunately, we were deemed not to be 'poor enough' and were refused financial support, so I had to leave. Luckily my sister's school was more accommodating to my mother's change in circumstances and her study there was not disrupted.

It was an abrupt and brutal end to what seemed to be the beginning of my entrance and progression into a new and privileged world. I did not get the chance to collect any of the items that remained in the boarding house or to properly say goodbye to my peers. It felt like I had done something wrong and was being punished. I also felt frustrated and confused because the school promoted itself as being a charitable organization, but here they were unwilling to extend this charity to me. *Bluebird House* also took my mother to court and put a charge on our home to ensure they would receive the outstanding fees. I now had a 'taste' and first-hand experience of 'how the other half' or, more accurately, a very small minority lived and I liked it and believed that I too deserved to be there just like anyone else. But, as an eleven/twelve year old, the removal from this world signified that although I was more than capable, as proven by not only gaining entrance to the school by passing their exam but as a student who excelled in the school, financial means (or lack of) was the only barrier preventing me from staying there. I also felt rejected and as though I was being told by the school that I was unworthy and undeserving of a place within such an elite space like *Bluebird House*. Looking back years later, I realized that this rejection contributed to the growth of an intense, internal hunger for opportunity, precisely because I had been deprived of this huge one. These feelings can manifest into internalized pressure and unrealistic expectations, as defined by some of the Black women in Chapter 3, and unnecessary stress, as shared in Chapter 6. I often wonder how my life would have been had I been allowed to stay at *Bluebird House* for the duration of my secondary education.

Bourdieu (1977) writes about how within the education system, (white) middle-class students have an advantage due to possessing additional resources such as financial, cultural and social capital which equates to knowledge, understanding and easy navigation of the education system, as well as influential connections. I contend that my mother *did* possess some cultural capital as she was able to understand the distinctions within the education system and prepare myself and my sister for the schools' entrance exams, as well as to find charities and organizations that could provide funding for my school fees. She also used her social capital to find that small, one-off payment towards my fees. However, in this situation, it was financial capital that was the most significant. My mother and I had the two-week Easter holiday to find another school for me to attend which proved to be a very traumatic, stressful and hectic time.

Being Black but not Black enough

My life seemed to turn upside down when I entered the state-funded, predominantly GM, all-girls', Church of England school *Holyway High*. Its inner-city location and sparse facilities contrasted a great deal with *Bluebird House*, but it was the only school that offered me a place in such a short time and with my mother's compromised financial situation. Despite being described as one of the best schools in the area, in an Ofsted report the school was characterized as:

> Very popular and oversubscribed … admit[ing] students from less affluent backgrounds … from lone-parent or low-income families. The majority are from minority ethnic backgrounds, with many students of African heritage, and around fifty different languages are spoken across the school.

Initially, I had a hard time fitting in at *Holyway High*. I was confused at how it could be so different from *Bluebird House*, and I was not accustomed to little encouragement, attention or interest from teachers, or the frequent disruptions during lessons. Also, although I was one of many Black British girls at this school, my lower-middle-class background and my previous educational experiences meant that I stood out. Apparently, according to my peers, the way I articulated and carried myself was like a 'neek' (an insulting term used for those that are deemed to be uncool, focused on studying and as a result, unpopular) and they often told me that I thought I was 'too nice' when learning of the previous school I attended. At this school, I quickly learnt about the pecking order in terms of Black girl beauty standards where the lighter your skin tone (preferably mixed heritage), the longer and wavier your natural hair, the more western your features and being of Caribbean descent meant that you were winning! These internalized Black girl beauty standards reeked of the interconnected traits of texturism, colourism, featurism and self-hatred as many of us didn't fit into all of those categories (Tate 2007). However, at twelve years old we didn't know any better and were merely upholding societal standards of beauty based on the images promoted to us by the media of desirable Black girls and women. This has been previously highlighted in a study by Muhammad and MacArthur (2015) who identified how Black teenage girls in America are influenced, styled and represent themselves based on media representations in a similar way that my Black girl classmates did. I also quickly found out that my style, as demonstrated by how I initially wore my uniform, my choice of bag and shoes, as well as my hairstyles, were considered unfashionable and not Black enough within this exclusive Black girl subculture of which I was now part. This created additional peer pressure and I quickly adapted to my surroundings and peers to prove that I was Black enough. This included, for example, changing my self-presentation and wearing the latest footwear - Kickers at the time - and the Nike 'just do it' school bag, as well as having the right hairstyles - slicking my baby hairs, wearing ribbons, bobbles and lollipops to adorn my hair. It also included adapting my language to incorporate the latest slang and learning about particular music genres and current songs to perfect the art of being Black (Alexander 1996). Though I had been exposed to some of these ways of being at my primary school, *St Clara's*, this had been diluted when I was at *Bluebird High* as I adapted to the subculture and surroundings of elite whiteness to fit in there. Looking back, being at this school was a true introduction to a distinct version of Black British girlhood with its own unique capital, which has influenced a huge part of British youth culture. I discuss this more in Chapter 3.

Interestingly, at this school, I was re-exposed to the diaspora wars and the divide between those of African and those of Caribbean descent- something that I had known about based on my own extended family interactions- and which was a feature of wider Black British identity (Daniel 2018). This meant that there was a lot of banter and casual insults flying around about negative stereotypical group traits. I grew up in a time when it wasn't cool to be African and therefore some African children would claim to be Caribbean. My classmates thought that this was what I was doing and they ridiculed me because they thought I was lying about being half Nigerian and half Jamaican. When they realized that I wasn't lying, I was often told to 'pick a side' which I would refuse to do as I had never done this before and I would proudly proclaim that 'I am both'.

Another distinctive memory I have about *Holyway High* was the lack of facilities available to us and the low quality of the facilities we did have. This meant that we often congregated in the classrooms at break times because there was simply not enough room for us outside in the school grounds. This was in stark contrast to my previous school, *Bluebird House*, which was situated 'on a 100 acre site in rural [name of county]'. For example, when it was time to do physical education classes, we would take a coach to a nearby sports ground. This sports ground was lent to the school by a local private, all-girls' school. On one of the occasions, when we were at the loaned sports ground, the students from the private school were also having a physical education class and I spotted a childhood friend amongst them. Like me in my previous school, she was one of very few Black girl students within the elite, PW space of her school. We were on either ends of the large mass of grass and the wired fence that separated us, but I remember excitedly waving and screaming her name to which she responded. Perhaps by doing this, I was trying to reaffirm that I did not belong in this school or with this group. I can remember the shock on my classmates' and teachers' faces – perhaps because I knew someone from such a prestigious school which was so far removed from the worlds that many of them inhabited.

As time progressed, my focus shifted to making friends and fitting in. My grades began to drop and my attitude towards education began to change. This was exemplified in my end of year school report, where one teacher wrote that 'there was no willingness to work hard which is a characteristic of the group as a whole'. I was no longer as enthusiastic or motivated as I had previously been. I was no longer stimulated or inspired to engage, and I felt a huge sense of alienation from the school and what it had to offer. My mother became both saddened and horrified at this change in my educational aspirations as well as with the quality of the teaching and school resources. After two terms, I left *Holyway High*.

Being Blackity Black

The introduction of the Education Reform Act in 1988 by the-then prime minister Margaret Thatcher provided parents with more freedom when choosing schools for their children as it put an end to catchment areas and fuelled competition. My mother, well aware of this right, utilized this in the selection of the final secondary school I attended, *St Bernadine's*, which was located quite a distance from my home. Scarred from my previous experience, my mother decided to try a school in the suburbs for me; however, the surrounding areas were questionable as, for instance, I remember walking past National Front graffiti signifying the presence of the extreme right wing, racist political group. *St Bernadine's* was a co-educational, Catholic, state-funded school which my mother believed to be better, in terms of resources, facilities and ranking than my previous inner-city school, *Holyway High*. For example, we didn't have to take a coach elsewhere to complete our physical education classes. Though it was not a private school, there were additional expenses such as the monthly travelcards for the train rides to and from the school. I now had to wake up extra early to catch the train because if I missed it I would certainly be late. For the majority of my time at this school, none of my peers lived near me and on those long train journeys I would often only have my iPod and the occasional book for company. At the time of my attendance, *St Bernadine's* was described in its Ofsted report as attracting students 'from a wide range of both relatively prosperous and less affluent areas'.

At *St Bernadine's*, which was PW, my racial and gender identity was the most noticeable in my experiences. After being initiated into a Black British girl subculture at my previous school, *Holywood High*, I brought the style and lingo with me to *St Bernadine's*. At this school, they perceived me to be Blackity Black and I became a target of anti-Black stereotypical insults (Wright, McGlaughin and Webb 1998, 1999). In the minds of my new peers, many who had rarely been in close proximity to a Black girl from the inner-city and clouded by largely negative media portrayals, to them, I just *had* to have gang-member friends and relatives and I just had to live on a huge estate, overrun with drug, knife and gun crime. These stereotypes were frequently projected onto me as I was constantly addressed by my peers with 'blud' and 'bruv', as well as mimicking gestures where they would constantly (try to) 'kiss their teeth' at me. Teachers also banned me and the few other Black girls that attended the school from wearing ribbons in our hair as, similarly to my peers, they believed them to signal gang affiliation.

Racial slurs were also commonplace from my peers, and on one occasion I was told to 'go back to Africa', that I had 'been under the sunbed for too long and was burnt', as well as the afro-texture of my hair being compared to 'bum-fluff'. When I wore my hair in patterned cornrows, it was referred to as 'embroidery'. I was also involuntarily included in debates and asked to be the spokesperson for all Black people to explain 'why white people couldn't say the n-word when (some) Black people do'. However, when I would defend myself, this often led to some of the teachers treating me more harshly, an example being that I was often sent out of the class or given a detention when responding to the racial slurs instead of the culprits. To adapt, I accepted this Blackity Black persona they put on me as it seemed to create a sense of respect mixed with fear that I would, for example, bring my 'people' to get them if they messed with me. I also found comfort in the friendships I made with the few Black and Global Majority girls in my year, the year above and the year below who understood and were also battling the same peer racism – though

I did make friendships with others. I also reasserted my Blackness in the space as both resistance and comfort in a similar way as I had done at the age of four when I attended the costume party as a *Black* Barbie at *Eaton Hill*. For example, I came up with the idea and, with the help of my friends, led the organization of a school-wide celebration of cultures and food to raise money for the selected charity of that year. I also made a proud statement when, at the end of my studies at the Prom, I teamed a traditional Nigerian head wrap, a gele which is worn on special occasions, with my gown. Prom was also the first time my mother allowed me to wear a full head, sew-in *weave* – a rite of passage for many young Black women – and I was ecstatic!

I stayed at *St Bernadine's* for the remainder of my secondary schooling where I finished with mediocre GCSEs. Unimpressed by the limited subject choices offered in the school's sixth form, tired of the long train journeys and craving a change in environment where I wasn't one of very few Black girls, I decided to go elsewhere to continue my studies. Luckily, I was able to gain a place at a reputable further education college, *Mountain Peak* and I could not wait to leave *St Bernadine's* to start my A-Levels.

Connections and turning points

I refer to my college and university experiences as a time of connections and turning points as they revealed to me just how disconnected I had been in much of my schooling experiences, particularly from the curriculum. Perhaps this is because there is more student choice in post-16 education. For instance, my time at *Mountain Peak* college was the first time I had felt seen in and connected to the curriculum. Transitioning into my undergraduate degree at the *University of Beddington* was the time when I found my feet within an academic setting, inspiring my desire to pursue postgraduate studies at the *University of Zodiac*, navigating the unknown to become an expert.

Being (un)seen in the curriculum

It was only when I got to my A-Levels at age sixteen, a good ten or so years after my primary school experiences, that I was able to celebrate and centre my own culture in an educational setting during my two years at *Mountain Peak* college. *Mountain Peak* was a well-ranked, mixed (in terms of social class and racial/ethnic makeup) state-funded, co-educational, further education college with excellent facilities, situated in a London suburb. It attracted a wide range of students as it offered a variety of courses such as the International Baccalaureate and A-Levels, vocational and technical courses, as well as apprenticeships and access courses. Though there were noticeable divisions between different types of students – for example, at break times, mostly Black students congregated in one canteen whereas another was utilized more by white students – I did like the fact that I had a choice of where and who I could socialize with. I also liked that there were spaces created to affirm, celebrate and be part of the organization and participation of Black History Month celebrations. Not only was this the first time, since primary school, that I celebrated myself and my cultures in an educational setting, it also showed that *Mountain Peak* catered to part of its student population by recognizing us in the space and facilitating cross-cultural learning with students from different backgrounds. The fact that there was a very involved and proactive youth worker, *Dwayne*, who often advocated for the Black students and oversaw the organization of the Black History Month showcase, may have contributed to the college leadership's interest and desire to lead and encourage our participation in such national celebrations. The experiences of Black British women in predominantly GM educational spaces and places is the main theme of Chapter 5.

Attending *Mountain Peak* was very refreshing and I felt a sense of belonging. Along with the extra-curricular activities, I attribute this to my choice of A-Level subjects where it was the first time that I had been taught the subject of sociology – the study of how society is organized and how we experience life (British Sociological Association 2022) – and I had three passionate sociology teachers across my two years, *Ruby*, *Amandeep* and *Jack*, who exposed the class to diverse sociological perspectives and topics. I was finally able to understand the underpinnings of societies through the lens of gender, age, social class and race/ethnicity. I was also able to engage in debates about the role of religion and education, and I discovered scholars like Bourdieu, Foucault and Gilroy, whose theories opened up new dimensions in my mind. It was at this time that I was also introduced to Black Feminist Theory and the concept of intersectionality along with previous research, particularly Professor Heidi Mirza's book, based on her research, *Young Female and Black*. I was able to see Black and Global Majority British people represented and that they could also be the subject and creator of knowledge in academic research. This was so very powerful to me. It was within these two years that my passion for sociology was cemented and I began to collect the intellectual tools that would enable me to think critically about society and its mechanisms, while learning how to effectively articulate my own thoughts about different perspectives and theories, both verbally and in writing. I was also allowed (by my mother) to perm (chemically straighten) my natural hair and wear weaves, so throughout the two years, as if to make up for the years when my mother wouldn't allow me to, I experimented with a huge array of weave lengths, colours and styles. College was also when I got into doing my nails regularly and my long acrylic nails were always changing as I expressed myself through nail art, different designs and techniques.

This was completely different from my time at my last secondary school *St Bernadine's* where I felt invisible and erased in the curriculum. For one of my GCSE subjects, I chose history because I craved being able to engage with diverse cultures, contributions and histories of people like myself, and I thought I would be able to gain this here. However, as a class, we were only taught about Black people in a limited capacity – particularly in the US, regarding slavery and the civil rights movement. I recall feeling frustrated with the ethnocentric, whitewashed curriculum because I did not see myself (or any other Global Majority people) represented anywhere in the school environment – until my cultural charity event. Although this type of curriculum was not unique to this school, the attitudes displayed by my peers, as mentioned previously, were. I remember challenging my teacher by highlighting the contributions of Black British communities and some of my peers reacted with sneers and responded by saying 'yeah right' and 'who cares?' I remember the teacher looking back at me speechless as he probably didn't know about this himself or have the interest or tools to learn and educate us about this. The erasure of Black British histories and contributions were evident in only being taught about the 1955 Montgomery bus boycott in America and not about the 1963 Bristol bus boycott in England, or not including the Black Panther's British chapters when discussing the American Civil Rights movement or their self-defence and social justice aims (Doharty 2018).

Overall, the all-rounded approach of *Mountain Peak* college where the teaching, resources and additional opportunities available were of a high standard meant that I thrived both socially and academically. Ironically, due to the diverse range of courses that *Mountain Peak* college offered, the student intake reflected a mixture of those I had encountered in each of my previous schools – possibly another reason why I felt so comfortable there. This was evident in my friendship group which consisted of like-minded and educationally focused individuals who, although mostly Black, came from a variety of social class and ethnic/cultural backgrounds such as Uganda, Dominica, Congo, Jamaica, Nigeria, Zimbabwe, etc., as well as areas around and outside of London. I thoroughly enjoyed learning and being at *Mountain Peak* college, and this translated to my grades and my academic growth.

Finding my feet at university

It was in 2011 and the year before the UK Government announced that university fees were to be tripled in the following year and because I did not receive the required A-Level grades for my course, I attended a different university and studied an unintended subject. Perhaps in previous years with my grades I might have still been able to retain my conditional university place, but in that year, the competition to avoid the increased fees was fierce. A gap year or resitting my exams were not options as my mother was convinced that I should follow the educational trajectory at the 'appropriate educational age-stage' (Hamilton 2018: 577) and due to her own educational experiences, she didn't want me to be held back resitting repeatedly when I did not have to. Luckily for me, both my mother and my sister played significant roles in supporting me to find an alternative place at a reputable university, utilizing their knowledge and connections. Their support was crucial as, when I received my A-Level results, I was completing a summer camp posting in rural New York state and unable to do the necessary and urgent running around after my rejection to secure a new place. As disappointed as I was to not be going to my first-choice, PW, elite university, I did gain a place at the *University of Beddington* – a good, PW, pre-1992, 'plate-glass' university (Beloff 1968). It turned out that being there was one of the best things to happen to me. As one of my *Mountain Peak* college teachers said as they consoled me when I first found out I had missed out on a place at my intended university, 'such unexpected detours, when we look back on them, become the path itself'.

I eased well into university where I read sociology, helped by my familiarity of being away from home as a boarder at *Bluebird House* and the academic independence of *Mountain Peak* college. I even joined (and quit) a sports team as Wednesday afternoons were also the designated time for sports like it had been at *Bluebird House.* My passion for sociology developed further as I thoroughly enjoyed the many modules which gave me insights into other related disciplines like social policy and anthropology, to name a few. In particular, it was my tutor, *Dr Osbourne,* who positively shaped my time at the *University of Beddington* through his constant support and sharing of opportunities which encouraged me to develop academically (Classens et al. 2017). Aside from my studying, I was able to engage with many different parts of the university, develop strong relationships in my department and beyond, participate in extracurricular activities, as well as holding down part-time employment throughout. I was also given the opportunity to participate in a year abroad in Hong Kong which I had never previously considered, and this opportunity really enhanced both my university experience and my life. I flourished during my undergraduate studies at the *University of Beddington.*

Looking back, I feel as though my gendered, raced and classed identities were valued during my university experiences as I was able to make sense of them through my course. However, coming from a single parent household meant that I was dependent on student loans, and I had to participate in part-time work to financially support myself, which fortunately did not impact upon my grades (Rokicka 2014). Additionally, my racial identity and cultural background did influence some of the extra-curricular activities I engaged with. For example, I was the African and Caribbean Society's (ACS) secretary in my second year, and in my third year during my year abroad, I co-founded a student organization called the Black International Community (BIC). Lastly, it was the combination of my identities and the ways that they intersected to influence my educational journey, along with the intellectual tools I developed in my study of sociology, which enabled me to think about the wider context and the experiences of other Black girls and women in the education system. This interest inspired the research topic for my final undergraduate dissertation and laid the seeds for my masters and doctoral studies. My time at university also led me to the decision to *loc* my hair – the culmination of my heightened consciousness initially instilled by my parents, shaped further throughout my education, and as a rejection of (white) western standards of beauty, as well as being a statement (to myself and others) of my full acceptance of my whole self, in readiness for the next chapter of my life.

Navigating the unknown to become an expert

Towards the final year of my undergraduate studies, I began to panic. I did not know what was next and the unknown scared me. I did not know what I was going to do afterwards, though I had considered a career as a lecturer. However, I did not understand the pathway to becoming a lecturer or whether I would be able to afford it as I did not want to take out another loan. The prospect of the next steps daunted me, so I booked a meeting with my tutor, *Dr Osbourne*. Due to the potential he saw in me, he provided reassurance and shared options for further study and the lecturer pathway. He also informed me about the Economic and Social Research Council (ESRC) 1+3 studentship – an opportunity which was not widely known about or advertised – at least in my circles! After attending an ESRC information session, I was really impressed as it seemed like a clear-cut route to assist with my initial ambitions of becoming a lecturer. Additionally, due to the topic I wanted to research, I would also get the chance to attend my first-choice university, the *University of Zodiac*, which had the relevant resources, and which I had previously missed out on for my undergraduate studies.

Dr Osbourne championed my application and I successfully gained an ESRC 1+3 studentship, with the added support of my soon-to-be ESRC studentship supervisor. I had become one of the small minority of Black British funded students, considering that between the years 2016 and 2019, 'of the total 19,868 Ph.D. funded studentships awarded by UKRI research councils collectively, 245 (1.2%) were awarded to Black or Black Mixed students, with just 30 of those being from Black Caribbean backgrounds' (Williams et al. 2019). This is unrepresentative of the overall population of the Black British demographic which the 2021 British census recorded as 4.2 per cent or 2.4 million in England (Office for National Statistics 2022).

In a similar way that I previously entered a 'new world' when I attended my private, PW boarding school, my predominantly GM, inner-city and my PW, suburban state-funded secondary schools, I was now entering the 'new world' of academia. Here, my race and gender identities were the most prominent in my experiences, as well as my age. I started the 1+3 studentship at twenty-two years old, directly after my undergraduate studies in a different higher education institution from the one where I completed my first degree. This institution was part of the twenty-four Russell group 'world-class, research-intensive universities' (Russell Group 2022), and I was able to enjoy the world-class resources and facilities available to assist my studies and professional as well as personal development. Unsurprisingly, I was the only Black British woman in my cohort as well as the youngest. I initially found it difficult to find a place in this space. I found it hard to relate to the other one-year masters students or my Ph.D. peers who were a mixture of international students and/or professionals with mortgages and caring responsibilities that I did not have. I also found that there was a huge jump from undergraduate-level to masters-level study due to the intensity, depth and increased expectations. My masters was also a research-intensive course to prepare me for the doctoral programme which was slightly different from a 'normal' one-year masters programme. There was also the added pressure of knowing that I had to successfully pass the masters (+1 part of the studentship) to unlock and proceed to the +3, Ph.D., latter part of the programme.

My confidence in my proven abilities began to dwindle so I looked for familiarity amidst this pressured chaos. Giving up was not an option because I had come too far. I was able to find familiarity in the friendships and networks that I made by joining and participating in the activities of student affinity groups and societies, especially a racial justice one, alongside my postgraduate studies which provided necessary solace, strength and affirmation. Many of my friends at the university were second and final-year Black British and Black international women undergraduate students who were of a similar age, and shared similar identities and experiences.

our Black British womanhood mixed with diverse African and Caribbean cultures bonded us in unexplainable ways as we studied at this elite, PW institutional place and intellectual space. The important role of friendship groups in educational experiences are discussed in Chapter 5. Yet, there were also differences in terms of the fact that we were navigating different levels of study and thus pressures. Nonetheless, we carved our own spaces and supported each other to supplement and successfully complete our studies. Such strategies employed for educational 'success' are spoken about in Chapter 7.

Completing a masters course is intense, so beginning a Ph.D. straight after was a challenge that I hadn't anticipated. During my postgraduate studies, particularly during my Ph.D., I experienced a lot of difficulties in terms of navigating the unknown. It was unknown to me as I had only known of one other Black British man who had a Ph.D. when I was growing up (he was the founder of a Black supplementary school I attended). As with every field, there are rules that one is expected to follow. However, I found out that many of these rules were unwritten and sometimes unspoken. Therefore, the importance of being part of different networks became clear. I experienced the common Ph.D. challenges of feeling alone and inadequate; changing supervisors; funding and time pressures and meeting the high expectations and demands placed on me by the programme and myself. To adapt, I observed and learned from other Ph.D. students and academics, I utilized the university's graduate school and the resources available, and I armed myself with many mentors (inside and outside of the university) who played different roles and showed me how to read and decode the unwritten rules so I could 'play the game' and win. These rules included networking, gaining publications *before* graduation, presenting at national and international conferences, developing teaching experience and so much more, alongside researching and writing my thesis. I had to do this as a minimum if I wanted an academic position which wasn't guaranteed. In some ways, the mentality of 'working twice as hard' to prove myself, being around different types of people and adapting to new and unfamiliar educational environments prepared me for my Ph.D. years.

Moreover, my parents stepped in to fill the voids that I experienced. While they did not pursue a Ph.D. themselves, they were able to help me to navigate, particularly institutional procedures and processes, due to their professional experiences and by investing time to familiarise themselves with the process of gaining a Ph.D.. They also supported me, alongside my sisters, mentors and friends, by becoming my sounding boards listening to my ideas as my research developed, using their contacts to help me to find appropriate places to complete my field-work interviews, reading drafts of my thesis chapters and bolstering my confidence when it faltered. This was all crucial to ensure that I finished my studies when this was jeopardised. I became the first in my family to gain a Ph.D. as well as becoming part of only "1% of 25–64-year-olds in the UK" (OECD 2019: 8) to have one when I submitted my thesis in 2019. On the other hand, it cost me my health and clear skin as my eczema consumed my body. I reflect on this in chapter 8.

Transforming experience, passion and expertise into a profession

As Osei (2019: 735) writes when reflecting on her own use of Black Feminist autoethnography, 'the deliberate act of writing ourselves, our histories, and the world through our eyes undeniably pushes against the traditions of social science and critical academic enquiry … to preserve and further archive my voice and lived experiences as a direct act of humanization within the exclusionary walls of academia'. This speaks to the aims of Blackgirl autoethnography employed in this chapter. My understanding of the process of 'becoming' includes reflecting upon the journey and experiences that shaped the current version of who I am. As exemplified in this chapter, my multiple and overlapping identities have influenced and contributed to my process of becoming. My identities have impacted the ways that I see the (educational) world, how I am positioned within the (educational) world and how I navigate in it. My educational story is an alternative narrative of the insights gained from my experiences and journey within the English education system. For instance, my attendance at multiple educational institutions illustrates the inequality and segregated nature of the education system. My educational experiences and journey taught me that 'people like me' are not supposed to 'make it' in a purposely skewed educational structure that facilitates differential access, quality of resources, educational outcomes and opportunities. I learnt that meritocracy is a myth because we are not beginning from the same starting point nor provided with equitable support or resources. This is explored further in Chapter 3.

I learnt that I had navigated the education system at the intersections of devalued identities that simultaneously dis/advantaged me across my educational trajectory. For instance, at my first secondary school, *Eaton Hill*, I was posh but not posh enough; at my second secondary school, *Holyway High*, I was Black but not Black enough, and at my final secondary school, *St Bernadine's*, I was Blackity Black. I learnt that, without the assistance of an audacious, knowledgeable, aspirational, determined, upwardly mobile and prayerful mother, who single-handedly refused to give up on realizing her child's potential, I would not have 'made it' to this position. I also learnt that to 'succeed', I had to fight to prove myself over and over again, I had to strategize, be focused, disciplined and determined – all requiring a great deal of additional energy, strength and stamina. I am indeed a 'Warrior' as Ray BLK lovingly sings, a constant reminder to me.

Most importantly, I learnt that my educational story is one of many which ignited a passion to explore others. I feel fortunate to be in a profession which builds upon my educational experiences and journey, my passion and my expertise gained from my studies and research training. Not only did I find myself and become Dr April-Louise, it led to the creation of sacred space to amplify the valuable knowledge of other Black British girls and women in an academic setting as well as to analyse and critique it. This has been advocated by Griffin (2012: 143) when she writes about the importance of 'Black women with access to academic privilege … [to] use BFA (Black Feminist Autoethnography) as a means to speak to, with, and at times for Black women'. This is done throughout the rest of the book, and, in this chapter, I have used Blackgirl autoethnography to share how I navigated the education system to get into 'a stranger's house (the academy), a white stranger's house, trying to tell my Blackgirl truth' (Boylorn 2016: 47), and those of others.

In the next chapter, the first of seven composite characters, *Shamari*, will represent some of the Black British women graduates' insights about the education system and its connections with wider society. *Shamari* will offer an understanding of what it is like to navigate within an anti-Black world and how this influences the depictions and positioning of Black women in British and American societies. She will also show how Black women experience social class. Ultimately *Shamari* will illustrate how this translates into the education system and impacts the journeys and experiences of many Black girls and women.

2

The Devaluation of Black Girls and Women

Figure 2 *Shamari*

It's a warm and bright evening topping off a long summer's day. It is quiet in this Black-owned nail shop which saw its last customer less than an hour before. However, it has stayed open for one of its most loyal customers who frequently had special after-hours appointments – a perk only extended to the co-owner and top nail technician's best friend. Disrupting the quietness with her anticipated presence, into the shop struts a tall, curvaceous and equally vivacious young Black woman in her mid-twenties. She quickly proceeds to greet her best friend with a hug and two air kisses before she wirelessly connects her phone to the shop's sound system, playing her favourite song 'Peng Black Girls Remix' by ENNY featuring Jorja Smith. Putting her handbag onto the nearest chair – never the floor – she bounces into the seat in front of the nail station, instructing her best friend, on the other side, how she would like her nails while showing pictures on her phone as examples.

Meet Shamari. Her bubbly, bright and friendly personality is infectious and draws you into her magnetic and disarming aura. She lights up the whole place with her presence which intensifies whenever she smiles, revealing her dazzling set of pearly white teeth, and her hidden smiley piercing. Since they could remember, Shamari and her best friend loved to pamper themselves and getting their nails done every two weeks was part of their self-care routine. But, after having so many disappointing – and sometimes traumatic – nail shop experiences, they became tired. This is exemplified in an article by Tso (2018), who writes about the long history of tension and conflict between some Asian and Black communities in the US in nail shops as an example. Unfortunately, there is little British research about this. Shamari and her best friend were tired of having similar experiences in England, spending their hard-earned cash where they were not valued as people, let alone customers. So, they decided that enough was enough. They decided to learn how to do nails for themselves and for others and opened up their Black-woman-owned nail salon. While only her best friend had completed the diploma in nail technology at the local college, Shamari had helped to open the shop, putting her business degree to good use as the other co-owner of 'BBYGRL Nails'. Along with their other Black women co-owners, it was truly a team effort and a collective enterprise utilizing their skills, qualifications and passion to offer the best nail care to their community and others. Though entering into this lucrative sector was risky, it was a bold, brave and necessary business move which was now paying off. 'BBYGRL Nails' provided investment in their community, careers to their all Black staff, as well as all the things that were lacking from their experiences in other nail shops like valuing and treating all their clients with care and excellent customer service; providing quality, cutting-edge and affordable treatment; and adhering to the latest health and safety measures. They were no longer just consumers, but contributors and beneficiaries of a booming UK nail industry, shaping nail culture via inserting and creating their own brand from the comfort of their 'hood.

* * *

Shamari is the first composite character who has been created to illustrate the insights gained from interviews with the Black women in my research. This chapter will highlight why and how Black girls' and women's capital is devalued by exploring the anti-Black world that they navigate daily, underpinned by intersectionality and misogynoir. Examples of how Black women are depicted and positioned in wider British and American popular culture, while considering how social class further influences these experiences will also be explored. The chapter will end by connecting these broad, societal observations to the education system, providing the premise which shapes the experiences and journeys of Black girls and women in it.

* * *

The outro for 'Peng Black Girls Remix' fades abruptly as Shamari's phone dies for lack of battery as her best friend finishes one of her nails. Choosing not to get up to charge her phone or to put on more music, as if soaking up and appreciating the lyrics of the last song, they begin to discuss the importance of their shop, reminiscing about their journey to this point as babygirls, best friends and now business owners.

The dialogue below that is italicized has been added for the flow of the conversation.

Shamari's best friend *It's just crazy that we had to create our own space to be valued within it!*

Shamari *It is crazy, but are you really surprised? I am just glad that we did something about it and we have our very own, successful shop! Big up us!*

Shamari continues to share her reflections and insights with her best friend who is now in concentration mode, as she completes the rest of her nails. Shamari knew this state well and that she would basically be talking to herself with the odd 'mmmm', nod or shake of the head, giggle or kiss of the teeth as responses from her best friend. Nonetheless, she continues to share her thoughts aloud, speaking gently while swaying her head from side to side, allowing her twenty-six-inch, body wave bundles to shimmy with her, sometimes sweeping over her perfectly laid edges.

Going all the way back to her schooling, she begins to retell her educational experiences to her best friend – who she had met at sixth form college, as if she were still journeying through it. Memories etched into her brain. Memories she shares have shaped her life, how she sees and moves in the world and how she understands her place within it as she reflects:

> You just learn your place in society through school whether that be good, whether that be bad, you learn quick and you learn what you can and cannot say and like I say, it's only something that I have recently come out of and even then, me saying this is still giving me anxiety.

As the youngest of five children, she remembers just following blindly in her older siblings' tried and tested footsteps as she did not have any other choice. Whichever school or sixth form college her two brothers and two sisters went to, so did she. Her eldest brother and sister would get new school stuff each year and pass down whichever stationery, clothes and shoes were still in good condition to the rest of them. She did not see anything wrong with this because she thought this was normal for families with loads of children, and she understood that her parents were doing the best they could, working multiple jobs, to provide for all five of them.

A bright student with so much potential, she was often encouraged by some of her teachers to do better and to be better until she worked hard to become the best in her classes, the best in her school. Because, as she says:

> As Black people, you have to be better than everybody else to get to the same level, so putting yourself at a disadvantage by not having the best grade is only impacting yourself negatively.

She recalls how her siblings used to tease her because she was 'different' – too smart, too consciously aware, too inquisitive. It was only after her A-Levels, when she went to university, that she was able to carve her own, fresh path – and that was only because none of her older siblings had chosen to venture to university in pursuit of a degree, opting for alternative routes or heading straight into the workplace. She had never thought that she would become a nail shop co-owner.

Navigating within an anti-Black world: the Windrush scandal and Black Lives Matter

Shamari, like many other Black girls and women, is navigating within an anti-Black world daily, which influences everything from her life chances, life expectancy and educational experiences and outcomes as a graduate. W.E.B. Du Bois' (1989: 6) double consciousness can be used to express how anti-Blackness creates an internal conflict felt by African-Americans whose Black and American identities are incompatible with each other because they represent 'two souls, two thoughts, two unreconciled strivings; two warring ideals in one dark body, whose dogged strength alone keeps it from being torn asunder'. This is a universal conflict experienced by many Black people, in mainly white societies in an anti-Black world.

Racism has multiple meanings, tropes, forms and levels. Many others like Sayyid (2017: 12) write that 'racism' as a term was first coined as the title of a German book by Magnus Hirschfeld in the 1930s to describe what the Nazis were doing to the Jewish populations; though as he notes, this was not the first time that 'racism' had been practiced. Based on the first usage of the term, what makes racism so destructive and important to understand is the power dynamics of those able to actively put racism into practice and those that are subjected to it. This is explained by the equation 'racism = power + prejudice' (Barndt 1991; Operario and Fiske 1998). Moreover, there are specific forms of racism such as anti-Gypsyism, anti-Black racism or Afrophobia, Islamophobia, Antisemitism, Xenophobia, and the resurgence of anti-Asian hate based on Covid-19, which are tailored to and impact diverse groups in different ways. Additionally, definitions of racism fail to incorporate much of its roots which are often, 'shaped by Europe's history of colonial abuse and repeated persecutions against minorities' (European Network Against Racism (ENAR) 2014). This is reflected upon in Chapter 3 using the curriculum as an example of how this is upheld. More specifically, the existence and operation of Afrophobia, also referred to as anti-Black racism, is characterized by the Council of Europe (2021: 4) as

> a form of racism that targets people of African descent and Black people and manifests itself through acts of direct, indirect and institutional discrimination, as well as violence, including hate speech. Based on socially constructed ideas of 'race' and reflecting the groundless belief that certain 'racial' groups are biologically or culturally inferior to others, Afrophobia seeks to dehumanise and deny the dignity of its victims.

Based on the previous definition, key examples of anti-Black racism are exemplified in the so-called Windrush Scandal of 2018 where, in Britain, it was revealed to the public that the Home Office had destroyed the landing cards and documentation of Black Britons of Caribbean heritage, who arrived in the UK with family members as children from the 1950s. No online records had been made of these documents and the individuals had not been told their documents had been destroyed. Triggered by the introduction of new UK legislation in 2012 to create a 'hostile environment', they were made to prove their entitlement to remain in the UK, and many were subject to the denial of rights, detained and threatened with deportation and experienced the loss of their homes, jobs and recourse to public funds. There were also many who had already been wrongly deported as confirmed by the Home Office's review in 2019, which identified that out of two thousand Caribbean people, 164 of them had been in the country before 1973 (and therefore were part of the so-called Windrush generation) and had either been detained or removed – or both – since 2002. What was happening was only brought to light when newspaper articles were written and prominent Windrush activists like Paulette Wilson began to speak up, pressuring the Government to action. Wilson's became one of the most well-known stories that illustrated the predicament and the injustices of this scandal. Summarized in a *Guardian* newspaper article written by Gentleman and Campbell in 2020, after arriving in the UK from Jamaica at age ten in 1968, she found herself being wrongly detained and on the brink of deportation. After successfully fighting to remain in the UK, she became a leading Windrush activist, helping to fight the UK government and to support other Windrush victims. Unfortunately, she died at the young age of sixty-four – possibly a consequence of all the stress and instability she endured in her quest for justice. Eventually the report, *Windrush Lessons Learned Review* by Wendy Williams was commissioned by the Government in 2018, and the Windrush Compensation Scheme was set up in 2019. But how much has really been learned when the Home Office was criticized for the inconsistencies, delays, lack of cultural understanding and decision-making of its case workers, and its compensation scheme has been described as complex and inaccessible with very few victims receiving a payout? The UK Government has also proceeded to put more Britons, mainly Black and Global Majority citizens and residents alike, at risk of the stripping of their citizenship and residence without notice, under the Nationality and Borders Act introduced in July 2021. Though there were many other victims of the Home Office's incompetence who were not Black or Caribbean, I frame it as anti-Black as it disproportionately impacted this group, in line with the historic underpinnings of this country (Martin 2020a, The United Nations, 2023) and seemed like a deliberate and targeted attack on Black Britons of Caribbean heritage who had ironically been invited by the UK Government to 'rebuild the country' all those years ago. They were now being tossed out, like rubbish, after they were deemed to no longer be of use. To make matters worse, in 2023, the current home secretary Suella Braverman reneged on going forward with implementing at least three of the Windrush report recommendations (Brown 2023).

The scandal was revealed in 2018 by Amelia Gentleman and it had been unknown to the wider public though many of the affected communities were suffering in silence for many years before that. As a grandchild of the so-called Windrush generation on my paternal side (though my maternal grandparents had also arrived in the UK in the same era), it resonated with me. I remember when the scandal was first emerging, not quite understanding its implications or severity so I asked my Jamaican grandma about her thoughts and she revealed to me that, in 1971 when the Government had started to change their nationality and citizenship legislation, she had gathered her money and completed the required documentation for herself and her family. I am eternally grateful for her foresight and action which prevented a huge amount of disruption to our family, but this raised uncomfortable questions and rocked my sense of belonging in the UK as a Black, supposedly 'British', woman.

On a global scale, the reemergence of the Black Lives Matter movement, after the public and brutal state-sanctioned execution of George Floyd in 2020, is another key example of anti-Black racism. Though the movement originates in the US, it spread globally as 'when we say "Black Lives Matter" we refer to the imperative to articulate and transcend nation-state boundaries' (Paschel 2017: 28). Moreover, violence and murder at the hands of those that are paid to 'serve and protect' (or similar variations) are not restricted to US contexts, despite the arguments of right-wing commentators in the UK who often make the claim that US and UK contexts are very different; on the contrary, UK cases such as Dorothy 'Cherry' Groce who was mistakenly shot in her London home by police and left paralysed in 1985; Sheku Bayoh who died after being restrained by Scottish police in 2015; Mohamud Hassan who died after being released from police custody in Cardiff (Wales) in 2021; Mark Duggan shot dead by police sparking the Tottenham riots in 2011, or Chris Kaba also shot dead in London by police in 2022 are a testament and make the point that they clearly are not. As Joseph-Salisbury et al. (2020: 22) highlight in their paper on the underpinnings of the Black Lives Matter 2020 protests and the movement in the UK where activists are 'turning our gaze to British racism: "the UK is not innocent" has become a rallying cry', and that 'the UK protests should be understood not only as inspired by the United States, but as the culmination of growing frustration in recent years. The racism underpinning the Grenfell Tower fire, the Windrush scandal and the unequal impact of the COVID-19 pandemic have all played their role … and exacerbated the over-policing of Black communities.'

What is clear from the Black Lives Matter movement are the ways in which Black skin is regarded as a threat, translating into excessive force, unequal treatment and a lack of empathy, care and justice exercised by those with authority, such as the police. It does not matter if that Black skin belongs to a child or a woman or whether the Black person is unarmed – they could even be asleep as was the case for Breonna Taylor in the US. There is a lasting impact on the lives of Black people globally as their collective pain and trauma is publicly amplified as newsworthy by the worldwide media, for all to see, over and over again. Then, the usual cycle of promises, pledges and messages of support shared by big organizations; and the Black squares as profile pictures and unified hashtags from individuals on social media, illustrate the performative solidarity but the lack of real, lasting change or social justice for Black communities. It must also be noted that anti-Black racism is not just a 'white issue' as other Global Majority communities also participate (Martin 2020b).

Remarkably, despite the many manifestations of anti-Black racism and its detrimental effects, of which I have only highlighted two, 'there is currently no EU or national policy developed specifically to combat racism and discrimination against people of African descent and Black Europeans' (ENAR 2021). However, small steps have been taken as, for example, in England the Labour parliamentary party (2021) created a

'Code of Conduct' to highlight and tackle Afrophobia and anti-Black racism for its members, and the Black Equity Organisation was launched in 2022 to 'dismantle systemic racism in Britain, drive generational change and deliver better lived experiences for Black people across the country' (Black Equity Organisation (BEO) 2022). In the United States, the George Floyd Justice in Policing Act 2021 was introduced in February of the same year to 'address policing practices and law enforcement accountability' (Congress.Gov 2021).

In academia, CRT as outlined in the 2021 book *Foundation of Critical Race Theory in Education*, has provided a way for discussions around anti-Black racism, specifically within educational spaces, to emerge via the discipline of BlackCrit which is an offshoot. In this area, BlackCrit scholars assert that there is a need for a 'critical theorisation of Blackness' which:

> confronts the specificity of antiBlackness, as a social construction, as an embodied lived experience of social suffering and resistance, and perhaps most importantly, as an antagonism, in which the Black is a despised thing-in-itself (but not person for herself or himself) in opposition to all that is pure, human(e), and white.
>
> (Dumas and Ross 2016: 416–7)

In other words, while CRT provides a powerful tool to critique the significant role of race, racism and whiteness as a resource that generates unearned privilege to those racialized as 'white', it does not give a deeper analysis to highlight the everlasting impact of transatlantic slavery, colonialism and the existing societal inequalities that are disproportionately suffered by Black diasporic communities globally (Dumas 2016; Warren and Coles 2020). Though focusing on African-American and African-Latin peoples, Sawyer (2008: 136) contributes four main tenets to articulate the trans-national operation of anti-Black racism:

1. A history of oppression and unequal incorporation in social, political, and economic life of the nation.
2. A negative and limiting set of stereotypes that operate to define that group.
3. Formal legal and informal barriers to achievement.
4. An ideology that justifies the domination and oppression of the group.

Referencing *Shamari*'s opening comment at the beginning of this chapter, her belief that to be Black means working harder than everyone else to get to 'the same level' is one that speaks to both tenet 1 and 3 of Sawyer's operation of anti-Black racism. It is a history of oppression which excludes Black children from being formally educated and then accessing education of a lesser quality to their peers once they were permitted to do so, which continues to this day (for historical depth, see Coard 1971; Gillborn and Youdell 2000; Wallace and Joseph-Salisbury 2022). This can explain the 'unequal incorporation' in other areas of the 'life of the nation', as well as the legacies of 'formal legal and informal barriers to achievement' which mean that Black people may feel they have to work extra hard to overcome. *Shamari*'s other articulations of anti-Black racism are described in the following extract which continues to reinforce some of Sawyer's observations:

> One thing that I haven't liked in this country is that I kinda feel like Black people kinda are invisible in this country, except for I think London ... London is the one place that I don't feel people are looking at me.

The belief that Black people are 'invisible in this country' describes both the first tenet of how anti-Black racism can operate according to Sawyer as *Shamari* states that she does not feel Black people are visible. This can evidence 'unequal incorporation in the life of the nation'. Moreover, the invisibility that *Shamari* states can also be interpreted as feelings of discomfort, possibly from her own experiences when in other places across the country and which is confirmed by her assertion that London is 'the one place that I don't feel people are looking at me'. This makes sense as statistics show that London is the 'most ethnically diverse region' in England and Wales (Gov.uk 2022d). However, this quote illustrates that Black people are invisible in the nation's culture which *Shamari* points out leads to people looking at her, presumably because she stands out as a Black person among mainly white people outside of London. The next excerpt exemplifies Sawyer's fourth tenet of the operation of anti-Black racism when *Shamari* says:

> It's like being British and being in a country where a majority of the people are white, you try and become someone who you are not amongst your journey, along the way, somewhere. It's weird, like we have all wanted to change our name ... I feel like that is a consequence of being Black and British because you are amongst white people a lot, and they look at you and ask you how you say your name, or they pronounce it wrong and you accept it. It's things like that, so the journey throughout life and especially education is very much confusing.

In some ways, *Shamari* highlights how being a Black person and a minority in a white-majority country means that you will inevitably try to fit in, which requires diluting markers of Blackness, such as names, which she goes on to explain. This implies an awareness that some white people may hold 'an ideology that justifies the domination and oppression of the group' which Black people must disassociate with to navigate. Through *Shamari*'s reflections, markers of Blackness like names seem to be treated as though they are culturally inferior and as if there's an underpinning assumption that getting a person's name right doesn't matter if it doesn't conform to mainstream white norms. Additionally, she describes the discomfort felt or microaggressions (Sue et al. 2007), and a reason why some Black people may wish to change their names, as some white people who are often unfamiliar with and mispronounce them can 'other' them in the process. This can also highlight a Black person's perceived difference and can question their belonging in whichever (white) space they are in. Moreover, this acceptance of the mispronunciation of names can indicate the lack of power felt by some Black people who choose not to assert the correct pronunciation of their names, as well as the lack of respect by some white people to learn how to say it properly. According to Kohli and Solózano (2012) who explore this within American educational contexts, they liken the mispronunciation of students of colour's names as 'cultural disrespect' and a manifestation of deeper factors originating from racism and racial microaggressions which have a lasting impact on Black and other students of colour. This lasting impact is articulated by *Shamari* when she shares that 'the consequences of being Black and British' are 'very much confusing'. But how does anti-Black racism manifest in gendered ways for Black girls and women?

The depictions and positioning of Black women: the 'bottom of the heap in both ways'

Shamari delicately holds her hands in front of her – even though her fingernails are dry. She switches positions so that her best friend can easily get to her toenails to continue her pampering session. Admiring the intricate nail art, new length, colour and shape, Shamari motions for her best friend to ensure that her toes are in sync with her hands after she has finished her spa pedicure. Thanking God out loud for her best friend and her skills, as well as their nail shop to which they both giggle, she looks briefly into space, as if she is deep in thought. Peering down at her best friend who has now started on her feet, she continues to talk, as though she has a lot more to get off her chest.

> I just think that being a Black woman is really difficult at times because you are at the bottom of the heap in both ways and there's that constant

> pressure to try and prove to yourself – cos you can prove to other people as well, but if you don't prove to yourself that you can do it, then it doesn't really matter. There is no point being Black, being a woman, being working class, you definitely do feel like there is a lot up against you and just trying to persevere through that is really important and there should be more emphasis made on that. There should be more emphasis on the fact that you are in a disadvantaged position but also, how to overcome that cos I don't think I realized how disadvantaged and how being Black and being a woman and being working class and all that has an effect on me, until I came to uni and it took me aback at times.

What *Shamari* describes is essentially the basis of 'intersectionality' as framed by Kimberlé Crenshaw (1989, 1991), when she outlined the ways in which multiple, overlapping and devalued identities come together at the same time, to influence and shape the lived experiences and realities of Black women. For *Shamari*, these experiences and realities include feelings of being at 'the bottom of the heap in both ways', 'constant pressure' and being 'in a disadvantaged position' which she reveals has taken her 'aback at times'. Mixed into these reflections is *Shamari*'s awareness of the role of her 'working-class' background as an additional dimension to her raced and gendered intersectional identities which slightly changes her thoughts on being 'at the bottom of the heap in both ways' as this means she is actually 'at the bottom of the heap in *three* ways'. She continues to explain her thoughts.

> Being Black is something that people can discriminate against you for, being a woman is another thing that they can discriminate against you for, so when you are Black and a woman it's like double whammy if that makes sense. I feel like I grow, I have a lot of strength in myself from it. I won't ever let – I refuse to let that be something that stops me if that makes sense or lets other people stop me.

The continued assertion of race and gender in *Shamari*'s reflections indicates the prominence of race and gender, more so than class (even though she is aware of it) in her lived experiences and reality which she shares is because

> I think it is hard to isolate race and gender so I'm not too sure where sometimes when I am approached in a certain way, I don't know whether it is because of my race or my gender or both so I really find it hard to [separate it].

While 'intersectionality' can also be applied to the lived experiences and reality of other racially minoritized women, the distinct and overlapping nature of both anti-Black racism and sexism in the lives of Black women cannot. As Lorde poignantly asks, 'what other creature in the world besides the Black woman has had to build the knowledge of so much hatred into her survival and keep going?' (1984: 150). This experience is further encapsulated by the term 'misogynoir'. Misogynoir, as defined by Moya Bailey (Bailey and Trudy 2018: 762), is 'the anti-Black racist misogyny that Black women experience' which translates to 'the specific hatred, dislike, distrust, and prejudice directed toward Black women'. In popular culture and wider society, concentrating on Britain and America provides a useful comparison for the depictions of Black women to illustrate misogynoir. However, misogynoir plays out differently in each context as the depictions and positioning of Black women in Britain can be characterized as one of invisibility and erasure in contrast to hypervisibility and negative stereotypes in America.

The erased and invisible Black British woman

In a thought-provoking 2013 article titled *Who stole all the Black women from Britain?*, the author Emma Dabiri grapples with a range of issues such as colourism, intersectionality, anti-Black racism and sexism. These issues plague the lived realities of dark-skinned, Black British women. However, Dabiri illustrates the media's role in perpetuating the constant erasure and invisibility of dark-skinned Black British women in popular culture and how this is transferred into *Black* British subculture too. The main example that Dabiri uses to prove her point is the frequent coupling of Black men with white women, light-skinned or mixed-heritage women in popular Black British music, movies, TV and radio shows who become 'the symbols of 'Urban' or 'Black British youth culture''. She also shows how these images filter into the minds of some young Black British men who begin to reject dark-skinned Black women – who are positioned as undesirable hence their erasure and invisibility – as partners, instead opting for white, light-skinned or mixed-heritage women. A strength of Dabiri's article is how she supports her argument drawing on wider contexts and theories such as the rising rates of the British mixed-heritage population, historical and colonial legacies of the slave trade and South Africa; along with Fanon and Black Feminist thought. An example of the phenomenon Dabiri describes is the popular YouTube show 'Chicken shop date' hosted and created by white, middle-class woman presenter Amelia Dimoldenberg who interviews celebrities in a London chicken shop. It received a lot of backlash with Black British women being some of the most vocal, as captured in a Refinery29 article where the author, Martin (2022), writes about the premise of the criticism:

> a lot of people seem to think that the show's format, paired with a middle-class white female host is problematic as UK chicken shops are seen as something that is typically rooted in working class and ethnic minority culture,

> and

> [t]he conversation is really about white privilege and access. People are wondering why it's so easy for white people to enter and succeed in our cultural spaces. Particularly, when many Black creatives and Black talent in the UK media industry are struggling to secure gigs and be seen, whereas white people can gain status and visibility in minutes.

Interestingly, what catapulted the show to success was Amelia's interviews with Black (British) male celebrities like grime music artist Ghetts – though she has gone on to interview a diverse range of other people, including Black women. However, yet again, Black British women are erased and invisible as content creators, in favour of a white woman, coupled with (mostly) Black men, discussing 'urban', youth (aka Black culture), from a space which they are and should be a visible part of.

However, Black British culture does not operate in isolation and there is constant exchange between it and wider society's dominant, mainstream culture which Dabiri believes to be evident in 'the basis of so much of Britain's somewhat depressing representations of mainstream youth culture, [which] borrows heavily from Black culture, yet sometimes both seem almost entirely devoid of Black women'. Importantly, Dabiri's article illustrates the extent of the erasure and invisibility of dark-skinned Black British women and raises questions about where they can find safe spaces to exist if they are excluded from cultures and spaces which are supposed to be their own. However, respectfully, I wish she reflected upon her own positionality as a light-skinned, mixed-heritage woman – though I do commend her for using her relative privilege to write about this important topic. This takes my mind back to primary school when in my english and creative writing classes, I went through a phase of constantly writing stories where the characters were families which always consisted of a Black dad, a white mum and mixed-heritage children. Not that there is anything wrong with such families, but at that time, this was my ideal family, possibly because I was subconsciously being influenced by what I saw represented in popular culture – despite this not being my own reality.

While the representation of dark-skinned Black British women in popular culture is slightly better in 2024, growing up as a young Black girl in Britain during the 1990s and early 2000s, it was very difficult to find mainstream representation of Black British women, both mixed-heritage and especially dark-skinned Black British women. I always yearned for Black British women representation so I remember being over the moon to see pop girlbands like the Spice Girls – especially band member Mel B – and Mis-Teeq's Su-Elise, Alesha and Sabrina on my TV. I was especially in awe and obsessed with supermodel Naomi Campbell, Keisha Buchanan from the girlband the Sugababes, singers Jamelia and Estelle, and more recently Misha B who appeared on the eighth series of the English version of the TV talent show *The X Factor*. To me, these women were beautiful and provided a rare glimpse of necessary representation for me as a dark-skinned Black British girl/woman. However, the media often depicted these dark-skinned Black British women celebrities in questionable and sometimes very negative ways. For example, Mel B's nickname was 'Scary Spice' given to her by a 'lazy' journalist because she was 'loud' (Lutes 2013), Keisha was accused of being 'intimidating' by her bandmates and often portrayed as the 'angry Black woman' by journalists (Aubrey 2020), in a similar way that Misha B was also depicted as aggressive and a bully on *The X Factor* (BBC 2020). This is also an important topic for *Shamari* who shared the following views:

> I wanna see more … more Black British women in [the subject of] english because I feel like that's the foundation of it all, you learn in english thus what can be shown in the world, it's like a microcosm of the world, you don't want – to me books are like a basic form of communication which you learn about and then you go out into the world, you have media, you have radio, you have different platforms where you can be seen and they are not showing us [Black British women], but where did you learn that from? You learnt it from the classroom, that's where you learnt it from.

Shamari's focus on the subject of english as well as the role of education in foregrounding the erasure and invisibility of Black British women in the media and wider society is a novel and important insight. In a similar way that Dabiri highlights the exchange between white British mainstream youth culture and Black British subcultures in her article, *Shamari*'s reflections argue that the erasure and invisibility of Black British women in the media, and the world, is ingrained and begins from 'the classroom'. I agree as, with my english and creative writing lessons in primary school, I would write stories which erased myself and others that looked like me. How children engage with and write stories, focusing on the importance of race is a topic explored by Chetty (2016).

On the other hand, thanks to rapid technological advancement, which has provided freedom to and access for content creation from previously excluded groups like Black women, there has been a deliberate re-centring of Black British women on platforms created by and for them. Such platforms include *Black Ballad, gal-dem* (now closed down) and *Cocoa Girl*, to name a couple. Growing up, I remember my mother taking me and my sister to events like the Afro Hair & Beauty LIVE, possibly to restore my sense of self and pride in my identity. Also, the rise of such platforms has been incredibly important to promote issues that particularly affect Black women which are then (sometimes) picked up and covered by mainstream media (Lundman 2003; Rhiney 2021) – usually after their loved ones and communities take it upon themselves to campaign and raise awareness (Black Ballad 2021). For example, Black British women being four to five times more likely to die in childbirth compared to white women (MBRACE-UK 2021). Another example is the Black British women victims who go missing or whose murders are unpunished, subject to police mishandling of justice like in the cases of sisters Nicole Smallman and Bibaa Henry who were stabbed to death in a London park in 2020 (BBC 2022). A final example is Blessing Olusegun who went missing and was found dead on a beach in Sussex also in 2020 (Etienne and Jichi 2022). This is no surprise, as it was reported in 2016, that British journalism in itself was predominantly white (94 per cent) and male (55 per cent) to begin with (Williams 2016) with slow progress in regards to racial and ethnic diversity (White 2019; Tobitt 2021) – which is another reason this is happening.

The hypervisible and negatively stereotyped Black American woman

In the US, Black women are much more visible to the population in mainstream media and popular culture compared to Black British women. These representations filter into the UK, and I was very exposed to and influenced by American depictions of Blackness as I grew up, for example via the reruns of NBC's 1990s sitcom *The Fresh Prince of Bel Air* (1991–1996). The global dominance of Black American culture, albeit with many other Black cultural influences, is one that has been written about by Hall (1992) and Gilroy (1993). However, deeper analysis reveals that this visibility is limited and through a number of fixed and racist stereotypes which can be equally as damaging. Leading Black Feminist scholar, Professor Patricia Hill Collins (2000) has written a great deal about the lived experiences of Black

American women and the racist stereotypes they are positioned to occupy. Collins explains how the stereotypical images of Black women serve as a tool to position 'U.S. Black women as the Other provid[ing] ideological justification for race, gender and class oppression' (Collins 2000: 70). She outlines, as below, that the five main depictions that Black American women are placed into are: the Mammy, the Matriarch, the Welfare mother, the Black lady and the Jezebel (Collins 2000):

> **Mammy** – the faithful, obedient domestic servant. Created to justify the economic exploitation of house slaves and sustained to explain Black women's long-standing restriction to domestic service, the mammy image represents the normative yardstick used to evaluate all Black women's behaviour. By loving and nurturing and caring for her white children and 'family' better than her own, the mammy symbolises the dominant group's perceptions of the ideal Black female relationship to elite white male power.
>
> (p. 72)

> **Matriarch** – the matriarch symbolises the mother figure in Black homes … women who failed to fulfil their traditional 'womanly' duties at home … spending too much time away from home, these working mothers ostensibly could not properly supervise their children and thus were major contributing factors to their children's failure at school. As overly aggressive, unfeminine women, Black matriarchs allegedly emasculated their lovers and husbands … From the dominant group's perspective, the matriarch represented the failed mammy, a negative stigma to be applied to African-American women who dared reject the image of submissive, hardworking servant.
>
> (p. 75)

> **Welfare mother** – a class-specific, controlling image developed for poor, working-class Black women who make use of the social welfare benefits to which they are entitled to by law … Essentially an updated version of the breeder woman image created during slavery, this image provides an ideological justification for efforts to harness Black women's fertility to the needs of a changing political economy.
>
> (p. 78)

> **Black lady** – middle-class professional Black women who represent[s] a modern version of the politics of respectability … this image may not appear to be a controlling image, merely a benign one … yet the

> image of the Black lady builds upon prior images of Black womanhood in many ways ... this image seems to be yet another version of the modern mammy, namely, the hardworking Black woman professional who works twice as hard as everyone else ... Highly educated Black ladies are deemed to be too assertive – that's why they cannot get men to marry them.
>
> (pp. 80–1)

Jezebel – relegates all Black women to the category of sexually aggressive women, thus providing a powerful rationale for the widespread sexual assaults by white men typically reported by Black slave women ... a Radicalized gendered symbol of deviant female sexuality ... a woman whose sexual appetites are, at best inappropriate and, at worst, insatiable, it becomes a short step to imagine her as a 'freak'.

(pp. 81–3)

The significance of these stereotypical images can be seen in many ways. For one, the fact that these five images encompass and connect with each other and to many aspects of Black femininity, from motherhood to sexual behaviour, shows the many restrictions placed on Black women identities in the US (Ladson-Billings 2009). Additionally, Collins (2000: 85–8) further indicates that these images have real-life implications as they filter into social institutions like the media, government agencies and the education system, as well as influencing standards of beauty which place darker-skinned Black women in particular at the bottom. It is even more concerning that these images continue to evolve in modern times with the same damaging consequences, becoming staples of both Black subcultures via music videos, reality TV shows, as well as in mainstream white media. At times, these images are internalized by some Black communities, especially Black girls and women because they 'serve as significant tools in socialising consumers to scripts of Black female sexuality', and reinforce 'the predominant media representations of Black women often illustrate[d] [as] racially-stereotyped, highly-sexualised images' (Coleman et al. 2016: 1165). For example, these stereotypes play out in particular ways like in Nelly's infamous 2003 'Tip Drill' music video where he literally swipes a credit card between one of his Black women dancer's bum cheeks completely sexually dehumanizing her. Additionally, reality TV shows like the VH1 franchises of *Love & Hip Hop* (2011–present) and *Basketball Wives* (2010–present), as well as the Bravo series of *The Real Housewives of Atlanta* (2008–present) and *The Real Housewives of Potomac* (2016–present), to name a few, continue to amplify these stereotypes albeit in slightly more sophisticated ways. Further stereotypical images of Black women such as being verbally aggressive (Glascock and Preston-Schreck 2018) and 'ratchet' (Pickens 2015) are also enshrined in both Black and white mainstream popular culture in the US.

As with the invisibility that characterizes the discourses surrounding Black British women, there are similar damaging implications caused by the negative stereotyping of Black American women. Steele (1997) asserts that stereotyping can hugely influence intellectual identity and performance which is highly relevant when thinking about how Black girls and women navigate in the education system and will be discussed further in the following chapters. Yancy (2000: 162) also demonstrates the damage caused by such images when he writes how 'Black women came to *know* themselves in terms of the destructive images created from within white imaginative spaces' [emphasis in original]. By shining a light on these damaging representations of Black women, Boylorn (2008: 414) writes in her paper about Black women, race and reality TV in the US,

> I am inviting other Black women to become critical consumers, using their gaze internally and externally (looking inward at their own lives and consciousness and outward at the images and depictions of Black womanhood that are currently available on reality television) to oppose and challenge rather than immediately and readily accept negative representations of Black womanhood.

Interestingly, though *Shamari* has never set foot in the US, due to the power and reach of US content, she is well aware of the negative Black women stereotypes and their damaging implications:

> You have to be thick skinned, you have to be able to overcome a lot of negative views, there are stereotypical views of you as a Black woman, you have to be able to overcome those views, you have to be strong to overcome those views and show that you know who you are – who I am as a person – yes my heritage and my culture are part of it but a stereotype does not define who I am. I don't like to be classified by stereotypes of my race or my gender at all and I think you have to be strong to overcome that in a world where that is what's thrown in people's faces and – like the media or … just wherever people get these stereotypes from.

Yet, in a similar way as highlighted in the UK, there has been active resistance to these limited, fixed, gendered, highly sexual and racist stereotypes of Black women in the US. For example, such resistance includes the establishment of Essence in 1968 – a lifestyle, news and music brand that boasts a magazine, festival and online presence where 'Black women come first' (Essence 2022); the BLACK GIRLS ROCK! network, movement and annual awards ceremony to empower, honour and provide Black girls with positive Black women role models; and the creation of the hashtag #BlackGirlMagic by CaShawn Thompson which became a movement 'to celebrate the beauty, power and resilience of Black women' (Wilson 2016). Moreover, the hashtag and campaign #SayHerName was created by Professor Kimberlé Crenshaw in 2014 to raise awareness and to fight for justice for the many Black girls and women victims of police brutality who are rarely spotlighted by the mainstream media (The African American Policy Forum and Center for Intersectionality and Social Policy Studies 2014). Notable Black women victims they campaigned for included Breonna Taylor who was shot and killed while she slept in her home in 2020, Rekia Boyd who was murdered in the street by an off-duty policeman in 2012 and Sandra Bland who was pulled over by police for an alleged traffic violation, taken into custody and never made it home alive in 2015, to name a few. The misogynoir directed at Black women also goes beyond both UK and US contexts as exemplified by the outrage from some Egyptians (and others) at the depiction of Cleopatra as a Black woman (though the actress that plays her is mixed heritage) in a Netflix series (Gharavi 2023). Not only has there never been the same level of outrage when white actresses have played Cleopatra, her being played by a mixed-heritage actress is most accurate as scholars (Diop 1974; Clarke 1984; Morkot 2000) have proved that early Egyptians were Black Africans.

It's cool to be a Black girl or woman – unless you actually are one: cultural appropriation, Instagram 'baddie' culture and Blackfishing

The invisibility of Black women in British mainstream popular culture and society along with their misrepresentation in fixed anti-Black racist and gendered stereotypes in the US is ironic when considering recent debates around cultural appropriation, 'the process of adopting an aspect of another culture and presenting it as one's own … usually received by the public as more acceptable than its original use by its creators' (Vaughan-Bonas 2019: 1). The emergence of Instagram 'baddie' culture which often goes hand in hand with 'Blackfishing' is illustrative of the cultural appropriation of Black women images. Journalist Wanna Thompson offers a powerful critique on this in her popular 2018 article *Black girls from the hood are the real trendsetters* and she is lauded for coining the term 'Blackfishing', explaining it in another 2018 *Paper* article:

> white women have been able to steal looks and styles from Black women … these women have the luxury of selecting which aspects they want to emulate without fully dealing with the consequences of Blackness … with extensive lip fillers, dark tans and attempts to manipulate their hair texture, white women wear Black women's features like a costume. These are the same features that, once derided by mainstream white culture, are now coveted and dictate current beauty and fashion on social media, with Black women's contributions being erased all the while.

The 'baddie' culture, as aided by the social media platform Instagram, parades and has, in recent times, made popular the cultural appropriation of these specific Black womanhood images by (mostly) white girls and women and is an under researched area. But as Cherid (2021: 360) argues, the 'baddie' culture is another way to show how 'Black culture is intentionally being made palatable to a white audience, with the goal of making a profit'. This can be seen by the blatant cultural appropriation by white, other non-Black women celebrities and even luxury fashion brands who incorporate distinctly Black women hairstyles like cornrows and bantu knots – which they rename as boxer braids and space buns respectively – promoting them as though it was them who discovered or created them, erasing Black women and their cultures in the process (Diaz 2019; Dirshe 2020; Kia 2020). Historically, these same, natural features saw Black South African woman Sarah Baartman paraded around Europe in circuses for profit as her curvaceous figure and protruding bum was made into a spectacle (Gordon-Chipembere 2011). Reversing these narratives about Black women is exemplified in the BLACK VENUS exhibition, beautifully curated by Aindrea Emelife, first debuting in 2022 at New York's Fotografiska and due to appear in London's Somerset House in 2023 (F. Pennant 2022). On the flipside, there was also legislation, like the one-drop rule, against passing as white in the US (Khanna 2010).

In light of the many ways in which Black girls and women are constantly policed by anti-Black racist school and workplace policies about how, for instance, they can or cannot wear their hair, these phenomena are particularly alarming and reek of misogynoir. It also sends a clear message that it's cool to be a Black girl or woman – unless you actually are one because Black women's style, features and even speech are only desirable and acceptable when used and worn by anyone but them. Moreover, rarely do these 'culture vultures' profiting from Black women in these ways, particularly white and non-Black women celebrities, use their platforms to advocate for Black injustices or share their resources with Black women publicly and when necessary (Persad 2020; Wallis 2020). This phenomenon is also in direct contrast to the open and public fetishization of Black men where the darker-skinned Black man is depicted and positioned as highly desirable, dominating popular culture, albeit as a 'cool', sexual object (Clennon 2013; Dabiri 2013).

It is unsurprising that popular culture and wider society would dictate how Black girls and women are depicted and positioned within the education system. After all, it merely replicates the beliefs and practices of the dominant (white) majority culture. It is important to emphasize that the greater availability and visibility of Black girl and women images in the US are not positive as they are assigned to fixed stereotypical and anti-Black racist images. But, fundamentally, both the invisibility in the UK and the fixed stereotypical and racist representation of Black women in the US achieve similar outcomes of silencing, misrepresenting and homogenizing their lived experiences. This is echoed by *Shamari* who shares how she experiences being devalued as a Black woman:

> I guess it is like reiteration of … it is definitely difficult. I think that focusing on Black girls and women, and not just 'Black in education' [is important] because it is very … it's a special one a very unique one … Because it's just, I feel like in general, the Black woman in society, in my opinion, you have variations … In this society that we live in, in the western world, I'm gonna say world, I'm gonna go ahead and say world, I think that the Black woman in general is at the bottom. Like if we are gonna look at a food chain of people of races and genders, the Black woman is at the bottom, and you can have variations like if you look at the Black Muslim woman, the Black LGBTQ+ woman, there is just something about a Black woman which is … for some reason, society has decided that she's the lowest, and she gets the most … I don't know, the most stick for decisions and stuff and I feel like when you bring that individual into the education system, which is founded on white middle-class male-hood, there is gonna be some tension there, so I think it is something that really needs to be looked into.

Having discussed the anti-Black and gendered relationship between the media, popular culture, wider society and how this influences the depictions and positioning of Black women in both the UK and the US, the following section will explore the role of class and its impact on the lived experiences of Black women. As will become clear, the education system doesn't make it easy for Black women to enter this space and make a difference.

'We came from the bottom so we have to work our way up': Black women and social class

The significance of social class is that it can greatly impact individual life chances, as well as future generations of the same family. This is outlined in Savage's 2015 book *Social Class in the 21st Century*, in which he argues that while social class is still significant in Britain, the groupings have evolved into seven distinct classes: the super-rich elite at the top of society at 6 per cent of the total population; established middle class; technical middle class; new affluent workers; traditional workers; emerging service workers; and the precariat at the bottom making up 15 per cent. The book, using the teachings of the French theorist Pierre Bourdieu's Theory of Practice, also illustrates the significant role of education, particularly how attending elite educational institutions provides families and individuals with resources to compete both on the education 'field' and within society, as they are armed with 'trump cards' of distinct 'habitus' (e.g. behaviour, speech, style – ways of 'feeling and thinking'), (Bourdieu 1990a: 70), and 'capital'[6] (e.g. cultural, social and symbolic) (see the Introduction and Notes at the end of this book) which facilitates the successful navigation of the education system. In other words, people who are brought up to speak, think and present themselves a certain way, with access to money and connections, tend to have more success in education and society by gaining better social class positions. I too draw on Bourdieu in my research as his theories are an important way to understand social life through his social class analysis and his sense of multiple trajectories through cultural space as expressed in his book *Distinction*. Particularly in education, Bourdieu is regarded as one of the most influential frameworks that offers an explanation to understand the divisions between social classes and it is a nice complement to intersectionality, which can sometimes come over in a mechanistic way. However, people interested in race and racism in British education tend to combine Bourdieusian understandings with CRT (Rollock et al. 2015; Wallace 2017; Tichavakunda 2019; Adewumi 2020). Much of Bourdieu's ideas have been dominant in the discourse and his theory is also useful as he used it to write on gender and ethnic minorities in France and North Africa (McCall 1992; Go 2013).

However, when discussing social class in Britain, it is important to recognize the differences between subjective and objective measures of social class which significantly changes categorizations. As Huang et al. (2017: 2) write when considering socioeconomic status (SES) in China, 'Objective SES is the economic and social position in relation to others, which is widely measured by using three indicators: income, education, and occupation.

In contrast, subjective SES is a person's conception of his or her position compared with that of others.' This is applicable across different societies like Britain. An example of subjective measures of where individuals feel they sit is captured in the British Social Attitudes survey and the Great British Class Survey – the basis of the data for Savage's book. Objective measures of social class in Britain can be found via The National Statistics Socio-economic Classification (NS-SEC) which has been the main tool used since 2001 to measure class and is largely based on occupations held, listing eight categories from 'higher managerial, administrative and professional occupations' to 'never worked and long-term unemployed' (Rose and Pevalin 2003; Office for National Statistics 2017a).

Additionally, it is also important to recognize that both subjective and objective measures of social class, especially government frameworks, are made for and by white people. Therefore, Black and Global Majority communities do not fit into the grandeur and they are an inadequate official measurement tool. Though, in recent years, there has been an emergence of visible Black British middle-class groups in the UK (Meghji 2017). Rollock et al. (2013) provide a useful mixture of subjective and objective categories to illustrate how some Black British Caribbean participants, all in professional or managerial occupations, identify in relation to the middle-class label. In their research, they provide five categories: 'comfortably middle class', 'middle-class ambivalent', 'working class with qualification', 'working class' and 'interrogators'. However, as class positions are often an intergenerational process, this formation is fairly recent and precarious as they have often been achieved in a lifetime. There is also reluctance from some Black people, who by society's standards are middle class, to claim it as, for example, they may not feel able to relate to the category due to its association with whiteness, their close proximity to Black working-class communities and family members or the lack of gaining the expected rewards (Vincent et al. 2012a; Wallace 2018). This is also the case for some in the Black community who do not really identify with working-class identities either (Lawler 2012). *Shamari* reflects on this 'stigma' in the following snippet:

> See this is … this is interesting because I've read loads of articles where the Black middle class don't actually want to identify themselves as Black middle class, simply because of the label and the stigma.

Additionally, due to the anti-Black racism experienced by many Black people, regardless of whether they have middle-class education levels, occupations, incomes and wealth, they are often still unable to access the full or same benefits and rewards enjoyed by their (white) middle-class counterparts, and studies show that Black graduates experience an ethnic penalty (Heath and Cheung 2006, 2007; Zwysen et al. 2021). In *Shamari*'s next account, she provides an example of how this can play out in the classroom:

> I had a module where people were from all over the place and there was a Black person who was from a middle–upper-middle-class background and you could tell that this person was very intelligent. But it took … it's not like the class underestimates their intelligence, but it just takes a while for them to realize that this person may have had a similar background to this guy over here so, what happened was the people from the white middle-class backgrounds, without a second thought, people weren't really willing to challenge what they had to say, and it took a while for the people with a Black middle-class background to achieve the same thing. So eventually he'd be at a position where people would be unwilling to challenge him, it's, I think, I find it really strange because even after months, people are still threatened by the differences in class which is a bit weird … In a sense where they are unwilling to challenge so, you've been studying the same degree for, I don't know, four, five months, what makes you think that this person over here knows more than you do just because of their background? And that's often what I see … it's bizarre.

Shamari continues:

> Class – so like I said, what I was tryna get across with that little anecdote is that a middle-class, white boy, unless he is challenged, what he is saying is going to be assumed to be correct – well that's what my experience has been, especially within my module, where someone, you can just open your mouth and say the stupidest thing and people will just be like 'yeah, yeah, yeah, sure' because you're well-spoken and you went to private school [laughs].

Shamari's anecdote helped to inform my understanding of Bourdieu's cultural capital, though the demographic in this book has not often been theorized using his ideas. For instance, she shares how her cultural capital brought to the education system is different to the white middle-class male student who is able to enjoy respect and power from others in the 'field' of the classroom, who validate his white identity and upper-middle-class background which dominates culture and determines what education is like through the acceptance of whatever he says. As the education system is tailored toward white, middle-class ideals, the white middle-class student's 'habitus' and 'capitals' match the 'field' and he is able to exist with ease in the space, or in this case the classroom. This power and respect, on the other hand, is not afforded straightaway to the Black middle-class male student in the same classroom by his peers even though the only clear difference between him and his white counterpart is skin colour.

Another reason for the reluctance to identify with middle-class positions by some Black people is due to an awareness of how previous generations came to call Britain their home. *Shamari* expands upon this in more detail:

> Most Black people are working class because we came here, most of us – well Caribbeans came here as working class, we came here to work and to build England, that's why we came here, to work for England after the war. We came here to work, that's why they brought us over here. So I just feel like it's just a generational … we came from the bottom so we have to work our way up, there's not a lot of Black people that are upper class or middle class, most of us are working class cos we came starting at the bottom and now we are working our way up and I feel like education is used as your way to work up.

What *Shamari* alludes to is that many Black Britons are products of postwar migration. However, it is often forgotten that in the case of Black Caribbean and Black African groups, there tends to be an assumption that they are all – and have always been – working class which does not consider the legacies of slavery and colonialism which created highly stratified, colourist and class-based societies in the colonies. Also, it must be noted that many Black communities experienced 'class-downsizing' as soon as they arrived in Britain (Rollock et al. 2015: 4) when they and their offspring were confined to working-class positions, by the state, to meet the labour market needs (Ramdin 2017). Indeed, international migration is a hugely disruptive process where many suffer from downward social mobility due to the lack of recognition of foreign qualifications and experience. Even so, it is important to note that most first-generation Africans have degree qualifications and professional jobs when arriving in the UK (Platt 2005a, 2005b, 2007). As *Shamari* shares, for some Black people, 'that working-class spirit' has become a big part of their Black British identity, regardless of any social mobility achieved:

> I guess I want to stay true to who I am and I think I have that working-class spirit where you have to work hard, you have to grind, y'know you have to do what you need to do and it's not like I am struggling in life, but like just understanding that struggle, I think that gives me a working-class spirit I would say.

Moreover, *Shamari* makes it known that even though education and gaining a degree are seen as one of the few ways to access upward social mobility in British society, and that many Black people subscribe to this by pursuing this pathway, there are still limits to the rewards and gains. For example, the position of hereditary and life peers in UK parliament, which is not on many Black people's radar at all, is an example of how the upper class is closed off to Black people who are more likely to be life peers and therefore unable to pass their title on to their children. Additionally, the Rt Hon Ms Diane Abbott, who is the first Black woman to be an elected member of the UK parliament (MP), as well as the longest-serving Black MP, is a perfect example of someone going through the education system, being educated at the 'right' institution to become an MP. However, she is still only partly able to enjoy some of the advantages of this status due to the misogynoir she has faced throughout her entire career (Palmer 2020a).

> Now obviously it's becoming normal for a lot of people to go uni where it wasn't before, so obviously a uni degree gives you more access to a job so theoretically that should mean that more Black people will get into higher paid jobs so we can move up, but at the same time, because it is becoming so common now, I feel like people are saying that it is losing value but … there's no reason why Black people shouldn't move up into middle class. Yeah there are hindrances, but I feel like if the education system, if you use it the best way you can, it can help you, but yeah I believe definitely from where we came from starting in this country, we can do way better.

Shamari's reflections also express that she feels as though the upper classes are closed off to Black people who can only make it to middle-class positions, though she does go on to say that Black people can 'do way better' perhaps to establish themselves firmly in the middle classes. In recent times however, the cases of Emma Thynn, Marchioness of Bath, and Meghan Markle exemplify how upward social mobility can also be gained by marrying into the upper class, gaining status and power. This suggests that some power and cultural agency comes from who you have access to and who you marry – though both Emma and Meghan also experienced anti-Black gendered racism – and colourism may have been a factor aiding their access to the circles that their partners occupy (Bailey 2021; O Neill 2021; Payton 2021). It seems that this is where racism, particularly anti-Black racism, comes to the surface and *Shamari* is not merely imagining the devaluing of the degrees possessed by Black and Global Majority graduates. This is discussed further in chapters

6 and 8 as I illustrate that Black graduates are more likely to experience ethnic penalties like unemployment, underemployment and pay gaps in the workforce. These ethnic penalties get even worse when gender is included and is also an issue that *Shamari* is well aware of.

> I feel like we have to fight, I feel like we do, when you think about the hierarchy of the pay scales, you have the white man, the white woman, the Black man and the Black woman y'know we are still at the bottom, we are still trying to make a way up and so regardless of what they are saying in terms of more diversity, equal pay and all that crap, actually, we are still fighting, we are still a minority y'know and so I think a lot more needs to be done, and I think because some of us kinda settle for the idea that 'yes we are a minority so let that be that', whereas I want to encourage people to be like 'actually you see me as a minority, but I am more than just what you call me, I can be more than that, I have a voice' and it's so important for us to get back our voice. I think we have lost it to some degree because we allow other people to overpower us, overspeak – speak on our behalf and what they are speaking is for them, not for us, do you know what I mean?

Ultimately, when it comes to social class positioning, for *Shamari* and some other Black British millennial women – 'approximately those born from 1980 to 1995' (BBC Bitesize n.d.) – make no mistake that while they may associate with a working-class 'spirit' or the fact that they experience limitations placed on their credentials, it does not limit their aspirations or 'vision', as *Shamari* reveals:

> I don't really class myself anymore, I don't really put myself in a social class as such cos my vision is upper class, upper middle class in all honesty, the only vision I've got is global, it's not local. But in terms of how it may have influenced, I think I controlled that as much as possible because even though we weren't privileged [growing up] or if anything the total opposite of that, I didn't want free school meals at school – I think I was entitled to it, but I never got caught up in the labels, I mean labels are so easily put on people these days, 'this person is most disadvantaged' and things like that.

Finally, the next segment will bring together the positioning of Black girls and women in the world within which they are living to illustrate how this impacts their positioning and depictions in the education system.

Unpacking the journeys and experiences of Black British girls and women within the education system

The education system is a reflection of wider society. Therefore, and as demonstrated throughout this chapter, the anti-Black racism, sexism and classism that is prevalent in society also underpins the education system. While many Black girls and women are largely erased and invisible in British educational research, they are hypervisible and negatively stereotyped in educational institutions and deeply affected by these 'isms' because their Blackness is devalued, their girl/womanhood is devalued and, regardless of their social class positions, their status is also devalued too. This has previously been illustrated by Fuller (1980) and in the book *Young Female and Black* by Mirza (1992) about the educational experiences of young, second-generation, Black British Caribbean women, and in her subsequent work (2006a, 2008).

Shamari's best friend has nearly finished decorating her feet and as if bringing her educational experiences and journey together, she proclaims:

> I mean the education system as a whole, ultimately it wasn't really made for all the people that are now entering it. It wasn't really made for women, it wasn't really made for Black people, it wasn't really made for working-class people – so working-class Black women – it really wasn't made for them at all, it wasn't so the structures of it don't allow people to flourish in it.

Reflecting on being a Black, British woman, as if she were digging deep into her soul, as if she has been waiting her whole life to say this, her eyes shine as they fill with tears that do not dare to fall. Shamari shares, in a near whisper:

> Number one, as I said, racism still exists so there is being Black, sexism still exists so there is being a woman, so we've literally got the double – and then class as well – triple and I think that's overlooked a lot of the time, and I feel also because in general statistically Black girls and women actually do better [compared to Black boys] and from what I have read in terms of data, Black girls and women do better and in a sense, we are overlooked ... I just feel you always have to be conscious as a Black woman because I feel in terms of racism, they are always highlighting the things that Black men face and Black women are always overlooked so even – just with the police, 'oh Black men are more likely to be searched'

> but what about Black girls and women, what we experience? And the fact that we are one of the main victims of sexual abuse but it's always overlooked like just these things where we are always overlooked and I think it's worrying as well cos it makes you feel as if you are not really valued and you are not really important.

Finally, a single teardrop slowly streams down Shamari's cheek. She does not bother to wipe it, instead letting it flow. This teardrop is a release. A very small release from the burden that she and so many other Black girls and women carry from an acute awareness that they are positioned and depicted as 'being at the bottom' of society and within the education system. But what can really be done? Shamari offers a solution:

> I don't know, I think this structure needs to be completely overruled and up-hauled and re-rooted in order for it to be fixed. That's what I think because at the moment, if it is founded on something which is so polar opposite to the Black woman, she is inevitably going to suffer the most.

Many Black girls and women continue to create and re-create their own spaces in order to recover and gain respite from society and as a consequence, the education system.

Shamari's best friend *All done!*

Shamari *Thanks girl! They look buff! We are actually so good at this! How about we open up a hair and beauty supply store next? Maybe our own school or at least invest our time and resources into the up and running Black supplementary schools?*

Shamari's best friend *'mmm-ed' in agreement going into deep thought, visualizing what that could look like.*

Shamari *We could actually do it as well. We are currently in a state of Black emergency!*

The effects of the anti-Black gendered racism and classism from society which filters into the education system and the unique struggles and challenges experienced by Black girls and women will be explored in the next chapter.

3

The Educational Steeplechase

Figure 3 *Eve*

'Point And Kill' melodically rapped by Little Simz and occasionally accompanied by Obongjayar plays from Eve's headphones. The song fills her headspace with conscious and cultural, unstoppable, traditional Nigerian vibes. It engenders strength, resilience and purpose in Eve – a great grounding for the content of this chapter ...

* * *

In this chapter, the education system will be explored through *Eve*, the second composite character who has been created to embody and illustrate how, using an athletic analogy, while some groups in the education system are participating in a marathon, many Black girls and women are competing in a 26-mile steeplechase. I assert that not only are they competing in a more difficult race compared to others, but many often do so with limited training (knowledge and understanding) and water supplies (accepted resources) while overcoming multiple obstacles (anti-Black gendered racism and classism).

* * *

Seven minutes late, bursting through the door, out of breath and panting as though she had just completed a 26-mile steeplechase in record time, she grabs her headphones from her ears, apologises profusely to her therapist for being late, explaining that it took her much longer than she had anticipated to find a suitable place to chain her bicycle. She proceeds to briskly position her bag on the floor, setting off a scented gust of the sweet, mixed flavours of fresh tropical fruits, coconut oil and cocoa butter.

Her head is covered in a patterned, material headwrap, fixed into a stylish turban with a section of her type 4 curls peeping out at the front in a volumized, fluffy fringe. She is adorned with chunky, gold hoop earrings which glisten as she moves, in sync with her tiny, double, gold nose studs which sparkle too. Her almond-shaped, dark brown eyes are framed by flawless threaded eyebrows and a set of long and thick eyelashes that look false, but could also be real. Her full lips are shiny and well-defined with the help of carefully applied lip liner and clear gloss. She is naturally stunning, oozing a calm and regal elegance.

After taking a few deep breaths and repositioning her headwrap, she eagerly awaits to spill her heart in her weekly therapy session. She had made this investment in her mental health following some challenging university experiences at a predominantly white elite university in the Midlands after reading up about the benefits and hearing from friends who also had therapy. Months later, she had remained committed to reaping better wellbeing, self-esteem, healing and inner-standing.

This is Genevieve or Eve, sometimes Gen, and occasionally Vivi, depending on who is speaking to her, as she explained at her very first session. She settled on Eve for her therapist to call her. The elder of two sisters, Eve grew up socialized to withstand and balance the high expectations and huge responsibility placed upon the shoulders of herself and other firstborn 'Strong Black daughters' (Nouroumby 2021). In some respects, this may have indirectly provided her with a slight advantage and another dimension to her experiences when entering and journeying through the education system. Though as BTP and CRT remind us, it takes more than just sheer determination to 'succeed'.

Eve intentionally opted for a Black woman therapist, though as Zora Neale Hurston famously said, 'all skinfolk ain't kinfolk', and so she had intensively quizzed her before agreeing to her services. At this stage in her life Eve needed an outlet and she needed someone with a similar lived experience, combined with culturally sensitive expertise, who she wouldn't have to over-explain what it was like to be a Black woman before unpacking and healing from her experiences. Over the moon and completely satisfied with her choice, she had built a strong spiritual connection and understanding with her therapist who had become a trusted guide and confidante as she made sense of her life. Today's session was dedicated to making sense of her educational experiences and the contexts underpinning the education system.

First, the ideals of meritocracy will be interrogated to introduce the concept of the educational steeplechase.

The myth of meritocracy and competing in the *educational steeplechase*

The English education system is internationally respected and regarded as one of the best in the world. Though this international reputation – which is increasingly eroding – has been gained from dedicated marketing strategies, certain private schools and universities, and not necessarily its state education sector (Binsardi and Ekwulugo 2003; Tapper and Palfreyman 2009; Sylvester 2021). It must also be noted that education systems differ between the four British nations of the United Kingdom – England, Wales, Northern Ireland and Scotland (Raffe et al. 1999; Phillips 2000; Taylor et al. 2013). My focus here and in the rest of the book is on the English education system which has created, and tries to retain, an established, ideal image as the bastion of meritocracy – a supposed reflection of English society as a whole.

The term 'meritocracy' was first introduced by Michael Young in his 1958 book *The Rise of the Meritocracy* and his original definition of it was **merit = IQ + effort**. Yet, when Young wrote the book, it was as a social satire predicting the future of a knowledge-driven, divided postwar British society, where men would be grouped according to their ability to pass exams which demonstrated educational 'success' resulting in better jobs vs. those that failed exams and would be confined to lower status jobs as a result. Meritocracy, if done right, was seen as an ideal way for governments to organize society where 'effective brain power planning is not only necessary to end one of the kinds of competition between employers that is wasteful, but gives the government strategic power to control the whole economy' (Young 1958: 67). However, meritocracy was accepted by many, particularly in the US and UK and 'its satirical and critical qualities were largely overlooked, or at all events discounted' (Breen and Goldthorpe 2001: 81). Additionally, as argued by Civil and Himsworth (2020: 375),

> in a seemingly post-aristocratic age, meritocracy offered a rationale for the role of elites in a liberal democracy, and a means to reconcile the tension between equality and liberty … the late 1950s and early 1960s can be characterised as a meritocratic golden age – a period in which politicians and public intellectuals imagined a future meritocracy, where

> white, educated men, imbued with a professional, rationalist ethic, would rise up the social ladder to selflessly serve the collective in the cause of efficiency, growth, and justice.

This same premise has evolved and still shapes English life to this day.

In fact, meritocracy was defined by former Prime Minister Theresa May in 2016, as 'a country where everyone has a fair chance to go as far as their talent and their hard work will allow'. However, when meritocracy is placed within neoliberalism – which encourages little government intervention and competitive markets fuelled by choice and profit – the results will inevitably be far from meritocratic. This is because, to bring BTP back into the conversation, individuals from different social classes and groups enter and progress in the education system (field) from differing and unequal starting points, with varying quantities and qualities of accepted resources (habitus, capital).

While the former prime minister acknowledged that reinvigorating Britain as 'the Great Meritocracy' would mean 'overcoming barriers that have been constructed over many years' and 'not being afraid to think differently about what disadvantage means, who we want to help and how we can help them', little has been implemented to level the playing field, certainly within the education system, or to truly 'help' those groups that disproportionately and consistently experience barriers. This is also ironic considering that she did not have jurisdiction over the other British nations.

In a thought-provoking paper, Reay (2012: 589) argues for the necessity of a socially just education system for all, focusing on the UK in the broader sense and England in particular. She centres social class inequality and retorts, as if forewarning the former prime minister's speech, that 'it is difficult for those genuinely committed to greater social justice in education to reconcile equality with elitism, fairness with rigid hierarchies, as our political leaders appear to'. Moreover, as Reay highlights, these inequalities are deliberately entrenched, widened and reproduced by, for example, the continued existence of private schools and the Government's uneven expenditure which pumps them up to the benefit of a very small minority (OECD 2012; Fairbairn 2019; Sibieta 2021).

Another area in which meritocracy falls short of consideration and a central aim of CRT is the role that race and racism plays. Critical race theorists challenge notions of meritocracy and the tenets of neoliberalism as they argue that both of these are constructed from a colourblind standpoint and fail to include the prominent and historical role of racism and race in advancing (mainly) white[7] groups, while disadvantaging (mainly) Black and other Global Majority groups – though the map of race, class, gender and how this intersects in educational achievement in England is complex (Lloyd and McCluskey 2008; Demie and Lewis 2010, 2011; Strand 2014a, 2014b; Parsons 2019). Of course, race does not operate in a vacuum and intersects with social class, gender and other identities too – also contemplated by Reay. In addition, it is important to note that meritocracy is often rooted in what CRT describes as a majoritarian story, evidenced by former Prime Minister May's 'the Great Meritocracy' speech. A majoritarian story is defined as:

> The description of events as told by members of dominant/majority groups, accompanied by the values and beliefs that justify the actions taken by dominants to insure their dominant position … Typically, majoritarian stories are constructed so that the responsibility for their own subordination falls on the subordinated people.
>
> (Love 2004: 228–9)

In the current English educational climate, which has seen increasing competition caused by school league tables, rankings and catchment areas (Ball 1993; Butler et al. 2013), the soaring prices of university fees which has in turn created huge student debt (Callender and Mason 2017), and Covid-19 algorithm grading scandals (Bright 2020), meritocracy can be characterized as well and truly dead. In fact, it has already been branded a myth, despite the Government's insistence and efforts to keep it alive. As van Djik et al. (2020: 256) state in their article to prove that meritocracy is indeed a myth, it has now 'easily become a cover-up for systems in which social inequalities accumulate'. Reay (2012: 592) previously agreed when citing and exploring in more detail that 'education cannot compensate for society' – a phrase originally from Bernstein (1970) that has a long pedigree in UK sociology. The publication of the UK Government's 2022 white paper 'Levelling up the United Kingdom' further promotes the myth of meritocracy as, by its own admission, it illustrates a need for their intervention as it attempts to 'spread opportunity more equally across the UK' (Department for Levelling Up, Housing and Communities 2022).

In addition, when the operation of anti-Black racism is centred, as Dumas (2014: 2–3) highlights,

> for many Black children and families, in the United States, Britain and elsewhere, schooling is a site of suffering … in which the possibility of educational [*sic*] access and opportunity seems increasingly (and even intentionally) elusive, even as the hegemonic and seemingly undeniable 'common sense' is that schooling is *the* sure pathway to improved life chances, not only for individual Black subjects, but for the Black collective (the 'race') as a whole. [emphasis in original]

Educational institutions as a distinct site of suffering further destroys the notion of meritocracy. Interestingly, despite the awareness of the entrenched inequalities in society, many Black families, like my own, still follow the ideals of meritocracy but believe that it is only achievable if we work twice as hard, though we may still get less. Perhaps this is because, as Dumas notes, doing well educationally is deemed to be one of the only ways to overcome at least some of the said inequalities.

As highlighted in the previous chapter, the 'intersections of race and gender that frame the category "Black women" generate a shared set of challenges for all women of African descent, however differentially placed in other social hierarchies we may be' (Collins 2000: 238–9). Refocusing on the athletic analogy used at the start of this chapter, the English education system can be viewed as a 26-mile marathon because to succeed requires a great deal of understanding and preparation, alongside stamina and perseverance. This understanding and preparation, primarily from families, is one that is often passed down from previous generations and can provide valuable resources to assist in the easy navigation of the education system. Additionally, there are many influences and constraints that determine which pathway one can proceed down as exemplified in the 'school to prison pipeline' or what I define as, the 'private school to private sector or parliament pathway'. This book seeks to offer knowledge so that a broader understanding can facilitate effective preparation and can be utilized to change the *educational steeplechase* back into a marathon. Currently, for many Black girls and women, it is truly a complicated and tiring feat to complete the *educational steeplechase* to become graduates. This was no different in my own educational journey and experiences and *Eve* also acknowledges the tiredness that still remains with her to this day:

> [I had] just been in education from the beginning to the end and I am tired [laughs] so yeah, I think I am done ... I'm not planning on pursuing a further degree so it's just ... I was never fixed on getting a masters or something so now I just ... the more I think about it, I am just like 'really, do I really wanna do this?' That, and I am just tired of the education system and I just wanna be out.

As *Eve* exemplifies, unfortunately, some Black girls and women are unable to withstand the *education steeplechase*, becoming too 'tired' to continue competing which can result in the choice not to pursue postgraduate study – or at least not straight away. While feelings of tiredness may be common for students to express towards the end of their undergraduate studies, as will become clear later in the chapter, *Eve* can be seen to be expressing 'racial battle fatigue', that is, the long enduring impact of coping with everyday racism (Smith, Yosso and Solorzáno 2011; Gorski 2019; Rollock 2021). Perhaps this is a protective measure as continued study will only take Black women on 'isolated, individual journeys into the heart of whiteness' (Casey 1993: 132). This can also be one of the many reasons why there is an existence of *The Broken Pipeline* as outlined in Leading Route's 2019 report about the barriers to Black Ph.D. students accessing research council funding, though a great deal of change through various dedicated initiatives has been created to address this since the publication of the report. However, there still exists a very small number of Black British women professors in academia in the UK (Rollock 2019), and as of 2023, there are only fifty-six Black British women professors in the UK out of a total of over 23,000 (Paper Whispers 2023). *Eve* explains in more detail how her tiredness has also been underpinned by many difficulties related to her multifaceted identity resulting in anti-Black, sexist and classist obstacles that she has had to navigate:

> The education system that I have been through has been a very difficult one for me and I think it wasn't of any doing of my own but of how people perceived and saw me and how they reacted to that, and I know for a fact that many other Black girls have probably had the same experience to me and have been completely misjudged, completely labelled and that has then shaped how they have been seen throughout the education system. Luckily, I had a strong support system and support network to help me, but a lot of other Black girls maybe won't have that and don't have that at home so I hate to think what happens to those who are also faced with the same things. So again it's difficult, as I say it's a very difficult road but I think there's a lot that still needs to be done to help with the quality and things like that but ... yeah it's difficult [laughs].

While *Eve* expresses individual and collective group experiences in her previous reflection, such experiences cannot be viewed without the contexts in which they emerge, as discussed in Chapter 2 and later in Chapters 4 and 5. In this way, the obstacles that many Black girls and women must overcome become integral parts of the unequal structures of the education system, with which *Eve* goes on to grapple in her next account:

> I guess now I would probably say it's due to the social structure, that is to keep the elites in their position and those who are lower class down. I am guessing – I don't remember actually experiencing that because I didn't know any different – but now, if that could've been changed then, maybe I wouldn't be trying to play catch-up now. I'm not saying I

wouldn't be where I am, but y'know, you would be a bit more equipped and there would be more Black women … doing this sort of thing and people won't look at them and be like 'Oh! You are doing a Ph.D.?' Do you know what I mean? It wouldn't be so odd.

Eve highlights the interconnected relationship between society, or what she refers to as 'the social structure', and the education system. In particular, she discusses the power of particular types of knowledge that can provide both understanding of the ways to navigate the education system and access to different types of opportunities like doing a Ph.D.. This is a key argument in BTP (Bourdieu and Passeron 1990) and is expanded upon in Chapters 4 and 5.

In the rest of this chapter *Eve* goes into more detail about the unique challenges and struggles that she and other Black women experience when journeying through the English education system. Her reflections include the constant awareness of being positioned as the 'other' through interactions and via Eurocentric, whitewashed curricula, as well as the internalized pressure of unrealistic expectations.

The merging of opposing cultures and the abrupt process of othering

Eve repositions herself in the chair, transforming from a slouch into an upright, more alert posture, as if she is ready to reveal her deepest, darkest secrets. But first, she swiftly tugs her phone from her pocket, scans the screen, possibly to check the time and for any notifications. Satisfied, she pushes her phone back into her pocket, looks up, clasps her hands together and begins, once more, to reason with her therapist about exactly why she believes her educational journey and experiences were so difficult and tiring.

Differences in ways of being

Being positioned in opposition to whiteness was an integral part of *Eve*'s educational journey and experiences. Such experiences have previously been analysed and articulated by DuBois (1989) and Puwar (2004). DuBois (1989: 6) terms this experience a 'double consciousness' to express the internal conflict felt by African-Americans whose Black and American identities are incompatible with each other. In other words, DuBois highlights how African-Americans have never really belonged in American society due to factors like racism which continuously position them as 'an outcast and a stranger in mine own house' (DuBois 1989: 6). Puwar (2004) describes the ways in which women and Global Majority groups enter into PW and male spaces, are not seen to naturally belong there and the processes in which they become marginalized in the space, and treated and seen as 'space invaders'. Entering the English education system means entering white spaces. As will become clear in the section that follows, *Eve* also demonstrates how this happens on numerous occasions, through her lived experiences, in both subtle and direct interactions and observations in educational settings. These interactions and observations demonstrate examples in which her natural ways of being – particularly her Black girl/womanhood – were perceived and positioned as different within the space. Phoenix's (2009) study about how Black Caribbean young women negotiate their racialized and gendered identities in education sees her write about the notion of education as a site of struggle. This builds on the research of Pratt (1991: 6) who found that classrooms become 'contact zones' as well as 'social spaces where cultures meet, clash, and grapple with each other, often in contexts of highly asymmetrical relations of power, such as colonialism, slavery, or their aftermaths as they are lived out in many parts of the world today'. Yet, for *Eve,* looking back, this clash in culture became a normal part of her experiences and started as soon as she entered into the education system.

> I think sometimes just little things y'know like with your packed lunch and the stuff you bring in and people are like 'rice is not packed lunch' [laughs] and like the hairstyles that you do and stuff [laughs] yeah what else? Just little things which are so normal in your household but when you get to school it's just so obvious when you are around like non-Black people it's like 'oh that's different' – stuff like that, you just notice you are different and that might have a negative effect on you later, from what I've heard anyway or [laughs] or you just don't notice because you are a kid and you are just playing and … and then you get into class and your teacher is talking to you about slavery and everyone is looking at you. Yeah, that's when it becomes obvious [laughs].

Eve suggests how distinct cultural (and sometimes racialized) markers such as food, hairstyles and histories become positioned as different within spaces and places that are dominated and underpinned by white, English, middle-class-ness. According to *Eve*, these differences not only become 'so obvious', but they 'might have a negative effect on you later', which was illustrated in the research of Nunn (2018) on the impact of gendered racism on Black girls which creates both strength and sadness in their educational experiences. Eve continues to explain how other cultural markers like language and ways of speaking become another way in which differences in ways of being are highlighted within educational spaces:

> When you have to explain the language that you are using like slang or things or it's got Patois in it or things like that and you are looking at it and you are thinking 'I don't want to have to explain my Blackness to you' just get it, just let me say it and you just understand, and so there are certain things that I'd say Black British Africans can use, the language that they'll use and they'll just get it and things that Caribbean people will say and they'll just get it but then you have to translate it across.

The additional efforts to 'translate' languages 'across' to others so that they can understand are not novel occurrences, as outlined by what Gumperz (1982) and Goffman (1981) defined as 'code switching'. In a paper about Black identities, race inequality and stereotype threat in the workplace, Boulton (2016: 139) shows how Black interns are constantly self-monitoring their own behaviours and must code switch within PW spaces 'to negotiate whites' racial stereotypes about Blacks while driving "the nod" underground to avoid stereotype threat because even the mere recognition of racial affiliation threatens to further exacerbate existing Black marginalisation'. For those unaware, 'the nod' is 'a subtle lowering of the head you give to another Black person in an overwhelmingly white place … it's a swift yet intimate statement of ethnic solidarity' (Okwonga 2014). This provides a glimpse of how style of speech can act as processes in which Blackness is 'othered' within white spaces. Eventually, as *Eve* reveals, this can lead to a process of having to 'adapt' to the space which includes learning to 'accommodate' and/or completely change language and ways of speaking – all of which can be an additional, tiring and frustrating process.

> You had to learn to accommodate, you had to learn to adapt the way you speak, there was a lot of slang that doesn't make sense [to white people] and I don't have time to explain myself or they [white people] used to find it really entertaining, they would be like 'Oh that's so funny' and you're like 'I am not tryna be funny, it's just how I talk', so you learnt a lot about having to deal with them [white people] because of the course I did, these were the people I was going to be working with. It wasn't a case of three years, 'sayonara, I'll see you again', and so it was kinda going ok, you are gonna have to work on finding something in common with these people because you are going to be doing long hours with these people, yeah.

Moreover, *Eve*'s recollections of her ways of speaking being ridiculed by others and the discomfort she felt by this are also evident in her extract. This connects with Fordham's (1988, 1991) concept of 'racelessness' coined after two studies in different schools that highlighted how some Black students felt that they had to distance themselves from markers of Blackness, such as speech, but also from whiteness, wanting to remain 'raceless' as a strategy to be 'successful'. Additionally, *Eve* went on to express her realization that she would have to do this for the rest of her life as being around white people and within white spaces, like the workplace, is inescapable. Next, *Eve* highlights the ways in which Blackness is accepted and recognized in particular ways and settings when referencing famous African-American rappers Tupac Shakur (1971–96) and the Notorious B.I.G, also known as Biggie (1972–97), but voices her frustration that this does not always extend to her ways of being, such as her hairstyles, within educational spaces as illustrated by the mockery from other white students:

> When I got to secondary [school] it was like we're different and we are different for a reason and there were some hateful girls in secondary school y'know, they would be looking at you like 'oh why's your hair like that?' or 'your hair grew, is it miracle growth?' and you are just looking at them like … these are white students saying it to Black students, and it's like, well I am understanding of your culture, you need to be understanding of mine, you start to realize that people don't wanna be. But they would gladly participate in cultural appropriation so gladly listen to Tupac and Biggie but you wanna be like 'oh your hair, why is it like that, why does it look like that?' Like those sorts of comments and that's why when at secondary school, you just realize that people are gonna be ignorant if they want to be ignorant and you either rise to it and try and correct everybody or keep moving, don't hold a grudge and don't start to develop hate.

This focus on hair is important as it should be viewed directly in relation to race, along with standards of beauty, according to Robinson (2011) who explored the relationship between race, Black female beauty and hair texture. The ways in which dominant groups often 'other', disrespect and disregard the ways of being of Global Majority groups like Black girls and women is emphasized by *Eve*'s statement 'I am understanding of your culture, you need to be understanding of mine'. As if coming to terms with why this is the case, *Eve* offers ignorance as an explanation as well as strategies that she employs to overcome this clash of cultures such as either correcting them or moving on and not holding a grudge to quell any hatred towards the perpetrators. *Eve* concludes:

> In terms of the identity of yourself, you learn who you are and you learn, like I said, what parts of your culture can merge with the British culture.

By entering and journeying through the education system, *Eve* vocalizes the ways in which, as her last quote shows, she learns who she is and who she is not and how to adapt, change or dilute markers of her Black girl/womanhood and culture which she finds is necessary in these educational spaces. *Eve* ultimately feels that such markers, like her language, speech and hairstyles, do not and cannot merge with white, British culture nor are they accepted in the educational space of her English school.

This process of 'othering' is embedded in many ways throughout and within the education system. Another significant way that this is achieved is via what and how certain topics are taught or erased from the curriculum. The following section will explore this in more detail.

Eurocentric and whitewashed curricula

The curriculum in educational institutions is another area that privileges and maintains whiteness. This is because it is 'a culturally specific artefact designed to maintain a white supremacist master script' (Ladson-Billings 1998: 18) and, therefore, the exclusion of other races and cultures – despite the importance of their contributions – is intentional. *Eve* affirms this intentional erasure of particular topics and the consequences that she feels filter into wider British society:

> I have a massive issue with how colonialism is taught or I should probably say isn't taught in this country, in the curriculum … I was never taught colonialism in my history education … I remember like a couple of years ago, I don't know if you watched *The Apprentice*, but last year they were making gin and the group thought they would call it 'Colony' and they basically romanticized this whole notion of like going to another country and stealing their resources. And I remember reading a poll showing that 41 per cent of the British public think we should be proud of the British Empire. So it's like there is nothing good about invading another country, stealing their resources, forcing your values on them and exploiting them further.

Eve's linking of the curriculum to wider British society through her mention of popular TV show *The Apprentice* (BBC, series 12, 2016) and a

YouGov public poll about British sentiments towards its empire which actually showed that 48 per cent of 18–24 year olds were proud of it (Dahlgreen 2014) emphasizes the lack of awareness of crucial parts of British history, and how this begins from the education system. She goes on to explain, in contrast, the ways in which Africa is often depicted when it is taught as part of the curriculum:

> The education system finds it … is comfortable enough to teach me about slavery within the educational system. You are taught about the continent of Africa being poverty stricken, full of conflict, full of rape, all these negative connotations are linked to Africa, in a way you get to a point where you think 'is Africa a continent or is it a country?' because you group the entire continent as one and you don't differentiate the different parts of the continent that has different histories and different experiences, and I think the way in which education – the curriculum – is shaped, it's biased and it's extremely Eurocentric and as a society you can see how the demographics have changed in London in particular, it's a lot more multicultural, the education system should reflect that because it's just in terms of intellectual curiosity, when you see someone that looks different to you, you wanna know more about them and as the demographics change, you should kinda instil that within the system and I feel even from primary school, I feel I would've wished to learn a bit more but then again, you can also say that education starts at home [laughs].

The power dynamics of a Eurocentric and whitewashed curriculum are very apparent from *Eve*'s statement in which she argues that the curriculum negatively characterizes and lumps together an entire continent and diverse peoples. According to Givens (2016: 1288), this is no surprise – he argues that schooling as a whole and the curriculum, particularly for Black students and the diaspora, function to transmit 'ideolog[ies] that would stunt their political, economic, and social progress; thus, supporting the goals of white supremacy'. Moreover, *Eve* once again highlights the importance of having a more balanced and reflective curriculum for the benefit of cohesion and understanding, especially in increasingly multiethnic and multicultural cities such as London, as well as the importance of having an education system that encourages and stimulates 'intellectual curiosity' beyond fixed and negative depictions of places deemed as 'other' and lesser. While she also notes that 'education starts at home', the interplay between the home and school are undeniable as they work hand in hand to influence both spaces as well as wider society. Once more, *Eve* links the ways in which the content of the curriculum influences white, British society's lack of accountability with its past and how this also filters into society's overall, skewed majoritarian story of itself.

> Yes as I said, I think in this country people forget – I think outside of London – people forget about Black people, we are just kinda pushed aside, I think, undervalued of our contributions … I think I remember that unemployment rates amongst Black youths are just extortionately high … I remember a couple of months ago [reading] that our criminal system is actually more racist than the [United] States and, I kinda feel like the fact that we don't address the racism that this country has done through colonization is not talked about. I remember when we talked about the KKK and slavery we were like 'America is so terrible', but it's like 'yeah but Britain did play a part in this, don't act like you are clean of this', and I kinda feel that yeah, colonialization is completely romanticized. I know white people here who think that even though bad things happened, overall 'we have improved Africa' and it's like 'Africa is a continent' and it's like yeah, but I don't think it's for you to decide, how would you like it if someone did it to you?

Eve calling attention to the established belief that Britain as a whole prides itself on not being as overtly racist as America highlights the lack of knowledge and accountability that the average white British person has in its own involvement and as a beneficiary of hundreds of years of slavery and colonialism, which is ludicrous. She also shows that despite this, she is very knowledgeable about wider societal issues that disproportionately impact Black people as she references Black youth unemployment which, in 2020, stood at 41.6 per cent of Black people aged 16–24 across the UK (Thomas 2021), and the racism that plagues the British criminal justice system (Ramesh 2010; Monteith et al. 2022). *Eve* also suggests how these established tropes of places like Africa in the curriculum have a direct connection to how Black people are treated, viewed and positioned in wider society, as well as the ways in which the operation of anti-Black racism are evident in unemployment rates, the criminal justice system and the existing 'white saviour' mentality around Africa. This is deliberate as what *Eve* has identified is stated by Givens (2016: 1290), to establish 'the exclusion of Black people from national identity within the modern state'. This extends to areas where one would think that the curriculum should be more balanced and reflective such as when Black History Month is taught. Yet, *Eve* shows her frustration in its limited scope and erasure of Black British people of Caribbean descent which, once again, fails to establish a wider understanding of the histories and immense contributions of Black Britons to the country.

> Yeah with Black History Month I was really frustrated, well for one we never did it every single year, well that was a bit of a cheek but, also it was never the Black British experience, like you never talked about the Windrush, you never talked about – it was always about Martin Luther King, Rosa Parks, never Malcolm X or the Black Panthers and it's like … well this isn't even my history, like we are learning Black History Month, but I'm Black and we are not even learning about Jamaican people or Caribbean people and it really frustrated me because it's like again where are …? How come we are not being represented? It really annoyed me.

Doharty (2018) finds similar sentiments in her paper which explores the experiences of Black Caribbean and Black African students learning about Black History which she asserts is littered with microaggressions which reflect the wider curriculum. Yet, it is through *Eve*'s discomfort of being inundated with a Eurocentric and whitewashed curriculum that purposely erases local and national Black history, dictating and upholding certain Black Americans that are deemed as acceptable to whiteness, which meant she was able to develop a deeper awareness of the education system as a whole and its institutions, as she explains:

> What I liked about it [the curriculum] in a sense was that it opened my eyes … it was more so it opened my eyes to quite a lot of things in a sense that …[I was able to see] how white the curriculum is for example and also you don't fit in within that institution, or you only fit in a certain way.

Eve's previous reflections illustrate the idea that Black girl and women students are being made to feel that they can only 'fit' into educational institutions in 'a certain way' which results in altering their identities to dilute markers of their Black girl/womanhood. This is further exemplified by the content of the curriculum and how it is taught, which will inevitably weave into the treatment that they receive. This also highlights the ways in which meritocracy cannot be achieved when the very foundation of the education system is experienced by different groups in diverse ways based on anti-Black, sexist and classist foundations. Another essential occurrence which *Eve* relays next is the additional obstacle of limiting beliefs and negative stereotypes, often held by those in authority like teachers but also from peers too.

Limiting beliefs, negative stereotyping and ultimately being misunderstood

In her widely cited writings, social theorist and leading Black Feminist thinker Patricia Hill Collins (1986) writes about the realities of Black girls and women in white educational spaces who have long been located in an 'outsider within' position. In other words, although Black women may now have access to academic spaces, they are not fully included and, alongside the differences in their ways of being and the Eurocentric, whitewashed curricula, another way in which they are positioned as 'outsiders within' are the limiting beliefs and negative stereotyping that they are subject to. This aligns with a whole body of literature in which Black British students are shrouded in discourses of underachievement and failure (Coard 1971; Gillborn 1997; Crozier 2005; Rhamie 2012; Tomlin et al. 2014; Hamilton 2018). Collins's notion about Black women as 'outsiders within' will be the focus of the next chapter. For now, *Eve* muses over the ways in which she has been subject to limiting beliefs in her educational experiences:

> I think they [white staff and students] expect us not to do well ultimately, they expect us to flop because y'know, 'women aren't supposed to be in school, women are supposed to be doing home economics and food tech' or whatever, and 'you are not even just a woman, you are Black and Black people aren't smart'. I mean I don't know people that have said it – they won't say it openly to be honest, but they will think it. But as long as they keep it inside, they think 'oh it's not bad' but still, your perception is wrong. Again the education's … education here is free, it's open to everyone so the same way you went to school and I went to school, you went to primary, I went to primary, you went to secondary, I went to secondary, we were at university, we both graduated, we are on the same level regardless if I am Black or I'm a woman, we are on the same level, we have been able to achieve the same thing, if not [I have achieved] more.

Eve's awareness that she is in a space where she is expected to fail or 'flop' in her own words, suggests that she has had to navigate hostility from both white staff members and her peers due to the limiting, established beliefs and stereotypes about women and Black people which she is doubly affected by as a Black woman. Moreover, while she notes that people may not openly express these views, the fact that they may just think it is disturbing as it can inevitably influence how she and other Black girls and women will be treated by others, particularly those with authority and power. When she also emphasizes how the education system is- certainly the state-funded part of the sector, she asserts that despite the limiting beliefs and stereotypes often associated with Black girls and women, in the same way that students from other raced, gendered, and classed backgrounds have been able to journey through, so has she. Interestingly, while she reminds us that 'we are on the same level' as 'we have been able to achieve the same thing', she aligns herself with meritocratic values, though UK Government statistics (Roberts and Bolton 2020) consistently show that there are differences in attainment between Black and other students. This is no surprise considering the very different educational experiences they have, which I characterize as an *educational steeplechase* for Black girls and women. On the other hand, even when Black women students do achieve good grades, it does not necessarily yield the same rewards – once again highlighting the limits of meritocracy. This is explored more in Chapters 6 and 8. *Eve* animatedly continues:

> People don't expect Black people to do anything extraordinary in education so I just feel like … not to play up to stereotypes, but I just feel like because it's not expected of you … like Black boys are expected to be good at sport, Black boys are gonna … they don't expect Jamal to be banging out A*s in physics even though he is more than capable. So I feel like a lot of the institutions and the systems don't give a lot of Black kids encouragement and I know a lot of Black boys especially as young as nursery are told off for being boisterous and stuff like that, so I think there's a lot of stuff that starts from such a young age that by the time you do get to testing stage … but I was reading this recent study saying that Black kids are failed and have declining marks up until GCSEs but then at GCSEs because we are marked anonymously, we do better than predicted because there's not the bias behind it and I do think that, even going to certain events now and seeing how many amazing young Black people there are that are really doing bits, that is so encouraging and I know it's changing, but at the point where I was at school, I just felt like it was a little behind.

Eve's previous recollection in which she provides examples using the fictional Black boy character 'Jamal' highlights how limiting beliefs work hand in hand with negative stereotyping. She also shows, in a similar way to what she highlighted previously with the role of the curriculum, how stereotyping through the example of Black boys as only good at sports acts to position them and restrict them to fit in a certain, expected way within the educational field. *Eve* also goes on to express some of the consequences she feels that these limiting beliefs and negative stereotyping have on Black students, such as little encouragement and bias which has damaging results. When *Eve* shares how she is only able to see different and more positive examples of young Black people doing well, presumably beyond educational spaces, as she rightly states, these limiting beliefs and stereotypes about Black students are reinforced by schooling and are 'a little behind' as they do not match or embrace alternative realities. *Eve* goes on to explain how there are particular negative stereotypes 'attached' to Black girls and women that she found within her own educational experiences stating:

> There's a lot of stereotypes already attached, like stereotypes of being disruptive or loud or rude blah blah blah but then also the expectation of failure.

Going into greater detail, *Eve* articulates the importance of being conscious of the differences in Black British girl student experiences, which she argues is a very diverse group. Yet, she also notes how this consciousness is often not the case as, from her experiences, Black girls are labelled and are stuck within opposing, fixed stereotypes:

> I think the stereotypes are still there for Black girls, but I think … it's weird because for me, like girls, there are so many different types of Black girls and some people don't realize. Obviously you can say 'Black British girl student' but … you don't really know the ins and outs, like there is so many different … going through the education system, in terms of university level, it kinda made me see the different types of Black British girl students and I think, I think in general, they are put in a box at times, they are seen as … labelled I guess, [as] either really smart, like really clever, really loud, aggressive or promiscuous or weird. I feel like that's what it was, they are put into these boxes so if they do this one thing 'oh you're automatically promiscuous', if they do this, 'oh you are really clever', do you know what I mean? I feel like that's what it is.

Eve also importantly shows how such negative labels and stereotyping act to position Black girls as [insert label] to the highest degree with the emphasis on 'really' and that these labels become fixed. Such labels and stereotyping of Black girls and women are established universally in the UK and the US as previously identified by Fordham (1993) in her ethnographic study about Black American girls in an inner-city high school where they are characterized as 'loud'.

> I think it can be difficult, at the end of the day, you are who you are, but because of what you look like, or what you do, people put you in those boxes and I think it can be hard to escape but ... and trying to prove to other people that you are not this or you are not that, I think, yeah it's difficult.

In a fascinating and insightful revelation, *Eve* also points out the ways in which limiting beliefs and negative stereotyping can also appear in intra-racial relations between different ethnic and cultural groupings all racialized as Black British.

> I just feel like there's still levels to it like even ... ok you're Black but ok are you African Black? Are you Caribbean Black? And there's obviously stereotypes that come with being Caribbean or being African y'know. Being African is like 'oh you are always gonna end up a lawyer' or 'oh your mum and dad forced you to do this' or 'oh you don't really wanna do this', and unfortunately with Caribbeans I feel like it's either 'oh well you don't have a dad and your mum forced you to do this and this, that or the other' or 'you lot don't really value education anyway' and 'you are probably just gonna all smoke weed', things like that and it's like 'No', there are Black British Afro-Caribbean and Caribbean women that are doing bits, you are just not finding them and celebrating them cos I know many business owners, many of them and they are doing it and they don't smoke weed, they are still married, they have kids, both the husband and wife still live together, their children have stable upbringings. If that's what you wanna classify it as, and there is no problem with that but because you don't wanna celebrate that and admit that there are people that are doing that, that becomes a problem in itself because they are left off those statistics cos you are not surveying the right people, cos if you try survey the right people then Lord knows the statistics will be higher.

Not only does *Eve* highlight the diversity in Black communities with reference to British Caribbean and African communities, she also suggests that there are contrasting stereotypes that they both fall under. Such internal stereotypes depict British African communities as being stricter and having higher aspirations when it comes to education compared to Caribbean groups. However, she does go on to dispel these negative stereotypes of Caribbean communities by highlighting the 'successes' of Black Caribbean women in particular. *Eve* also implies that these stereotypes have been internalized from outside sources when she refers to 'statistics' and 'surveying the right people', potentially referring to national measures or the media which are in charge of disseminating such information. These insights from *Eve* connect well with research by Lam and Smith (2009: 1266) about how British adolescents of African and Caribbean heritage self-identified according to national and ethnic labels highlighting that 'theory should move away from conventional notions that have tended to homogenise each minority group by equating its racial label with one culture and one identity'.

Overall, it is evident to see how limiting beliefs and negative stereotypes influence the experiences and journeys of *Eve* and many other Black girls and women. The final section of this chapter will communicate the ways in which *Eve* internalized pressure – the basis of which originate from societal, familial and cultural expectations.

Internalized pressure and unrealistic expectations

Eve's phone vibrates and once again, she swiftly slides half of it out of her pocket, just enough for her to peep at the new information that has just appeared. A small, affectionate smile lights up her face as she explains to her therapist that her little sister, who has just started her A-Levels, has messaged her. She proudly sings her sister's praises, sharing how she has steadily been improving her grades, with a lot of effort, noting that this has been a gradual, challenging process which involved changing her little sister's mindset from demotivation and uninterest to an enthusiasm for learning and the possibilities it could open.

But Eve reveals to her therapist that she does not really blame her sister for becoming demotivated or uninterested because she can relate to her as she also went through a similar phase. Like her little sister, with a lot of effort, she too had to push through and jump over the obstacles until she could finally exit the educational steeplechase upon graduating with her English degree.

Being the first in the family as the eldest sibling is not easy and Eve also divulges to her therapist how it was actually her little sister who had been a key motivator for her to 'succeed' or to at least appear to be! Now she says, after going through it herself and after taking on the responsibility to do well so that her little sister had no excuse not to, Eve shares that she made the decision, from an early age, almost like a mission, to encourage and support her little sister in the best way she knew how. She knew what it was like not having a big sister to do the same for her. She knew what the overwhelming sense of pressure felt like and she vividly remembers that it was a heavy load to carry, whilst competing in the educational steeplechase. She admits that this pressure came from a number of sources like the constant awareness of how to be within white educational spaces or what she defines as finding and being 'the middle ground':

> As a Black girl or woman, from my perspective, we've got to fit in, so in the academic environment, I wouldn't say you would act white because that word is a bit ... but you've got to present yourself in a certain way, you've got to show that you are worthy of being there but still keep your roots, it's a balancing act and that can be in any environment actually, not just academically. But y'know ... and we [Black girls and women] have a lot to deal with actually, because you've gotta be the middle ground from both sides of the coin.

For *Eve*, this 'middle ground' is what she describes as trying to also remain true to herself but knowing the limitations of doing so within particular spaces and places.

> So as I say, for me I want to stay true to who I am and where I am from and so on but I couldn't go to my workplace or an academic institution and be like 'yeah bruv, you get me though?' Not saying that that's a bad thing, cos I don't particularly speak like that anyway but y'know, you don't wanna sound like an arse [laughs] yeah ... so ... but again that's my perspective as how I would like to present myself, somebody else may not be like that but it doesn't mean they are not qualified to do the same thing y'know, and, I think as a Black woman in the educational environment, you want to be an example for your other Black girls to follow and look up to, so I think there's a lot of pressure, there is that with men too but then with the Black woman, you wanna kinda get out there and accomplish something.

This constant awareness and feeling of not fitting into educational environments as a Black woman and therefore having to constantly adapt to ways that are deemed to be acceptable, or closer to accepted versions of whiteness, can be challenging feats. *Eve* also shares that she strives to remain true to herself and keep her identity within the space which she previously described as a 'balancing act'. Interestingly, she internalizes the ways in which stereotypical markers of Blackness, such as certain speech styles, are perceived as unacceptable within academic spaces, as well as in workplace settings, mentioning how this difference in speech styles should not be used to determine a person's capabilities. Marsh (2013) finds a similar occurrence happening amongst the young, academically, successful Black women she centred in her research who also wish to remain true to their Black woman identities. Marsh discovers that through participation in what she calls social clubs, they are able to find spaces within the white educational setting to consciously identify as Black, and to develop and demonstrate versions of Black womanhood that allow them to negotiate diversity. Other strategies employed by Black girls and women will be explored in the following chapters.

In a similar way that *Eve* has expressed how her little sister became a motivating factor to succeed, she once again clarifies how many other Black women experience the pressure of trying to be good examples to inspire other Black girls along their own educational journeys. The importance of Black women role models is touched upon in Chapter 7. This may be particularly important and a role purposely taken on in order to counter the limiting beliefs and ways in which Black girls and women are negatively viewed and treated within educational spaces. *Eve* went on to explain the specificity of trying to gain knowledge while also learning about herself and how she is perceived by others as a Black girl and eventually woman within the education system:

> Yeah, it's been tough [laughs] it's been a journey, because with education you're learning about yourself which is a learning process in itself. That's education in itself – learning about yourself, and you are trying to fit in as well, and you are trying to take as much knowledge as possible which can be stressful. And you are also acknowledging that people already have a perception of you so you want to prove people wrong and I think that's so tough – like even just looking at my face, it's just so tough because I want people to know like 'listen I am going to succeed' – not even – 'I am succeeding right now, you need to believe it, I'm doing well right now!' And irrespective of the fact that I am Black or British or I'm a woman, take all of that away, me and you are on the same level.

Despite *Eve* revealing the difficulty in her experiences, she passionately asserts that it has not held her back and that even though she has had to overcome obstacles, she believes that she is on the same level as others who may not share similar identities or face the same challenges. This also suggests that her self-esteem had not been tarnished, which it has been documented as being for many other Black girls and young women in the English education system (Fuller 1980, 1982; Coultas 1989; Mirza 1992). This passion and motivation to make sure she succeeds is a quality that has been socialized into her as she explains:

> From young, I was always taught 'aim high', even if it's hard, keep going – aim to be the best, you have to do the best you can, so I guess that's what keeps me going. I have this thing on my wall at home, it's a picture of African parents saying 'succeed or don't come back!' so … [laughs] that is literally … everyday I'm like, 'succeed or don't come back!' Like I have to do the best I can – that's my mentality.

As she rightly admits, this socialization and the pressure to succeed educationally and to meet familial expectations, despite the difficulty in doing so, has become part of *Eve*'s everyday mentality. Moreover, she shares that she has internalized the idea that there is no other option but to keep going. Next, she explains the role of mothers in upholding this:

> I think especially with the women I've noticed, the 'push on, deal with it, you must do what you must do' is something that I've noticed from my Asian friends' mums and my Black friends' mums. It's just the mentality that we seem to have yeah … I think it was just, overall the oppression, systematic and otherwise is similar, I think the struggles in our communities are quite similar, I think we have a similar cultural mentality.

Eve echoes what Byng (2017) explores in her article *Failure is not an option: the pressure Black women feel to succeed.* By broadening the internalized pressure from familial expectations to what she defines as a collective and shared 'cultural mentality', which she extends to include Asian as well as Black girls, passed down by mothers, *Eve* illustrates the intergenerational impact and influence of constantly having to navigate racialized and gendered inequalities within hostile, white educational contexts. That is, many Black and Asian women are very aware that such intersectional barriers exist, but that they must find ways to overcome them. The significant role of Black mothers in educational experiences and journeys of Black girls and women will be explored in Chapter 7. What's more, *Eve* shares how these intersecting gendered and racialized pressures are also transferred onto her by other women family members like aunts:

> You need these things to be valuable in a sense but when you get to that stage and it's like 'ok well I have done everything now', I've passed my driving test, I've got my first job, I am paying bills, doing all these things but you're complaining because I am not going out and I don't have a boyfriend [laughs]. So it's just a very, a very … it angers me a lot but I've had to pick and choose my battles, I've had Aunties, I remember when I

> was studying and my Aunt said to me 'if you finish and you haven't got a boyfriend, I am bringing someone for you'. I was literally twenty-one years old, like … and even now … I've got goddamn time, there's no rush!

The cultural and gendered expectations of having a partner by a certain age in order to start a family, as well as gaining an education which is deemed as necessary, is another added pressure faced by many Black women like *Eve*:

> I think it's … I think it's unique. I almost feel that all my successes are even bigger than they would have been because as a woman and then as an ethnic minority I just feel like every big achievement I make is that much more of an achievement so I'm alright with that. Because people didn't expect it of me and one of the biggest problems I have in general is with expectations, when people expect a lot of me, sometimes I buckle and so it's kind of … not having I don't know … it's like I can make people more proud easily, it could be problematic for some people but I don't choose to see it that way … I think that it's a unique experience to prove something … I just feel like I have to just work ten times harder. I was having this conversation with my friend about this the other day and we were just saying that you just have to prove yourself, especially in settings like this … you really have to prove yourself.

As *Eve* illustrates, there are multiple pressures that are internalized by Black girls and women as part of their educational journeys and experiences. These internalized pressures are underpinned by expectations from the white educational spaces they have to navigate, as well as being conscious of the unequal positionings and perceptions due to being Black and women, as well as meeting high familial and cultural expectations. It is very likely that the aforementioned obstacles will have mental, as well as physical health implications for Black girls and women. In fact this has already been documented by Geronimus (1992, 2023) in her 'weathering hypothesis' where she highlights that the health of African-American women may begin to decline prematurely in early adulthood, compared to other racialized women, due to encountering a combination of socioeconomic disadvantage, racism, stress and being more likely to live in highly deprived areas. I believe that this can extend to Black women living in England and other British nations. The impact on mental health will be explored in the upcoming chapters.

* * *

Eve's therapist, who has been listening intently, provides her with a number of strategies to aid in her healing, acknowledging Eve's journey and the pain expressed in this part of her life. She also offers Eve the opportunity to pick this up again in future sessions. Feeling a little bit lighter, Eve thanks her, grabs her bag, puts her headphones back in and allows the session to marinate in her mind as she walks to her bicycle and rides away.

* * *

In the next chapter, Collins's concept of Black girls and women operating as the 'outsider within' will be applied to illustrate experiences and journeys of 'being the only one' in PW educational settings.

4

Being the Only Black Girl or Woman

Figure 4 *Chika*

Chika's high cheekbones and dimples are visibly noticeable as she beams at the mirror, delighted with what she sees looking straight back at her. Finally able to stretch her legs, she stands in front of the mirror, admiring her reflection and gassing herself up via her signature pose which reveals her tongue piercing, before excitedly rummaging through the small pot of hair adornments – beads, hair cuffs and cowrie shell rings – as she attempts to decide on the ones to add to her fresh, intricately cornrowed Fulani braids.

She has desired this hairstyle for a very long time. She was ecstatic to finally land an appointment at this hair salon with the baddest hairstylist who was known for her superior handiwork that is quick but quality, resulting in the masterpieces that she lovingly creates upon each and every one of her clients' heads – every. single. time. These hair rituals – install, maintenance and take out – requires time, skill and cost.

Chika had been sitting for hours and hours, enjoying the process of her hairstylist formulating structure into her afro and retrieving the small sections of extensions Chika carefully passes to her which are entwined with her natural hair, producing each tiny plait. It can also be painful – though Chika does not mind withstanding occasional pain due to her tender head as the familiar mantras 'beauty takes time', 'pain is beauty' and 'you can't rush perfection' highlight. Besides, she had come prepared with food, snacks, drinks and reading materials to supplement the scattered conversations with her hairstylist, to occupy herself and to last the duration of her stay – anywhere from two to eight hours, depending on the thinness and length of the braid style desired.

Once she has finally chosen the pieces that will decorate her crown and accentuate all of her Black girl magic, Chika waits for her hairstylist – who has briefly stepped out – to return and fasten them onto her braids to complete her transformation. Whilst waiting, Chika can't help but to stroke the fine braids from her scalp all the way down to the tips that dangle and sweep the top of her waist. She hums the melody of her favourite song, 'BROWN' by mystical hip-hop duo OSHUN, utterly embodying the song lyrics.

The plaiting of Black women's hair illustrates multiple sources and enactments of heritage and identity. For Chika, the hairstyles which she takes months to decide upon and hours to complete, are an expression of her heritage, a reminder of erased histories and a celebration of the cultural artistry that have survived the many attacks, over generations. They are also an ode to her past self. The self that was not always confident to wear such hairstyles with pride. The self that did not have the words to explain 'what is on your head?!' The self that struggled to find the energy to fake a smile whenever she was made into a spectacle as something 'exotic'. The self that literally had to swerve to avoid the unwanted hands of someone feeling compelled to touch her hair without permission. The self that had to navigate whiteness while simultaneously diluting her Black, girl/womanhood in an attempt to be accepted.

* * *

In this chapter, I braid together the experiences and journeys of young women to create the composite character *Chika*, plaiting together the data from their accounts to retell how they have and continue to navigate all or parts of their educational journeys within PW educational places and spaces as the only one or at least one of a very small number of Black girls and women. In particular, *Chika* will articulate the operations of whiteness and how it was experienced by students and remembered by graduates in certain educational institutions that tend to be PW. This includes institutions such as schools outside inner cities in suburban or rural areas, as well as grammar or private schools and sixth form colleges in those, and elite or pre-1992 universities. This will also extend to educational experiences and journeys of 'being the only one' in certain university subject areas and undergraduate courses.

The white, English education system

The overwhelming whiteness of the English education system is a feature that cannot be ignored – regardless of the type of educational institution that Black girls and women like *Chika* attend. To be clear, there isn't a single education 'system' as it is in fact highly differentiated and fragmented. For instance in higher education, there are departments and faculties that have overwhelmingly 'non-white' or Global Majority student demographics (Gamsu and Donnelly 2017; AdvanceHE 2021: 138). However, I refer here to policies and the systems of ideas and ideals which implicitly (and sometimes explicitly) privilege whiteness and are deeply embedded within the English education system (Bhopal and Pitkin 2020). This is exemplified by the unique struggles and challenges that make up the *educational steeplechase* outlined in the previous chapter. Recently, with the emergence of *Critical Whiteness Studies,* not only has whiteness become a visible category, it has also been declared as a valuable resource or to use a Bourdieusian lens, as Rampersad (2014) has, 'racialised facilitative capital'. This type of capital is responsible for providing 'unearned benefits and advantages' to individuals and groups racialized as 'white', based on a system 'normed and standardised on white-European values, with most of the structures, policies and practices of the institutions being situated in such a manner as to pave the road for white individuals while creating obstacles for other groups' (Sue 2003: 138). To understand the central foundations of *Critical Whiteness Studies,* Nayak (2007: 738) offers the following principles:

1. Whiteness is a modern invention; it has changed over time and place. (For a better understanding, see books by Allen 1992; Ignatiev 2009; Guglielmo and Salerno 2003; Roediger 2018).
2. Whiteness is a social norm and has become chained to an index of unspoken privileges.
3. The bonds of whiteness can yet be broken/deconstructed for the betterment of humanity.

It must be noted that there are exceptions to the 'whiteness' rule in that, as highlighted by Dottolo and Kaschack (2015: 179):

> while whiteness generally carries privilege in European-American contexts, the extent of such privilege depends greatly on the principles of intersectionality or mattering. That is, white women and men of different classes, disabilities and sexual orientations are not equally privileged in equivalent circumstances.

Additionally, it is widely known that in England, Gypsy and Traveller groups who look 'white' still experience what has been defined by Bhopal (2011) as 'white racism' in schools – this also extends to Eastern European groups. In this way, while there are different versions of 'whiteness', it primarily benefits the status quo who employ 'race' 'as a decoy offer[ing] short-term psychological advantages to poor and working-class whites, but it also masks how much poor whites have in common with poor Black and other people of colour' (Guinier 2004: 114). What Guinier is describing is the CRT concept of 'interest divergence' (Bell 1980) which has been applied in English educational contexts, particularly around the 'true racial victims in education as 'white working-class' children, especially boys' (Gillborn 2013: 480; see also Sveinsson 2009; Gillborn 2010). 'Interest divergence' is often employed by those in power to silence any attempts of racial justice and equity, particularly for Black students, diluting the argument and decentring race to highlight that social class is indeed the main barrier. This logic of 'interest divergence' is also used to divide Global Majority or racialized minorities when the educational 'success' of the so-called 'model minority' British Chinese and Indian groups are frequently used to 'justify the equity of the established system' (Wong 2015), while blaming the 'bad Black students' and their communities for their educational outcomes. Whiteness must be understood as a global system that is reproduced, maintained and operates through white supremacy, which has been characterized by Ansley (1997: 592) as:

> a political, economic, and cultural system in which whites overwhelmingly control power and material resources, conscious and unconscious ideas of white superiority and entitlement are widespread, and relations of white dominance and non-white subordination are daily reenacted across a broad array of institutions and social settings.

This daily reenactment of whiteness is institutionalized via the positioning of Black bodies as outsiders within educational spaces and places through many subtle and direct processes such as microaggressions (Joseph-Salisbury 2019); 'the maintenance of power, resources, accolades, and systems of support through formal institutional structures and procedures' (Bhopal and Chapman 2019: 102); and through nationwide education policy (Gillborn 2005). For many Black girls and women, this plays out via the constant awareness of being positioned as the 'other' through interactions and Eurocentric, whitewashed curricula, as well as the internalized pressure of unrealistic expectations, as identified in Chapter 3.

All individuals and groups are complicit in this system through a 'racial contract' that is unique because it 'is not a contract between everybody ("we the people"), but between just the people who count, the people who really are people ("we the white people")' (Mills 1997: 3). This means that those racialized as 'non-white' who are the Global Majority are affected as they do not have the same level of power in this 'racial contract' which the global system upholds. Over hundreds of years, this contract has established a racial hierarchy where those racialized as white are at the top, and those who are Black are at the bottom, with other groups in between. Moreover, to the average person, whiteness is still very much invisible due to its insidious nature which is difficult to penetrate (Dei et al. 2004).

There are many distinct challenges faced by Black girls and women like *Chika* navigating within the institutionalized whiteness of educational spaces and places which will be explored as this chapter progresses. Such challenges include restricted access, particularly into elite white educational institutions, and remaining 'outsiders within' the space. However, there are some 'advantages' if one is successful in navigating elite whiteness – though this is limited due to the intersections of the anti-Black racism and sexism Black girls and women encounter in the education system and beyond (Crenshaw 1989; Bailey and Mille 2015; Johnson 2019, 2020; Sobande and Wells 2021). Still, some 'advantages' include becoming an expert in navigating whiteness, as well as acquiring different types of knowledge, support and resources.

Infiltrating elite, Predominantly white (PW) educational spaces and places

There are 2,366 fee-paying, private (or independent) schools in England; in comparison, there are 20,249 primary and secondary state-funded schools (BESA 2021). This means that only a small minority of children have the opportunity to study in private schools as 'the independent sector educates around 5.8% of the total number of school children in the UK and around 6.4% of the total number of school children in England' (ISC 2021). This is also the case for the twenty-four elite universities across the UK who are part of the Russell group where in 2016/17 it was reported that 632,010 students were studying in these universities, which is only 27 per cent of the UK's student population (Advancing Access 2022). Therefore, though there are hierarchies of private schools and elite universities, I define them as spaces of exclusivity due to their restricted access, and underpinned by elite whiteness as their purposes are to educate, and maintain, the future generations of the status quo. When understanding white spaces, Anderson (2022: 14–15) explains the difference between what he refers to as 'white space' and 'deep white spaces':

> For Black people in particular, white spaces vary in kind, but their most distinctive feature is the overwhelming presence of white people and the relative absence of Blacks. 'White space' is a perceptual category that assumes a particular space to be predominantly white, one where Black people are typically unexpected, marginalised when present, and made to feel unwelcome, a space that Blacks perceive to be informally 'off-limits' to people like them where on occasion they encounter racialised disrespect and other forms of resistance. 'Deep white spaces' are settings which Black folk are seldom if ever present and are unexpected.

In many ways, his 'deep white spaces' are what I call here elite, PW educational institutions. Also based on his observations, as I argue, Black girls' and women's presence within these places and spaces can be seen as infiltrating them. Remarkably, it has been revealed that at least twenty-nine of England's most elite schools – Eton College, Christ's Hospital school and Liverpool's Blue Coat grammar (Adams 2023), as well as a number of universities like Cambridge (François 2019) (and others across Britain) – have profited from millions of pounds in donations from compensation that white enslavers and their families gained from the Slave Compensation Act 1837 when slavery was abolished in Britain in 1833. The irony lies in the fact that many Black students are essentially excluded from being educated within these elite, PW institutions that were literally built and maintained on the backs of many of their enslaved African ancestors! Clearly the profits of the slave trade and slavery have permeated all levels of British society, and while many generations of white people have been advantaged by this, on the flipside, many generations of Black people have been disadvantaged. Perhaps a starting point for such educational institutions could be similar to what the University of Glasgow in Scotland has committed to doing with their Historical Slavery Initiative, or the creation of ring-fenced scholarships for Black students like Yale University has done in America with its Pennington Fellowship (Shelton 2022). However, any reparative justice based on slavery across the UK *must* include Black students in Britain, Africa, the Americas and anywhere else where the legacies of slavery remain.

In this section, there are parallels with my own story as told in Chapter 1, and *Chika's* accounts which will explore the educational experiences and journeys of other Black girls and women within elite, PW educational spaces and places.

* * *

Chika has spent her entire education – from primary school to university – 'being the only one' in such educational institutions. In many ways, this matched her experiences at home as the only child – both a blessing and a curse. A blessing in that she was able to indulge in and be indulged by all of her parents' love, attention and resources. Minus the love, this was similar in her schools and at university. She merely had to utter whatever she desired, and soon enough, it would be in her possession. But she wasn't spoiled – just immensely wanted and cherished as it took her parents many years, procedures and prayers to conceive and birth her. A curse because she was one of one and never got the chance to experience the intimacy, rivalry and camaraderie of siblings – though her cousins came close to providing this to her. Still, another unintended blessing of being an only child was that she had more time for reading as she didn't have siblings to play and fight with, which facilitated the unrestricted exploration of different worlds, guided by diverse characters and plots. From a very young age, with no siblings to discuss her discoveries in her books, she would often engage in intense conversations with her father – who had most probably given her the book – to decipher the hidden messages, articulate her points and to suggest alternative avenues.

She also benefited from the intellectual environment of her parents' professions which overflowed into her household and stimulated her mind way beyond her years. Chika's parents migrated to England in their mid-twenties and came from comfortable backgrounds in Nigeria, but they had to regain this comfort once more as first-generation immigrants, through hard work, strategy, sacrifice and dedication. As a professor and a barrister, they had managed to regain and maintain their stability to provide their only child with extra comfort.

Like most parents, they wanted the best for their daughter and, rightly or wrongly, this included using their generous resources to fund the best education which coincidentally resulted in Chika's educational existence in PW, elite spaces. This desire has been explored by Ayling (2021) *when illustrating how four, middle-class Nigerian fathers sought to provide their children with better futures by educating them abroad to gain what she describes as 'Western capitals', which simultaneously reinforces the hegemonic discourse that the 'West is best'. Ayling shares that the capitals these fathers seek by sending their children to study abroad are institutional (acquired by attending a Canadian university), embodied (gained via mastering the English language) and symbolic (receiving Canadian citizenship). While Chika's parents had already migrated to England where she had been born years later, in the same way as the Nigerian, middle-class fathers in Ayling's study, they too focused on placing Chika in white, elite, educational institutions to provide her with the right capitals in the hopes of bypassing the seemingly unshakeable 'isms' and 'schisms' for an advantageous future.*

However, to access and gain a place within these educational institutions required a great deal of preparation, which *Chika* remembers in the scattered conversations she had with her hairstylist:

> Yeah it was my parents cos my mum was very new to the whole [English education] system … it was just her with the books you get from WH Smith's and just Saturday … like after school prep kinda thing, that was the main preparation they did. Obviously … they did all the school searching and all of that. I had no idea what was going on at that time, it was just like 'well these are the places you are gonna be sitting the exam' [laughs] and 'these are the schools, ok? Pick one'.

For *Chika*, the initial experience of entering into these PW, elite educational institutions were choices that were not hers to make – though she was able to input her preference according to the pre-selected options presented to her by her parents. In her own words, she 'had no idea what was going on at that time'. Moreover, this highlights how entrance into elite, PW educational spaces are conditional, based upon meeting the financial, examination and interview prerequisites – all of which require a great deal of preparation – especially if you have not had previous generations existing in the space to help you to navigate it with ease. *Chika* shares how her parents were very much determined and focused on ensuring that she was prepared for the exams – first juggling the preparation themselves before seeking outside assistance from the educational tuition company, Kumon:

> I think at one point they even got – I can't remember, but I think I had a tutor for a little bit … I did one or two sessions then but it was mainly my mum and dad sitting me down and making me do extra … they made me do Kumon as well for a little bit.

Once *Chika* successfully passed the first stage – the exam – she details her experiences of being further tested, the second stage, via an interview at the school, an additional step she had to take to gain entrance and acceptance into this elite, PW space:

> So you did an exam and then you did, you had an interview actually, you had to read a passage at one point and then one of the teachers asked you a few questions like what you like to do and what your hobbies were and it was very similar to uni, like my uni interviews, but dumbed down for

> ten year olds but very much 'what kinda things are you into?' I think to just try to get to know you, but I think by the time you did that interview, you'd already passed the exams and they were kinda a get-to-know-you as a real person kind of thing so mainly it was just an entrance exam which consisted of three exams or something like that … yeah, there was maths, english and there was like a verbal/non-verbal reasoning.

Though *Chika* and her parents were able to gain entry through successfully passing the exams and interview, her existence within this space was one that must be maintained by the payment of school fees and associated costs. This is a big undertaking usually eased by family trust funds and knowledge of charitable organizations to offset the costs – a quick Google search will show the many trust fund providers ready to assist with options and the opening of one. Unfortunately, this wasn't the case for *Chika*'s parents as she explains:

> It was effectively like paying another mortgage a month. I am just thinking about how much it would've cost, but because they had planned a long time ago, they had actually saved towards it when … let's say three/four years before they had saved towards it and so obviously it still wasn't easy, but they'd already had some money for it.

This illustrates the often precarious positions of many Black British families who may have migrated and/or gained their middle-class statuses during their lifetime and therefore do not have the generational support via wealth and knowledge to employ for future generations – though they still try to carve their own paths and create strategies for their children (Vincent et al. 2012a, 2012b, 2013). *Chika* is aware of her parents' immense sacrifices and the financial pressures that come with keeping her in elite, PW educational institutions and so she shares that she opts to work part time during her university studies:

> I worked throughout uni to … cos my parents were paying for my fees and my accommodation but because I didn't want to take out student finance and have additional loans, which I could have, because they were doing their best for me to come out of uni without any debt so I thought it would be best for me to work whilst I am in uni and use that as my spending money rather than taking out additional loans.

However, as a lot of students have to take student finance and have to work, *Chika* not taking out a student loan is describing being in a position of advantage rather than disadvantage. Another downside of operating within these elite, PW educational spaces is the distance that becomes evident between an individual and their wider communities who are not a part of this new space that Black girls and women like *Chika* now occupy. This new distance is reflected upon by *Chika:*

> I wish I stayed closer with family, like my wider – not cousins like blood cousins but y'know the wider community, I just … people thought I'd moved to another country – cos also my accent changed, I started sounding a bit more like the people around me and they were like 'where have you moved to?' and I was like 'only up the road' [laughs] yeah I'd say that's a regret.

It's almost as if this new elite, PW place that *Chika* finds herself in is the complete opposite to her community, an occurrence discussed by Casey (1993: 132) when she explains how young Black women's journeys into elite, PW educational spaces and places mean that they become

> separated from their families, from their cultural communities, from their system of signification, from their existing Black identities, [and] these young women's passages turn out to be isolated, individual journeys into the heart of whiteness.

Chika's accounts also suggest that being immersed in the elite, whiteness afforded by her entire education may have altered her own sense of self and connections to her community, using a figure of speech to denote that her school was literally just 'up the road' and therefore not far but located in an entirely different space. This also shows the restrictions of entering into elite whiteness which is not for everyone to enjoy as it is a privilege that decides future social positions and maintains existing ones which are 'strategic emplacements, fortresses to be defended and captured in a field of struggles' (Bourdieu 1984: 244). This also moves such educational institutions from more than just places into all-encompassing, restricted spaces – regardless of their geographical location and proximity to diverse neighbourhoods and communities where *Chika*'s extended family live. While many people have a 'home' identity, and a 'school' or 'university' identity, there are plenty of upwardly mobile working-class people who experience a growing distance from their home roots, and who have two selves as a consequence. This is illustrated in research by Reay et al. (2009) who, using the Bourdieusian concepts of habitus, field and cultural capital, explore the experiences of nine working-class students in an elite university. They document the tensions between the students' working-class backgrounds which are at odds within this unfamiliar, elite space and how they adapt and respond, ultimately retaining their working-class identities. However, I make the case that anti-Black gendered racism alongside classism creates unique experiences for Black girls and women – even if they have similar social class statuses as those in elite, white educational institutions. This disconnect is perfectly exemplified by Collins (1986, 1990, 1999) in the notion of the conceptual contribution of Black women as the 'outsider within'. I will use this concept to frame *Chika*'s understandings and experiences of 'being the only one' within PW, educational spaces and places.

'Outsiders Within': Black Girl/Woman- PW, elite, educational space

Chika excitedly repositions herself back in the chair as her hairstylist returns to add the final touches to her Fulani braided crown. Chika had more than enough time to admire what was on her head and to visualize how she wanted it to be with the adornments in her hair. She had finally settled on creating a beautiful, beaded fringe at the ends and dispersing the hair cuffs and cowrie shell rings across the cornrows. Chika explains this and watches, from the mirror, as the hairstylist reaches for the needle, thread and rubber bands in preparation to begin the skilled process of decorating each and every tiny plait with beads and fastening the cuffs and rings.

Chika's hairstylist *I am currently considering a local PW private school for my daughter who is turning three, but I am not sure. I know you went to a private school and went to an elite, PW university – what were your experiences like?*

Chika *Hmmmmmm … I have never actually articulated it before … let's see …*

In English contexts, there is little theoretical framing of the experiences of being the only Black girl or woman in white, elite educational spaces and places, though books such as *Taking Up Space: The Black Girl's Manifesto for Change* and *A Fly Girl's Guide to University: Being a Woman of Colour at Cambridge and Other Institutions of Elitism and Power* have begun to explore and document such experiences, albeit focusing on higher education settings. Therefore, I have had to look to the US, which has more detailed theoretical explanations about these experiences particularly Collins's 'outsider within' conceptualization (1986, 1990, 1999) which articulates and identifies the marginalized status of Black women within white educational spaces and places as a result of 'the social hierarchies of race, class, and gender that create outsider-within social locations in the first place' (1999: 86). Though she notes that there are many different racialized women groups that can also be 'outsiders within'. Yet, Collins argues that due to different group histories that position them in these ways, as well as the intersecting power dynamics at play, some 'outsiders within' are clearly better off than others, as 'not all "minorities" travelled the same path en route to these new rooms, nor are "people of colour" interchangeable when they get there' (Collins 1999: 86–7). In this way, she highlights the unique experiences of anti-Black gendered racism or misogynoir (Bailey 2021, Bailey and Trudy 2018) which often supersedes social class identity in the daily lives of many Black women. Moreover, Collins asserts that the 'outsider within' position emerges from and is located in the wider discipline of Black Feminist thought, which communicates Black women's collective and distinct standpoint for understanding self, family and society (1986: S14). Even though the 'outsider within' status as well as Black Feminism as a whole is rooted in an American context, it is useful and applicable to other western nations like England as well as Black British girls and women who it also seeks to represent and champion (Collins 2016: 135). Here, the 'outsider within' status is represented in elite, PW educational institutions via experiencing a disconnection with Blackness.

Disconnection with Blackness: self, others and the wider community

Chika points out that a major consequence of being in PW, elite educational spaces and places and assuming an 'outsider within' status can be a disconnect which can infiltrate perceptions of what it means to be Black. This was indicated by her earlier when she stated that a regret she holds is not staying closer and more connected with her community, which she expresses here again:

> I've always been that parallel of being 'too white for the Black kids' and 'too Black for the white kids' sorta thing. I hate to use that phrase but I've always had to defend who I was, what my [social] class was, why my parents did this, why my parents did that – like whenever I say my parents paid for my private schooling, it's the shock that you get cos you automatically know … and the trouble is there is so much perceptions behind private school, people … but as soon as I start to explain my story, that makes me feel vulnerable because of people's reactions …

Chika suggests that not only does she feel that her Blackness is not truly accepted in white, elite educational spaces and places, but she also feels that the entrance into these spaces has alienated her from Black spaces and places as well. In essence, she now straddles two distinct, opposing spaces as an 'outsider within'. She goes on to share that this disconnect and struggle has been a feature of her entire educational trajectory:

> I would say that for me, even in university as well, I would say my whole education, I have kinda struggled with what it means to be Black in a sense that growing up around a lot of white people, there were a lot of things that growing up with them, I felt like I was a part of that culture in a sense, but then there were a lot of things that … for example my mum would just not let me do, so it was like what is it? And I did get teased as well in secondary school like y'know 'you sound so white', 'you're a coconut', they'd make fun of my name … this is white people saying it to me, I would be called a coconut, an Oreo, they would make fun of my name and they would make rhymes to make fun of it and when you are a kid, that stuff is so deep it's like the worst thing that anybody can say to you and it really made me question 'am I Black enough?' My hair is the way Black people's are, but I don't talk like what a typical Black person would talk in a way I don't know, I talked like a 'white' person, I wasn't from London as well and then when I got to university it was like completely different, it was actually one of my friends, she was born in West London which is different to like South London so she said like for her, she doesn't talk like the stereotypical Black Londoner and she was the one that kinda got me to see that being Black is whatever you decide it is and you don't have to act like a Londoner, you don't have to act – just be yourself and that is enough, nobody can take the fact that you are Black away from you, you get to define that.

By citing her mother, who she deems to be stricter than her white peers' parents, and being labelled as a 'coconut' and an 'Oreo' – an offensive term to denigrate Black people who although appear to look Black/brown on the outside are perceived to be 'white' on the inside – *Chika* illustrates that although she 'sounds' and 'speaks' like those from the dominant culture in the space, she is still ridiculed by her white peers as being inauthentic. This is possibly based upon negative notions surrounding how Black people should be, speak and sound (Rollock 2014; Schwarz 2016). When she mentions that her name is also a point of ridicule that is also used against her, it contributes to her questioning her Black identity. She also provides clarity on her earlier comment of 'being too white for the Black kids' when she explains that she does not fit into the London-centric Black identities that are often used to exclusively portray Black British people. *Chika* is sharing her actual experience within PW, elite educational settings where she goes through an identity crisis and feels discouraged as the 'only one' in these spaces. She also illustrates that she is unable to thoroughly become enculturated into the cultural habits of these places as she is constantly reminded of her difference. Somewhat of a loner, as she does not mention being a member of a friendship group, it is only when she becomes friends with another Black girl at university – the end of her educational journey – who also does not fit with the stereotypical 'South London' trope that she is able to remedy her internal identity struggle and accept her own version of Blackness.

In a similar way to what was highlighted in Chapter 3 regarding the merging of opposing cultures and the abrupt process of othering, *Chika* delves deeper into this, building upon the unique experiences of Black girls' and women's 'outsider within' positions within elite, PW, educational spaces and places, where such othering is more blatantly obvious. She reflects on being made into a spectacle and 'othered' through the behaviour towards her hair:

> Within education but not specific to being educated so just like within school, it depends if you are the minority within the school as well cos then it's like 'oooh, can I stick my hand in your roots?' sorta thing, that was always a thing like touching your hair. So, the one day I came to school with an afro it was like 'wow, it's so spongy' and it's just like … the fascination to the other extreme where it's like 'I can't see the board!' and it's like 'calm down, I'm 2 rows from the back anyway'. But yeah, I guess it's sorta like always a fascination of hair and questions like 'so how do you wash your hair?' 'Do you wash your hair?'

The significance of hair for Black girls and women cannot be downplayed due to its historical and current ties to standards of beauty (Tate 2007; Thompson 2009; Oyedemi 2016), and the policing and regulations of how it should or should not be worn in particular spaces and places (Dash 2006; Joseph-Salisbury and Connelly 2018). So, when *Chika* shares what she describes as the 'fascination' that others had with it, it can be understood by the rarity of its presence within the space. Such distinct racialized and gendered educational experiences have been researched by Proweller (1998: 96) who notes in her study of American private school culture and the centrality of whiteness in them that students of colour are 'forced on a daily basis to mediate and negotiate racial contradictions that have been cleverly obscured through their institutionalisation'. On the other hand, the urge to touch *Chika*'s hair can be viewed as a violation of personal boundaries and basic levels of respect, which is a familiar experience for many Black girls and women as exemplified in the 2016 chart-topping song *Don't Touch My Hair* by the African-American, grammy-award winning artist Solange featuring Sampha. *Chika* also shares that this 'fascination', which for the most part can be seen as curiosity, can also have negative undertones through the positioning of it, by others, as an obstruction to learning and through the questioning of her hair grooming practices. *Chika* continues to reminisce about her experiences when participating in extracurricular activities:

> There's always that and then you don't notice it so much in sports, I feel like in sports it's less obvious cos I always did sports [and] music – to do music … cos I did classical guitar, I was the only Black girl ….it was interesting cos I even did [names prestigious school] guitar ensemble cos I was in the top group so we'd play [names prestigious place/event] and stuff, and again I was one of three girls and the only Black girl out of the sixteen of us, so it was always just like … [and] doing stuff like hockey I'd say I was the only Black girl and they would be like 'oh she's so fast'.

Interestingly, *Chika*'s revelation that her hair is not as much of an issue when she participated in musical and sporting activities – despite still being the only Black girl – is due to it being displaced by her obvious talent and exceptionalism. These provide her with the merit and acceptance when engaging in such activities within even more restricted sub-spaces, superseding the need to highlight or 'other' her difference via her hair. *Chika* continues with another incident centring her hair:

> I remember with girls, cos one time, I had greased my hair to slick it back, they were like 'we could fry an egg off that!' And it's just the little comments that always reiterated to me that I wasn't very much like them. So, in situations in schools like that, money talks more than anything – doesn't matter what race, creed, etc. you are – if you're rich then you're accepted, that's the first thing. Second thing is race … so race and prettiness which sorta intermix, so if you were skinny, white and blonde you ascertained [*sic*] to the social norms and then popularity came after that. But I was neither rich, neither skinny, white or blonde and I didn't really have the money to do the cultural activities that they did, so a lot of the time I just felt isolated cos at first I was being invited to things but bit by bit, when they saw I couldn't reciprocate, I just stopped being invited to things.

When describing the negative comments that were made when *Chika* decided to style her hair in another way, she once again highlights the 'othering' effect that it has, reinforcing her 'outsider within' position within the space which she further clarifies via her awareness that she finds herself 'caught between groups of unequal power' (Collins 1999: 85). Incidents like *Chika*'s have been identified by Fordham (2016) in her book *Downed by Friendly Fire: Black Girls, White Girls and Suburban Schooling* when she highlights the 'female-centred bullying, aggression and competition' within such educational places and spaces which 'directly relate to the structural violence embedded in the racialised and gendered social order'. For *Chika*, being a young Black British woman means she is obviously in opposition to this elite, PW space and the young white, rich, English women who occupy it. Therefore, she is judged by standards that she will never meet in terms of her hair, her Blackness and her perceived 'prettiness' in relation to a white standard. While she also discusses money and being 'rich' as another criterion that qualifies an individual to be in the space, though her parents are relatively financially comfortable compared to other Black British families, *Chika* does not see herself on the same financial level as her peers which is further trumped by the other qualities she does not possess. This, she shares, results in her gradual isolation and the establishment of her 'othering' in the space as a true 'outsider within', or in other words, 'part of the whole but outside the main body' (hooks 1990: 149). In order to come to terms with her 'outsider within' positioning, *Chika* discloses a strategy she quickly developed to operate and exist within these PW, elite, educational spaces and places:

> I think as the years went by, you very much got used to it, you became your school self when you were in the school gates and at school functions, and then when you got down the hill back to where you lived, you became – and you weren't the only Black person for ten miles – you became [laughs] very … you reflected back into your old self. But when you first start … we [Black girls] just accepted that this is going to be the norm for you … because it becomes your norm, you are used to being the only Black person in that class really, you are used to there being only two of you, and you just keep it moving and be like 'Fine, this is it today'.

As highlighted in Chapter 3 by *Eve*, this merging of opposing cultures is not always successful as *Chika* shares she instead has to separate and compartmentalize her two existences in what she refers to as her white-accepted 'school self' and her normal, Black 'old self'. Through the lens of a Bourdieusian analysis, by creating and presenting two selves in different spaces and places, *Chika* is engaging in 'strategy and struggle work within the logic of practice for the purposes of recognition, legitimation, capital and access to capital within the symbolic and material world' (Mahar et al. 1990: 19). Additionally, to bring a racialized dimension to *Chika*'s strategy, what she describes is also outlined by DuBois (1989: 6) as the everyday experiences of African-Americans who have to develop 'double consciousness' due to their African and American identities being incompatible to each other. These experiences continue for *Chika* as she ventures into university:

> Coming to uni ... yes, of course it was gonna be a bit different but I didn't expect there to be such a barrier, I feel like ... honestly I had to explain my Blackness before any white person was ... I don't know willing to befriend me ... I don't know if that makes sense, I feel like I had to show that as a Black girl 'oh I'm not loud' or 'I'm articulate' or whatever before – there's just a barrier before I speak that I have to show – when I open my mouth it's like 'oh she's like that' sort of thing.

Though she is familiar with being in elite, PW educational spaces and places, she finds that she still remains an 'outsider within' and has to exert additional energy to convince 'any white person' that she isn't a stereotypical Black girl and that she is just like them in order to gain their friendship. Therefore, part of her experience is having to actively counter these stereotypes. Anderson (2022: 48) identifies that this is a normal experience of Black people in white spaces as 'the impermanence of this position is owing in part to the fact that ... the Black person will likely encounter many more people who need to be impressed ... to be convinced that the presumed identities do not apply'. Yet, once she has gained friendship from some of her white peers, *Chika* reveals that despite how close they may even become, she still finds that there is a disconnect:

> There is always some sort of disconnect I find anyway, like one of my best friends, I'm always having to, as I say, to explain things and she doesn't just understand when I say certain things because culturally we are slightly different and again that can be hard because again you feel out of place sometimes, especially when [at] a top university ... you are on your own, there's only five of you in the whole year, I would want to see a bit more diversity ... that's one thing I think really does need to change in education, especially in top universities.

Chika ascribes the 'disconnect' to cultural differences, once again highlighting the ways in which opposing cultures are not always able to completely merge and how this results in feelings of being 'out of place', on the margins and an 'outsider within'. This is further worsened by *Chika*'s awareness that she is one of a very small minority of Black girl students in her year in this elite, PW university, as well as her desire for more diversity which she essentially believes would alleviate the disconnect between peers, the imbalance of the space, along with the burden experienced by the few Black and Global Majority students there. Additionally, she confides that disconnects are not just with other white students but can also extend to other students of colour beyond university campuses into student accommodation:

> I had to live with one girl who is (white) Welsh and one girl who is Pakistani but grew up in Kenya and so for example just doing my hair was an eye opener. I use coconut oil in my hair and the girl was like 'but isn't that what you use in food?' And I was like 'it is not the same tub that I use to cook with and put in my hair' and … you try and explain to her why I use coconut oil in my hair and why I have this coconut butter moisturiser – that kinda thing which didn't need explaining when I lived with my other housemates and it's just that kinda realization of 'oh yeah well we are really different' … or why I season chicken and she doesn't, she was so confused … they used to ask a lot of questions cos for them you're the first person of whatever that they felt comfortable enough to ask such a question.

While *Chika* once again highlights and understands the curiosity of her housemates and attempts to educate them about some of her cultural practices, it can be both tiring and intrusive to have to constantly explain herself and her actions, considering whiteness is rarely interrogated in the same way and is accepted as the standard. However, there is definitely beauty in people from diverse backgrounds living closely together and feeling comfortable enough to ask specific questions in order to gain new understandings which can bridge differences and divides. *Chika* agrees by viewing these interactions as unique and sometimes useful in order to truly educate others:

> I think that it's a unique experience to prove something because even with everyone I relate to, even the friends that I've made and stuff, I can educate them on my own experiences and I feel like even with my housemates … having gone to uni with me, they got something extra … just an understanding how things can be different for someone from an Ethnic Minority group cos like my – one of my best friends at uni said I'm the first Black person she'd ever had a long conversation with, she was like, 'I'd literally honestly, it just, I didn't realize until my mum was

asking about my friends' and she was like 'and actually I never realized you're the first Black person I've spoken to'.

On the other hand, the fact that *Chika* doesn't need to ask her white friends about their cultural practices shows that she has been so immersed in them already that they are taken for granted. Next, *Chika* expresses some of the benefits and advantages that she feels she was able to gain by 'being the only one' and an 'outsider within' for most of her educational experiences navigating within elite, PW spaces and places.

The 'advantages' of enduring PW, elite educational spaces and places

Chika is no longer afraid to experiment and enjoy the versatility that her afro textured hair provides or the inevitable fascination, curiosity and questions she is likely to be asked by her white and non-Black work colleagues when she next returns to work. She believes that while things may not have changed much in elite, PW spaces and places, her mindset certainly has compared to how it was as a Black girl and young woman who had to successfully navigate it as a requirement in her education. She is self-assured and reaffirmed, developed through years of training, adaptation, 'othering' and being the 'outsider within' throughout her educational journey. Now, she is able to straddle comfortably in multiple spaces and places as her authentic (Black woman) self. Collins defines this state as the different dimensions to being an 'outsider within' where those that have gained access within these elite, PW spaces can obtain advantages such as becoming 'privy to some of the most intimate secrets of white society' (Collins 1986: S14). Such advantages include becoming an expert in navigating elite whiteness, as well as acquiring different types of knowledge, support and resources.

Chika's hairstylist *Wow! There is so much to consider – thanks for sharing. Is there anything else I should know?*
Chika *Definitely … it's not all negative depending on how you look at it …*

Becoming an expert in navigating elite whiteness and learning about the true power of networks

To be educated within elite, PW educational spaces and places is to face and deal with the barrier of navigating whiteness to survive. Therefore, it can be argued that acquiring this ability is a valuable skill. This is because the ability to navigate whiteness is what Yosso (2005: 80) terms 'navigational capital – the ability to manoeuvre through institutions not created with Communities of Color in mind'. *Chika* hints at this when she remembers being more comfortable in elite, PW educational spaces and places compared to other Black girls and young women she encountered along the way:

> My experience is … so a great example is I met someone who … she's from [the inner city] … we had different school experiences. Her primary school and secondary school were predominantly Black, so coming to university for her was really a shock because she's like 'I actually don't think I have been around this many white people and I feel so isolated'. Whereas that wasn't a shock for me, it was more the sorta, more nuanced things actually trying your identity so, I can't – I don't think you can pin it down to anything cos actually some people have that shock later. They actually are … like the identity thing and feeling out of place might not even happen in school, they might be chilled until then and then they might go to uni and be like 'Wow!' My friend's friend said that shock only happened to her in the workplace.

Withstanding such a 'shock' and becoming accustomed to elite, PW spaces and places is a skill precisely because not everyone can manage to do it and *Chika* clarifies her insights as to why:

> I guess [in my school] we had the luxury of having a place where you had the teachers, the time and the resources to do anything, that's the difference. So, I think it definitely shaped my view of the world in terms of thinking that everyone matters and that everyone should have the opportunity. It also definitely made me feel sad cos there were some people there who were excellent, who were so smart – some of the smartest people I've ever met where the environment of the school – cos they were from working-class backgrounds, they'd got – their parents had hustled, decided to get them in, people that may have been the next … I don't know cured cancer or something, but the environment that they were in at home just did not allow them to function in that school and ultimately some of them dropped out. It's sad because if they can't function where some people actually want them to succeed, they might not even function in somewhere where people have little time for them.

By discussing her working-class peers that were unable to function within PW, elite educational spaces and places, *Chika* highlights how elite whiteness can also be restrictive and hostile to any groups that do not fit into the mould. A similar occurrence happens for white working-class boys in British secondary modern schools due to the class culture which is in opposition to their own as highlighted by the groundbreaking study by Willis (1977). Though Willis's study was conducted in the 1970s when boys left school at fifteen, it highlighted key themes such as social mobility and how 'respectable' working-class identities were alien to them. Willis's ideas are so powerful that they have influenced and impacted a tradition of British social science thinkers of anti-social working-class boys. A more current study by Ward (2015) continues to explore the marginalization of white working-class men navigating the labour market, a shrinking economy and the increased importance of educational qualifications. *Chika* also confirms that in her current workplace experiences she is still able to withstand the PW space – which is occupied by the same people who she spent her educational years with. Interestingly she notes how these same people are unfamiliar with a Black woman like her:

> I feel like if I didn't have that kinda middle-class background, there are a lot of situations that I would've felt uncomfortable, so even for example where I work now, it's very middle class, like very Oxford/Cambridge, white man who has been to every continent since he was a child so I feel like in a sense, I am able to relate a bit more especially when I am in the office and I speak and they hear my – well I don't think I have an accent, I think everyone sounds like me, but when they hear my accent, they kinda, they are a bit taken aback and I don't know what they expect, maybe they expect me to sound like I am from, I don't know … but that is always quite funny to me yeah. I know exactly … I had a private school education, sometimes it makes me feel a bit good to be a bit underestimated and then when I speak my Queen's English it just baffles them and they don't know what to make of it at all!

Another advantage of successfully operating and navigating through elite, PW educational spaces is the different types of knowledge that are available within these spaces. Perhaps this is one of the main reasons why certain parents desire for their children to be educated in these types of spaces and places as they are closely connected to social class positions and the kinds of opportunities that one is able to access in the labour market. For example, *Chika* shares that she learned very early about the value of membership into the right networks:

> Yeah, you were taught networks were the way you get further and unfortunately I think that's a failing within the education system cos

> sometimes we try and lie to people and say 'it's your academic ability'. No it's not, there's some mediocre people doing great jobs that they should definitely never be in, but they had good networks and I think that's the difference. I think that is one of the key differences between private school and normal [state-funded] secondary schools as well, they don't lie to you about that, they tell you 'it's the networks so go out and make them'.

She identifies the value and power of specific networks when explaining the real ways that they can provide opportunities. Bourdieu (1986) describes this as social capital, which are connections and resources that are accrued from membership into certain social networks, for example the infamous Old Boys' network.

> I just started working in my company and I was talking to my friend the other day and he had a similar kinda educational experience to me but his dad knew someone who worked in the agency who just hooked him up with a job at my current company straight away. So, I feel like we [Black women] have to go through the whole like paper procedure whereas other people can escape that part because of someone they know and sometimes I feel like because of ... you might not look as good on paper as the other person, if you wanna get somewhere education is the only way – well one of the ways in order to better your social status and class.

Interestingly, *Chika* has been unable to bypass the formal processes of securing a job in her current company with a 'hook up' like her white, male counterpart despite having a 'similar kinda educational background'. What *Chika* highlights with this example is that it's not because he is white and male that he gets 'hooked up', as that's not the whole story; rather she is illustrating that it's the network and class connections that are the crucial difference. Though the network and class connections are held almost exclusively by white middle-class people, it does also exclude the majority of white people from lower social-class backgrounds and Black people regardless of their social-class positions. In other words, the underlying point is that money can buy the elite education, but not the elite connections which are intergenerational. While she does possess some degree of privilege to even be able to know about and apply for her job, as Bourdieu (1996: 21) explains:

> a particular mode of acquisition: what we call ease is the privilege of those who, having imperceptibly acquired their culture through a gradual

> familiarisation in the bosom of the family, have academic culture as their native culture and can maintain a familiar rapport with it that implies the unconsciousness of its acquisition [emphasis in original].

Yet, as illustrated by *Chika*, little changes for Black women from middle-class backgrounds who possess similar cultural capital and habitus to the field who often 'have their cultural and social capital devalued, rejected and treated as illegitimate' (Vincent et al. 2012b: 350). Yet, these are practices that often happen despite attempts to have fairer recruitment processes which is evident when the educational backgrounds of most of those in top professions are scrutinized (The Sutton Trust and the Social Mobility Commission 2019). This also speaks to the types of resources, encouragement and support that are more readily available in elite, PW educational places and spaces compared to others. Unfortunately, the educational game is rigged, but at least *Chika* has acquired some knowledge of how the rigging happens.

Acquiring different types of resources, encouragement and support

In a English study by Abrahams (2018), building upon the work of renowned American theorist Lareau (2003, 2009, 2011) who created the term 'concerted cultivation' to explain how middle-class families and schools purposely provide middle-class children with the right tools and experiences to navigate the education system and society, she explores and categorizes three types of English schools: private, state in an affluent area and state in a disadvantaged area. Abrahams finds that there are marked distinctions in terms of subject-choice provisions at GCSE and A-Level stages, the kinds of career advice and guidance given, as well as the facilities available to the different cohorts of students in each of the schools. This leads her to categorize the private and the affluent state schools as engaging in 'institutional concerted cultivation' in comparison to the disadvantaged state school which exercises 'constrained cultivation'. Though it must be noted that there are two types of private school – run-of-the-mill and elite, with the latter providing a lot more social capital. Another example of these resources is in the book *Privilege: The Making of an Adolescent Elite at St. Paul's School* by Khan (2012), an ethnography of an elite, PW boarding school in America, which provides another example of how a select few students are prepared for 'success'. *Chika* details the kinds of encouragement and support that she was exposed to before entrance into her secondary school:

> I remember when I was in primary school, the secondary school that I went to, one of the heads came to the school and spoke to us all and

> kinda encouraged us… when we do our exams that these are the types of things that will happen when you come to the school. Whereas, I am not so sure that would've happened if – you could see like the progression – whereas if it was the [state-funded] school round the corner from my house, I am pretty sure the head didn't go to that school, so [I was exposed to] those little things that really do make all the difference.

This kind of encouragement and support or 'concerted cultivation' or 'capitals' that are provided and developed continue when *Chika* became a student at her secondary school where she was encouraged and supported to develop particular interests and skills alongside her studies:

> The one reason why I think I liked my school a lot was because they really pushed us to care about social issues and that's still the thing that they talk about now. It's their big difference about them cos there are a lot of standard private schools, but this is the one thing that I do actually do well, and I was really getting out there and being part of the community, caring about people, caring about what they are doing, everyone had to volunteer – there wasn't even really a choice in it. People would either be doing – oh I used to teach elderly people how to use computers after school, and we used to have kids come who were doing sorta – it would be like booster classes, literacy schemes on Saturdays, they would come to the school and we would help them through it and y'know just … and that was just embedded into what we did.

Moreover, *Chika* remembers that her school had a lot of resources available to develop each student through extra-curricular activities which they strongly encouraged and tailored for them:

> Extra-curricular activities were very much encouraged because all your friends did it so you kind of all went. So with the netball, all my friends played netball so we all used to go together because if you didn't you'd be the only one going home by yourself anyway. But we were very much actively encouraged, they tried to have a society for literally everything so there was even a language lot who wanted to do extra-curricular languages, there was … cos they used to have language week – suppose it's now seen as an international week in school so we very much could get involved in that. If it was reading or poetry or writing, they had a thing for you, so you could get involved. It was very rare for you just to sit, it was very rare for you not to do anything but it was kinda hard because there was so much available to you that 'why not?'

Chika reveals that this type of encouragement and support is due to the small size of her year group which also has other benefits such as being in a close-knit group, at least at the beginning of her secondary school experiences:

> It's very small, there were only seventy of us in the year, everyone was everyone's friend, we would all roll as a batch of sixty-five [laughs] it was nice, you were all young, confused, you didn't know what was going on, this whole idea that you had to move through your class was lost so yeah at the beginning, before people's personalities and the pseudo fights and whatever comes with girls' school, what broke out, everyone was quite good friends so yeah it was quite … there was no expectations, I think when we go to like uni and onwards, you've formed your personality, when you are eleven/twelve, you don't have that much of a personality yet, there wasn't so many issues so everyone was quite nice to each other at the beginning.

Additionally, *Chika* recalls the expectations along with the dedicated support and encouragement by a teacher when choosing what to do at university:

> Around choosing whether or not to go to uni, I wasn't too sure whether to go to uni or not, I just wasn't sure I was feeling it cos the only problem in my school was there was this expectation of 'you have to go to a Russell group' and 'everyone has to apply to Oxford and Cambridge' blah blah blah and that was the only thing, it was very pushy, everyone was very … and actually I was like [inaudible] maybe I just want to start working, maybe uni is not for me … no one ever did that, everyone just went to uni and it's cos I was a little bit … I thought I should go and do actuarial science cos I thought I'd make money and then it was my English teacher who sat me down and was like 'are you sure about actuarial science?' like 'you are kinda a people person and that's not a people person kinda job, so maybe you should do something different?' And it made me think so I did rely on them to sorta give me a reality check, I am ultimately glad I did go to uni, I don't regret going at all, I loved it.

* * *

A mist of hairspray covers Chika's head as the hairstylist finishes her hair session. She smiles in delight as she embraces the hairstylist and thanks her for her services. The hairstylist also thanks Chika for sharing her educational experiences and journey within PW, elite educational institutions which will aid in her making an informed decision about where to send her daughter. Chika packs away her things and puts on her jacket, gently lifting her long braids so that they hang freely, swaying down her back as she walks out of the salon. Whenever she moves – even an inch – all the adornments glisten and shimmer as the beads clang and click together. She is on her way to meet her friends and cannot wait to show off her new hairstyle.

* * *

Chika's educational experiences and journey have shaped her in many ways. Collins's concept of 'outsider within' illustrates *Chika*'s experience as the only Black girl and woman in both PW spaces as a result of her PW, elite education. The experiences she shares, particularly at the start and end, bring home beautifully that she has been able to integrate these experiences into a strong sense of identity as a Black woman, but clearly it was a challenge for her to do so. The nature of that challenge is highlighted in the disconnection she felt with her Blackness, her peers and her wider community which she is eventually able to make sense of. *Chika*'s story also demonstrates some of the advantages that can come from learning how to negotiate PW, elite spaces, such as becoming an expert in doing so and acquiring different types of resources. However, it must be noted that the strength of anti-Black gendered racism and classism means that, in many cases, the advantages and rewards that others may gain from being educated in these elite, PW educational places and spaces are often not fully enjoyed by Black girls and women.

Additionally, while it is fantastic to see the philanthropic endeavours of Black British celebrities like the musician Stormzy and footballer Raheem Sterling who are providing financial support to ensure that more Black British students are educated within elite, PW educational institutions like Cambridge, the University of Manchester and King's College London, I am sceptical in fully celebrating these great moves. Firstly, it is *not* the responsibility of individual, rich Black British celebrities to right the historic, systemic, anti-Black racist wrongs of England and Britain as a whole's past; instead the government and institutions should take accountability and responsibility to ensure that Black British communities, who also pay their taxes, receive better access, treatment and outcomes in education, as a starting point. Secondly, educational inequalities are entrenched before university and such celebrity-created initiatives should support Black British students to enter into elite, PW educational institutions from nursery and primary schooling. Most importantly, as demonstrated in this chapter, being and navigating within these elite, PW educational spaces and places is not an easy feat, and if Black British celebrities who have taken it upon themselves to do something wish to *really* change the game, dedicated support for Black British students is another investment that is needed from the point of entry and even beyond completion of university courses. Lastly, Black British celebrities could work with Black experts of education to create alternative, quality, Black-centred institutions for Black British children and young people. Otherwise, these educational institutions will continue to remain elite, PW spaces with privileges that are reserved for white people.

But what are the experiences of Black girls and women in predominantly Global Majority (GM) educational spaces and places? Chapter 5 will explore this in more detail.

5

Being One of Many Black Girls or Women

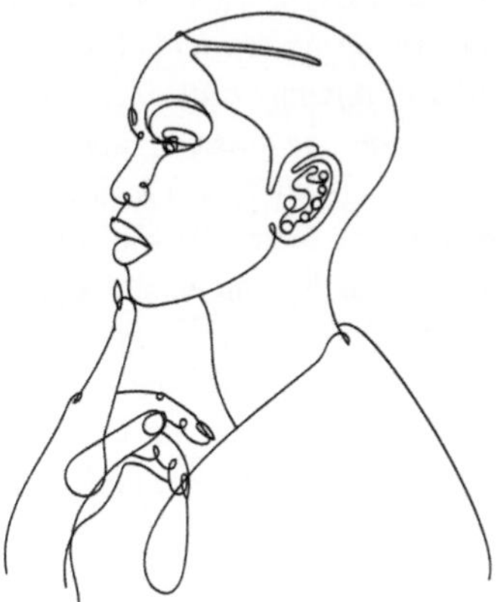

Figure 5 *Nia-Elise*

She holds up the canvas, moving it slowly in the air, viewing how it reflects the light. Unhappy with what she sees, she places the canvas back down and swishes her paintbrush, mixing and blending the different colours on the palette to achieve the shade she is after. She finds painting an intriguing and therapeutic activity as it allows her to recreate the visions in her mind's eye onto a blank canvas, and as of late, she has ventured into painting and printing her art onto clothing and crockery, as well as taking orders to draw and produce art tailored to the needs and wants of her clients – mainly friends of friends. Drawing on her learnings from her fashion degree, she has just set up an Etsy seller account which is doing quite well and receiving a lot of interest and requests. She has hopes of expanding her customer base and enabling her heart, via her work, to travel far and wide while gaining exposure and creating a nice side hustle to provide another source of necessary income in this day and age. Eventually, it is her ultimate goal to paint and create full time, letting go of her unfulfilling 9–5 which has never really stimulated anything but her pockets. She dreams of being invited to showcase a collection of her pieces at somewhere exciting like the Tate Modern in London or Biennale Arte in Venice. For now, she works on her latest artwork collection as part of a temporary exhibition in a local community space. This collection is her best yet and is connected via the theme 'being one of many', titled 'Babygirls inna, but not of, Babylon'.

'She' is Nia-Elise – twenty-two years young and living in the Midlands with her parents. She is number four of six, sharing two siblings with the same parents, plus two sisters from her mother and a brother on her fathers side. She grew up enjoying her big, blended family, particularly cherishing having bonus parents and plenty of nieces and nephews, courtesy of her three half siblings – though she despises the term 'half' because they are very much 'fully' her siblings. From a young age, she had always been creatively inclined, which she simply regarded as a family trait since her father was a tailor, one of her brothers was a musician, the other a graphic designer and one of her sisters was a pastry chef. This creativity was highly visible in her style which she was constantly switching up. Currently, she is rocking her hair in a low, bright ginger fade with a side parting and matching ginger eyebrows of course! This colour contrasted beautifully with the undertones of her dark chocolate brown complexion. Nia-Elise always had the latest and noticeably unique trainers which she would order from around the world and sometimes still customize further to ensure that no one else had anything remotely similar. Nike was her favourite brand by far, but if another competitor made a pair that she was really feeling, she would not hesitate to add it to her huge and ever growing trainer and sneaker collection.

The soulful and defiant words of 'I Owe You Nothing' by Seinabo Sey plays softly in the background as Nia-Elise resumes work on her blank canvas once she has finally achieved the shade that she wanted. The song, along with a combination of smells from her burning incense – rose musk, pink sugar and sweet harmony – set the scene and lead her into a trance-like state of maximum concentration for her newest illustration that will be added to her 'Babygirls inna, but not of, Babylon' collection.

Her plump lips are slightly parted as she sucks in the air around her, assisted by her full, button nose, enabling her to pace her creative energy along with her paintbrush strokes. Perched onto a stool, she leans forward with one hand holding the paint palette and the other directing the paintbrush on the canvas securely held up by an easel. Nia-Elise occasionally squints her round eyes as she moves her head slightly to view her progress from different angles to ascertain whether she is on the right path of recreating her internal vision. She keeps another thin paintbrush behind her right ear – an additional tool and adornment along with the shiny silver studs that decorate both ears from the lobe, all the way up to the top of her cartilage. She emits a natural and subtle attractiveness defined by her distinctive Caribbean features, a mixture of the many peoples of the region. Her face is bare because the paint she is working with is guaranteed to splatter and end up decorating it like make-up by the end of this particular painting session.

She has stumbled in and out of her artistic talents and expressions throughout her life, but Nia-Elise was never really provided with the right types of resources, support or exposure in her formal education at local, predominantly GM schools, limiting her understanding of her ability – which was way beyond her peers- or how to nurture it. Yet, during her schooling years, she could never stop doodling at the back of her exercise books or filling countless notebooks with her vivid, colourful and stunning creations. She always loved to design and showcase elements of Black British cultures, particularly centring Black femininity and girl/womanhood in ways that paid homage to their existence in a variety of formations. Finding joy in the reactions of her friends, family and peers, who were profoundly moved when she showed, gave or produced her artwork to/for them, she had now come to finally accept that this was her calling, leading to her focused investment in it. A while ago now, during her latter educational years at university, she had utilized social media platforms and YouTube to find her art tribe and to become acquainted with creative communities to learn, nurture and develop herself as the artist that she is and has always been.

* * *

Nia-Elise is the fourth composite character who will narrate what it is like 'being one of many' Black girls and women being schooled and studying within predominantly GM educational spaces and places. Such institutions, which have higher numbers of GM student populations, are typically found in inner-city state-funded schools and sixth form/further education colleges, as well as post-1992 universities. *Nia-Elise* will illustrate the positives gained from such spaces and places like the appreciation and understanding of self and cultural diversity, as well as the strength in numbers which can provide valuable connections, solidarity and affirmation. On the other hand, she will also reveal how predominantly GM educational places and spaces are still largely controlled by white authority and how Black girls and women are positioned and treated as 'unruly' within them. Lastly, she will interrogate whether predominantly GM educational spaces and places limit educational opportunities due to the racialized, classed access and the inequality of resources which stunt the growth and exposure to worlds beyond their own for predominantly GM students, specifically Black girls and women.

Predominantly Global Majority (PGM) educational spaces and places

The English education system is highly segregated along class, gender, religious and racial/ethnic lines as evidenced by the existence of grammar,[8] private, single-sex and faith-based schools; as well as elite, pre- and post-1992 universities. The geographical location of educational institutions also plays a huge part. As stated by Coldron et al. (2010: 20) when looking at why English schools are socially segregated, 'schools in England have historically served different groups in society with the responsibility for provision being shared between religious or philanthropic groups, and the state'. This is evident in the foundations of the modern English education system which laid the seeds for this established division beginning with the introduction of the 1944 Education Act. The Act organized state-funded education in England and Wales, until the 1960s, into a tripartite system of grammar (academically selective), technical (trade-focused) and secondary modern (mixed ability) schools; and private schools (independent of the state and usually fee-paying) were largely unaffected. From 1965, comprehensive schools were introduced, replacing secondary modern schools and this also saw a decline in grammar school provisions. Through the Learning and Skills Act 2000 and the Academies Act 2010, a new type of educational provision – academies which are partly state-funded but independently run by trusts – was introduced (West and Wolfe 2018).

While social class divisions are often the focal topic when looking at the divided English education system, the intersection of race and gender cannot be ignored. As Critical Race theorists assert, race, racism and whiteness are an underpinning and important feature which permeates society both in the US – where CRT originates, and in the UK where it has been transferred (Ladson-Billings 1998; Gillborn 2008; Leonardo 2009; Warmington 2012). Race, racism and whiteness are important considerations because, as Gillborn (2005: 498) highlights, when characterizing education policy as an act of white supremacy, 'race inequity and racism are central features of the education system', and the intended consequence of education policy, in the case of England and other western societies, is to 'support and affirm the very structure of racist domination and oppression' (hooks 1989: 113). Though whiteness is not always highly visible in predominantly GM educational spaces and places, it does not mean it is not a key feature shaping access, educational opportunities and experiences due to 'the complete racialisation of daily life' (Leonardo 2005: 405). Chapter 4 provided some insights into how Black girls and women experience racialized, gendered and class differences when studying as 'the only one' in PW, in some cases elite, educational spaces and places. In this chapter, both positive and negative experiences of Black girls and women as 'one of many' in predominantly GM educational institutions will be explored.

Due to the higher concentrations of these GM communities in England, they often reside in certain areas; thus there are pockets of schools where they are in the majority such as in Slough, Luton, London, Leicester, Birmingham, Manchester and Bradford (Mitchell 2022). In addition, when race and social class intersect, similar issues such as unequal access, quality of resources and lower outcomes remain prevalent and further represent the unequal English education system (Office for National Statistics 2020). From a historical standpoint, this can be seen as an attribute of both systemic and institutional racism where GM children were more likely to enter into schools of lesser quality and, particularly Black Caribbean students, were disproportionately labelled 'educationally subnormal' and disproportionately excluded by being placed in special education programmes away from 'mainstream' schooling – which continues to this day (Coard 1971; Hamilton 2018; Wallace and Joseph-Salisbury 2022). Additionally, academic scholars conclude schools to be racially and ethnically segregated (Bagley 1996; Johnston et al. 2004; Burgess and Wilson 2005; Burgess et al. 2005; Johnston et al. 2006; Weekes-Bernard 2007; The Challenge et al. 2017). This ties into the fact that school segregation can lead to inequality from the point of entry. Strand (2010: 290) analysed whether different types of schools in England narrow or widen attainment gaps and highlighted that there is an overlap between achievement, poverty and ethnicity as well as the fact that Black children are more likely to attend schools of lower quality, during their (state-funded) primary schooling. It has also been illustrated that ethnic and racial segregation continues into secondary schooling in a English report by Weekes-Bernard (2007) about school choice and ethnic segregation, in which contributor Claire Alexander writes in the foreword (p. II) that many Black, Asian and Minority Ethnic parents (which I refer to as GM) are restricted to selecting schools for their children due to a combination of

> structural barriers to accessing necessary information, institutional constraints on the kinds and quality of schools available to those families living in deprived areas, the demand for ethnic, gender or religion-specific provision and less tangible considerations around location, safety and reputation.

Moving onto the Higher Education (HE) literature, Pásztor and Wakeling (2018: 984) observe that 'despite the formal abolition of the binary divide between universities and polytechnics, England continues to have a diverse and informally stratified HE system'. This informally stratified HE system refers to the different kinds of higher education institutions available to study in, the different qualifications that can be achieved and the different kinds of students that attend them. In terms of the different institutions available to study in, universities occupy different levels of prestige based on when they were established, rankings and research intensity. This has previously been highlighted by Brown and Scase (1994) who researched the experiences of students in three different British universities, as well as recruiters to illustrate the importance of social capital to succeed in a changing economy, finding that privileged students are more likely to have access to them from their universities and families. More recently, the *Paired Peers* project by Bathmaker et al. (2016) looked at the experiences of two sets of students over a three-year period at two different universities in the same English city. The project demonstrated the power of social class distinctions and how universities reproduce them. This is because the same subjects have different status according to the type of institution they are gained from (Bathmaker et al. 2013). Also, different higher education institutions provide different subjects. For example, no post-1992 university has a medical, veterinary or dental school, nor do they have classics degree options, and most pharmacy degrees are in post-1992 universities (Purcell et al. 2009; Boliver 2015). Through the highly stratified nature of universities in England, a similar process of social segregation, specifically in regard to race, ethnicity and social class, as experienced in schools, occurs. At the point of entry, according to Croxford and Raffe (2013: 173), factors such as 'different qualifications of applicants from different backgrounds' limit participation and reinforce inequalities in higher education in terms of which institutions are occupied by which groups, as well as which subjects are chosen to study. In fact, Mirza (2006b: 2) notes how GM women students are most likely to enrol in 'lower status universities and [be] concentrated in particular subject areas'. This concentration into lower status institutions and subject areas like health and social sciences for GM students as a whole is not a coincidence. Boliver (2016: 262), who analysed university admissions data, illustrates 'that ethnic minority applicants are less likely than comparably qualified white applicants to receive offers from Russell Group universities, especially in relation to degree programmes that attract disproportionately high numbers of ethnic minority applicants'. A great strength of the previously mentioned *Paired Peers* research is that they followed two student groups at an elite university and a post-1992 university in the same English city, studying the same degree courses which further illustrated differences in admissions, experiences, resources and outcomes in the labour market.

Taken together, it is important to acknowledge that in spite of 'the myriad policies and practices that restrict access of students of colour to high-quality curricular [and] well-equipped schools', in western societies, 'some students of colour have been able to penetrate these barriers to educational opportunity' (DeCuir and Dixson 2004: 28). *Nia-Elise*, who is herself a recent graduate from a post-1992 university and studied a fashion degree, represents how many Black British girls and women have been able to do this and what they encounter along the way. With this in mind, *Nia-Elise* shares the positives gained from predominantly GM, educational spaces and places starting with gaining an appreciation and understanding of self and cultural diversity.

Appreciating and understanding self and cultural diversity

An interesting report by the Demos Integration hub (2015) states that 'ethnic minority children … are substantially more likely than white British children to attend schools in which ethnic minorities are in the majority' and they also state that 'across the country, around 94 per cent of white British students are in white British-majority schools'. Johnston et al. (2006: 975) put forward in their article about ethnic school and residential segregation that such processes are a disservice to a multicultural society where

> [s]ociety will be 'better' – fairer, more tolerant and culturally richer – if children mix and make friends with students from other ethnic groups than their own in school milieux where they learn tolerance face-to-face in a nurturing, guided environment and then take these favourable experiences forward into adult life.

These observations can extend beyond schooling to encompass the entire education system. Moreover, in a study conducted by Rhamie (2012: 178) exploring how students make sense of their identity and understand diversity at secondary school, they find that the students they observed were 'very aware of the value of different cultures in enriching their own lives [and] the importance and value of learning about other cultures was a key element of pupils' responses … considered to be crucial for understanding different people and their backgrounds'.

* * *

The room that Nia-Elise is painting in is now silent as she answers her ringing mobile phone, puts it on loudspeaker and perches it on a nearby flat surface. She is being interviewed by a journalist from a local magazine for an article to promote her upcoming 'Babygirls inna, but not of, Babylon' exhibition.

As if Nia-Elise is engaging in deep conversation with the image she is bringing into existence upon her canvas, she greets the journalist and begins to delve into the inspiration behind her exhibition, while continuing to swish her paintbrush. Nia-Elise begins by reminiscing about her memories of her primary school located in a large city, in the heart of a GM community with predominantly GM peers:

> [My primary school] was very diverse but I think that it opened my eyes up to the way the world is I suppose. At a young age I started to realize that we are all different and we all have different cultural backgrounds because I remember talking to someone in primary school, we were quite young, and we were talking about things we eat at home and I was like 'rice and stew, it's amazing' and they were looking at me like 'what are you on about? What's rice and stew?' And that's when I was like 'Yeah you guys don't eat the same thing as me.' So, it's like 'Ok, what do you guys eat at home?' And the Filipinos would be like 'Yeah we have noodles or we have rice but it's not with your type of stew.' Whereas, some of the white kids would be like 'Yeah I have bangers and mash or fish and chips or I have a casserole or ….' So, that's when I started to realize that 'Oh wow!' we are all different people, but we are still the same at the same time.

The awareness of differences as highlighted by interacting with fellow students from other racialized and ethnic backgrounds about food in primary school was a positive experience for *Nia-Elise* as 'it opened [her] eyes up to the way the world is'. In a classic study in America, Heath (1983) explored how language is used by children from two working-class communities, one Black and the other white, at home and in school. One of her key findings was that 'the place of language in the cultural life of each social group is interdependent with the habits and values of behaviour shared among members of that group' (p. 11). This is useful when understanding *Nia-Elise*'s memory as it also provides an example to show that while the names of the 'stew' and 'casserole', for example, may be different, they are both very similar in that they are slow-cooked tough meat. It also shows how an appreciation of others can be gained by being in close proximity and becoming familiar with other ways of being through finding common ground in a diverse group. Moreover, in this case, different food dishes decentre white norms as it is not the only point of reference. Educational institutions can be great places to facilitate shared understanding and cultural awareness. In their report, encouraging the teaching of citizenship and diversity in schools, Ajegbo et al. (2007: 23) assert that 'all pupils are entitled to education for diversity and that their school experience should offer opportunities to explore, in the first instance, their own identities in relation to the local community'. When *Nia-Elise* reflects upon her own identity and what she eats compared to her peers, through her curiosity to engage and understand others, she evidences how she is able to 'locate [herself] within wider UK society, [be] comfortable in [her] own skin and alive to the individuality of the diverse people around [her]' (Ajegbo et al. 2007: 23). The other pupils will be able to learn about Black cultures too due to the exchange with *Nia-Elise*. In Chapter 1, I shared how a similar appreciation of cultural diversity was fostered at my second primary school, *St Clara's*, when teachers organized a cultural event. Moreover, by being able to discuss and compare cultural practices, such conversations can shape 'difference' and diversity as a benefit from an early age which can provide richer understandings of the world and others in it. In a Danish primary school, Dinesen (2011) makes a similar case after observing the children in his study, concluding that ethnic and cultural diversity creates more trust between white and non-white Danish children which facilitates good relationships in later life. When focusing on her secondary school experiences *Nia-Elise* shares the following:

> In secondary school it was a bit more Black, definitely a bit more Black I think cos as you get a bit more older you start to … you start to appreciate your culture a bit more and that's when y'know, you have the Caribbean/African banter and you know only certain people can get with it and you start to listen to certain music which is more inclined with your culture and things you have grown up around. So it was definitely more Black but at the same time because I kinda describe myself as a social butterfly where I like learning about other people so I did have a variety of friends, but my core friendship group was definitely more Black.

For *Nia-Elise*, studying within a predominantly GM educational environment where she is able to have a friendship group that consists of people like herself who are mainly from Black Caribbean and Black African backgrounds contributes to her identity development. The engagement in cultural 'banter' and the listening to specific musical genres as 'one of many' enables *Nia-Elise* to begin to appreciate who she is as a young Black woman, beyond her household, and to embrace her groups' distinct and shared cultural markers and practices. I touched on this process in Chapter 1, though my introduction into a 'Black girl subculture' was not initially positive at my second secondary school *Holyway High*. As Furlong (1984) discovered when exploring pupils' interactions and knowledge of school life and with each other, there is a variety of shared understandings of such things as teachers and the curriculum which develops when interacting with others. Despite Furlong's study being over thirty years old, this process is still evident in *Nia-Elise*'s reflections of the shared Black experience she describes. Importantly, these encounters are not 'othered' or positioned as alien – though from her account, it is not clear how she or her friendship group are viewed in the wider school. However, based on *Nia-Elise*'s recollections, she is able to gain mutual understanding with other Black students who are also able to cultivate a sense of belonging with each other.

On the other hand, predominantly GM educational environments are still located within the context of a white-dominated society and education system, and *Nia-Elise*'s core, Black friendship group can be seen as a way to cope 'by creating and using formal and informal, social and academic identity-affirming counter-spaces as a resistance strategy to buffer experiences with racism and other forms of discrimination' (Carter 2007: 543). Following on from that, when looking at school cultures and practices and why GM students may stick together, Crozier (2015: 36) asks whether such friendship groups are self-segregation or the result of enforced exclusion. For *Nia-Elise*, as will become clearer later in the chapter, it is a mixture of both. This theme was explored in more detail in the American study and book by Tatum, *Why Are All the Black Kids Sitting Together in the Cafeteria?* (1999), which was re-released in 2021. In it, she illustrates how Black and white students develop their racial identity in a racially mixed public school by focusing on the importance of the creation of Black spaces, via friendship groups within them. What I also find fascinating in both of *Nia-Elise*'s memories of primary and secondary schooling is how it is implied that these interactions are made beyond the classroom, created in an organic way, over time with those from similar and different backgrounds to her own. Based on these experiences, *Nia-Elise* is contrasting primary and secondary school, imparting how diverse educational spaces, particularly predominantly GM ones, can also positively impact how teachers conduct their interactions with ethnically diverse students. She goes on to reminisce about her sixth form college experiences:

> Having some kinda cultural education – I don't know if they may do it now – but I feel like they [white teachers] need to be very much aware of different cultures and how different children will act and learn. Cos like I said, when I went to my sixth form college where there were more Asians and Blacks, overall the teachers' response was completely different and

> I felt like that's because they had more experience with children from different cultural backgrounds. They knew that I wasn't being rude or y'know messing around but culturally I was probably a bit more vibrant, I was a bit more outspoken and they didn't take that as me being rude, they took that as personality. So, again I feel like getting to know different types of children from different cultures will help them [white teachers] to understand and to not just straight away label the Black child as being problematic and naughty.

Besides having Black teachers, which will be discussed in Chapter 7, *Nia-Elise* highlights the importance of cultural understanding and awareness between mainly white teachers, who work in predominantly GM educational spaces and places, to properly fulfil their duties as educators. In research conducted by Hyland (2005: 432) on four white teachers who worked in a predominantly Black school in the US, she demonstrates how 'sometimes racism is inserted into schools simply by doing what is normal in those schools that primarily serve students of colour'. But therein lies the problem as, according to one of the fundamental tenets of CRT,

> [r]acism is – except in its most extreme forms – so *ordinary*, so business-as-usual, that its very existence is routinely denied. This denial entails strategic *colour-blindness*: a deliberate misrecognition of racialised relationships and practices. Schools, universities, welfare systems and police forces deny their institutional racism by depicting their own cultures and practices as *race-neutral* and meritocratic.
>
> (Warmington 2020: 24; emphasis in original)

Also, by being around predominantly GM people, it does not necessarily mean that teachers will automatically become more culturally in-tune as it requires additional effort and a willingness to want to learn on their part. It also requires active engagement and the adaptation of teaching practices around an ethnically diverse student cohort. Moreover, when mainly white teachers educate GM students, they 'may subtly and sometimes obviously – but surely unwittingly – serve the purposes of whiteness and white racism' (Hyland 2005: 432). This will be highlighted later in this chapter by *Nia-Elise*'s reflections of particular perceptions of certain students by teachers which influence how they interact with them. An example of white teachers putting in additional effort to understand their predominantly GM students is in a book by Pearce (2005) titled *You Wouldn't Understand: White Teachers in Multiethnic Classrooms*. Pearce shows the transformation and the results of 'multicultural capital' on a white woman teacher who reflects internally upon her own ethnic and racial background, making changes that engender better understandings, teaching and treatment of her predominantly South Asian, Muslim pupils.

Being educated in predominantly GM educational spaces and places is valuable according to the idea of 'multicultural capital' as expressed by Reay et al. (2007). In their study, they extend Bourdieu's concept of capital in their investigation of white middle-class families who opt to send their children to multicultural, multiethnic, inner-city secondary schools. They describe 'multicultural capital' as a highly sought-after resource because it instils 'tolerance, understanding and proximity' and is preparation for 'the global economy [which] requires individuals who can deal with people of other races and nationalities openly and respectfully' (p. 1049). Reay et al. also mention that along with white middle-class students benefiting, GM students also gain from mixing with them and therefore 'capitals can move in both directions' (p. 1050). This chapter focuses on the gains of 'multicultural capital' as acquired by Black women who completed most of their educational journeys within predominantly GM educational contexts.

In this section, how heightened appreciation and understanding of self and cultural diversity can be gained from being educated in predominantly GM educational spaces and places was demonstrated. In the next section, *Nia-Elise* will illustrate how being 'one of many' Black girls and women studying within predominantly GM educational spaces and places can also provide strength in numbers via the creation of connections, solidarity and affirmation.

Strength in numbers: connections, solidarity and affirmation

The confidence and self-esteem of Black girls and women are often undermined throughout their educational journeys and experiences due to what Evans-Winters (2016: 143) describes as the 'complex and subtle gendered, racialised, and classed exchanges occurring in schools' which rarely value or empower their identities. In this way, in predominantly GM educational spaces and places, *Nia-Elise* as 'one of many' Black girls and women, is able to find ways to ensure that she creates connections and solidarity with people like herself in order to affirm a sense of self which, I suggest, is vital when navigating within the (white) education system. As *Nia-Elise* proclaims with pride:

> I had the 'Dark & Lovely' crew [laughs] that's what we called ourselves ... I had a good friendship group as well, there were probably about three

> or four of us that were really close. I am always talking to everyone and get on with most people, but you have your selection of friends that you are – whatever break you do, you go together and stuff like that. But yeah the 'Dark & Lovely' crew was an interesting … [laughs] it was all girls and all dark-skinned girls, all Caribbean. But everyone kinda had groups so you might have the Ghanaian girls kinda stick with the Ghanaian girls, the Jamaican girls stick with the Jamaican girls.

Nia-Elise shares how her friendship group was made up of other 'dark-skinned' girls from similar cultural backgrounds to herself and that they called themselves the 'Dark & Lovely' crew. This is such an important name for a 'crew' as the name not only references a hair care product range that states on its website 'was created to help Black women express and embrace their individual styles', it shows that *Nia-Elise* and her friends align with the brand and use it to affirm their identities. In this way, I view *Nia-Elise*'s friendship group as a safe space for Black girl identity development which is significant because 'in finding their space [they] create a community where they are central, important and highly visible and indeed often politicised' (Weekes 2003: 50). She also reveals the distinctions between ethnicities in the same racialized Black group such as Ghanaians and Jamaicans when highlighting how everyone had their own core groups based on shared cultural heritage – though it is important to note that even in Ghana and Jamaica there are many distinct, smaller groupings. Through these spaces, confidence and self-esteem can be maintained at high levels. In fact, *Nia-Elise* explains how this is made possible in Black and specifically Black girl/women friendship groups:

> Having Black friends … say for instance for me is a good thing because it allows me to talk about the issues that I face separately as a Black girl/woman if that makes sense … and knowing that they'll be able to relate to me, to understand those problems I've had or things going on in the media, they'd see it the same way sometimes to how I see it, whereas a friend from maybe another ethnic background may not see it the exact same way that we do if that makes sense.

In Chapter 3, *Eve* mentions that one of the challenges for many Black girls and women throughout their education is constantly having to explain who they are – a theme also described by *Chika* which is a prominent feature when in PW educational spaces and places. Therefore, the fact that *Nia-Elise* can have friends who understand her is invaluable in her educational experiences. She continues to explain the value:

> It was nice to have people who came from where you came from and had similar names to you and who ate similar food to you, it was nice to have some elements of home when you are basically in a very, very, very far away place from home, it was very nice to have people with elements that are similar to you.

In *Nia-Elise* 'being one of many' Black girls and women studying within PGM places and spaces, she summarizes the power of being able to cultivate Black girl/women friendships throughout her entire educational trajectory – which is not always possible when studying within PW educational spaces and places:

> I think the Black British girl/woman experience – uni, sixth form, secondary school – is sticking together. I think there's a lot more of a sisterhood, even like from my primary school, that even though I didn't use the word, it was a sisterhood at the end of the day, the fact that I could go to … and I wanted to be in this group of Black girls, it was very specifically Black girls that I wanted to be a part of and it wasn't just because 'oh y'know we can talk about …' I just felt a lot safer with them and I don't think there was … nah there wasn't like a solid … it must be Black boyhood, I don't think there was that … Black boyhood thing, there would probably be a white guy tagging along or an Asian guy but with Black girls it was very sacred like it was very much, 'this is our space'. That's from like ten year olds as well, and I think secondary school, when we became fifteen, the breaking offs were still like Black-centred as well. Even if my other best friend's Asian, there was still that clinging to Black women kinda thing and then, of course when I got to uni that's what I wanted, I wanted genuine open discussions which is what I got with Black women who I could share and be like 'oh this has happened, has this happened to you?' Whatever! Yeah I think that's one thing, we do – one thing about the Black British girl/woman experience is not just having, but seeking it out and like building a sisterhood and then like making it bigger so it's not just like 'oh my friendship group' but like 'there's this event and then there's this', do you know what I mean? It does reach out a lot more, so yeah.

Nia-Elise describes the friendships that she created with other Black girls and women as 'sacred', akin to sisterhoods and actively and highly sought after by many Black girls and women. She demonstrates that they provide valuable and vital fictive kinship, that is, self-selected close relationships with peers in hostile educational spaces and places – regardless of whether they are predominantly GM or white (Tierney and Venegas 2006; Greyerbiehl and Mitchell 2014; Cook and Williams 2015). As stated by George (2007: 127), when researching friendships in an urban schooling setting, 'it is unsurprising that Black girls, with their different history and heritage rooted in past racism, as well as different futures dictated by institutional racism, will make friends with girls who share similar backgrounds', in comparison with other friendship groupings, as highlighted by *Chika* in Chapter 4. This network or sisterhood enables Black girls and women to not only carve out a space, but to define its boundaries and to own and belong to something bigger and greater than their own individual existence in educational institutions (Carter 2007; Kynard 2010). This, I argue, provides strength in numbers. In addition, these friendship groups exhibit Black Feminist principles, namely the ethics of caring through being a space that allows 'personal expressiveness, emotions and empathy' (Collins 2000: 263), tailored towards Black girls and women to connect, be heard, nurtured and affirmed.

Being educated within predominantly GM educational settings means that Black girls and women are not alone and are able to gain some comfort through gaining an appreciation and understanding of self and cultural diversity, as well as strength in numbers providing deep connections, solidarity and affirmation. The work by Fuller (1980, 1983) on Black Caribbean girls in a London comprehensive school highlights both the deep inequalities they were aware that they faced, as well as how they still managed to maintain positive senses of their gendered and raced identities. However, 'being one of many' studying within predominantly GM spaces is not without disadvantages as many Black girls and women are still subject to white authority where they are negatively positioned as 'the unruly Black girl'. Further discussion of this follows next in this chapter. They also may find that they have limited educational opportunities because of their existence within these racialized, classed, unequal spaces and places because of structural inequalities and historical legacies.

Blacker space, white authority

In Anderson's book aptly titled *Black in White Space*, he defines Black space as 'a perceptual category, indicated most remarkably when Black people claim and occupy white space beyond its "tipping point", so that whites avoid the space as "too Black"' (2022: 15). While he is describing American society, his definition is relevant in an English context as a report compiled by the Institute of Community Cohesion (Cantle 2009: 17) identified that in places like Sunderland, Bristol and Blackburn, to name a few of the thirteen areas it studied, 'white flight' happened where white parents moved their children when they believed they were outnumbered by GM pupils. Even though *Nia-Elise* has always studied within predominantly GM educational institutions, she was always confronted with white authority – the most obvious manifestation being her mainly white teachers – though governors, kitchen staff, teaching assistants and more also play roles. So, while the white pupils may leave, the staff within these predominantly GM institutions remain mainly white, particularly in senior leadership (Tereshchenko et al. 2020). As Anderson (2022: 15) reminds us, 'whereas whites usually stay out of Black space, Black people cannot avoid white space' – or authority, even when they are in the majority. This is unsurprising as in 2018, 85.9 per cent of all teachers in state-funded schools in England were white British compared to 0.9 per cent who were Black African and 1 per cent who were Black Caribbean (Gov.uk 2020). The numbers are significantly lower in senior teaching roles as there are, for example, only two hundred Black Caribbean headteachers out of a possible 22,400 (Gov.uk 2020). This is less than the working age population based on the 2011 census and this may or may not match the overall Black population in England which stands at 3 per cent – though the 2021 census data includes Scotland, Wales and Northern Ireland in this total (UK population data 2022).

In *Nia-Elise*'s experiences, she and other Black girls were frequently positioned as 'unruly' in educational settings by teachers who were not racially literate. But how can educational institutions with predominantly GM student populations have unrepresentative, white staff and leadership? As NASUWT and the Runnymede Trust report, in the entire English education system, 'there is a chronic shortage of BME teachers in relation to the BME pupil population' (2017: 9). This is an issue which is prevalent and reflects the overwhelming whiteness of the education system regardless of the type of educational institution that Black girls and women like *Nia-Elise* attend. In fact, *Nia-Elise* noticed this imbalance too:

> [I remember that] the school was predominantly – cos of the area – the school was predominantly Black, basically Ghanaian, Nigerian and Caribbean. There were like two white people or three white people in our year [laughs] but all the teachers were white.

Though she had positive experiences with some white teachers as mentioned previously, she also had some negative ones- especially at secondary school. She reflects further on both the wider contexts and how mainly white teachers in predominantly GM educational spaces and places can be detrimental to the experiences and journeys of Black students as a whole:

> Because ultimately the institution of schools are set up in a certain way that you are always gonna be well … the first thing is, we live in very urbanized areas predominantly, so the schools that we go to are usually the most underfunded ones anyway and then historically, y'know especially let's say, for example, Black boys, you see them on the street in their hoodies, people instantly think they are up to something wrong so that factors into it. So, the stereotypes of life factor into your school like your [white] teachers have lived their lives [somewhere else] and have done things so they still see you in the same way and I think that one of my primary school teachers is a great example. She was … even though the school she taught in was predominantly Black, she still saw some of us as these 'troublemakers' and she would probably never shake that … the ones that she liked more were the ones that were viewed as more 'white'.

Nia-Elise points out how, in her primary school experiences, her white teacher still held negative stereotypes towards Black students due to external influences which reinforces such stereotypes, despite working in a school that serves predominantly Black children. In this way, her teacher should be both culturally aware and familiar with Black communities on a more personal and everyday basis as someone who works with them closely. But as mentioned previously, this proves that white teachers need to actively put in additional efforts to unlearn the internalized stereotypes of Black and other Global Majority people. When analysing race and racism in English schools, Joseph-Salisbury (2020: 7) points out, amongst other factors, the need for the mainly white teaching staff to develop what he defines as 'racial literacy' which is 'the capacity of teachers to understand the ways in which race and racisms work in society'. It also involves having the language, skills and confidence to utilize that knowledge in teacher practice, and that this role should not fall on just GM teachers alone, but the entire workforce. With such awareness and racial literacy, *Nia-Elise*'s teacher would reject and resist what they were taught even though, as she mentions, many white 'respectable working-class' teachers often 'have lived their lives' away from these communities and schools that they teach at. *Nia-Elise* highlights how these negative feelings and stereotypes were felt in terms of how the teacher labelled and viewed some Black students as 'troublemakers' compared to those that she viewed and treated more positively who happened to also be 'more "white"'. It is evident that the teacher, as *Nia-Elise* asserts, could not 'shake' off the external influences and negative stereotyping of Black children which she transferred into her teaching practice. *Nia-Elise* shares that she also experienced similar sentiments in her secondary schooling:

> I do feel it was a bit negative in secondary school in a sense that I feel like some teachers had this idea of who I was. So, they would associate me with certain type of people and just be like – they wouldn't try as much as they could have with me, but otherwise I think it was ok.

The behaviour, views and interactions with 'certain teachers' due to associating *Nia-Elise* with 'a certain type of people' negatively impacted her secondary schooling experiences as she felt that, because of such beliefs, she was not given as much teacher encouragement and support – a vital component of the learning experience. This is similar to my own experience, as outlined in chapter 1, at my state-funded, PGM school where my teacher implied that me and my mainly Black girl classmates didn't want to work hard or in other words were lazy. However, as stated previously, Nia-Elise was able to gain support from the friendship groups she established and interactions she had with other students that tended to look like and relate to her. According to Youdell (2003: 17), who explored how learner identities are constructed, for Black British Caribbean students 'their Blackness renders them undesirable learners' to the mainly white staff members. *Nia-Elise* essentially identifies how this happened to her. She also provides an example of how the mainly white teachers used their authority and power to impact the trajectories of Black students through, what she terms, 'selection and separation' during secondary school:

> I feel probably – but I don't know if it relates to … cos of my background or cos of somebody's background, but just in terms of selection and separation of those who would perform well and those who wouldn't perform as well, and it was a bit sad to see those who didn't perform too well were a mixture of Afro-Black students and I felt – actually, one of those classes I was in, I was actually in there [laughs] and they were kinda like shoved a bit, 'Do well, get your Cs and Ds'. Whereas the others, unfortunately were white and I don't know, maybe Asian, and it was a friend who actually told me what the discussion was like in that class and y'know it was like 'get your As, get your A*s, you guys are gonna do really well!' so that I suppose is the distinction that I can remember.

The difference in attainment between Black students and those from other ethnic and racial backgrounds, along with social class, is always a point of contention. However, there are processes in educational institutions, such as setting and streaming along with teacher support and encouragement, which contribute to these attainment differences (Gillborn and Youdell 2000). *Nia-Elise* shares how mostly Black students like herself are placed into classes where teachers have low expectations of their abilities which is further hindered by, for instance, being prepared and entered into lower-tier, foundation-level exams in the old General Certificate of Secondary Education (GCSE) system (introduced in 1986) where they are only able to gain a top grade of a C – even if they get full marks in comparison to the higher-tier exam where an A* could be achieved. Gillborn et al. (2017) has focused on the impact of GCSEs on Black Caribbean students in particular, linking it with attainment gaps between Black and white students. In 2010, GCSEs were replaced by the English Baccalaureate (EBacc), but problems around attainment between different groups still remain (Gillborn 2014). *Nia-Elise* also notes that, in other classes dominated by mostly white and Asian students, such teacher expectations and support are much higher and the students are encouraged to gain top grades of A and A* possibly because they are entered into and prepared for higher-tier exams. Note that this is happening in a predominantly GM school. Yet, this is unsurprising as there is a long history of such processes in schools as revealed in a study by Tomlinson (1981: 56) looking at educational subnormality where it states that 'tracking processes ... left Black Caribbean young people over-represented in lower ranked sets and sustained racialised and ethno-cultural hierarchies among students in "normal" schools'.

Nia-Elise reiterates her disappointment with her educational experiences and path due to the educational spaces and places she has studied in, as well as relaying the importance of an ethnically diverse and representative staff and leadership workforce in the entire education system, especially in predominantly GM educational institutions:

> Yeah, I don't like the English education system, I kinda feel like unless you have private schooling, or you go to a grammar school, you're not forced enough ... like supported enough yup, and I feel like when I think about someone like me ... so when I think about myself, had I have gone to a grammar school or private school, I feel as though I could've been a better me at the moment do you know what I mean? I found that being in an [inner-city, predominantly GM] state school, you kinda ... you don't get as much support as you would've had had you been in a school that is predominantly focusing on your performance and nothing else. Do you know what I mean? And it's sad because I don't feel like, yes there is gonna be weaker people, there is gonna be stronger people, but I don't think everyone gets an equal chance in terms of learning because I mean you have inconsistencies with teachers, so you have supply teachers today, supply teachers tomorrow, you're not having consistency in learning and the children are not being pushed enough and it's sad

> and then they expect them to do ... they are predicted to get A*s but they are only capable of a C and then, the statistics then become inconsistent and inaccurate because actually you predicted somebody who you knew would never ever get that high achieving and it just makes you look like you are failing y'know and it's just sad. And even in university as well, I understand that it is all about independent learning and pushing yourself but at the same time, I feel like there is more diversity needed in the education system – not just Black teachers, but Chinese teachers, Asian teachers, whatever it may be just so you feel represented and actually a form of – a sense of belonging, there is so many times you feel like you can't approach certain teachers because of the way they look or how they view you or whatever it may be. So a lot more needs to be done getting more people involved in the education system to help us be the best we can be.

There is much to unpack from *Nia-Elise*'s self-reflection on her own educational trajectory within predominantly GM educational institutions. While she mentions grammar schools, there are few English Local Educational Authorities (LEAs) that still have them, which represents their exclusivity. In some ways, she laments over not being provided with the same support or encouragement that she believes is standard in private and grammar schools which tend to be PW and/or elite educational spaces and places. As *Chika* shares in Chapter 4 about her own educational story, though not without disadvantages and challenges, she does confirm that such academic and extra-curricular support and encouragement are more readily available as experienced in her educational journey in PW and/or elite institutions. *Nia-Elise* characterizes her own educational experiences journeying within predominantly GM educational spaces and places as unequal chances, limited support and encouragement, along with inconsistent learning due to a lot of supply teachers who do not really know or understand the students. This inconsistency in teachers, she argues, leads to unrealistic and unmet predictions, and a lack of teacher diversity, resulting in feelings of disconnection and not belonging within educational settings, despite 'being one of many' Black or GM students. All of which *Nia-Elise* feels has and continues to hinder students like her from being 'the best we can be'.

Another consequence of white authority in predominantly GM educational spaces is *still* being positioned and treated by mainly white teachers as unruly and delinquent, deserving of harsh disciplinary treatment, as well as encountering over-surveillance in an effort to 'tame' and remind Black girls and women of their inferior place.

The unruly Black girl

As the educational field is highly stratified, one's habitus – behaviours, speech, style, knowledge and understandings of the world – can reinforce or hinder one's placement in an institution. This is because 'different habitus confer and facilitate access to different amounts of capital, so that the unequal positioning of players in a field is typically reproduced over time' (Brosnan 2010: 647). When focusing specifically on Black girls and women, *Nia-Elise* believes that she had often been treated and viewed, by her mainly white teachers, as an 'unruly Black girl'. This is a collective Black girl and woman characterization often placed on them, in both American and English contexts, which includes having an 'attitude', being rude or too assertive, being overly-aggressive, loud and unmanageable (Crenshaw et al. 2015: 24). This can be based upon existing stereotypes of Black girls and women that was previously discussed in Chapter 2, using Collins's (2000) characterizations of *Mammy, Matriarch, Welfare mother, Black lady* and *Jezebel*, which have since evolved to 'the Strong Black woman' (West et al. 2016), 'the Superwoman' (Reynolds 1997), 'the Angry Black woman' (Jones and Norwood 2017) and 'the Loud Black Girl' (Adegoke and Uviebinene 2020; Fordham 1993). This stereotyping reinforces teacher bias and one particular way that this manifests is by what Fergus (2017: 172) refers to as deficit-thinking, that is, teachers 'discount[ing] the presence of systemic inequalities as the result of race-based processes, practices, and policies ... plac[ing] fault in a group for the conditions they find themselves experiencing' and navigating within. 'Unruly' needs to be understood in the context of adultification 'which disproportionately harms Black children, presenting them as older than they really are and thus not treating them with the care and protection that should be afforded to minors' (The Commission on Young Lives 2022: 21). The case of Child Q is an example of where such negative perceptions and positioning of Black girls as 'unruly' can lead when:

> [i]n 2020, Child Q, a Black female child of secondary school age, was strip searched by female police officers from the Metropolitan Police Service (MPS). The search, which involved the exposure of Child Q's intimate body parts, took place on school premises, without an Appropriate Adult present and with the knowledge that Child Q was menstruating, because teachers believed she smelled strongly of cannabis even though they didn't find anything when they searched her belongings.
>
> (Child Safeguarding Commissioner 2022: 2)

Additionally, it must be remembered that such positioning of Black girls and women is based on historical legacies where these stereotypes of 'controlling images' reflect 'the dominant group's interest in maintaining Black women's subordination' (Collins 1990: 71). The unruly Black girl positioning also feeds into perceived notions about the 'ideal' student in educational contexts which is often 'a young (white) man from an upper-class or middle-class background' (Leathwood and O'Connell 2003: 598). As shared by *Nia-Elise*, regardless of the fact that there may be more GM students in particular institutions, the perceptions of the 'ideal', white student remains prevalent. This also speaks to the need for a more representative and ethnically diverse staff workforce in educational institutions and particularly those with higher rates of GM students. When reflecting upon her own educational trajectory, as *Nia-Elise* identifies, many white teachers lacked cultural understanding or racial literacy (Joseph-Salisbury 2020), sensitivity and awareness of the lived experience and cultures of Black girl and women students. *Nia-Elise* brings to life how these stereotypes about Black girls and women are projected onto her and thus how she is positioned in her school.

> I feel like the whole detention thing and the whole feistiness, a lot of my Black girl/women friends have had that. I suppose when my teacher said you developed 'the look', I was like what does that mean? This was year 9 and it was genuinely because he said something which was, to me, quite out of order and I just went 'What?' And I gave him 'the look', but apparently, it's a very 'Black girl look', and I was like 'ok that's a little bit racist, but I'll let it be.'

Nia-Elise uses 'the whole detention thing' as an example of the consequences of herself and other Black girls' and women's perceived 'feistiness' as interpreted by mainly white teachers. She also reports that while her teacher may be used to being around Black girls and women, he is over-familiar as demonstrated by inappropriately remarking that she has developed a 'Black girl look' after offending her with a comment that he has made. Her reaction of asking for clarification as well as giving her teacher 'the look' is read as defiant due to her teachers' negative and stereotypical perceptions of Black girls as a group. Similar Black girl experiences have previously been highlighted by Morris (2007) in her study on the perceptions of Black girls in the classroom where she finds that being reprimanded for subjective, behavioural offences is commonplace. However, it is normal to react when offended and so 'the look' – according to her teacher – is a reaction, but *Nia-Elise*'s account provides an insight into the reality of many Black girls' experiences where they are 'constantly being policed and punished for menial transgressions which are sometimes subjectively determined as problems' (Wun 2018: 433).

Nia-Elise continues to recount how she experienced and was positioned as unruly in her educational experiences:

> Sometimes the way we [Black girls] speak or say things, they [white teachers] would say 'why are you being aggressive?' or when you are having – not even an argument – but you just don't agree, let's say you don't agree with the teacher or agree with a student, and then it just seems like you're causing disruption or people feel awkward or tense around you and they label you. It's like 'why are you angry? What issues do you have today?' or 'something is going on at home' and stuff like that. That's one of the key ones especially being in school and I think especially for [Black] girls, especially the whole angry thing – 'why are you so angry? Why are you shouting?' You're walking with your friends or … 'why's your face …' – that 'bitch-resting' face? 'Why do you look like that? Why are you never smiling?' I think that's another thing we [Black girls] can relate to and then teachers and stuff would get worried. I even remember with one of my friends, they said that she is always looking angry and they called home and they even wanted the social services involved … declaring that she has issues when there was nothing wrong with her, that was literally just her … she is fine but they just see that there must be something wrong with you if you are not always smiling or happy or you have to put on a fake smile.

As Wun (2018: 433) identifies from her study, mode of speech, walking with friends and facial expressions are not recognized formally as warranting discipline. Yet, as *Nia-Elise* reports, all too often, she feels that it is normal to be reprimanded over such things based upon how Black students, particularly Black girls, are perceived by mainly white staff. She also illustrates how the usual racist tropes and the labelling of Black girls as 'angry', 'aggressive', 'loud' and 'disruptive' are once again at play. Despite 'being one of many' Black girls studying within a PGM secondary school, *Nia-Elise* reveals that she and other Black girl friends are still positioned as 'unruly' as exemplified by the 'look', which she now refers to as a 'bitch-resting face', which is ascribed to them by teachers who are essentially viewing and reinforcing the idea that Black girls are naturally angrier and more aggressive than others. Although having a particular facial expression does not hurt anyone, there are real consequences that can come from this. As Francis (2012) recalls from her investigations, 'teachers often make subjective judgements about student behaviour, and these behaviour perceptions may influence their decisions', which seems to be the unfortunate case for *Nia-Elise*'s friend whose facial expression is deemed to warrant the attention of the social services. Importantly, *Nia-Elise* also demonstrates how the policing of herself, her friends and other Black girls in terms of how they should act, speak and their facial expressions are, in effect, encouraging 'Black girls [to] deny who they are and adopt the characteristics of the majority culture … [but] this logic is problematic in that it teaches Black girls that in order to be successful, they cannot be who they are organically' (Ricks 2014: 14). In influential work by Judith Butler (1988, 1990, 1993), her concept of 'performativity' is useful here when looking at gender, which she explains:

> [i]s instituted through the stylization of the body and, hence, must be understood as the mundane way in which bodily gestures, movements, and enactments of various kinds constitute the illusion of an abiding gendered self.
>
> (Butler 1988: 519)

Such performances are 'a constructed identity, a performative accomplishment which the mundane social audience, including the actors themselves, come to believe and to perform in the mode of belief' (Butler 1988: 520). Therefore, the white teachers encountered by *Nia-Elise* have come to view, read and place them (and their other Black girl friends) in 'the unruly Black girl' category and therefore deserving of harsher discipline or intervention. It also seems that regardless of how the Black girls behave, the 'unruly Black girl' becomes '"the script" … already determined in this regulatory frame, and the subject has a limited number of "costumes" from which to make a constrained choice of gender style' (Salih 2002: 55). *Nia-Elise* expresses the limited 'costumes' she feels all Black students, but especially Black girls, have, which are unruly, aggressive, disruptive and angry. Other scholars (Tate 2005, 2014; Chadderton 2013; Clammer 2015) meaningfully extend Butler's concept to foreground race. *Nia-Elise* also points out that there is a misunderstanding of Black culturally acceptable behaviours and ways of being, including non-verbal cues and how similar behaviours expressed by white students are treated differently by schools; for example, being outspoken is viewed as confidence when expressed by white, middle-class students but as bad and challenging school authority when displayed by Black students (Wallace 2018). Historically from slavery, imperialism and colonization, Black people have been expected to accept white authority without any challenge, and if they did resist, there were dire consequences. *Nia-Elise*'s narrative attests to how she and her friends were mocked by teachers due to being perceived as unruly:

> I just think that they [white teachers] just thought that we had a bad attitude and they always used to tell us 'oh you guys think you run the

> school' like 'you think this is your school' – well it is our school [laughs]. And I used to think 'huh?', yeah they always used to say 'you walk around here like you own the place' and … when they were talking about 'ah you lot think you run the school', it was me and the rest of my friends – three other Black girls or mixed heritage girls – I don't know how they would describe themselves – but yeah.

Nia-Elise remembering how she and her other 'Black or mixed heritage' girl friends were viewed as having 'a bad attitude' and frequently reminded by teachers that they 'think they run the school' upholds the stereotype that Black girls are unruly and need to be put into their places, which can also act to 'other' them. As *Nia-Elise* says, it is *their* school as they are students there, but the assumptions in these teacher statements suggest otherwise. In their research, Archer et al. (2007: 565) assert with regards to the role of race, gender and class in the inner-city secondary schooling experiences of young women that their participants' 'embodied identities clashed against a dominant discourse of the idealised middle class female pupil', which is similar for *Nia-Elise*, her friends and other Black girl students. The importance of cultural understanding and awareness, as well as the cultural clashes and power struggles as a result of the historical legacies that remain in the education system – regardless of the type of educational institution or the student demographics in it – are summarized nicely by *Nia-Elise*:

> This goes into behaviour that I have seen in the classroom and some things that have happened to myself as well. But I feel like we [Black people] are taught to tell the truth from our culture, I am not saying that other cultures aren't … but I feel like we are very truthful like unfiltered so if you have something on your mind, you say it, don't let it fester or harbour but just let it out and I feel like that is interpreted by a lot of the white teachers as being arrogant, as being rude and being blunt but ultimately you are just saying what's on your mind … I haven't seen it as much with African students, I can only say what I saw at school and if a teacher should disrespect somebody or say something that was a bit out of line cos teachers can do it, then a lot of the Caribbean students would be like 'Don't talk to me like that, that's rude' [laughs]. I didn't see that a lot with the African students if I am being honest, it's just what I saw and I can only equate that down to being from a Caribbean background because if someone was to chat to me in a rude way it would be like 'who are you talking to?' But like I said it's a power struggle, it's really odd, it's almost like the remnants of the past have come to play … The power struggles and that whole 'you had us, now you lost us',

> [laughs] 'I'm gonna speak my mind now, you can't hold us down' then you've got the ex-colonizer saying 'no actually you are in my system now, you are gonna learn what I want you to learn and you are going to respect me' … I don't know why it happens because I am gonna compare this now with Asian students who also had a colonial background but they didn't speak up as much. When I saw the majority of students in detention, they weren't Asian, they were Black and they were usually from a Caribbean background so it's interesting to see what you've been taught, compliancy, do you speak up? When do you speak up? And I do think it's a cultural thing.

In her recollection, the difference in cultures between Black, particularly Caribbean, students is more evident in her PGM secondary school which operates under white authority. *Nia-Elise* also shares the way different racialized and ethnic groups, by way of Caribbean, African and Asian students, in her narrative respond to white authority. Once again, the expressiveness and ways of being typical of Black, Caribbean students are misunderstood and negatively viewed as 'unruly' which *Nia-Elise* believes is a cultural trait. She also notes that white teachers can also be disrespectful to Black students which makes sense considering that they may hold negative, stereotypical views which will inevitably manifest in how they interact and treat them. By calling it out and defining this process as 'power struggles' and by invoking histories of white oppression and domination, as Bourdieu (1996: 264) confirms, the education system is a 'field of forces structurally determined by the state of the relations of power among forms of power, or different forms of capital', therefore, 'a field of power struggles among the holders of different forms of power' is inevitable as highlighted by *Nia-Elise*, which she attributes to her strong Caribbean culture.

The interactional styles of teachers are important to bear in mind as it is their perceptions and treatment of Black girl and woman students *Nia-Elise* exemplifies in her accounts. This emphasizes the significant role that teachers play as social agents within educational spaces and places and in the reproduction of stereotypes, and consequently inequality and disadvantage in the experiences of Black girls and women. The role of Black teachers in particular will be focused upon in Chapter 7. The inequalities and disadvantages that are faced by Black girls and women in predominantly GM educational spaces and places are considered by *Nia-Elise* next.

Limited educational opportunities?

Nia-Elise's artistic development, which is now in full force due to her having the freedom to develop and practice it, was hindered in her educational experiences. As a Black, working-class girl and now woman who attended inner-city predominantly GM schools and a post-1992 university, her educational opportunities may have been limited due to the lack of availability and resources she had access to within such places and spaces. Though she had to learn english, maths and other academic subjects as standard at school and she was an average student, it really was not her thing. She was a free-spirit, imaginative and expressive, and painting and creating was her thing, the thing that allowed her to be her most authentic self. Though there were art classes at her school and she was able to choose art and design for her GCSEs, it was never really taken that seriously by either her teachers, who did not really have the skills or expertise, or her peers, who saw that class as a time to hang out and gossip. But art – whenever she could do it – was how she learned to understand the world, to make sense of the texts she read and was inspired by in english lessons, to solve the problems– beyond equations in her maths classes – to find and create her own space and to include and invite whatever and whoever she wanted to see within it, namely Black British cultures, centring Black femininity and girl/womanhood. That's what she always wanted to do and she was able to begin to do so at university when completing her fashion degree which she continued on her artistic journey once she graduated. Either way, this was her life's path and the time was now for her to show up and be the artist, the creator, the designer, the true Nia-Elise after completing her fashion degree with a 2:1. But what would it have been like if the educational spaces and places she studied in had identified and actively nurtured her talent for art? Would she still be having to learn some of the basics of her craft now?

* * *

Unfortunately, due to the hierarchical nature of the neoliberal (white) education system, as Mirza (1992: 2) highlights in her study about Black British young women in English secondary schools, the 'central role of the education system [is] in maintaining social and economic disadvantage', enabled by 'institutional constraints to equality of opportunity'. In fact, an Organisation for Economic Co-operation and Development (OECD) report in 2012 stated that UK schools were among the top of the most socially segregated in the developed world and that 'among the children of immigrant families in the UK, 80% were taught in schools with high concentrations of other immigrant or disadvantaged pupils – the highest proportion in the developed world' (Coughlan 2012). Additionally, many predominantly GM schools tend to be characterized as low status due to the kinds of academic support provided which is limited by the quality and level of resources, guidance, advice and even encouragement for students. As summarized by Hollingworth (2015: 44), 'this differentiation both between and within schools is widely known to map onto racial and class divisions, where minority ethnic and working class or poorer students are over-represented in lower ability groups; "failing" schools; "newer" universities and so-derided "Mickey Mouse" courses'. These institutional differences create barriers to accessing additional educational opportunities in the future. As discovered by Weekes-Bernard (2007: 43–4), many GM parents with the knowledge and the means to do so seek to enrol their children in 'schools identified as high achieving and, by definition, with a largely white pupil population', due to the awareness, amongst other factors, that 'the commitment of staff in Black/Asian majority schools was often particularly low … in view of … their perception of BME children as under – achieving and problematic'. This reality is illustrated in *Nia-Elise*'s journey.

Racialized and classed access into unequal educational spaces and places

The racialized and classed access into 'urban' predominantly GM secondary schools is alluded to in a chapter in James (2017). Combining the findings of two research projects looking at how such schools are seen as an educational resource for some white middle-class families, James defines them as going 'against the grain' when choosing these 'urban' schools as they tended to be low-performing. However, he finds these families saw them as advantageous for exposing their children to diverse backgrounds and making them better all-rounded citizens and that they still held high aspirations for their children to enter into middle-class professions like doctors. What must be noted from this study is the privilege that these families have, which enables them to choose 'urban', predominantly GM schools, and the fact that their additional resources will assist in their white middle-class children having very different educational experiences and outcomes to their white working-class and GM peers. Additionally, in a report by Horgan (2007: 1) on the impact of poverty on young children's experience of school, he states that 'how most children experience school is determined by the level of disadvantage they face', which is also closely associated with racial and ethnic identity (Tackey et al. 2011). BTP puts forward the idea that society is made up of a variety of social spaces defined as fields (Bourdieu and Wacquant 1992: 97–8). Within each field, individuals and groups 'play the game' through differing understandings of the rules, made easier with the possession of power by way of habitus, capitals and trump cards or educational credentials (with varying value based on the field). The education system is one such field with many subsections and dimensions based upon the many different types of schools, post-16 institutions and universities that 'each has its own unique, established and taken-for-granted practices that effectively define the range of possible and acceptable (or orthodox) actions and behaviour available to individuals operating within it' (Watson 2013: 414).

In addition to this, along with individual habitus which defines the dispositions, behaviours and thoughts that are embodied and entangled with history in which players enter into a field, influencing the way they 'play the game' (Bourdieu 1990a); institutions also have their own habitus. According to Reay et al. (2010: 109) when writing about UK higher education (which can translate to all educational institutions), they outline institutional habitus as

> a complex amalgam of agency and structure … understood as the impact of a cultural group or social class on an individual's behaviour as it is mediated through an organisation … [which] have a history and have in most cases been established over time … [based on] academic status … curriculum offer, organisational practices, and less tangible, but equally important, cultural and expressive characteristics.

In other words, as universities have historically been made for and dominated by white, upper- and middle-class students, the institutions are reflections of them and are tailored to meet their needs from the organizational practices to the curriculum and beyond. However, it will be interesting to see how this may or may not change due to the cuts in university funding and the need for financially lucrative international students (London Economics 2021). The academic status of the institutions that *Nia-Elise* and many other Black girl and women students attend tend to be lower than others. *Nia-Elise* points to the complicated application process for entry into schools in England as a way that may limit equal educational access and opportunity:

> [When I applied to secondary school] she [my mum] was like 'we are gonna apply here, apply here' and we got rejected from all of them, not just me, my friends I grew up with who I am still friends with to this day, they got rejected from the schools they applied to … and then we got put into [names school] which at that time had a 28 per cent pass rate when it came to A*–C GCSEs … [we went through the whole process] it's a bit like when you are doing university or you are picking a

> college so basically you have like a prospectus for something, you go to the different open evenings and then you just sort of get a feel for what you like and then obviously your parents will be with you as well and then you put down the ones you want to rank highest so, the criteria is the catchment area [*sic*], which schools they feel will fit, closest to your house and things like that. Apparently they go off grades from SATs, I think that's rubbish, I just think they saw where you were from and they put you in a school because they felt that's what suits you best, if I am being completely honest because there was a boy that lived down the road from us and he was white and he got a place at [a well-performing, state-funded school].

For *Nia-Elise,* her secondary school fate was in the hands of the local authority who assigned her with the most suitable school based on criteria which she did not quite understand and left her feeling both confused and unfairly treated when she and her friends (who are also Black) were denied a place at a well-performing local state secondary school at which her white neighbour was successful in gaining a place. The demands of school marketization and rankings, as Coldron et al. (2010: 23) state, filters into school selection criteria where it is 'in the school's interests to attract children who are, because of their social characteristics or prior attainment, more likely to perform well in … tests', and that schools also consider 'the reputation of the residential areas from which they come'. This inevitably leads to inequality in educational opportunity and access as the better performing schools seek to select and create an institutional habitus for 'ideal' pupils and students who are often white and middle class in opposition to undesirable Black pupils and students (Youdell 2003; Rollock 2007; Hamilton 2018). Moreover, the fact that there is proven school segregation in terms of race and ethnicity, as well as class, suggests that this phenomenon may be occurring across the country (Bagley 1996; Johnston et al. 2004; Burgess et al. 2005; Johnston et al. 2006; Weekes-Bernard 2007; The Challenge et al. 2017). *Nia-Elise* continues to share her educational experiences studying in a predominantly GM, state-funded secondary school which she describes as low-performing:

> [The secondary school I went to] … had such a bad reputation and she [my mum] was like 'put down your head and work' and that's what I did, I just worked through it … and then the school turned into an academy and it just shifted focus from … they stopped caring about the kids in my opinion, it was more about the results and you could see it in the way they dressed us, in the way they talked to us, the lunch times being cut down, it was very much academic, very much hit your quota so we can

> get our funding and yeah … but it did, well it boosted it up from 28 per cent to 98 per cent so it worked but at the same time the relationships with teachers were never the same … I would've loved to experience a grammar school, I know a lot of people that have been to grammar school and their outlook on the world is completely different to the ones I went to secondary school with … it's just like I said, when you're in a mediocre, just-getting-by school and you're the best in that school, then you feel like 'yeah, I'm the don, I'm amazing', whereas they [students at grammar school] have to fight dog eat dog to get that grade, they understand the whole cat nature of the world, it's not about you're a big fish in a small pond whereas they are in a big ass pond and they've gotta start swimming quick and you can see the difference when you start to get into the real world and the work platforms, when you are applying for jobs, it's not the same, they've got more velocity, they want it whereas we want it but when the hard work comes we are like [makes voice high-pitched] 'oh no' [laughs].

The marketization of the English education system means that good results are the main priority and supported by *Nia-Elise*'s account of when her school transitioned to become an academy.[9] While in some places, *Nia-Elise* has mentioned wanting to be pushed and to be held to high standards, she also expresses regret when the school adopted methods that helped boost students' academic achievements. This is because she talks about the new emphasis on dress and behaviour which speaks to the idea that many working-class and/or Black, GM pupils are 'perceived within dominant frameworks of values as being deficient' (Exley 2013: 78), and therefore in need of harsher disciplinary school policies to supplement their perceived inadequacy. In US educational contexts, Kupchik (2009: 294) expands on Bourdieu and Passeron's (1990) notion of cultural reproduction explaining that the:

> [s]chools' disciplinary practices mirror … state punishment … [where schools for] mostly lower-income youth and youth of colour prepare students to live under close watch by the State by subjecting them to frequent police surveillance and harsh punishments for misbehaviors; in contrast … schools with mostly wealthier, white students teach skills that empower them to avoid, manage and control such risks, or to use these elements of control to their social, professional and economic advantage.

Nia-Elise fantasizes about the educational opportunities and the kinds of academic support that she feels would have been available had she attended a grammar school. This speaks to *Chika*'s educational journey in Chapter 4. It also speaks to Abraham's (2018) research in a English city about the real differences in academic support in three types of schools: one private, one state in an affluent area and one state in a disadvantaged area. These different experiences are underpinned and intersect with social class. *Nia-Elise* discusses her sixth-form experiences:

> My sixth form was in the poorest area of [names area] so there was like just Asians and Black people, not a lot of white people … same as my primary school and maybe that is I dunno, a reflection of injustices in the educational system, the fact that, Asians and Black people are concentrated into one particular area, one particular school whereas, perhaps the white kids were in better flourishing schools. Do you know what I mean? Just that concentration in itself could be a reflection of inequality, but I still got my grades! Sooooo … [laughs] do you know what I mean? I beat the system in that sense.

While not all PW schools are 'better flourishing', *Nia-Elise*'s account shows the strong connection between poverty, race and education in England. In another OECD report (2018: 6) about student experiences, when looking at 'immigrant students' (assumed to mean GM and perhaps white Eastern European students, though it is unclear who they are including in this group) 'one in three were socio-economically disadvantaged'. This is further compounded by internal challenges such as teachers' low expectations, negative stereotyping and harsher treatment experienced by Black students, which *Nia-Elise* encountered and is able to reflect upon when discussing what it was like to study within predominantly GM educational spaces and places. Moreover, she shares how despite the inequality and disadvantage of the location of the sixth form and her treatment within it – which she sees as a reflection of the wider local area – she was still able to achieve the grades required to move onto university. In this way, according to her, she 'beat the system'. *Nia-Elise* also displays another way that the internal processes within predominantly GM educational institutions can further disadvantage Black students by sharing her mother's first-hand experience:

> Yeah cos when I think about my mum obviously, she works in a school and she tells me some of the stories about how they treat her students and one thing she always says is that y'know they are trying to do interventions for white young boys cos they are underachieving but my mum, she goes 'yeah but the Black boys are also underachieving so how can you then separate … why not do interventions for boys in

> general then or for everybody to help everyone achieve the best they can?' And just that separation in the schooling can actually influence that and impact that Black young boy who didn't get that extra support because he wasn't white do you know what I mean? So I feel like these indirect, very subtle differences for instance in the schooling system between white and Black could actually trigger an effect to actually why Black boys or Black people in general albeit Caribbean or African are underachieving in comparison to their white peers.

The moral panic about 'failing' white working-class boys and the more recent attacks on 'chavs' (Gillborn 2010; Jones 2012), the backlash against feminists in education (McRobbie 2009) and the fear of the British National Party (BNP) and Combat 18, as accepted by the UK Government (UK Parliament Education Committee 2021), is captured in *Nia-Elise*'s quote above. Essentially, she highlights how such debates and actions based on her mother's firsthand experiences in her job, means that 'transformative reform is lacking and communicated outcomes overly focus on "white working-class" boys, obscuring issues common across groups' (Adjogatse and Miedema 2022: 123). *Nia-Elise*'s use of her mother's work, as a teaching assistant, in schools shows a number of key insights, namely the importance of having Black teachers to interrogate ineffective processes as well as to speak up on behalf of Black students, and how decisions and choices are actively made to benefit and support particular groups deemed as deserving and worthy – regardless of the type of institution.

The existence of differing qualities of educational provision and opportunities, along with the racialized access into them is clear evidence of inequalities and the ways in which many Black girls and women are forced to exert additional energy, devise many strategies and to compete in an *educational steeplechase* in order to gain 'success'. Chapter 6 will consider what is meant by educational 'success' when focusing on Black girls and women. An additional way in which Black students may be disadvantaged is through the lack of exposure and the resulting stunted growth as a consequence of studying within predominantly GM educational institutions.

Lack of exposure and stunted growth

Power et al. (2009) outline how different secondary schools provide varied provision and participation in out-of-school learning which can contribute to students' exposure to new insights and their growth beyond formal curriculum and classroom-based learning. Interestingly, the study reveals that 'different levels of provision are not randomly distributed but relate to the different characteristics of schools', as well as 'gender and ethnic dimensions to patterns of participation' (p. 459). Additionally, in a report by Horgan (2007: 1) on the impact of poverty on young children's experience of school, in relation to Power's findings he shares that 'the experiences of school for children from poorer families were narrower and less rich. For example, children in disadvantaged schools had limited access to music, art and out-of-school activities that children in advantaged schools generally took for granted'. This is part of the inequality that underpins many predominantly GM educational spaces and places.

* * *

Nia-Elise stands up, using her foot to gently slide the stool to the side. She glides around the small room, her eyes fixed upon her canvas, musing about whether she is satisfied with her creation. It isn't finished yet, but she does like what she sees, and she intentionally decides on the finishing touches that will make the key messages pop to ensure it will be perfect for her latest collection. She needs a little break from painting though.

Nia-Elise *So, that's some of the themes I wanted to get across in my exhibition, focusing on 'being one of many' throughout my education and what that meant.*

Journalist *That's so fascinating and powerful!*

Now holding her mobile phone – which is still on loud speaker – she slouches on the small couch in the corner of the room, scrolls to see if she has had any new Etsy orders. They say hindsight is a wonderful thing and Nia-Elise cannot quite believe how far she has come from the days when she lacked confidence in her artistic talents, could not access the right support or resources and literally had to follow her passion which led to her creating her own networks, her own learning and her own development as an artist. Honestly, if her friends and family had not believed in her or appreciated her work, she would not have continued to pursue it. Today, she is able to be confident in her abilities and to flex with pride due to the dedicated cultivation of her unique style and visually pleasing and thought-provoking pieces. She is filled with gratitude and vision for herself, her friends, family and her community, as expressed in her creations. After a short while, she positions her mobile phone back onto a nearby flat surface and resumes painting and continuing to talk directly to her creation, as if speaking life – or at least her experiences – into it. The journalist continues to quietly listen on the other end of the phone line while taking detailed notes.

* * *

In Chapter 4, *Chika* highlights the commitment and encouragement given to her to participate in extra-curricular activities within her educational journey, as well as the different types of support, encouragement and exposure she gained as a result of this. This was very different in *Nia-Elise*'s experiences and she frequently wondered whether her educational experiences and journey within predominantly GM educational spaces and places limited her exposure to others beyond her community, and may have actually stunted her growth – though she was able to proactively kickstart it again once she chose to immerse herself in her art:

> So when you kinda restrict yourself to a certain type of social group, you tend to feel uncomfortable outside that social group and during my experiences at university, I kept myself within a certain social group. However there's two friends I still have now who were not part of that social group in a sense and we got on cos the friendship was beyond social, it was like a combination of things but yeah. For instance when you kinda keep yourself to a certain racial group, you find it hard to communicate with others and that's what I experienced during my first and second year, it's only until third year when I thought do you know what? I need to learn more and it's just that intellectual curiosity to just broaden out and I learnt this is what I should've done during my first year cos also it would've been much easier cos we are all in the same boat and I think in a sense, that's one thing I can say you're programmed … I feel as a Black girl/woman you are programmed to do throughout your educational experience … kinda like 'stick to your own' that's how I feel like when I went to secondary school –but when I went to secondary school, all the Black people just went together cos you felt comfortable, sixth form – all the Blacks went together cos you just feel comfortable.

When reflecting upon her university experiences, *Nia-Elise* speaks of how she largely stuck with social groups and settings that reflected her background and identities due to the comfort she wanted to create – though she was able to have two friends who didn't share similar identities or backgrounds. This could also be a habit developed from her previous educational experiences where her friendship groups consisted of mainly other Black students as revealed earlier. On the other hand, *Nia-Elise* expresses that one disadvantage of keeping to those from a similar 'social' or 'racial' group and not mixing is being unable to communicate with or to bridge the gap with others. In some ways, this can be interpreted as a lack of 'multicultural capital' (Reay et al. 2007), in that being within predominantly GM educational spaces and places has limited their confidence in and understanding of how to meaningfully interact with others from different racial backgrounds such as white people. It is also notable that once *Nia-Elise* realizes this, she proactively makes an effort in her latter university years to mix with others beyond her social and racial group for the sake of her 'intellectual curiosity' and to 'broaden' her understanding of the world by interacting with different people. She also realizes that doing so may have been much easier at the start of university when everyone is new and 'all in the same boat'. She points out that she feels that this is a collective experience for Black girls and women who she feels are more likely to hang around Black people. She goes on to confide why such things as conversations may be quite difficult for many Black girls and women who may be unfamiliar with interacting with people beyond their communities:

> I think one of the things that I noticed is that I feel that … I think I've learnt how to adjust, but I can see that some people are really awkward, it's just being able to relate and speak to other people and not just your own. Sometimes I can see that some Black girls/women don't know how to make conversation, not just small talk, but just conversation not based on, I don't know, your favourite shows and the music because that's something that Black girls/women can relate to, hair, music and all that other stuff and also like educational stuff. But, other people can't relate to that so then how do you communicate? How do you make conversation? How do you start a conversation? I think that's one thing that I've noticed with Black girls/women yeah.

Nia-Elise makes an important point showing that she feels that she has little in common with other non-Black students during her university experiences. It is not so much *how* to converse with others that she initially finds difficult but more so *what* to say when having conversations with others, despite the myriad of student topics like getting a job, student life and academic work. Perhaps there is a disconnect as the 'awkwardness' may stem from being uncomfortable with other identities, experiences and cultures and can translate to a lack of effort, on both sides, to bridge the differences. While she proactively learns to adjust, she admits that other Black girls and women may not, which makes such interactions 'really awkward' and become another reason why they may just stick to socializing with people like themselves. Once more, *Nia-Elise* brings her mother's teaching experiences to provide more context and to summarize the importance of exposure for all students, regardless of background:

> So my mum used to take her [school] kids to the Lake District once a year and she was like that was the first time some had gone away in year 7 and

I think there is where the introduction of more activities are available. So, I think it's sad that they get introduced to these things when they are much older and when people already have a mindset of 'oh that's not what people [like me] do', the mindset is just [names poorer area] high street as opposed to if I introduce it to you when you are seven [years old], race doesn't become a thing for you, you don't mind doing horse-riding, rock-climbing or whatever ... both [Black and white kids] need to be open and both need to know that on either side of [names richer area] is [names poorer area] and [names another poorer area] and I don't think that they [richer, white kids] are aware that either exists because they are like 'have you been to [names poorer area]?' and I am like 'just walk a little down the road and you will be there, just buss a right!' And I think both with the Black kid there needs to be an acknowledgement that there is a lot more to your high street, and with the white kid – this bubble that you live in doesn't exist for everyone – it's a nice bubble to be in – don't get me wrong, but it's not a bubble for everyone. I think when they [richer, white people] do acknowledge [Black] people, it comes across as condescending, they [richer, white people] need to know that they have positives and negatives just like they [poorer Black people] do, it needs to happen on both sides. It is very easy to do a trip to the Tate [gallery], but I don't know how they can't just do a school trip to [names poorer area] high road but y'know they [richer, white students] need to know that there are other people outside of their cushty bubble ... Looking at the Black kids from my experience, when they got to uni they were very taken aback by some of the things that [white] people do, but if you had been doing it when you were ten, eleven, twelve, thirteen [years old], it would be normal and not so strange.

There are many ways to learn and *Nia-Elise* comments about how being exposed to different places and participating in a variety of activities is one such way. When reviewing school trips and their value to education, Behrendt and Franklin (2013: 237) define them as being key to providing experiential learning which they define as 'authentic, first-hand, sensory-based learning'. However, *Nia-Elise* reveals how for many Black students who may come from deprived backgrounds and live in deprived areas which their schools are a reflection of, they are rarely given this additional dimension to their learning experiences. This is a central finding of the *Paired Peers* project mentioned previously, where they explore the differences in resources and opportunities for working- and middle-class students studying in two types of universities in the same English city. Perhaps in hindsight, *Nia-Elise* can see how limited exposure is not something that is just detrimental to Black students – though it may impact them the most – but also how more privileged white students are also being disadvantaged via the restrictions of the 'bubbles' that have been created for them and which they rarely venture outside of. Ultimately, both sets of Black and white children in *Nia-Elise*'s account are disadvantaged in different ways which lead to stunted growth. *Nia-Elise*'s reflections align with the research of Marchant et al. (2019) who find that there is a strong link between child health, wellbeing and curriculum-based outdoor learning and education. In their study they share how the children aged nine–eleven and their teachers felt about outdoor learning which included feeling free from the restrictions of the classroom, exposure to environment and safety, and increased pupil engagement from a wide range of pupils, including those with additional learning needs. They also note that there were many benefits for pupils and staff such as better behaviour and key skills development. However, they also note in their paper that organizing outdoor learning is largely based upon teacher motivation, accessibility to natural resources and the level of school, governor and parent support, all of which will inevitably be dependent on the type of school attended.

* * *

A big bright smile lights up Nia-Elise's face along with all the different colours of splattered paint all over it. She has now finished her phone interview and her painting, her newest baby! The different shades of brown – from the lightest to the darkest hue – shine on the canvas with the assistance of her LED ring light. The final piece is magnificent and depending on the angle it is viewed, it boasts both abstract and figurative elements. In many ways it is akin to the confusion and chaos of Babylon, or in other words 'oppressive Western modernity' (Niiah 2020) and 'the corruption of the white consumerist society' (Sabelli 2011: 139). These elements of Babylon are evident to see in every part of society, including the education system which Black girls and women like Nia-Elise are forced to navigate. Even though they may not agree with such a system nor enjoy navigating within it, they must do so as a societal requirement. However, Nia-Elise and many other Black girls and women are constantly reminded – through being positioned as unruly and being given lesser quality educational resources and opportunities – that, regardless of the safe spaces they create or how they mix and try to integrate, like the title of her collection, they are, and will always be 'one of many' Babygirls inna, but not of, Babylon.

* * *

So, what happens when Black girls and women have jumped over the many hurdles and barriers of the *educational steeplechase* to navigate through the (white) education system in PW and predominantly GM educational institutions? Do they gain 'success' or is it all just a load of unnecessary stress? The next chapter will explore this in more detail, as well as alternative options.

6

Educational 'Success' or Unnecessary Stress?

Figure 6 *Yaa*

It is a grey, gloomy miserable day outside, the perfect opportunity – if you are able – to stay inside, wrapped in a blanket, on the sofa or in bed, sipping on a hot, sweet beverage, reading a book or watching Netflix. Yet, a small, impenetrable enclave lies within the gloominess, remaining unaffected. This enclave is a small apartment, in a sky-scraping tower block. Perhaps it is the fact that all the rooms of this one-bedroom apartment – the kitchen, bathroom, the bedroom and even the corridor – are filled with different species of house plants, big and small, from aloe veras to cacti to peperomia and pothos, providing natural energy, as well as vibrant greenery, which counters the gloominess of the weather and the surrounding housing estate.

Yaa has lived here for a couple of years now, obtaining the keys in her final year of her three-year sociology and criminology course after deciding that she could no longer bear to live with anyone else. She was thrilled to bits to have her own space away from her family home which she had grown and flown away from. She had ideas of how she wanted it to be, but she had never imagined it to become a green oasis, an urban jungle, full of her beloved plant babies. As a proud and dedicated plant mum, she has a carefully established routine to ensure that every plant is nurtured according to its needs, and on her designated days, she spends hours repotting, trimming and feeding them. It happens to be her designated day and she resists the urge and opportunity to snuggle the time and gloom away; instead she joyfully sashays across her apartment, tending to her nature-filled surroundings, with the added assistance of her specially curated Spotify playlist – on shuffle – creating the right ambience for the task at hand.

As if in perfect sync, Yaa finishes watering the latest addition to her plant family, a large kentia palm, just as the outro of 'Reality Check' by Noname featuring Eryn Allen Kane and Akenya harmonically flitters away. This song is a reminder to Yaa of her internal power and light which has seen her through the toughest challenges of life as a young Black British woman in this day and age, particularly when navigating through university when she felt the most alone.

The truth is, Yaa's devotion to plants began when she needed to find peace and a purpose. She had heard about the many benefits of plants in the home such as improving one's mood, dealing with dry air to ease dehydrated skin and clear sinuses, and the lowering of stress and anxiety, and she decided to see if it was true. She brought a single, small aloe vera plant and it became apparent that she could actually find some solace in nurturing it. It turned out that she was actually pretty good at it too, as evidenced through her first plant growing and growing, even producing a flower – which is very rare. That was the moment her plant collection of a variety of species began and continued to expand. She also drew parallels and familiarity between lovingly tending to the plants and lovingly tending to her hair.

Yaa places the now-empty watering can down with one hand while the other holds back some of her tightly coiled, thick and full strands of hair as they escape from her loose, scarf-turned-headband. She swiftly re-ties the scarf – more tightly this time – to secure her hair back and away from her face. In the same way that her plants had grown and grown after dedicated, tender, loving care, so too has her hair which she is currently wearing in an enviable twist-out. Yaa's plant journey coincided with her natural hair journey when she also found solace and peace in rejecting chemicals and learning how to love and care for the different textures that grew from her scalp. As she learnt about different fertilisers and plant food, she also learnt about the best shampoos and conditioners as well as how to showcase the versatility of her natural crown. As well as being a fully-fledged plant mum, she was now also a proud natural-haired babygirl – an advocate and expert of the twist-out which she had now perfected after much trial and error. Though Yaa was petite in stature, her full and natural hair gave her both height and grandeur as people always admired and anticipated seeing which style she would morph her afro into. She had a unique, intriguing and ethereal beauty which screamed a combination of Asase Ya (Mother Earth) and African Queen, accentuated by her green fingers and beautifully cared-for natural hair.

Yaa grew up as the youngest child amongst her cousins with her Aunt replacing her mother who had died when giving birth to her. While she had grown up internalizing the deep, initial trauma and pain of being a motherless child, her Aunt didn't treat her any differently from her cousins, and she had never let it stop her, though she was very quiet – an introvert. She often reflected and daydreamed, in her quietness, about what it would have been like to know, speak, hug or even smell her mother. In some ways this longing for her mother had resulted in her commitment and connection to being a mother to her plants and her natural hair.

Yaa had a lovely gap between her two front teeth – just as pronounced as the American model Slick Woods. She always wore an Adinkra symbol – which originated from the Akan people of modern-day Ghana and Ivory Coast – somewhere on her person as if it were an amulet warding off the isms and schisms she fought on a daily basis. The duafe, which looked like a wooden afro comb, was her favourite one, symbolizing femininity, love, hygiene and care.

Guided and protected by the spirit of her mother along with her other ancestors, Yaa had managed to navigate to the end of the educational steeplechase, obtaining what she believed to be 'success'. Though, nearly two years after graduation, she was finding it difficult to decide what it is she wanted to do and desired a job that reflected her hard work, skills and credentials. She was tired of the moving goalposts and burnt breadcrumbs from the white (wo)man's (stolen!) table that she and many other Black British women graduates were told to accept and be grateful to receive. I use burnt breadcrumbs here as a metaphor to convey and build upon the existing notion of the remnants of graduate-level labour market opportunities and slow progression beyond 'successfully' completing education. Not only are the burnt breadcrumbs or limited options for Black women graduates small to begin with, they turn out to be really of no value due to the struggle it takes to get them and the slow progression they encounter once they do. Yaa had settled by working for an education charity and her preoccupation with her hair and plants were still providing her with vital peace, solace and purpose that were missing from her schooling, university and now labour market experiences.

* * *

In this chapter, I am using *Yaa* to embody some of the many Black British women graduates who have done what they should – sometimes more – to be educationally 'successful'. Through her reflections, *Yaa* will interrogate how educational 'success' is often defined by the government, educational institutions and the labour market, while highlighting the unnecessary stresses it takes to gain it. She will also reflect on alternative options with the aim of illustrating the need to redefine educational 'success', especially when it pertains to Black girls and women.

Achieving educational 'success' and becoming a Black woman graduate

England is characterized as being a knowledge-driven economy (Castells 1994; Brown et al. 2003; James et al. 2013). This means that possessing an academic degree has become a basic requirement to obtain many jobs in the labour market. This is also the principle of human capital theory (Schultz 1961), which Tomlinson (2008: 50) sums up as 'participation in education and training as an investment that yields both social and private returns'. In this way, being a graduate signifies that a person has a particular and desired set of attributes and skills (Bridgstock 2009) as defined jointly by higher education institutions, employers and the government. In fact, graduates are seen as 'one of the most common talent pools and many top-performing organisations view them as a key source of high potential employees' (McCracken et al. 2016: 2728). As stated by Devaney and Roberts (2012), societal expectations and labour market competition for academic degrees mean that nowadays 'employers can now choose between three types of graduates: those straight from an undergraduate programme, those who have completed an additional postgraduate course or those who have taken a postgraduate conversion course after a first degree in something else' (p. 233).

On the other hand, 'graduate' can be seen as a generic term that hides additional factors surrounding it. With the expansion and marketization of higher education, the increasing number of first-time graduates has created a competitive and hierarchical system where value as a graduate increases or decreases according to degree subject, degree grade and institution attended (Bowl 2018), individual/group identity (Archer and Hutchings 2000) and 'positional conflict theory' (Brown 2000) which is explained as 'the "rigging" of the market for credentials and the way individuals in the market are "ranked"' (Brown et al. 2003: 116–17). This is further compounded by socioeconomic barriers to accessing higher education due to student loans and debt which both deter and create different university experiences (Bachan 2014; Evans and Donnelly 2018). As Ingram and Allen (2019: 724) highlight, there still remains an 'ideal' graduate who is privileged because they 'embody certain valued capitals', and this results in 'graduates from socially disadvantaged backgrounds experienc[ing] considerably worse employment outcomes than their middle-class peers, including rates of employment and earnings, even after completing the same degrees from the same universities'. They note that these factors also converge with disability, racial and gender identities. This was previously stated by Hinchliffe and Jolly (2011: 581) who write that it is also important to acknowledge that a graduate identity is transitional and 'can be seen as the cultural capital acquired prior to entering an organisation', which replaces a previous student identity.

Therefore, regardless of graduate status, it may not alleviate exclusions from the labour market disproportionately experienced by certain groups (Harvey et al. 1997; Carmichael and Woods 2000; Bhopal 2020; Zwysen and Demireva 2020). What's more, individual and group experiences and journeys that lead to becoming a graduate are important to consider when exploring the broad-ranging term (Bowl 2001; Reay et al. 2006; Tett 2010; Arbouin 2018). As previously researched by Mirza (1992, 1997b, 2006a, 2006b, 2008) the pursuit of educational 'success' comes at great cost and sacrifice for Black girls and young women who have to survive and navigate within hostile white spaces. Mirza (2008: 136) also asserts that there is a deep connection between race, gender and educational aspirations which she terms 'educational desire', underpinned by 'educational urgency' – 'the desire to succeed against the odds' (Mirza 2008: 144).

Yaa fills up her watering can before continuing to feed her plants, as usual, she strokes and she talks to each one, reciting a deep and complex story, she recalls her own educational desire and urgency when thinking about her experiences in the education system:

> [There has always been] that pressure that we [Black girls and women] can't .... – there was just no room for us not to be achievers ... y'know cos we had got so far against whatever obstacles and it was like there is no room for failure here which is good in moderation. But it's like when that's – it's the whole ... it's who I am, the confidence thing, and it just cripples us because it was that whole part of my self-identity and I think that's a lot of the case for all the [Black] girls that I met, because I was talking about it with my friend the other day, I mean a lot of us [Black girls and women] – obviously this is not everyone's story, but a lot of us, if you grew up a bit like the ugly duckling, then being clever was

> your thing, do you know what I mean? Like if you weren't pretty, the boys weren't following you, but you were smart, so you know that was our thing. So, it was like 'yeah we're smart though' so it's all right, and then later you are like 'ok I don't look bad now', but then you still have that accolade … do you know what I mean? … Education was the most important and I think especially for [Black girls and women] that just got through to us so much more clearer as well.

Yaa's revelation that she believed that there was 'no room for failure' and that being educationally 'successful' was closely connected to her confidence and self-identity echoes *Eve*'s reflections of the internal pressure that she experienced on her own educational journey in Chapter 3. In their study, Blankenship and Stewart (2017) measured whether there was a link between the marginalized identities of their three groups of participants and the impact upon both their academic achievement and their sense of self-worth which they term 'academic contingencies of success'. They find that 'the centrality and internalised stigma of an individual's identities will relate to academic contingencies of self-worth differently, based on their constellation of identities' (p. 112). While Blankenship and Stewart's research is within an American context focusing upon Asian/Pacific Islanders and white participants, it can assist in explaining *Yaa*'s own feelings that she must prove herself by gaining educational 'success', as an 'ugly duckling' as well as a Black girl or woman. Therefore, for many Black girls and women, gaining educational qualifications is regarded as one way to overcome this. *Yaa* also demonstrates how educational resilience and success are part of her self-identity and her habitus, which Dumais (2002: 46) explains 'influences the actions that one takes … generated by one's place in the social structure; by internalising the social structure and one's place in it, one comes to determine what is possible and what is not possible for one's life and develops aspirations and practices accordingly'. Moreover, *Yaa* discusses the gendered dimension to the pursuit of education which she defines as an 'accolade' that can supplement for her perceived lack of beauty as she grew up – possibly influenced by media representations of beauty standards, as explored by *Shamari* in Chapter 2, which rarely include dark-skinned Black girls and women. However, the constant equation of *Yaa*'s value with academic achievement and continuous resilience in coping with the pressure can be crippling, as she said, leading to difficulties with mental health and wellbeing for many Black women in their educational journeys and experiences. Additionally, the great costs and sacrifices in obtaining academic qualifications is understood by *Yaa* to be closely connected to privileges that she did not have, namely financial, as exemplified in her memories of university:

> In terms of the privilege that I saw, I saw a lot of kids come to uni who had their parents paying for their course and they squandered it all on drugs and I just thought 'see what happens when you get everything handed to you on a plate?' Maybe it was just me being bitter but, I was just like you didn't have to apply for anything, you didn't have to work for anything, you got it and you don't realize the value of it. Whereas, I realize the value of everything I have, it's kinda been devalued by the society we are in, but I value what I have. I know what I have been through to get that piece of paper and what it can lead to, what I want to do with further studying and whatever in the future. But like I said, it definitely gives you a fire, like I said you don't wanna ... and it's not to diss what I had because I was happy, I don't want to make it seem like 'oh my god I had nothing!' I was very happy to play outside doing whatever, I was very happy doing whatever with the family I had and with the background that I was from, but ultimately, you know that that can only last for a certain amount of time, when you are getting older, you wanna get a house or you wanna get this stable income coming in and that traditional roles are just not cutting it anymore – not saying that graduate roles are, but at least it's a bit better than that, and I know what you have to do to get it. And then because I am a creative person, I also know that you can't rely on your art to get ahead, so I had to have a back-up plan if anything was to go wrong, at least I know I have got my degree.

Within the education field there are constant struggles taking place between agents in which dominant groups are able to navigate more easily due to sharing similar habitus – the dispositions, behaviours and thoughts that are embodied and entangled with history – to the institutional setting (Bourdieu 1990a). In addition, possessing the 'right' capital such as whiteness and middle-classness is another way that enables a better fit in the educational field for some students compared to others. *Yaa* voices this when she talks about being around privileged people who did not have to bear the additional financial worries of university and how, because of this, she felt that they did not value the opportunity as much as she did as exemplified by jeopardizing their financial resources on drugs. She also reflects on her own experiences to get there and the high stakes involved in getting to university and 'successfully' completing her course. Yet, *Yaa* highlights how the differences in her experiences compared to her other more privileged peers provide her with what she calls 'fire' akin to motivation or urgency and desire as Mirza stated, to keep going despite the odds. In many ways, *Yaa* shows that although she is not part of the privileged group, she too is able, through her own habitus, to survive within the field even though, as she notes, it is a struggle made harder because she knows that it will unfortunately be 'devalued by the society we are in'. This devaluation of *Yaa*'s credentials, despite how hard she has worked to gain them, can be explained by Vincent et al. (2012b: 350) who conducted a study on how Black middle-class parents support their children in schools – they write how 'in white dominated fields … [Black middle-class parents and their children] have their cultural and social capital devalued, rejected and treated as illegitimate'. While *Yaa* does not identify as middle class or privileged, she is illustrating that despite gaining the same qualifications as her more privileged peers, she may still be disadvantaged when applying for jobs. This can also extend to the white dominated workplace which *Yaa* also comments on when she declares her degree as a 'back-up plan' that she hopes will provide her with a route into a 'stable income'. She also demonstrates how rigid the pathway to educational 'success' is, premised upon an academic pathway and a degree. I argue that in a better society, educational 'success' should be measured and judged in other ways, which will be discussed later. Nonetheless, *Yaa*'s relief to finish her degree course is obvious when she remarks:

> I am happy, I am just happy that I made it out alive and I've got my degree, nobody can take it from me … just you know when you have had to work so hard for something and you just think that all of this for this piece of paper, but knowing what that piece of paper meant, like after I finished my undergrad it was like, 'Ok!' Everything I've done so far is worth it because I've gotten what I was meant to get.

Yaa stating that she is grateful that she 'made it out alive' is an indication of the immense effort she employed within her studies and is a striking phrase that can relate to the ways she felt under threat during her university time. Yet, for some students, despite achieving educational 'success', they are still unable to acquire the expected advantages they are supposed to (Brynin and Guveli 2012; Elevation Networks Trust 2012; Boliver 2015; Trades Union Congress 2016a; Khan 2019). This once again raises further questions about, first, the validity of meritocracy – a fine idea only for elite white men and an empty theory without any regard for race, class and gender inequalities, as previously explored in Chapter 3. The second question is the true value of educational 'success' for Black British women graduates when moving into the workplace. This question is explored both in this book and in the joint report by the Fawcett Society and the Runnymede Trust (2022) *Broken Ladders: The Myth of Meritocracy for Women of Colour in the Workplace.* While the report explores the experience of thousands of women across the UK from a range of ethnicities and religions, it does focus on Black women's experiences where, for example, they state that 'Black women of African heritage were most likely to change by "a great deal" or "quite a bit" their clothes (54% did so), the language they use (50%), the topics they talk about (46%), their hairstyle (39%), and accent (29%)' (p. 59). Additionally, the current model of educational 'success' characterized by individual choice and hard work that 'good' grades and qualifications come to symbolize upholds dominant discourses of 'success' shaped by white middle-class ideals (Yosso 2005; Spohrer 2016). This fails to acknowledge or legitimize other forms of 'success' beyond academic routes or utilizing different methods and ways of knowing, or the sacrifices made, against the many odds, to enter and survive within a white dominated, hostile education system (Love 2006; Evans and Moore 2015; Chapman and Bhopal 2019; Kwakye and Ogunbiyi 2019; Olufemi et al. 2019).

Unnecessary stress: working twice as hard to get half as far

Despite the additional efforts that go into navigating through the education system for many Black girls and women, as outlined in previous chapters, as Roscigno and Ainsworth-Darnell (1999: 161) assert, 'it is unclear whether Black students are rewarded in the same manner as their white counterparts'. This is why educational 'success' needs to be critiqued, as currently the definition does not consider the differing positions individuals and groups enter the education field from (Bourdieu 1977; Harker 1990; Hirsh 2007); or the *educational steeplechase*, as defined in Chapter 3, that is competed by Black girls and women which includes the many obstacles that are overcome to reach the point of graduation (Mirza 1992; 1997b, 2006a, 2006b, 2008; Chavous and Cogburn 2007; Ricks 2014). It also does not consider whether good grades truly open up opportunities in the labour market (Hilpern 2008; Foley and Brinkley 2015; Trade Union Congress 2016b). Therefore, educational 'success' is narrowly defined and elusive for certain groups like Black women graduates. This argument can contribute to debates around 'equality of opportunity' – ensuring that opportunities are both available for all and are of the same quality (Terzi 2014: 490) vs. 'equality of outcome' – 'equalising where people end up rather than where or how they begin' (Phillips 2004: 1). Ringrose's (2007) research also contributes to these questions when she states that the educational 'success' of girls is often pitted against boys' disadvantage/success which fits into an individualized neoliberal discourse that obscures the role of identities such as race, ethnicity and class in issues of achievement. Additionally, in many Black households the mantra, ethic and rule to 'work twice as hard' is imparted to children from an early age, as a guide, a necessary requirement and what many Black parents and older relatives practised themselves to succeed – or at least get by – within a white-dominated society (Pennant 2023). This is something that *Yaa* can also relate to, describing it as a 'lesson' that she learnt from an early age which she brought with her into the education system:

> [There are] certain lessons I believe a Black child is taught at home that they then carry with them into school. So having the lesson instilled in you that you have to work twice as hard to get half as far, I've heard that from a very young age. I'm not saying that I felt disadvantaged as such, but I knew that I had to put in extra just to … Cos I knew that even if I accepted it, there are still so many people out there who see me as Black first rather than seeing any value I have.

Yaa illustrates how she is already socialized to understand that being Black may hinder her full acceptance and the way she is able to navigate within the educational 'field' due to the underpinnings of both whiteness and anti-Blackness, as exemplified in previous chapters. Bourdieu's (1984) concepts of habitus and capitals as resources are useful to explain the ways in which different groups navigate within the education system or 'field'. Usually, white, middle-class students, supported by their families, are able to activate their habitus and capitals – including their whiteness and social class – which are accepted and enable them to navigate with ease. When a CRT lens is employed alongside a Bourdieusian understanding of habitus and capitals in the educational 'field', we see how *Yaa* brings attention to how people may devalue her due to her Blackness (habitus) and that any resources (capitals), like her qualifications, that she may have. For this reason, her family has prepared her by sharing their own rules to help her to understand the nature of the 'game' and how to play it. One such rule is that she will have to 'work twice as hard to get half as far', or in other words, she will constantly have to prove herself by exerting a lot of effort to, in most cases, get a lesser return on her extra investment and not as much as she truly deserves.

Yet, with this established mindset, it also shows that to 'work twice as hard to get half as far' is a lot of pressure and is not sustainable because it will lead to stress, burnout and poor mental health and wellbeing; this could induce illnesses such as high blood pressure, which Black women suffer from in high numbers. This has been proven in the high-profile study by Geronimus (1992, et al. 2006, 2023), an American professor of health, who identified the 'weathering hypothesis' which shows that due to socioeconomic inequality coupled with racial stress, Black women's health begins to decline from early adulthood, impacting upon maternity and infant mortality. Black men also experience similar impacts as Black women. Another American study by Smith et al. (2011) found that, particularly in historically white universities, Black men's encounters of gendered racism which led to blocked opportunities resulted in mundane, extreme, environmental stress (MEES). They argue that these all lead to 'racial battle fatigue' or the 'excessive strains … additional energy redirected from more positive life fulfilling desires for coping with and fighting against mundane racism' (p. 67). Such findings can extend to Black girls and women like *Yaa* who resort to 'working twice as hard for half as much' as one such strategy against the gendered, anti-Black racism and classism they experience. *Yaa* also goes on to reveal an example of what 'working twice as hard for half as much' looked like for her during her university experiences:

> I think the joint experience is, if you are someone who wants to be on it, you have to work doubly as hard to show that you are really great for people to respect you for that, so you will be the one that they will always ask to do the bits, to do the panel, to do this, do that and at the time you are like 'of course I will'. But then [you] do it and [they] maybe [do] not acknowledge it as much. You do a lot for your acknowledgement compared to maybe what a white woman, a white man or sometimes even a Black man would have to and I don't think that's the issue … the [issue and the] consequences are our confidence … I think the consequences are our confidence to feel like 'yeah we are great' cos we are great but then also the confidence to say that out loud and not look like you are up yourself cos even me sometimes, if someone is like 'I am just the most amazing person' I'm like 'well that's a bit much' and I think 'well why is that a bit much?' But we [Black girls and women] are also socialized into it, to feel like we need to tone it down.

Yaa uses the colloquial phrase 'on it' to describe how she had to be active and intentional about gaining 'success' alongside her studies. For her, this included always 'working twice as hard' which she feels is a collective experience shared by many other Black girls and women. It also means putting herself out there more, in order to gain 'respect' and feeling the need to take on extra responsibilities to 'work doubly as hard' in order to prove that she is not just great but 'really great'. However, she emphasizes that in return, she feels that she does not receive the same 'acknowledgement' from others like peers and staff for the additional effort she has made compared to others. She also highlights the consequences of such an experience as being her confidence because, instead of being able to bask in her exceptional multitasking and resilience, she doesn't want to be viewed as arrogant or 'up yourself' and it becomes an expectation that going above and beyond is her minimum. Yet, despite being 'great' by any standards, due to the social conditioning and British values of modesty as explained by Mangan (2006) who writes that 'most British people would genuinely rather cut their own throats than crow about themselves' – as well as her earlier socialization, *Yaa* and many other Black girls and women continue to 'work twice as hard for half as much' silently. *Yaa* opens up further about the additional consequences of constantly working twice as hard which triggered her mental health:

> I went through a lot in uni, first year to third year I had counselling the whole three years and no one knows, not a lot of people know that. A lot of people think I am strong, but uni nearly broke me. Not only did the education … just striving to be successful – it was like you've gotta do this … your friends are smart … it was the pressure of it and … cos Black people are like 'we don't have mental health issues', so there's always a stigma with it. So I was like I need to talk to someone and I didn't really want to talk to my [Aunt] cos I knew she would worry, and I didn't want to talk to my [cousins] cos I knew they would worry and they're not there so what could they do? They'd just be worrying and it's like I didn't really wanna put them through that, so it was hard. But at the same time, looking back on it, it taught me a lot about myself, it taught me … it made me stronger … the counselling definitely helped, it definitely helped. It made me realize a lot about my personality as well and the way I deal with things.

As highlighted by West et al. (2016), when exploring Black women students at university in America, the internalization of the 'Strong Black Woman' by many of their participants resulted in negative effects on their health as it included being independent and self-sacrificing. While *Yaa* does demonstrate this in some ways, the fact that she does get counselling is promising and shows she is trying to heal from her experiences to change this narrative. Though, she also divulges that due to the stigma of mental health within the Black community, as well as not wanting her family to worry about her, she felt unable to confide in those around her and instead relied heavily on the counselling support available at her university. However, despite the counselling she received during university, her experiences had a lasting impact on her even after she graduated:

> [Uni was] traumatic … it literally … I think even now, it took me a while to … after graduating, which is why I didn't do any … I think it took me

> [some time] to really start to recover from that because that … I had to really build myself up again … like literally in that final year, I remember saying to myself 'ok *Yaa*, if you get through this yeah, we are gonna do something that makes sure we are not in this situation again', and a lot of what I wanted to work on was loving myself and y'know why I was tearing down my own self-esteem, and why I believed that I couldn't do the course when I was passing, do you know what I mean? So, it really … it was traumatic, but it really highlighted all my issues and I think I was really clear on what was going on with me, but I just didn't know how to heal it and how it would work, so I really took a vow to sort that out … because I was like 'no no no … I'm not doing this again!'

The lasting impact of *Yaa*'s university experiences, which she describes as 'traumatic', is caused by the constant pressure of always having to prove herself and working twice as hard in the process. While there are other English and wider UK studies that indicate that even the most advantaged students are finding university really hard (Macaskill 2013; Shackle 2019; Cage et al. 2021), which rose significantly during the Covid-19 pandemic (Office for National Statistics 2021), it must be indescribable with the additional pressures *Yaa* describes. For *Yaa*, this means that she had to invest even more energy to heal and recover after her studies. However, it is not clear whether she was able to gain professional help without access to a university counsellor to do so. Along with trying to recover and heal, as a graduate, *Yaa* is expected to also compete in the labour market to gain a job. This reveals additional challenges such as the realization that the acquisition of educational credentials does not always lead to ease in accessing opportunities in the labour market:

> I think Black people know that it is harder for them so we all share that common grievance with the world I suppose like 'why is this happening to me?' y'know 'why is this going wrong?' and I think when you come out of uni and you try to apply for jobs and things like that, you start to realize that the grade you got doesn't really matter. They are now looking at your name and who you are and I think we know that, so the pressures that Black people put on themselves are a lot whereas some people in uni, daddy's set them up for life or mummy's set them up for life and it's like, 'don't care if I get a job because mum said she is gonna get me a job in whatever empire' or … but a lot of us [Black women] don't have that to fall back on, and a lot of Black people are like that as well. I think in that experience, in the sense of the emotions around university, I feel like Black people have a lot more appreciation for education and I think we appreciate it more and we value it more so in that sense the pressure that we put on ourselves is a lot more to be great and to show people that,

> 'look, you might have underestimated us, but trust me you don't wanna do that, you wanna take us seriously.' But I don't necessarily think the journey is the same cos obviously some Black people would've done IB and some do A-Level and some do BTEC and things like that, so in terms of the pressure and the strive for success, I think we've all experienced that and we all go on the same journey to do better.

Yaa communicates that she feels that her degree becomes devalued in the labour market where other identity markers are instead considered more important. She believes this to be a collective Black experience which she once again contrasts with the experience of her white, more privileged peers who are able to depend on the established networks that will provide secure, workplace opportunities. In his chapter 'Outcastes on the Inside', Bourdieu (1999) explains the ways in which the supposedly democratized education system that encourages the participation of all, in actual fact forces different groups into an educational pathway that is set in a pre-arranged hierarchy, and thus impacts the kinds of labour market opportunities they will have. This is the process that *Yaa* has named when mentioning the different educational qualifications – IB, A-Level and BTEC[10] – as one way that certain groups are kept in inferior positions because, with the inclusion of once-excluded groups into the education system, 'after an extended school career, which often entails considerable sacrifice, the most culturally disadvantaged run the risk of ending up with a devalued degree' (ibid., p. 423).

Unfortunately for many Black women graduates, during their education and in spite of their acquired educational credentials, they are often viewed as being culturally disadvantaged and deficient (Carter 2003; Yosso 2005; Wallace 2017a). In this way, the additional pressure they put on themselves contributes to the 'working twice as hard to get half as far' mentality they have been socialized into, as well as the value placed on educational 'success'. This is an example of the core distinction between tacit and technical knowledge and skills which is so central to sociological research on work and education (Stephens and Delamont 2010). In *Yaa*'s case, she shares her eventual realization that all the stress she went through to gain her grades was not really worth it when she went to apply for jobs. This realization is evident in previous research by Delamont (1989) exploring gender and social class divisions in the US and Britain and the role of education in reproducing and maintaining the positions of elite women in certain professions, showing how difficult it can be for women from lower classes to break into them. This difficulty in breaking into certain professions for women is described by Rowe (1977) as 'the Saturn's Rings Phenomenon' which Delamont uses to explain her own findings as, 'the subtle barriers that operate against women in the learned professions and in science Saturn's Rings … as Saturn is partially obscured from us by its rings – whirling particles of dust and ice – so the real nature of much professional work is obscured from many marginal recruits (such as women and ethnic minorities)' (Delamont 1989: 252). While Delamont focuses solely on women, Rowe includes Black people too and these studies are still relevant decades later in the case of Black British women, as *Yaa* demonstrates. More recent statistics and studies in the UK confirm such findings and indicate that certain British Global Majority graduates like Black African, Black Caribbean, Pakistani and Bangladeshi disproportionately experience ethnic penalties in the labour market (Berthoud 2000; Li and Heath 2010, 2020; Morris 2015; TUC 2016a; Zwysen and Longhi 2016, 2018; Weekes-Bernard 2017; Li 2018; ONS 2019). Moreover, and specific to Black British graduates, it was found that they are most likely to come from and to go on to live in poverty as 'Black households (54%) were most likely out of all ethnic groups to have a weekly income of less than £600' (Gov.uk 2022b). Even when there is a graduate head of a Black household, it is true that they will still earn significantly less than their white and Asian counterparts (TUC 2016a; Social Market Foundation 2021; Mirza and Warwick 2022). These ethnic penalties in the labour market are further exacerbated when gender intersects (TUC 2006; Nandi and Platt 2010; Hills et al. 2015; Breach et al. 2017;). For Black British women, these intersecting oppressions are most apparent in the fact that as a group, they are most likely to be in insecure and low-paid employment by way of zero-hour contracts and temporary jobs (TUC 2016c). But if this is the case, what are the alternatives?

Peering out into the grey gloominess from the green sanctuary she has lovingly created, Yaa sighs in relief. Relief, or more accurately reassurance and relaxation, is what she feels whenever she is in her little space, which is just big enough for her and her plants. Often, she thinks deeply about the importance of her place and the significance of having her own space. After all, in the big city where she lived, having your own place was a luxury that not many could afford. While she knew that others would think that it was not much because her apartment was in a big estate and on the higher floors of a tower block, she often chuckled inside when she looked at the luxury apartments, also in a tower block, that were recently built, right by the estate, divided by a walkway and a wall, boasting lavish properties that are unaffordable to people like her. She would remember her privileged peers at university and wonder if they would own places like those. Maybe, she thought, they would be attracted to live there as it was located in an area deemed to be 'hip', 'trendy' and 'cool' – though these definitions did not extend to the majority of the long-standing residents.

Maybe, she thought again, they would own such properties for investment purposes to add to their generational wealth. Must be nice. It really must be nice to have options and to be able to assign value to something just by owning or living within it. This was the purpose of gaining an education – well at least for people like Yaa, it was seen as the opportunity to be of value to society, to gain value in society, and therefore to have options and the freedom and power to choose your path.

Education as a means to an end and championing alternative options

According to Givens (2016: 1288), education 'has played a tool of white supremacist colonial commandment on the one hand, and … a liberatory Diasporic practice on the other'. This has previously been highlighted by hooks (1994: 4) who also differentiates between two types of education: 'education as the practice of freedom and education that merely strives to reinforce domination'. For many historically oppressed groups such as Black women, the notion of education as a liberating tool is shared and signified through the earning of qualifications alongside the subsequent access it is *supposed* to provide like opportunities, financial gains and more stable positions within society (Fordham 1996; Smith and Middleton 2007). Additionally, being from a historically oppressed group and educated does not only supply individual benefits, but generally also engenders pride and is regarded as a huge accomplishment amongst one's family and wider community due to the challenges that are frequently involved in obtaining it. Also, the pursuit of educational 'success' and the emphasis on academic routes in Black communities should be viewed within the context of eugenics, race and intelligence (Chitty 2007), as well as the historical exclusion in England, Britain, and its colonies which prevented Black participation in formal education, and unequal experience as students once they were eventually allowed in (Coard 1971; Malisa and Missedja 2019). As Mirza (2006a: 152–3) reminds us:

> The struggle for humanity, as the Black and Asian community know, is fundamentally linked to the struggle for education. For a Black person to be educated is to become human … education … is not about the process of learning or teaching it is about refutation.

In this way, as expressed by *Yaa* and many other Black women who may or may not be aware of these historical contexts, going through the education system and being educated to become a graduate is a means to an end as it is the achievement of doing so that represents something much greater. As *Yaa* describes:

> I feel like we are more knowledgeable about what education can do for you rather than just getting a standard job and then you're just capped at a level because you can't move up … don't get me wrong, there are other ways obviously to progress but education is not the only way, but I feel like it's something no one can take away from you, that thing you will always have is your degree.

Both the possibilities of gaining an education and getting a degree such as how it can ensure that you are able to navigate in the workplace, beyond a standard, dead-end job suggests *Yaa* views education as a vehicle. On the other hand, *Yaa* also illustrates an awareness that there are other options to progress other than education and that the possession of a degree not only symbolizes capabilities, but it also provides ownership which as *Yaa* emphasizes, 'no one can take away from you'. Providing a critique of the processes of the education system which she has journeyed through, however, *Yaa* indicates the other options that she wishes that she was provided with other than the traditional academic university route:

> I feel like as … the education system is … I feel like it is very rigid. You have to study in a certain way like exams, essay, you are required to write in a certain way in order to get the highest grade, so it's like you have to follow a certain criteria [*sic*] and pattern, it's like … I don't know, some people aren't very good at academics so it's like if you are not good at that then y'know you have to fall into other vocations of work [*sic*] which may not be as respected as if you were doing a degree or something. So, I feel like it's hard for some people … it's hard because I think that's the way it has just been set up … [laughs] They made other … what's it called? Routes for people, other different types of qualifications, but they will never be as respected as the traditional [academic ones]. That's just life, you can't really do much about it.

Yaa's view that the education system is 'rigid' and forces people to adhere to particular standards in order to achieve educational 'success' is a criticism that has been levelled previously. For example, Freire (1973, 2008) described this approach as 'banking education' where students are not equipped with the critical skills to make any real changes, instead they are fed particular sets of ideas from teachers to keep them passive and thus to maintain the status quo. When *Yaa* talks about the fact that academic routes are seen to be more 'respected' than vocational routes this is because it has mostly been the case that 'students considered to be at the higher end of the ability range have chosen [and been encouraged to take] the academic route' (Conlon 2005: 299). This can also show why there has been a push for Black women to gain access to academic routes as previously they were prevented from doing so and had to find 'backdoor entry' to higher education through choosing particular courses and/or returning back to the education system at later stages in life (Mirza 1992, 2006a). Despite this push and the high regard placed on academic routes, *Yaa* still calls for additional options to be made available:

> I feel like there needs to be more in place to teach young people that, ok, yeah uni is one avenue but you can work, there's apprenticeships, there's other forms of education that you can do, you can go on courses and you can still get that qualification to … y'know depending on what you want to do, of course! But it's not the end of the world or the only way. I just think there needs to be … yeah there definitely needs to be more support with smaller groups not like a … three hundred people and one person talking at you – no, it needs to be personable if they can, one-to-ones maybe or just small intimate groups on 'why do you want to go to uni?' 'what do you want to do?' 'why do you wanna … where do you want to go?' 'where do you see yourself in ten years, five years?' There wasn't a plan, it was just like 'ok off you go, it's the next step, move on' like, 'here comes the new kids, the new year'.

Yaa highlights that many students are not given these alternative options or the support in their educational trajectories to make different choices, which can be influenced by the type of school that they are educated in (Abrahams 2018), as well as parental understandings of the education system (Ball and Vincent 1998; Ball 2003; Brown 2013; O'Donoghue 2013). For instance, *Yaa* wishes that the next steps and options after school and college were better explained to her, and coaching provided to prepare her or at least provide a way to make informed decisions. However, this is also compounded by what Pugsley (2004) already defined as the increasingly market-orientated and highly differentiated higher education sector in the UK and how it can be a challenge for students from different social class backgrounds, along with their families and schools, to engage with choosing universities in such a climate. Additionally, there has been a shift to promote and encourage other routes than the traditional academic school-to-university pathway, for example by way of the UK Government's reform to boost 16–19-year-old vocational provisions (Department for Business, Innovation and Skills

2014) and the push to do apprenticeships instead of degrees (Department for Education, 2023). Still *Yaa* recognizes that there may be some slight improvements in the education system when she refers to a conversation she had with a younger Black girl:

> It's getting better from what I am hearing from when I was at school, I feel our generation lacked quite a lot of things just in terms of surviving outside of school y'know mortgages, all those kinda things. I know you can do your own research but I feel there is more to learn than maths, english, science – those kinda subjects cos when you get into the real world that's when the learning starts. I feel … and speaking to my [friend's little sister], there are a lot of things she is learning that I wish I would've learnt at her age, like debit cards and credit cards, she is only thirteen years old but those things are vital at that age, she has a card herself so it's good to know how to manage your finances at such a young age. The housing market, that's quite important to know, at this stage it is just blowing up. What's going on in the world? Politics? Ok it is a bit boring to some but it's still important, it's all around us, so certain things that we hear about on the news or the *Financial Times* should be brought into lessons.

As *Yaa* rightly notes, the importance of providing learning that will aid understanding of real life/world topics and challenges will assist in being able to navigate in the wider world and ensure that all students can truly be global citizens, which is therefore a worthy argument for being taught in schools as part of the curriculum. The UK Government's inclusion of citizenship education in the English education system as part of its national curriculum is supposed to engender and incorporate such learning (Department for Education 2014). However, what use are these alternative options if they still will not include or be tailored towards the realities and needs of different groups of students? *Yaa*'s alternative suggestion deals with creating an affirming space in the education system for herself and other Black students:

> I lacked interest because I never saw myself on the page … only being self-taught that, and not experiencing it with other young people my age who are learning it at the same time … I could've lost my identity … I think that could've happened. Maybe we do need to open our own [Black] schools, just putting it out there, it's not … Y'know I see it happen in the Sikh communities, I see it happen in the Muslim communities they don't see themselves represented in the syllabuses, so they open their own schools, why are we so afraid to do so? It's not a cult, we are not teaching our kids with Black Panthers but we are not teaching them

> anything that's ... we are teaching them to be them and why are we such a threat to you? To the system that feels so happy to oppress us on a daily basis? I wonder if we would have had a different opinion on ourselves if we had been in the same school together without any other influences?

Yaa's idea to start 'Black schools' is not a new one and speaks to the influential and significant history and existence of the Black supplementary school movement in the UK, which she seems to know nothing about even though Black supplementary schools began from the 1950s onwards. Chapter 5 explored experiences within predominantly GM educational settings, which are still controlled and underpinned by whiteness; Black supplementary schools were social movements which represented struggle and resistance against this but often took place after school on the weekends or evenings (Mirza and Reay 2000; Andrews 2013, 2016). They were powerful tools, alongside the fight for the creation of policies by Black Caribbean communities (with others) to address inequalities in the education system and wider British society (see The Race Relations Act 1965, 1968, 1976; The Race Relations (Amendment) Act 2000). *Yaa* wanting full-time 'Black schools' performs a different function to Black supplementary schools which she envisions as replacing all the other options and, in her extract, she conflates such schools with existing faith-based Muslim and Sikh schools, highlighting their ability to transmit cultural, religious and affirming norms and values to their students. While in America there is the existence of Historically Black Universities and Colleges (HBCUs) and African-American, Black-led charter schools, English law only permits schools on religious grounds and not race (Long and Danechi 2019). However, the English Government's 'free schools' policy could address this as community and faith groups and/or parents, amongst other groups, are legally able to set up and run an all-Black school with Black staff and Black students (Gov.uk 2022e).

* * *

Yaa puts on the kettle to make her favourite drink – hot chocolate with condensed milk – very fitting for the type of day it was! She grabbed her laptop as she remembered that there was a big online sale that had just started at a new plant store – of course she had to have a browse. She promised herself that she was not going to buy another plant because she simply had no more space to house it! But perhaps she could find some inspiration for how she could reposition and rework her space and the kinds of pots and accessories available when she wanted to freshen up her apartment. Relaxing into her giant beanbag, she pressed 'play' on another of her Spotify playlists, clicking and scrolling along to the rhythms in the background.

Redefining educational 'success'

In neoliberal contexts, meritocracy and competition are a widespread belief that isn't true, foregrounded as the fairest way for all to gain educational 'success' usually identified by opportunities in the labour market that grades unlock (Souto-Otero 2010; Au 2013; Guinier 2014; Meroe 2014; Mijs 2016; Crozier 2018; Rottenburg 2018; Warikoo 2018). Yet, the meritocracy that underpins educational 'success' in most societies 'has been used to establish a link between individual effort and desert, mediated through education' (Souto-Otero 2010: 399). This meritocratic ideology means that 'whites believe equal opportunity is the rule and that the free market operates fairly and impartially. Therefore, according to this view, material [and educational] differences between whites and Blacks represent differences in merit' (Rousseau 2006: 124). As *Yaa* states:

> I just feel like with the education system, grades define people too much which I don't agree with, like through school I tried my best, I got the good grades but I always looked at other people who were so smart – literally smarter than me, like they were really smart, but they just never got the grades and I just feel like as a result of that, they didn't get the opportunities to go to uni and everything but it's not because they are not smart, but they will never be looked at in the sense … I feel like people come to uni because it's just expected now and coming to uni is just seen as a success, but coming to uni, there are so many people out there that didn't come to uni and just because they're not … they might not be exam smart or whatever but it doesn't mean that they are not smart and I've had a lot of friends that are like that, literally so bright but exams were just not for them and as a result of that it's just shaped everything afterwards.

The view that 'grades define people too much' in the education system is linked to university being seen as the main option which grades mostly unlock access to. While she does not explicitly say who she is referring to when she talks about how others who are equally smart may not get the grades or make it to university, she asserts that this is not an indication of their intelligence. *Yaa*'s assertion aligns with Hamilton (2018: 3) who writes about how English educational contexts and the way educational 'success' is managed disadvantages groups like Black Caribbean students because, instead of acknowledging and addressing historical ethnic and racial inequalities, it blames attainment on the individual, positioning them as having 'the inability to compete with their counterparts in a meritocratic system'. As illustrated by previous chapters, there are many examples of the ways in which race, gender and social class intersect and negatively position Black girls and women within different educational contexts, along with the overwhelming whiteness of educational institutions that continue to marginalize and disadvantage Black students as a whole. Ultimately, this will inevitably have an impact upon Black girls' and women's performance and thus whether they are able to gain educational 'success' as it is currently defined.

Additionally, it can also be said that the established existence of both gender, race and ethnic work penalties – which doubly disadvantage Black women entering and competing in the workplace – do not make their often complex and difficult educational journeys worthwhile. Therefore, it is unsurprising that the inequalities of the education system, as highlighted in this book, do not cease, but instead continue in the labour market. In this way, unfortunately, for many Black British women, they will continually find it difficult to escape the 'sticky floors' and break the 'glass ceilings', or more accurately 'concrete ceilings' that keep many of them trapped at the lower rungs of the labour market – even if they are armed with their qualifications (Christofides et al. 2010; Tan 2017).

When redefining educational 'success', meritocracy as an ideology and concept needs to be characterized as an unrealistic goal to desire because it is certainly a myth (Themelis 2008; Crawford 2010) and a white middle-class privilege as highlighted by Knowles and Lowery (2012) and Crozier (2018). Even though previous chapters suggest that many Black women like *Shamari*, *Eve*, *Chika* and *Nia-Elise* buy into meritocracy, there are currently few other systems or alternative options, and they still notice and highlight its limitations according to their lived, educational experiences. *Yaa* is no different as she too reconsiders meritocracy and how the power of grades is used as one of the main measures of educational 'success'. But she is also asserting that educational 'success' needs to include the plight of many Black girls and women who, despite the odds, still achieve it:

> So, there's this thing I keep hearing called a glass ceiling and I am just like really? Who does that stop? It's not stopping me. It may exist but you really think I am gonna come this far to let somebody say that because you are Black you can't get past a certain level, or because you are a woman or because you are from [names area] really? No! But I have seen it, I have seen certain people say 'Oooh, I didn't expect you to be Black', 'I didn't expect you to have …' 'Oooh you're from [names area]' 'Oooh, I never saw that coming'. That's your business, that's your perception of what you thought I was gonna be and I can't alter that, I can only be me and prove you wrong.

Yaa is using the metaphor of the 'glass ceiling' to explain the invisible inequalities that typically disadvantage women in the workplace. She also displays her strong drive, resilience and resistance which is a sensible attitude for her to have to succeed and has aided her to 'come this far' and graduate. It also demonstrates that she is unwilling to be limited because of such inequalities and that she is redefining 'success' by creating her own standard and criteria. *Yaa* is no longer accepting being underestimated or the word 'no' because of the immense hard work she has put in to get to where she has. However, *Yaa*'s determination may be overly ambitious as an individual person cannot shatter the 'glass ceiling' or what has been described as a 'double glazed glass ceiling' (Meeting of the Minds 2020) or a 'concrete ceiling' (Teixeira et al. 2021) for Black British professional women in the workplace as structural change is required instead. By listing her Black woman identity as well as the area she is from she illustrates the intersectional oppression she faces, as well as the way others perceive her and thus her capability and her potential because of it. Yet, *Yaa* defiantly lets it be known that she does not care about such negative perceptions because she does not feel that that's her 'business' as she can only prove others wrong via her 'success'. This is echoed by Carter (2008: 478) in the US who discovered that high performing Black students in her study used educational success as an act of resistance. *Yaa* also hints at the renewed self-esteem that she and many other Black girls and women now have after graduating from the English education system:

> I feel like we are valuing our worth more, we are understanding that we can also be powerful, we are not trying to let anyone suppress us. I might live in Britain and my prime minister might be white, and a lot of people around me are white, and my manager might be in a good position and I am probably doing the job better than her, all these things. But I feel like we [Black women] are valuing it more to the sense like, 'look I have gone through the education system and I have tried damn hard to get where I am, so no one is gonna stop me!' It's empowering because that means the next generation of Black British women are also gonna be that way and they are gonna improve on that and grow on that and eventually in the next years, hopefully we will start seeing 50% of these FTSE 100 companies having Black British women CEOs and people on the board. It's inspiring, I will say that, but it's not easy, it is hard and it is a lot of pressure especially if you don't succeed in the education system as a Black British woman – you are looked at like 'What is wrong with you?'

Yaa goes into more detail about the types of inequalities that she currently experiences in terms of being a minority within a PW society and workplace, as well as how this whiteness, embedded with unwritten boundaries and rules, excludes people like herself from accessing particular positions which she frames within a wider and collective Black British woman experience. It must be noted that *Yaa* was talking about a white Prime Minister *before* Rishi Sunak became the first Global Majority leader of the UK Government in 2022. For instance, according to the initial findings from the *Green Park Business Leaders Index 2021*, there are no Black Chairs, CEOs or CFOs at FTSE 100 companies. Yet, she sees the progress that has been made before her, and which she has contributed to, as facilitating her self-confidence in her worth, value and abilities which her educational qualifications bolster. *Yaa* also shows how she positions herself beyond educational contexts though the 'seeds' for such a transformation were planted within them. In essence, she is asserting that she has met the existing societal and educational standards despite the difficulties and so she refuses to be restricted. She also highlights that instead of the unequal education system being critiqued, it is Black girls and women who do not achieve educational 'success' that are critiqued instead.

The high value placed on education as signified by the acquisition of qualifications, along with the obligation and motivations that implore Black women like *Yaa* to succeed are evident. In this sense, it can be argued that educational credentials become what Bourdieu and Wacquant (1992: 98) have referred to as 'trump cards' in that they are 'valid, efficacious in all fields – these are the fundamental species of capital – but their relative value as trump cards is determined by each field and even by the successive states of the field'. In this way, as has been demonstrated previously in this chapter, the huge investments made in the pursuit of education become a basic element precisely as these qualifications are 'a species of capital … efficacious in a given field, both as a weapon and as a stake of struggle, that which allows its possessors to wield a power, an influence, and thus to *exist*, in the field under consideration, instead of being considered a negligible quantity' (Bourdieu and Wacquant 1992: 98; emphasis in original). Not only is *Yaa* motivated and empowered to continue to succeed against the odds, she also sees her relatively disadvantaged position as lessons which make her more hungry:

> I literally will grab any opportunity that comes my way and even if I have a doubt, I'll still go with it cos of my upbringing. I haven't really got the best result in life but that shouldn't stop me, it should motivate me more – challenges as well as failures – it pushes me even more to go out there.

It is this formidable attitude as illustrated by *Yaa* and many other Black British women graduates that needs to be acknowledged, respected and bottled as a secret ingredient to serve to others! However, the current version of educational 'success' leaves Black women both practically and theoretically excluded as they frequently assert extra energy and effort to achieve it. Yet, doing so still does not always unlock the expected rewards when compared to other groups. Alternatively, a different future needs to be envisioned. A future where the education system is dismantled and rebuilt in an intersectional and socially just way that does not force Black girls and women to constantly have to prove themselves by having to 'work twice as hard to get half as far'. *Yaa* illustrates that the real success has come from her creativity, and from developing a strong sense of self, rather than the pieces of paper she has achieved through university and the limited job opportunities it has given her.

* * *

After hours of browsing and being both delighted and inspired by all the plants and accessories on offer, Yaa has made an online store account and is saving the items she likes for another day. She is super proud of her strong discipline as she did not add anything to her virtual basket – though she was tempted to on many occasions. She has just sipped her way through the last of her third cup of hot chocolate, savouring the extra sweetness from the condensed milk – a drink that was also her late mother's favourite, as she had been told, and so, through making it, she feels a connection to her every time, often smiling internally as she gulps it down imagining her mother doing the same.

A loud ringing, out of the blue, abruptly interrupts her; she isn't sure what it is and so pauses her music to hear more clearly and the ringing continues. Jumping out of her beanbag, she realizes it is her intercom so she goes to answer it. Yaa is pleasantly surprised to hear her aunt's warm, sweet and comforting voice through the receiver – she was in the area and wanted to pop in to see her niece. Yaa pushes the button to automatically open the downstairs door to let her in, refilling the kettle to boil as she waits for her aunt to take the lift all the way up to her floor. After a short while, she hears a tapping at her front door and goes to open it. When she opens the door her aunt is standing there, smiling and holding a snake plant in a beautifully decorated pot.

Yaa's Aunt: *I saw this and thought of you, I thought it would make a lovely addition to your collection.*

Yaa grins in appreciation whilst inviting her aunt in, taking the plant with one hand and embracing her at the same time with the other. As she leads her aunt to the front room, the grey and gloominess outside began to disperse, punctuated by the sunlight shining directly into her enclave.

After the dark must come light, and though she always found her way in the dark, sure enough, the light always came out for Yaa – or perhaps it had never left because she was her own light.

7

Strength, Resilience and Black Women's Education Power

Figure 7 *Hamda and Hodan*

This is the day that they had all been waiting for! The day they would finally get to meet, eat and chat with other Black British women graduates about their educational experiences and journeys. A dedicated time to reflect on the good and the bad; the ups and the downs; the trials, tribulations and triumphs; as well as the lessons learned and the tools gained from educational trajectories in the English education system, from primary school to their (undergraduate) university experiences. This forum to speak and to share collective educational secrets and stories was provided by the fictitious, award-winning and nationally known podcast 'Choppin' & Chattin' Babygirlz', hosted in England by the fabulously fashionable and witty twin sisters Hodan and Hamda, with a diverse range of Black women guests. Starting their show on the podcast hosting platform Podbean during their second year of their undergraduate degrees in physiology and anthropology respectively, it had risen in popularity from an underground, grassroots show, shared via word of mouth and focusing on a specific community, to capitalizing and attracting a nice slice of the huge UK market which stands at nineteen million podcast listeners as of 2021 (Statista

2022). They needed a space to make sense of their, and other young Black British women's experiences, particularly as it pertained to their subject areas in the sciences and humanities, student lives and the additional pressures of eagerly pursuing 'success' within an unfair and challenging education system, as discussed in previous chapters and explored within this one. They recorded shows in bunches, slowly releasing them bi-weekly. Sometimes they did video episodes along with their standard audio ones; they also recorded additional 'specials' and multi-part episodes if the content was really juicy and beyond their usual 30–35 minute slot.

Hodan and Hamda wanted to facilitate conscious conversations through insider insights by and for Black women – their ideal podcast listeners. But they also wanted their messages to be shared near and far to a wider audience to create awareness and intersectional social justice – hence the utilization of a commercial podcast platform like Podbean where over the year, they worked their way through the four-tiered pricing model from the free, basic plan to the business one as it grew in popularity and they were able to begin monetizing it with advertising and sponsorship. They also wanted to facilitate an open, safe and good vibes space, to bring about laughter, joy, affirmation and, if necessary, healing to their Black women guests. They used the episodes to tease out and address both individual and collective difficulties, themes and experiences that many Black British women graduates endured – it would seem as a requisite to being inhabitants of England. The episodes were also solution-focused, inspirational and motivational. In many ways, their podcast could be characterized as a mixture of popular podcast shows Dope Black Women, Therapy for Black Girls, Comfort Eating With Grace Dent and Surviving Society. However, they devised a slightly different format, a podcast show with a twist, curating an extended experience with the inclusion of food in which each guest of the podcast was required to bring a dish that represented them. Everyone would share and eat the food whilst getting merry and building rapport before delving right into the topic of the episode. Today's topic is 'strength, resilience and Black women's education power'.

Due to the episode topic, Hodan and Hamda, who usually had someone in mind to be a guest on their show, had instead put out a call, advertising for Black British women graduates who had completed their undergraduate degrees within three years and wanted to discuss their experiences. Overwhelmed by responses from interested women who came from across England and the UK, they decided to choose five women, plus themselves, which would total seven. They thought that this would be a nice number for a conscious conversation and ultimately a great episode. As recent graduates themselves, they were as excited to hear the wisdom and different stories of all the other Black British women graduates as they were to indulge in the variety of dishes that would be brought in just a few hours. While preparing their studio space to welcome their guests (which was the open-planned kitchen and sitting area in their shared house), the sounds of the very fitting song 'Babygirl' by Chlöe x Halle, which they would always blast on loop when they were about to record an episode, filled the space, alongside the smells of bariis and hilib ari that was lovingly being cooked and would make up Hodan and Hamda's dish contribution, representing their proud Somali roots.

Affectionately known by their family and friends as 'HoHam', Hodan and Hamda are identical twins. So inseparable, they may as well be one person, they were doing life and most things within it together. They went to the same schools and were in most of the same classes, they attended the same university but did different degree courses – Hodan doing anthropology and Hamda doing physiology, and they shared the same friendship group. They do, however, have different personalities and, only slightly differing but overlapping passions and styles. Hodan, the elder twin by about two minutes – a fact she was full of pride about and which she never let Hamda forget – is loudly confident and unapologetic, she is a fierce leader who has a lot to say and, more importantly, she believes that she has every right to say it. In fact, the podcast was initially her idea, stemming from her love for exploring human life and researching different cultures – hence her choice of anthropology for her degree. On the other hand, Hamda is calm and collected, very humble and quiet – at least when compared to Hodan! She is intrigued with the human body and enjoyed getting to explore it as part of her physiology degree. They balance each other out like sweet and sour sauce, fried chicken and syrupy waffles, yin and yang. They were two sides of the same coin. Hodan can disarm people with her infectiously brash personality and humour which leaves others believing in their own sauce, while Hamda would do the same but with her contagious warmth and kindness which made others want to be kinder and better human beings. They both take their Islamic faith seriously, adhering and making steps to achieve the five pillars11 and, alongside their British Blackness, Somali-ness and womanhood, it played an important role in their educational experiences and journeys.

Both fashionistas in their own individual right, today Hodan's shoulder-length, wavy hair is styled in neat bantu knots with triangular partings. Hamda on the other hand wears her headscarf wrapped in a low bun, intentionally tied to reveal her gelled, swooped, baby hairs as well as her large silver hoop earrings. Where Hodan loved to have her face heavily made up, or as she would say 'beat to perfection', at any given time, Hamda only occasionally wears make-up and when she does, it is very lightly applied. Regardless of the amount of make-up each sister chooses to wear, as anyone who sees them in person or by glancing at their podcast website or social media profile pictures knows, none was actually needed. They had gorgeous natural features – a narrowly set nose in between prominent cheekbones and beneath cat-like, bright eyes, on top of heart shaped lips. Hodan and Hamda's delicate, caramel skin – which seemed like it would forever remain youthful – frequently gained compliments which intensified their purposeful, beacon-like glow and commanding auras – perhaps it was the secret that drew an abundance of Black British women, and others, towards them and their podcast!

One by one each podcast guest began to arrive bringing both main and side dishes with them – a fusion of cuisines from across the Black diaspora. Of course, all allergens had been checked beforehand and all the food was halal. First to turn up is Shamari, then Yaa. Next, Eve wanders in and shortly after, Chika arrives. Lastly Nia-Elise strolls in. The complete Choppin' & Chattin' Babygirlz menu consisted of:

- *Somali bariis and hilib ari*
- *Jamaican brown stew chicken, white rice and potato salad*
- *Ghanaian style grilled tilapia with fresh shito*
- *West African inspired – with a twist – jollof-couscous with a side dish of fried sweet plantains*
- *Eastern Nigerian cuisine of Abacha and Ugba accompanied by elélé also known as moin moin*
- *Cross-Caribbean infused dishes of seafood and meat rotis, saltfish fritters, mac 'n' cheese pie and bakes*

Apart from Yaa who doesn't eat meat and only fish, the rest of the women can enjoy it all.

Marvelling at all the dishes, Hodan and Hamda welcome the women – or fellow babygirls, in line with their podcast title – introducing themselves as well as the plan for the rest of the afternoon. They warm up the dishes and provide their guests with different flavours of soft, non-alcoholic sparkling drinks or fresh fruit juices, as they sit down around a wonderfully laid, African-print-clothed and accessorized table. Each babygirl then proceeds to explain to the others the dish(es) they bought with them and why. The space is suddenly filled with excitement, curiosity and ease as they all help themselves to the selection of dishes on the table. They get merry, build rapport with one another and line their stomachs with wholesome, homemade, delicious food before delving right into the episode topic.

The women finish their feast and proceed to the circle of seven chairs and microphones that have been set up in the sitting area, eagerly awaiting their bums and mouths. Some grab their drink as each of them take one of the seats behind the carefully positioned microphone stands. Now experienced podcasters, HoHam go around the circle to reposition the microphones to ensure they are a good distance from their guests' lips. Comfortably in place, the 'record' button is pressed and the 'Choppin' & Chattin' Babygirlz' podcast jingle plays. In normal fashion, Hodan and Hamda introduce themselves, the topic of the episode and allow their guests to do the same as well as briefly teasing the listeners' taste-buds when sharing the dishes they each brought and the reasons behind their choices ...

* * *

In this chapter, the composite characters of *Hodan* and *Hamda*, in conversation with *Shamari*, *Eve*, *Chika*, *Nia-Elise* and *Yaa*, will personify the experiences of Black British women graduates. In particular, this chapter will narrate the resilience and power of Black girls and women characterized through the strategies they develop, and the importance of their role models of mothers and (Black women) teachers/lecturers, in contributing to their educational 'success'. Lastly, they will impart the crucial wisdom they learnt from their educational journeys and experiences to their younger selves which will also be useful for future generations of Black girls and women.

The dialogue that is italicized has been added for the flow of the conversation.

Strategizing to cultivate strength and resilience

Resilience has many definitions but is widely understood to be the ability to adapt, withstand and persevere when confronted with stress, trauma and difficult situations (Luthar 2003; Unghar et al. 2013). The cultivation of strength and resilience is a necessary part in the lives of Black girls and women across the world, particularly in western societies like England, as Chapter 2 illustrates, and within the education system, as explored within the rest of the book, where they are frequently exposed to anti-Black, gendered oppression. In Chapter 5, we saw that this resilience can manifest in Black girls and women taking on the stereotypical roles of the 'Strong Black woman' (West et al. 2016); 'the Superwoman' (Reynolds 1997); 'the Angry Black woman' (Jones and Norwood 2017) and 'the Loud Black Girl' (Adegoke and Uviebinene 2020; Fordham 1993), or positioned as 'unruly'. Yet, being continuously strong and resilient can have detrimental effects on health and wellbeing, as discussed in Chapter 6 and 8. However, in this section, I demonstrate examples of strength and resilience as an individual and collective process, providing necessary empowerment in the educational trajectories of Black British women graduates. This is particularly useful when empowerment is viewed as 'a process in which individual, relatively powerless persons engage in dialogue with each other and thereby come to understand the social sources of their powerlessness and see the possibility of acting collectively to change their social environment' (Young 1994: 91). In doing so, as an American study by Goodkind et al. (2020) argues, resilience can be redefined and resistance reframed as it pertains to Black girls and women. Drawing on Young's (1994) definition of empowerment, Goodkind et al. focus on thirty-three Black girls participating in a year-long empowerment programme. Based on Black Feminist principles and critical consciousness theory, they assert that by being able to reflect collectively and critically on their oppression, while developing positive gendered racial identities as part of the empowerment programme, this can provide 'an alternative, collective form of resilience' (p. 327). Goodkind et al. put forward that this is in contrast to the typical individualized process of resilience, which negatively impacts mental health and enables Black girls' proactive resistance to injustice. Building on this, I find that the Black women in my research are aware of the barriers to their educational 'success' and therefore actively develop strategies of strength and resilience over time through having a positive but determined mindset, as well as drawing upon the power of their cultures, ethnicities and religion/spirituality within their education.

Positive but determined mindsets

Hodan (in excitement) *Ok, Ok, Okkkkkkkkk Babygirls, as you all know, many of us as Black women have had to work extremely hard to become graduates. So, what would you say were some of the ways that you managed?*

Hamda *Yeah, we have all had to work extremely hard in our own ways! So, I guess building on from Hodan's question, what were some of your strategies to 'success'? And by 'success', I mean getting to the end of your education and having the degree in your hand?*

The rest of the women 'hmmmmed' in unison as they agreed strongly with the 'working extremely hard' statement, going into deep thought to conjure up some of their strategies. Eve answered first simply stating how she had relied on having a positive mindset which strengthened her resilience. She explained further:

Eve I don't dwell on negatives so anything that's negative, I find a lesson in it, or I find something that shines within it, and therefore almost all negative experiences become positive to me, so it's a way of me balancing. Like, how I explain it to people is I am obsessed with the colour orange, but orange can only exist when there's a balance of red and yellow. Now red for me is passion, pain, drive, success, devastation, all those different things, and then yellow is safety, joy, happiness, cheerfulness, everything like that and then when you … if I have a red situation I look for my yellow, so if I am not happy, I look for something that's joyful or I look for a lesson in it. If I have a yellow, I seek red because I don't want to become complacent and think that happiness will exist all the time. I have to look for another goal, I have to look for … probably from when I was fifteen/sixteen that's when my connection to the colours really got stronger.

Eve reveals that the strategy she drew upon meant that she constantly looked past the negative situations in order to either learn from them or find positives, which ultimately helped her to move forward. By going on to explain how she did this using colors, *Eve* is actually utilizing and using on herself what is known as colour therapy – 'an alternative remedy that employs color to balance the body's energy centers, also known as chakras' (Butler and Grace 2021)[12]. While *Eve* doesn't share how she was introduced to colour therapy, employing such an ingenious strategy from the age of fifteen/sixteen illustrates how ahead of her time she was, as well as how her educational experiences and journey drove her to have to seek such unconventional ways to cope.

Nia-Elise *Funny you should say that, because that really resonates with me, Eve. I feel as though I subconsciously used my style, particularly at university as my own way to be the strongest version of myself.*

Nia-Elise continues to open up …

Nia-Elise I don't want to conform; I want the things that make me different to stand out so that you can see it. I think that's why I have my nails as long as I want or I have my hair as natural as I want it to be and I wear bright colours in corporate colour environments, because it is becoming more ok for you to be yourself. But I'm also seeing it as being unapologetic about being who I am and being authentically me because there's more value in that and it's more sustainable. In the education system, in terms of at university you don't have a uniform so you can

> see it from the things people wear and me coming to lectures … and I'll wear my Afrocentric earrings without thinking about it because that's the style I want to wear, and seeing other Black girls who act in the same way … so I think it is about becoming, because they are doing it independently themselves, then the things and the environments that they are going to such as the education sector, they will bring themselves with them. I think that there is an integration between the two because that accepting yourself allows you to then move into different environments and then be yourself.

Being unapologetically authentic and true to herself was *Nia-Elise*'s strategy, particularly within her university experiences and 'in corporate colour environments' which are typically dark, muted colours and/or plain. By boldly announcing that she does not want to conform and that she does this through her adherence to a style that is not (white) mainstream which includes her length of nails, her natural hair and wearing bright colours, she shows how that allows her to be resilient and strong as, she believes, 'there's more value in that and it's more sustainable'. She also acknowledges that she is only able to do this fully at university as there is no required uniform, which highlights how uniform policies in school can disproportionately discriminate against Black students, particularly Black girls (Joseph-Salisbury 2021). She also alludes to collective practices of resistance using style by herself and other Black girls at university through the deliberate wearing of 'Afrocentric earrings' and 'bringing themselves', their whole selves into the white space (Anderson 2022). This strategy has previously been written about in the book *Dressed in Dreams: A Black Girl's Love Letter to the Power of Fashion* by Ford (2020), which amplifies how she employed fashion and style, along with many other Black girls and women as 'a form of empowerment for her interconnected identities but also how she experienced and navigated oppression and microaggressions related to fashion, appearance, and her Blackness' (Matthews and Reddy-Best 2021: 99–100). For *Eve*, her mindset turns into actions.

Hodan *Thanks for sharing Eve and Nia-Elise! I also agree with what you have both said about seeing the positives in everything and being unapologetic. It's actually the main reasons why we started the 'Choppin' & Chattin' Babygirlz' podcast! How about you Yaa?*

Yaa I feel like it's important to find that zeal and motivation in order to do well and, because we are not given that platform to do well, i.e. given university where nobody was pushing me to my fullest potential, I just find it elsewhere. I feel like if every Black female had that in university,

> they could be doing big things right now cos I think it's in our spirit – resilience. It's in us to keep pushing for things. I think if you go back to the whole slavery idea, y'know, we've overcome so much to get us to where we are today and so naturally, we are always willing to fight, we are always in fight mode to try and do the best we can.

While *Yaa* notes the importance of finding both 'zeal' and 'motivation' within educational spaces, she shares how she didn't feel able to gain this from her own experiences, particularly at university which led her to 'find it elsewhere'. In research by Katz and Acquah (2022: 11) about the schooling experiences of Black girl teenagers, the authors report that their informants also said they encountered a lack of support resulting in having to find a sense of community as 'ways to resist feelings of entrapment and gain a sense of freedom by supporting themselves, working to remain positive, forming trustworthy and supportive connections, and looking forward to the future'. Though Katz and Acquah are focusing on schooling experiences, this is similar to *Yaa*'s account of her time at university. There is also a sense of disappointment emphasized by *Yaa* who believes that many other Black women university students have also been restricted due to a lack of institutional support which is where resilience, ingrained in Black girls' and women's spirit, according to *Yaa* kicks in. This deep-rooted Black girl and woman resilience and determination is explained by *Yaa* when remembering historical injustices that have been overcome by Black people, and a willingness or perhaps necessity to always be 'willing to fight' and to be 'always in fight mode' which is exhausting.

Hamda [sighing] *That's so true.*

Hodan *For me I know I have to fight too as I am aware of my gender yes definitely largely because being a woman, I feel like again we are so marginalized, we're just faced with … just like so many inequalities as well and I feel like being a Black woman as well, is harder because I don't know, there are two sorts of discrimination that you are facing, being a woman and being Black as well. So, again that has really pushed me to want to empower women, that's why I think I am so passionate about women's rights.*

By using her own experiences and awareness of racial and gender inequalities and discrimination, similarly to *Yaa*, *Hodan* is able to remain positive but determined as well as motivated to empower other women. But why must Black girls and women be responsible for reversing the inequalities they did not create? As argued in Chapter 6, structural change is required instead. Another strategy that the women recall is drawing on their cultural, ethnicity, spiritual and religious resources.

Gaining power from culture, ethnicity or religion/spirituality

Hamda I would say, I look at stuff in an Islamic perspective more than anything. So, I think … I'm just trying to think of an example, but I don't know … but like standard things, I don't know how to say … it's just so … like the fact that I got rejected from Medical school, it was more like 'ok, maybe it was just meant to be' but, when I was like … I know people that would say … 'it's probably because I'm Black'. I don't really know how to express myself like that, and all that which doesn't … it's quite stereotypical I think, but some people would look at it like that 'oh it's because I'm Black and Muslim' whereas, I was like 'oh, it just happened', it's looking at it from a different perspective I guess.

While there remains a dearth of research about the lived experiences of Black British Muslims in general, and specifically within educational settings, *Hamda*'s account provides a novel contribution and can contribute to the work of scholars like Johnson (2018) who centres Black Muslim women in Britain. These rare insights into the experiences of Black Muslims is recounted within a blog post by Godfey (2018) where she interviewed *Adna*, a Somali student who completed a year abroad in London who spoke about it characterizing how

> within the global imagination, people have constructed the idea of what a Muslim person "should" look like. People believe that Muslims are all Southeast Asian or Arab, and that Black Muslims do not exist. I'm Somali, and people also believe that Somalis simply are not Black.

This blogpost interview further highlights the complexity and diversity within Blackness according to racial, ethnic and religious identity. Though *Hamda* went on to study physiology, she brings up her Islamic faith to demonstrate how it helps her to look at situations differently as part of her strategy. She chooses to see, for example, her rejection from medical school as not being caused by her raced and religious identities. As the British Medical Association (2015) acknowledges, only '20 per cent of secondary schools in the UK provide 80 per cent of all applicants to medicine', though they also note that 'by 2013 more than half of all medical students were female', but, 'data for 2013/14 shows that nearly two-thirds of medical students in the UK describe themselves as white, just under a quarter identify as Asian and a mere 2.86 per cent as Black'. This suggests that there is an under-representation of Black British students on UK medical courses and doesn't capture the added dimension of religious identity. This had led to the creation of the charity *Melanin Medics* by Trueland (2021) to attract more Black British students to medical degrees. There is also a rise in Islamophobia across and within UK higher education which is described as 'a form of intolerance and discrimination motivated by fear, mistrust or hatred of Islam' (Stevenson 2018: 7). *Hamda* also shares the important role that being a member of her university's Islamic society played in her experiences which she felt provided her with a 'home away from home'.

Hamda At university I belonged and was part of the Islamic society. I learnt a lot in the Islamic society like, Islamic values and they're just, you know … we share common values, you share like … there's a, I can't explain it, there's just this bond that we have … it just feels like a home away from home kind of thing.

In another insightful blog post, Abdulaahi (2019) reflects on the discomforts some Black Muslim students frequently feel with ISOC (the national student-led Islamic society in most UK universities) and the important role of Somali student societies at universities to discuss and highlight issues such as 'anti-Blackness in the Muslim community'. It's good to see that this did not impact *Hamda* based on her reflection, but it is nonetheless still an important consideration which future research should explore.

As a Christian, *Eve* smiled as she reminisced about her own experiences.

Eve I'd say Church as well, I've got people who I pray with at Church, I've got a really good prayer group, I also went to a Church near my university and I think that's really good actually because they did like student lunches and stuff. You could go and speak to them, they had a support network and stuff and they would pray for you and stuff like that yeah, that was really helpful.

Nia-Elise [chuckling] *Eve, you remind me of my uni friends!* At the time, while I wasn't very religious, I felt like some of my friends definitely had their religion that helped them! Some of my friends were super Christian so they'd be like 'nope Jesus is not going to fail me' y'know and that got them through. They believed it. 'Nope, I don't care', do you know what I mean? 'If that marker goes to write 5, God will just take their hand and do 7' [laughs]. My friend used to literally say that, and that's what got her through. But I didn't really have that religious standpoint but I used to read spiritual and self-help books and that helped me.

In evoking how Christianity, faith, prayers and the church were key strategies used by both *Eve* and *Nia-Elise* in their education, especially at university, they confirm what previous research highlights. According to Witherspoon and Taylor (2010), their study illustrates how four Black American women school principals draw on their Christian faith which they employ as spiritual weapons to contest the status quo and educational administration in US schools. Similarly, in a comparative study about the educational achievement of Black male university students in the UK and US, Byfield (2008) illustrates how a major factor in their success was their church communities which provided alternative forms of social and cultural capital and their strong faith in God gave them religious capital. In a study about the significance of faith for Black men's educational aspirations, Dumangane Jr (2017) illustrates how Black British Caribbean men in elite higher education institutions in England and Wales are also able to use their faith as a 'capital' and resources to succeed. *Eve* illustrates the ways in which her church community provided the capitals Byfield and Dumangane Jr indicates. *Nia-Elise* shows how her Black girl university friends also did the same while noting that she preferred to read spiritual and self-help books – which also contributes to cultivating strength and resilience to complete her studies.

Shamari [laughing] *I think we all had or have friends like that! What helped me was my culture ....* The Jamaican culture's very much like ... Jamaicans don't give up and they're boasy [excessively proud] bad! If we are gonna do it, we are gonna do it good sorta thing so, it's just like that has very much been a driving point of remembering where you went from.

Chika [giggling] *L-O-L!* I beat the system and l feel that that is because Nigerian parents drill it into you [laughs] [Nigerian accent] 'the people that are getting A* and A, they don't have two brain' [*sic*], so I thought to myself, no matter what school I'm at private, public, state-owned – whatever, I need to put the work in and get good grades in that sense!

Yaa *Yes girl, yesssssssss!!* I feel like I was born to go to university – like from the womb y'know African parents – well my aunt who raised me – she would always tell me y'know [Ghanaian accent] 'you need to go to university, y'know we wasn't able to go!' Y'know they say African parents want you to study hard or all African parents want you to be a doctor or a lawyer, those things are similar. It provides motivation – but also pressure!

The significant role of cultural background, behaviours and practices are another dimension to their Black Britishness, feeding into the educational strategies they employ as drawn upon by *Shamari* who talks about Jamaica, *Chika* who refers to Nigeria and *Yaa* about Africa in general and Ghana more specifically. However, it must be noted that while *Chika* and *Yaa* discuss their Christian faith, across Africa and particularly in Nigeria and Ghana there are sizeable Muslim (and other religious) communities. This has previously been referred to as 'ethnic capital' by Modood (2004) when summarizing the educational success of British South Asian and Chinese students – though a key weakness is his play into the 'model minority' trope and failing to consider fully the historical and structural barriers like anti-Black racism, that prevent other groups, like Black British students, from enjoying similar 'success'. In that regard, Hylton (2003: 104) offers the novel view that Black identities are imbued with spirituality as, 'the African and Caribbean approach to individual, family, and collective provisions includes a strong emphasis on a unified approach that encompasses many aspects of individual and group life cycles'. Though it is important not to essentialize or stereotype Black communities who are diverse.

Based on my study, I contend that for some of the Black British women, spirituality was a key resource within each of their educational trajectories, along with their cultures providing them with motivation to succeed due to the expectations along with the pride and the joy in doing so. Though understandings of the self-identity of Black British African girl students has not been as frequently explored, for Black British Caribbean girl students, there are long-established studies that show that they maintain high levels of self-esteem strengthened by their racialized and ethnicized identities – in spite of all the processes that seek to counter these within the education system (Coultas 1989; Reid 1989, Mirza 1992). Next, *Chika* provides a fuller picture of how her Nigerian culture was an important strategy that she was able to utilize.

Chika *They say pressure makes diamonds and look at us all SPARKLING and SHINING bright!* I feel like I can't speak for other African countries but Nigeria, I definitely know that families value education. They treat it like gold. They are always tryna … like a lot of my family, some of them live in Nigeria but they want their children to come here for uni or A-Levels cos they value the education and they understand that it's kinda a gateway to other sections of life. So it's definitely that and some of my mum's siblings – well they all went to uni – but there were people in my family who did not necessarily get an education because of different reasons and so they understand the struggle that they had had to go through and that's why they try and tell us like, 'look you have to go to uni' cos they have been through it and they don't want us to go

> through it. So, it was definitely like two things that Nigerians take very seriously: church and education. I don't underestimate that at all, they are the two things, and secondary to that is family and everything else. But if you have God and you have education, it's like I can conquer the world really, so definitely being Nigerian has definitely influenced that a lot and it's just like, be the best person you can be, and don't make the mistakes of the previous generation or the generation before that.

The awareness of the huge value placed upon education in some Christian Nigerian households is perfectly summarized by *Chika* who likens it to gold, the main way out of poverty and thus struggle, and only slightly below, sometimes on par with religion/God. Though as noted previously, not all Nigerians are Christian. Coming into the education system with this type of awareness and constant reminders will certainly provide the strength, resilience and power to at least try to succeed. This has not gone unnoticed as *The Financial Times* (2020) dedicated an article to exploring *What makes Nigerians in diaspora so successful?* Also, a report by the Migration Policy Institute (2019) found that in the US in 2018, Nigerians are the 'most highly educated of all groups with 61 per cent holding at least a bachelor's degree compared with 31 per cent of the total foreign-born population and 32 per cent of the US-born population'. Back in the UK, Demie and Mclean (2007) and Demie (2021) studied Black African children's educational achievement and concluded that the high value of education passed down from parents was a huge factor. This coincides with the previous accounts.

Hodan *So, you all talked about how your mindsets and being able to lean into your religion or spirituality, as well as your cultures are some of the strategies which assisted you in your journey to become graduates …*

Hamda *Are there any other influences that you would also credit with your 'success'?*

Shamari *Other Black women, of course!*

Honouring key Black women in educational journeys and experiences

Black women are often overlooked contributors in both the education system and student journeys and experiences (Mirza 1997; Mirza and Reay 2000a, 2000b; Bruce-Golding 2020). This section begins to redress this by focusing on the testimonies that show how Black women as mothers, teachers and lecturers play significantly powerful roles, both inside and outside the classroom or lecture theatre, to support and uplift Black girls and women students. In research carried out by Peters and Nash (2021) on Black women school leaders in America, they cite that what makes them truly unique and valuable within the education system as a whole and specifically for Black girl and woman students is their intersectional style of leadership which is made up of personal experiences of discrimination, an ethic of care, resistance, activism and social justice. I extend this leadership style to include Black mothers who are leaders within their homes and display similar qualities.

Supportive Black mother and daughter relationships

The 'strong mother' is a recurrent trope in many autobiographical accounts of educational 'success' (Owusu-Kwarteng 2019) including my own as demonstrated in Chapter 1. As will become apparent, the women's data presents rich accounts of the role of their mothers. However, a lot of these examples have previously been captured, especially in America, in terms of immigrant parents as a whole who have particularly high aspirations for their children (Jung and Zhang 2016). For example, in Chinese communities, mothers have been characterized as 'Tiger mothers' (Chua 2011; Guo 2013) and there are works that demonstrate how Latino mothers (Ramirez et al. 2020) and African-American mothers (Collins 2000; Herelle 2022) are also fiercely proactive in ensuring their children's 'success'. These contradict narratives that 'parents of colour are often considered hostile, non-participatory adults with minimal understandings of education' (Chapman and Bhopal 2013: 568).

The insights in this section will build upon similar, previous research to redress the negative depictions and deficit thinking of Black families, particularly mothers. Also, it must be noted that though in my full study (Pennant 2020a: 233–4) Black fathers are also mentioned and present as playing significant roles within educational journeys and experiences, here I have chosen to centre Black British mothers. Moreover, I argue that Black mothers have unique experiences compared to other Global Majority groups due to the anti-Black, gendered oppression they encounter and have to navigate themselves and as parents. According to Reynolds (2020: 5), who has researched and written extensively about Black mothering in the UK, for Black mothers

> [T]he care and nurturing we provide our children are underpinned by a deep-seated fear that we are raising children in a society that seeks to denigrate them, fails to protect them, and that does not recognise their worth or contribution to society. A central component of Black mothering is therefore, adopting strategies to challenge racism in their

own and their children's lives. This includes, for example, talking to Black children from an early age about the impact of racist oppression and identity politics so that they can successfully navigate the environment and institutions that place them at a disadvantage.

With this in mind, the composite characters will illustrate the manifestations of their own mother's support within their educations.

Without pausing to think Shamari begins …

Shamari My mum. She was an influence because she always wanted me to go to uni, she wanted me to have the best options for myself that she didn't have. So yeah, she was just always giving encouragement, always on my case. I remember there was a time in – when was it? Both … actually, secondary school and college when she realized that I was slacking and I hadn't revised, she sent me to my nan's for like a week and I stayed there to revise for my exams. She was like on my case! My mum would always help me make schedules for myself, she was involved in everything, very involved in all my education.

In this extract, *Shamari* acknowledges how her mother's university aspirations played a big role in motivating her to want to go, as well as how her encouragement and support, alongside her grandmother's, helped *Shamari* to stay on track to get there when she experienced difficulties. By being 'on [her] case' and actively 'rolling up her sleeves' to assist her with her studies, I credit her mother with providing *Nia-Elise* with aspirational capital, that is 'the ability to maintain hopes and dreams for the future, even in the face of real and perceived barriers' (Yosso 2005: 78).

Hamda *Awww, how sweet.*

Chika *My mum was also very influential in my education – especially the kind of schools I went to …* My mum actually told me a story, so when I was in primary – literally going from nursery into primary school, one of my teachers said that I was smart but that I wasn't smart enough to get into this particular secondary school and my mum, she said that she made a promise that day that I would – this is … I must've been maybe six or seven, and she was like 'you are going to go to that school, because that teacher said you are not' and cos it's the best. My mum, obviously being very religious as well, was like 'I rebuke that for my child, she is definitely gonna go there.' So, I always knew in the back of my mind that that was the school I was going to go to.

Chika also recounts something similar to *Shamari* when she expresses how her mother's aspirational capital dictated her educational trajectory into the best secondary school, despite opposition from her schoolteacher. While it is not clear from this particular extract why her teacher held limiting beliefs about *Chika*'s abilities, this, combined with her mother's religious faith, provided impetus to ensure that she eventually successfully gained entry into the school. Additionally, by retelling the story to her daughter, *Chika*'s mother may be consciously raising her to be a 'resistor' and fearless to limiting beliefs and obstacles – crucial attributes to have when navigating the education system, as found in a study by Ward (1996) about African-American mothers and daughters.

Hodan *The power of Black mothers and their prayers is unmatched!*

After taking a quick sip of her drink and alerting people with her hand that she wanted to speak next, Eve beams into the microphone …

Eve I depended a lot on my mum and my good friends in uni cos it was weird, uni was the biggest trial for me … it was mostly my mum cos I had to learn to be humble then. I never wanted to admit to anyone that I didn't know it, it was when I got to A-Levels so … and then even at A-Levels, it was more like the teachers I had weren't really influencers, they were more like there to just guide me. So it was really my mum who I went to and was like 'mum I can't do this' and she was like 'yes you can', 'mum I can't do it', 'yes you can' and she'd sit with me and she'd try and understand what I was learning and yeah it was mainly my mum and I do owe a lot to her in terms of my educational experiences, it was mainly mummy.

The additional role of mothers, alongside teachers, is evident from *Eve*'s experiences, particularly as she didn't have the required extra support or encouragement that she needed – hence why she turned to her mother. This can be one of the many ways that anti-Black gendered racism can occur and *Eve*'s mother not only counters it by instilling self-belief, she also, in a similar way to *Shamari*'s mother, actively 'rolls up her sleeves' to hold her hand and walk with her so that she stays on track. Powell and Coles (2021), in a paper on Black mothers making sense of and supporting their children in the anti-Black, US education system, write how they actively resist anti-Black narratives by not internalizing them. I believe *Nia-Elise*'s mother practises this when she counters her self-doubt. Resuming from where she had left off and building on from *Eve*'s story, *Hodan* marvels at the huge influence her own mum had been to her and her sister within their education.

Hodan Yeah 100 per cent, I think my mum got it from her mum which is why I got it and I am probably going to give it to my kids and it is probably gonna trickle down, but I think with my mum, she was very much … she just wanted the best, like she still wants the best for us and when you are younger is when you can influence them more. If she was to wait until uni to start tryna be an advocate for my education, I probably wouldn't have got anywhere in life. So, I view education as the foundations of life because it is a lot harder if you can't read or write, because if you do want to become a business owner and you can't read contracts, you are gonna get swindled out of a lot of things, or when you go to uni and you get like your student finance and stuff, if you can't read them or depend on other people, your life is now in the hands of someone else. So, reading and writing is not the only thing that you take from education, it's those basics and my mum was like y'know 'education is everything, you don't want to ever feel disadvantaged because you haven't done something'. So it doesn't mean to say that you need to do A-Levels, it doesn't mean to say that you need to go to uni, but I do believe that from reception to year 11, those years especially are important, especially because that's when you are taught the basics of life like maths and English, y'know writing proper sentences and grammar and maths, just learning basic adding and subtraction, multiplication, division – it helps and I think my mum was just like 'you might hate it now but trust me you'll look back and say thank God I did it!'

By invoking the intergenerational resilience, support and encouragement passed down from her grandmother to her mother to her, *Hodan* illustrates the high family value placed on education and how 'for centuries, Black families have fought against these [anti-Black] narratives and the systems that these narratives have given birth to' (Powell and Coles 2021: 91). She further emphasizes how the high value on education, which she was raised to have, is due to it being seen as one of the few ways to have 'the best'. By going on to discuss 'education as the foundations of life' that provides 'the basics of life like maths and English', which, although it is the case for every student, when thinking about the histories of Black communities, has additional meaning due to the fight to be formally educated. In this sense, education is regarded as a life source as it was often historically denied, in a formal setting, based on not viewing Black people as intellectually capable or fully human. Therefore, Black women view education as an obligation to obtain, precisely because of the significant and political role it has played in former times as well as in the present day.

Once again, all of the women 'mmmmmmed' in unified agreement as Shamari also clicked her fingers.

Nia-Elise My mum has always pushed our education and I think it's because … because she was very aware of the fact that in her educational experience, that her race and ethnicity played a big part in it and she didn't want that to be true for me and my siblings so she pushed us a lot and we were never really given scope to think that we could be failures or that our race would be part of our failure, so when I heard that in school, it didn't make sense.

Nia-Elise shows how her mother's own experiential knowledge in the education system is a huge contributor to her desire for the same barriers not to exist within her children's trajectories. Interestingly, by highlighting the contradictory messages she received from her mother that failure was not linked to being Black, versus hearing that it was in school, shows the role that educational institutions can have in reversing the positive sense of self many Black families spend a great deal of time equipping their children with (Vincent et al. 2012a, 2012b).

Hamda *Thanks babygirls, I appreciate you all for sharing this! I think we all need to make sure that we tell our mums how much we love them after this!*

Everyone looks at each other nodding.

Hodan *So, I wanted to pick up on what you said Nia-Elise about the discrepancy between your mum teaching you at home, that your race should not be thought of as contributing to your failure, but how at school, failure was often attributed to race as that's all you heard. Can any of you babygirls think of and share any examples of when you felt your race, ethnicity and/or gender was affirmed in the classroom or lecture theatre?*

Shamari *Again, I can only remember being truly seen and affirmed by Black women teachers or lecturers.*

Being seen and affirmed by Black women teachers/lecturers

As argued by Howell et al. (2020: 27) in their paper that develops Black Gaze Theory by centring Black women educators in the USA, they are crucial in Black educational journeys and experiences because they simply 'humanise Black students in their classrooms'. In this way, they are reversing anti-Black, gendered racism which erases and/or positions, views and treats Black girls and women as non-human, such as positioning them as 'unruly' as discussed in Chapter 5. However, it should not be forgotten that Black women teachers and lecturers are also susceptible to the anti-Black gendered oppression that influences the experiences of Black girl and women students, and they are unsupported as well (Pitts 2021). Here, the ways in which Black students are seen and affirmed by Black women teachers and lecturers will be explored.

Nia-Elise *Good question Hodan. Ms Robinson* was my favourite teacher at school, she just … she was like a mother to us, she really treated us well and she gave credit where credit was due and she taught very well and she knew how to … I wanted to say … she used to pattern us but she used to keep us in line all the time – oh and *Miss Achebe* cos they came as a pair cos they were best friends so one was like … probably cos she was African as well, the *Ms Robinson* was Caribbean and *Miss Achebe* is African and she would be like 'Listen I will sort you out' whereas, *Ms Robinson* would pattern you but *Miss Achebe* was more closer to home I guess cos the way she would approach it is like how my aunt, who is like a mum to me would approach it.

The fact that *Nia-Elise* mentions the cultural backgrounds of her favourite teachers suggests that she may believe that this is a key reason why she appreciated their teaching practice. This can be linked to them having a deeper understanding of *Nia-Elise* and other Black students' upbringings which can create extra rapport. By remembering how her two favourite Black women teachers 'treated us well' while also 'getting them together' and in line when they misbehaved to 'pattern us' provided both discipline as well as support, and illustrates balance and how, you could argue, all teacher-student relationships should be.

Hamda *How about the rest of you babygirls? What about you, Shamari?*

Shamari So actually there was this Trinidadian science teacher, she was actually Asian, but she was Trinidadian and she came here in her teens, so she had a very mixed-up accent, she called herself Trini. So, she had an assembly one day talking about home and talking about music from the Islands and people were like 'which islands are you referring to?' So the concept of her being Asian and Caribbean was just lost to the white kids in school, but to the Black Caribbeans amongst us, we got it, to everyone else, they were confused … She actually used to look out for us Black lot, subtly, whether she did it on purpose or not I don't know, but I think there was an element of trying to make sure that the ethnic lot stayed. So you know when we got around year 10, people kinda start to lose their minds [laughs] and started to stay out a bit too late, she kinda made sure people stayed on track and she'd keep you on that path – not that she didn't do it for the other kids – but I think she knew that if it went left for them, mum and dad could save them, they would just give them a business or a house, it would be fine [laughs] but for us, we didn't have that background option, this was it, if we did well we'd be fine, if we don't do so well things could be harder for us and so there was … she was one of those few that made sure that we kinda stayed on the path we were supposed to stay on.

Even though *Shamari*'s teacher is not racialized as Black, her cultural background of Caribbean and Trinidadian can be seen to be located in close proximity to 'African Diasporic Blackness' (Andrews 2016: 2063). Moreover, based on *Shamari*'s account, the teacher in question identifies and connects with the Black British students, particularly of Caribbean heritage, in ways that white teachers cannot. This calls into question how the prominence of nationality, race, ethnicity and culture can interchange in particular contexts, along with how political Blackness may provide 'strategic essentialism' (Spivak 1988, 1996), that is 'a political strategy whereby differences are temporarily downplayed, and unity assumed for the sake of achieving political goals' (Eide 2016: 2). In a similar way to what *Nia-Elise* experienced, or in this case educational 'success', *Shamari*'s teacher also seemed to provide more encouragement and support to the Black students as she was aware that 'things could be harder for us' and ensured that they 'stayed on the path we were supposed to stay on'.

Eve *I didn't have those experiences in school.* But I remember a Black woman lecturer at university … she was really helpful, she taught me in second year, she was on one module, it was just so refreshing to be in that lecture. It was the second half of second year – this is the point where I was literally like 'I actually want to drop out' – not even joking, before her, before that half of the semester, the first half of second semester I was so over it. The only thing that saved me during the first half was Caribbean poetry – that was massive for me and that literally kept me on, I was ready to go except for that module … The fact that she could put that on the curriculum, the fact that we would have lectures or we had to sit and watch *Formation* [American superstar Beyonce's music video, released on 6 February 2016] and talk about Black hair and Black women and … she made it so it wasn't like 'ok this is for all the Black people' even though there was like one row of us just sitting down and enjoying *Formation*, but it was still like 'now we have watched it, go and talk to someone about it'. Seminars were never just dead, cos I don't know how it was in the rest of uni, but in my seminars it was just … you could sit and not do the reading and be fine in the seminar, but she would never allow that, so that was good.

The fact that *Eve* states that she was considering dropping out of her course before she had this particular Black woman lecturer highlights her significant role. This is because, before she came, *Eve* felt disconnected from the curriculum as she was unable to relate to it. Not only was she able to see someone who looked like her, but with the arrival of her Black woman lecturer came a more diverse and inclusive curriculum through centring Blackness via music, hair, women, etc. which she could finally relate to. This impact of whitewashed curricula and identity within teaching is touched upon by Hancock et al. (2020) who showed how many Black women teachers are 'aware of how this white-male perspective viewed Black students and other nonwhite people … [and] felt it was her duty as a holistic teacher to use cultural influences, relevant media and music, as well as alternative perspectives, to educate her students' (p. 412). It seems that *Shamari*'s lecturer was doing the same and is similarly apparent in the next extract from *Yaa*:

Yaa Yeah, I had one Black lecturer, *Nancy*, and I really liked her … because she was teaching my seminar. So, she was teaching my course and I feel like that's when I first really got introduced to Black Feminism and stuff in my second year. So that was when I was properly introduced to alternative ways of feminism and it just … yeah it was kinda like a stepping stone or something, it's like you knew – like I knew about these things before but it's just the ways to incorporate it within my degree. It was just like 'ok, I can incorporate it' and I think since then, my narrative – cos I did an essay on third world feminism or girls yeah, and that was really heavily impacted with Black feminists and stuff … so like my narratives changed in terms of how I like … it's just kinda the outview. There was one other Black woman, she's a Canadian lesbian woman and she taught us as well and that was on … again on gender narratives, that was really interesting and the thing is as well, she kinda introduced a lot of new material and a lot of new thoughts into seminars – it doesn't necessarily have to like … the thing is with the two Black women seminar leaders I had, they really used their seminars to really talk about race and all that stuff which was sadly missing from the rest of the course.

Yaa begins by naming one Black woman lecturer, *Nancy*, before highlighting a second to illustrate how both were crucial when it came to including Blackness within the course content. She also shows how the introduction of topics such as Black Feminism within the course assisted her in changing her narratives and being affirmed to include it within her essays and thus learning. For Lane (2018), much of what *Nia-Elise, Shamari, Yaa* and *Eve* describe about their Black woman teachers and lecturers can be defined as a 'politicised ethic of care' in that, they 'cultivate viable social and academic identities … to engage in critical and culturally responsive forms of caring for these youth' (p. 285).

Hodan *I get what you mean about feeling disconnected from your course at uni and searching for ways to see yourself and your experiences within the content! It's crazy how it is left, in most of your experiences, to the Black women lecturers to include it!*

Nia-Elise *Exactly, you are so right.*

Eve *It's a damn shame.*

Hamda I don't know … with some seminar groups you would mainly be the only one or maybe one of two Black girls in your seminar and you would be very conscious of that. But I was really quiet and I didn't really speak and it's funny cos I had one seminar – a Black leader and I feel like she was really on my case to … to speak and I felt like … do you know when you just feel like there's that teacher that's picking on you cos they want you to do well and just not fade into the background? And I think it was because obviously she was Black and I was Black, I don't know, I just feel like you are always aware that you are a Black woman in the education system and you are … consciously you just have a perception of what someone is thinking of you, which then influences how you act, so yeah … she wanted me to take up space and use my voice.

Hamda credits her Black woman seminar leader as getting her to speak in seminars as she didn't feel confident to do so due to her other seminar experiences. This suggests that while other white seminar leaders may have left her to be quiet – possibly due to limiting beliefs about Black women students, her Black woman lecturer held high expectations and encouraged her to 'take up space and use my voice' and thus validating her existence in the class. Watson (2018) finds in her research that Black women educators employ a 'Praxis of politicised care' which she suggests has three parts: 1) soulful and politicized purpose driving high expectations; 2) building relationships through vulnerability, encouragement, communication and recognition; and 3) redefining success and envisioning paths for the future. *Hamda*'s Black woman lecturer was exercising a similar praxis to her. This aligns with a study by Gershenshon et al. (2016) in America which concludes that Black women teachers have the highest expectations of Black students.

Hodan *Maybe there is a correlation between the lack of Black teachers and lecturers in general, and specifically Black women ones, and why the curriculum is so white and why Black students are so disconnected. But also why other students do not respect our contributions because they don't really understand or know about them as they were never properly or consistently taught about it!*

Eve *You are right, and it's a damn shame!* [shaking her head along with the others].

Hamda *On that note, let's take a short break and come back for the final section.*

The women take the opportunity to unwind a little. While some of them decide to get some fresh air in the garden, others go to nibble on the feast leftovers, and a few take it in turns to use the bathroom. It is a nice break, filled with deeper connections and laughter, as now the women are completely comfortable with one another after eating together and divulging their personal educational histories in a space where they felt safe.

[shouts] *Aight babygirls! It's time to begin again!*

Hodan *They all take their seats, reposition their microphones and proceed to remember, reflect and share.*

Speaking to our younger selves and future generations of Black girls and women

For Collins (2000: 251) a key component of BFE is 'lived experience as a criterion of meaning' or, in other words, that 'knowledge claims made by Black women who have first-hand encounters about what they share and can also cite examples increases credibility'. Additionally, Collins (2000: vii) also writes that 'oppressed groups are frequently placed in the situation of being listened to only if we frame our ideas in the language that is familiar to and comfortable for a dominant group. This requirement often changes the meaning of our ideas and works to elevate the ideas of dominant groups.'

Based on this, as well as the overall educational journeys and experiences of the Black women graduates as narrated via the composite characters of *Shamari, Eve, Nia-Elise, Chika, Yaa, Hodan* and *Hamda,* and due to the power of their wisdom, I will allow the words of advice to their younger selves – which will also be useful for future generations of Black girls and women – to speak for themselves.

Hodan *So babygirls, it has been so delightful hearing about all of your educational experiences and journeys! We discussed how we all had basically created different strategies to give us strength and resilience. It was so fascinating to hear how Yaa used colour to find balance and to create a positive mindset. It was also so fascinating to hear how some of you gained power from your cultures and religion or spirituality. I loved the African accents which brought your examples to life!*

Everyone bursts into laughter as they remember.

Hodan *I personally found it so lovely to reflect and hear about the supportive Black women who played such important roles in our education. Particularly our mums, oh and Black women teachers or lecturers – who rarely get a mention! What would we have done without them, please?*
Shamari *For real!*
Hamda *So based on all your wonderful insights, I am really intrigued to hear about what you would say to your younger selves?*
Hodan *Oooooooh, I like this, Ham! So, if you could picture yourself, perhaps at four or five years old, you are just about to start primary school – I think you already mentioned being around this age when a teacher told your mum you weren't smart enough to get into that secondary school, Chika. But yeah, you have all your hopes, dreams and are excited for all the possibilities as you begin your educational journeys.*
Hamda *Exactly! What would you tell that little Black girl or another Black girl or young woman who is currently journeying in the education system that you have just left, based on all that you experienced and now know?*
Eve *What a great but big question!*

There is a short pause, filled with a collective 'hmmmmmm' as they all think long and hard.

Shamari [raising hand] *I don't mind going first.* I think with a lot of young Black women, we feel we have to be exceptional; we have to be magic because if we're not all these things, we're not good enough – do you get what I mean? It's ok … even though I scream 'Black excellence' with vim, it's ok to be 'Black mediocre', 'Black ok.' It's just ok to be ok, you don't have to be the be-all and end-all. You don't have to be first!

Yaa *Yesssssss! I hear you and I agree!*

Nia-Elise *I would say* … never stop learning! I am still learning to this day, I did one course after uni and I am looking to do another course soon and like little bits and pieces. So never stop learning but also be thankful for every day that you've got. I have lost people close to me over the last couple of years and I never thought I would – it's weird – so take every day … you do something, set something to achieve and do it even if it is something small, like going to the bank and finally depositing the money that you have had in your purse, do it. Set something to do – if it is complimenting four people a day – do it! Set yourself tasks and actually do them and I think just be yourself. Be true to who you are, don't think that because you don't act a certain way that you're not a good person or you're not doing what other people are doing cos people who work for charities are always on LinkedIn or Facebook like 'yeah I am doing a social run this week and I have raised £5,000'. Don't think that cos you are not doing it you are not making a change in the world – you are, you are making a change!

Hamda *That's beautiful, I like that, definitely never stop learning!*

Eve I think maybe something about taking time for yourself outside of … whether it's at sixth form, uni – taking time for yourself to just relax, just get what you need to get done, like a chunk or whatever, go home, just do what it is that you need to do just by yourself. I think for me, it's what I needed during the time where things were really difficult. I just needed to spend some time on my own, even when things were fine and I had like ….say if I had work to do, I just wanted to be by myself and get the work done, but it's ok to be by yourself. It's ok to y'know … to just take some time out for yourself and just have a night in, do what it is you need to do.

Hamda *That's great advice, Eve!*

Hodan I'd say work hard – work as hard as you can! Cos you may think 'ah this is really hard right now', but the next stage is always harder like GCSEs, like A-Levels are always harder than GCSEs, uni's always harder than A-Levels and stuff like that. Just be sure about what you want to do before … don't go to uni just because it's like 'ah everybody else is going' – make sure you have a plan and know why you are doing that degree.

Yaa *On that note, I would say*, pay attention in class! Yeah, pay attention in class, probably read more … read more and different types of things,

I always like to read but probably … say you are doing something in social science, read a bit more around that…and be more aware as you can about things and how it affects you as a Black person because I find now, it's only now I am maybe able to offer a contribution about certain topics and I think that not being able to participate in conversations earlier was because I wasn't in the social settings that had that kinda conversation so, I just didn't know. I couldn't offer anything to it because I didn't know anything about it and even now, I wouldn't say 'oh yes I know about such and such' but I mean, at least you can listen, offer an explanation or not, so that's the advice I would give my younger person, and in terms of like assignments and academics, get the work done early and then you can relax after rather than putting yourself under pressure, because I found under pressure, some things you can perform better, but other times you can't because you are stressed out and you can't enjoy it and it becomes a burden and I think the anxiety of completing it stresses you out [laughs].

Shamari [laughing] *If only I was told that!!*

Chika I'd say embrace the experiences, don't enter anything thinking that you won't come out of it because you will. Listen to what people say and how people say it, but YOU at the end of the day get to decide whether you keep that person around. At the end of the day, the decisions are yours in terms of what you want to be and what you want to become. You can't depend on anyone else to make certain life choices for you. Learn from absolutely everything, good, bad and indifferent and I'd say don't get caught in the clouds, ride the valleys. I mean I'd listen to coaches and stuff and they talk about mountains and valleys and you can't have a mountain without a valley so you have to go low before you can go high, so I definitely believe in riding the rollercoaster … but also I would say to my younger self, don't internalize everything cos it's only going to be detrimental to you, and forgive as quickly as you can.

Hodan *What about you, Ham?*

Hamda The best is yet to come. You go to uni and you think 'oh my god, this is life, I am gonna leave home and I am gonna work, that's all I'm gonna do, then I'm gonna get married and have kids and that's all I'm gonna do', and you start to think like that. But honestly, when you leave uni – the experience you get just interacting with the world, and actually being an adult and having to manage your own finances and all these things. Don't be afraid. Definitely don't be afraid and don't think that you have experienced it all. I think that when we are at uni we think 'oh my God!' and you think that you have gone through it all, like 'oh my God this is so hard! Life only gets harder from here!' But you haven't, there is still so much more to experience!

Hodan *That's so true and a wonderful way to end this amazing episode! Thank you all for taking the time to participate in reflecting on 'strength, resilience and Black women's power in education'! You are all truly amazing, strong, resilient, powerful and beautiful babygirls! May you continue to rise – regardless of the circumstances!*

All the babygirls thank Hodan and Hamda as they share their gratitude and compliments. In normal fashion, the 'Choppin' & Chattin' Babygirlz' jingle plays, signifying the end of the episode and the button is pressed to stop the recording. The babygirls, now feeling reaffirmed, even more powerful and inspired, hug, chatter and exchange contact details to stay connected.

8

Now Is the Time to Overstand!

Figure 8 *Every babygirl should be supported to become a happy, healthy and fulfilled Black woman graduate*

Based on the insights shared throughout this book about Black women in the English education system, I argue that **now is the time to Overstand**. Here, I borrow from the style, sound and wordplay of Rastafari Dread talk (Pollard 1979, 1982), 'where the lexicon changes to reflect the philosophical position of the speaker' (1982: 20). To 'Overstand' 'implies more than basic understanding, something like having "the big picture"' (Marley Natural 2022). In more detail, to 'Overstand' signifies 'when certain Ights (heights) of knowledge and wisdom have been reached, Rastafari say that something is Overstood, in the sense that if InI[13] understands something, then InI are not underneath the knowledge, InI are over it, so InI say Overstand, never under' (Sobers 2016). This philosophy and language has travelled across the Black diaspora through music, texts and movements forming 'Black counterhegemonic circuits of knowledge in the UK' (Palmer 2020b: 98) where, 'redefining and reconstructing the dominant language can only become a form of self-empowerment' (Henry 2012: 362). It is hoped that this book will move readers towards a 'certain Ights (heights) of knowledge and wisdom' about how the English education system operates, through the experiences and journeys of some Black British women graduates.

This final chapter will make sense of the previous chapters, illustrating that the problem lies not with me or you as individuals but in the way the education system, the labour market and wider society works. I will also reflect on how we can learn and heal individually and perhaps collectively from the educational journeys and experiences of Black British women graduates – which may be personally relatable. Lastly, I will end by speaking to my younger self to release my own educational trauma in the hopes of beginning to heal. But first, I will illustrate when I began to Overstand the education system.

* * *

It was Wednesday 25th September, in the year 2019. That was the day, exactly three years since I had started my Ph.D. and right on my minimum period of study.[14] *I was tired. No. I was actually exhausted. Burnt out. Mentally, physically, spiritually, emotionally, intellectually, and any other '-ly' there was! My cup was well and truly empty – and so was my teapot and kettle. However, I had already notified my university's research office of my intention to submit at least three months in advance. I couldn't stop now or, it would seem, anytime soon. I had never stopped to be honest. All I knew how to do was to 'keep going', to 'never give up', to 'do my best' and to 'never stop'.*

'Don't stop' even if it is difficult.
'Don't give up' even when you are rejected.
'Keep going' even if you are the only one.
'Do your best' even if you are tired.
Whatever it is, 'never stop'.

Perhaps what it really meant, and what I always knew it meant is that I, of all people, could not afford to stop or to give up. Because if I did (and if I ever do), where would I be? Who would I be? Maybe, I would become part of the statistics that get thrown around to back up negative narratives about the failure of Black people – narratives that I had worked and sometimes even fought my entire life to remain out of.

In the weeks leading up to submission, I scrambled to complete all the required finishing touches to my thesis, like printing out several copies and then taking the hardcopies to the campus print shop to bind, etc. Though I was nearly finished, I was running into delay after delay, for example, issues with printing, despite my meticulous planning. As always, my mind and body went into autopilot, remembering how I could not stop and that I must keep going, as I determinedly used the little energy I had left to lift myself over each final barrier, to pass the finish line, in the hopes of receiving my just rewards.

At around 1pm on that same day in September 2019, I submitted my thesis and, after a prolonged six-month wait, at the start of the global Covid-19 lockdowns in March 2020. I passionately defended my thesis in a virtual viva voce, passing with minor corrections.

Alone, in a victorious and disbelieving solitude, I joyfully and tearfully danced in my living room, praising the most high to the gospel song 'I Made It' by Fantasia featuring Tye Tribbet. I could not believe that I had made it to this point or that my hard work, dedication and effort had resulted in passing. After more than twenty years of continuous formal education, from primary school until doctoral study, I had finally completed my own educational steeplechase.

I had done good, succeeded against all the odds, done the remarkable and the unexpected, made myself and everyone else proud. I had exuded #BlackGirlMagic and #BlackExcellence.

I had made it right?
So why didn't I feel like the cat with all the cream?
I had made it right?
So why did I feel like a boxer who was battered after completing twelve rounds in the ring?
I had made it right?
Or had I really?
Tell me, what more could I have done?

It's not *you* or *me*, it's the education system, the labour market and society at large

After my own experiences completing the *educational steeplechase*, I could not wait to leave the education system and be done! But, because I had been navigating the education system for the majority of my life, I was very much institutionalized and could not imagine a life without the rules and regulations, the structures and deadlines, or the strategic planning for the next stages, to build upon the previous ones. But, after completing my Ph.D., I now Overstand that there was **nothing more I could do** educationally. Not only had I exhausted the academic route and achieved the highest qualification, I had exhausted myself. I had *just* made it to the end of the end. I may have also been going through post-graduation blues also known as graduate blues or post-university depression (and other similar variations) which many graduates experience after the completion of their studies – 'a kind of depression, non-clinical, but significant, a combination of restlessness, confusion, and a sense of lacking place' (Stamp 2020). However, little did I realize that the inequalities and barriers that I had managed to navigate and overcome within the education system simply continue in the 'congested and competitive graduate labour market' (Tomlinson 2008). It seems that there, identities and background also become additional measuring and separating tools, regardless of grades, impressive CVs or institutions attended, particularly for Black British graduates who are especially disadvantaged. For example, a report about graduate outcomes in London by the Social Market Foundation (2021) found that Black graduates earn less than their white, Asian and mixed-heritage counterparts six months after graduating. The report also highlights that only 25 per cent of Black graduates earn above £25,000 per annum compared to 38 per cent of Asian graduates and 30 per cent of white graduates. When it comes to securing graduate jobs, in 2021 it was reported that Black British applicants were three times less likely to gain a place on the UK Government's Civil Service 'Fast Stream' elite graduate scheme, compared to their white counterparts (Mohdin and Thomas 2022). When it comes to progressing in one's career, a report by The London School of Economics (LSE) and The Inclusion Initiative (TII), stated that, after analysing results from a seventeen-year period, the team of researchers, Almeida et al. (2021) showed that Black women are the least likely to be among the UK's top earners compared to any other racial or gender group. Nonetheless, one way that Black women have acted to redress this has been done in America through the creation of the National Black Women's Equal Pay Day, celebrated on 3rd August in 2021, 21st September in 2022 and 27th July in 2023 to call attention to the fact that 'Black women must work an additional 214 days to catch up to what white, non-Hispanic men made' (Corbett 2021; National Today 2022). Perhaps a similar day is needed in England!

As argued in Chapter 2, society was not made for or by Black women. Neither was the education system as demonstrated in Chapters 3, 4, 5 and 6. Therefore, it is no surprise that the labour market is not made to accommodate us either. Once we do enter the workplace, we may go on to encounter experiences of 'pet to threat' which Thomas et al. (2013) identifies as a common experience for many Black women early in their careers who are 'seen initially as likeable, moldable novices, [and] become more suspect as they grow in their jobs and exert the influence and authority they have earned. Their increased agency is perceived to threaten the status quo in a culture typically dominated by white males'. This can also lead to Black women graduates experiencing the 'almost impenetrable "concrete ceiling"' which would halt career progression (Teixeira et al. 2021).

While I briefly had some time as an employee in the corporate world away from academia, as if coming full circle – where I had run away from academia due to my challenging Ph.D. experiences – despite my goal to become a lecturer, and the disturbing prospects for Black women academics (Rollock 2019, 2021), I ran right back! I craved intellectual stimulation, creativity and independence. I craved a profession – defined by my parents as a stimulating role where your skills and expertise are asked for, instead of a dead-end job where you just follow instructions. My wish was granted when I was supported to apply for and was offered an academic position, albeit a fixed contract, focusing on my passions which also provided me with the time, resources and guidance to write this book. For me, while the academy is far from perfect, hooks' (1994: 207) words ring true to my experiences when she reminds us that 'the academy is not paradise. But learning is a place where paradise can be created. The classroom, with all its limitations, remains a location of possibility'. My time in the corporate world provided me with space, time and first-hand experiences to help me to Overstand the relationship between the education system as well as the labour market, the plight of many Black British women graduates, including myself, and that we needed, wanted and deserved way more than what I termed *burnt breadcrumbs*, as described in Chapter 6.

Once I Overstood the relationship of the education system and the labour market with Black women, it reignited my motivation to do something about it. First, I started with myself. I decided to stop giving my everything to organizations that would continue to exhaust me and trigger such things as mental illnesses in which Black women are more likely to suffer from (Geronimus 1992 and 2023, Gov.uk 2017). I decided to learn how to rest – a process I am still learning – as I did not actually know how to. In fact, the words of Lorde, 'caring for self is not self-indulgence. It is an act of self-preservation, and that is an act of political warfare' (Lorde 1988: 205), became my encouragement.

The education system is unequal, problematic and unfair. It needs more than pockets of collective, community-led and individual resistance; it needs change – but it must be top-down, structural change. I can't make it change and neither can you individually – but we can Overstand and act accordingly while collectively creating and finding alternatives to create an education system that operates differently while also protecting Black youth.

Making sense of the educational journeys and experiences of Black girls and women

Over the course of this book, the composite characters of *Shamari*, *Eve*, *Chika*, *Nia-Elise*, *Yaa*, *Hamda* and *Hodan* are created in line with the CRT method of counter-storytelling to amplify overlooked stories and experiences. They lend themselves to analysing and challenging the unequal power wielded in the dominant, white, societal and educational narratives (Delgado 1989, 1993) and they come to life 'by taking elements of intersecting stories to create the foundation for a character' (Cook and Dixson 2013: 1246). Their hairstyles and features, their settings and relationships, their personalities and educational experiences and journeys are the foundations that, alongside references to key songs by Black women artists from across the diaspora, centres, affirms and celebrates this unique but overlooked group. Through the composite characters, I merge the individual educational stories of the forty-two Black British women, as told in the in-depth interviews in both my masters and Ph.D. research. In a similar way to that outlined by Solarzano and Yosso (2001: 488), the goal 'is to engage the characters in a real and critical dialogue focused around ... findings from the interviews, literature, and experiences', to offer 'an accessible and critical insight to this set of concepts, ideas, and experiences'. The composite characters aided in narrating and answering the original research question which was:

What are the educational journeys and experiences of Black British women graduates?

More specifically, my research sought to explore and gain a clearer understanding about:

1. The characteristics of the educational journeys of Black British women graduates.
2. The key decisions and choices that have shaped their journeys.
3. The role of the family and extended networks in shaping these educational journeys and experiences.
4. The role of ethnicity, cultural background and social class, along with race and gender in mediating the aspirations, strategies and decision-making of Black British women graduates throughout their educational journeys.

In Chapter 1, I employed 'Blackgirl autoethnography' as defined by Boylorn (2016: 46):

> to discuss and situate a way of being in and seeing/experiencing the world through a raced and gendered lens … as a way to talk about embodied, critical, and culturally situated research that begins and/or ends at home, in the bodies we live in, the people we live with, and the social circumstances we live through.

By doing this, I provided the context of the education system, through my own educational journey, illustrating the different types of institutions I attended, and how this shaped my experiences, alongside the important role of my intersecting raced, classed, religious and gendered identities, my cultural background and ethnicity. I also showed the important role my family and networks played in helping me to navigate all the complexities and challenges I encountered, as well as my choices, aspirations, strategies and decision-making. In line with BFE, I purposely engage in this self-reflexive interrogation through autoethnography to provide readers with an understanding of my positionality and how it influenced my life and this research. In doing so, I am 'taking into account the situated nature of knowledge and [my] identities in relation to [the] research participants', and 'influence of social position and the politics of identity on the interactions between researcher and research participants, and the role of power and identity in everyday lives and research' (Kohl and McCutcheon 2015: 751–2). My positionality is important because it motivates my research interests and indicates why I speak, write and focus on this topic. As I also use a CRT framework, autoethnography facilitates utilizing my experiential knowledge to 'speak back' to the dominant (white) majoritarian story (Solarzano and Yosso 2002). Reflexivity is also strongly advocated by Bourdieu whose theory of practice also informs this research (Bourdieu and Wacquant 1992; Maton 2003; Kenway and McLeod 2004). Additionally, my educational story is another contribution to the insights shared by the forty-two Black British women graduates featured in this book, charting my journey from primary school to Ph.D. and it is a way for me to bring my whole self to the book as, in the words of Lorde (2009: 182–3), 'if I do not bring all of who I am to whatever I do – then I bring nothing of lasting worth, for I have withheld my essence'. However, this book does not seek, nor claim, to represent or speak for all Black British women graduates – which is an impossible task. This is the power of intersectionality, which is embedded within BFE and CRT, and weaves throughout the research. It is through intersectionality that an increasing awareness that there is no single 'Black woman' story in such a diverse group is illustrated (Arya 2012).

The aim of Chapter 2, where I provide the background for why Black girls and women are devalued in school and higher education, is to provide a broader context about the conditions within which they navigate. *Shamari* invites readers into the anti-Black world that fails to respect or protect Black peoples' humanity and how this manifests over and over in events like the Windrush Scandal in 2018 and the reemergence of the global Black Lives Matter movement in 2020. Narrowing the focus, I then illustrate the depictions and positioning of Black women who are erased and invisible in British contexts, in contrast to being hypervisible and negatively stereotyped in America. The intersection of Black women's raced and gendered identities is considered in relation to social class which again highlights the prominence of anti-Black racism and how it influences their status, regardless of the resources they may or may not have access to. Based on all these observations, the chapter ends by foregrounding the rest of the book, showing why it is no surprise that the education system, which is a microcosm of society, is also anti-Black, sexist and classist.

Chapter 3 delves deep into what an anti-Black, sexist and classist education system looks like as operationalized by my metaphor of *educational steeplechase*. While others are competing in a marathon, many Black women are running in a 26-mile *educational steeplechase*, with limited training (knowledge and understanding) and water supplies (accepted resources); jumping over multiple hurdles (anti-Black racism, sexism, classism); as well as devising unconventional strategies to overcome other unexpected barriers that may emerge as a direct consequence. Therefore, it is truly a complex and tiring feat for this group to complete the *educational steeplechase* to become graduates in the English education system. *Eve* assists in presenting the argument that meritocracy is outdated and abstract and was never created for an equal society, yet alone education system. In the absence of acknowledging or rejecting meritocracy, it is no surprise that in such an unequal education system white, upper- and middle-class boys, men, girls and women will continue to be privileged and aided to progress. *Eve* then talks us through what many Black British girls and women endure when having to merge opposing cultures and how they encounter the abrupt process of 'othering' in the education system – which happens via an awareness of the differences in ways of being, the Eurocentric and whitewashed curricula and the limiting beliefs and negative stereotyping that ultimately leaves Black British girls and women being misunderstood within educational spaces and places. *Eve* also provides insights that fulfilling the desire to win the *educational steeplechase* is not made easy by the internalized pressure to fit in, alongside the unrealistic expectations to do well which fail to see how the group's raced, gendered and classed identities put them at a disadvantage within white educational settings.

Chika is the voice of Chapter 4, detailing what it is like being the only Black girl or woman within PW educational places and spaces. In many ways, similarities can be drawn to what Anderson (2022) observes in his book about the enduring impact of people of colour as Black bodies in white space. Such educational places and spaces include schools outside of inner cities in suburban and rural areas, as well as grammar or private schools and sixth form colleges within those, and elite or pre-1992 universities. This also extends to educational experiences and journeys characterized as 'being the only one' in certain university subject areas and undergraduate courses. She articulates the ways that whiteness in particular manifests within these spaces, specifically focusing on elite whiteness that shrouds private schools and elite universities and the knowledge, preparation and financial resources needed in order to circumvent the restricted access. Once inside these PW educational settings, many Black girls are left feeling like what Collins (1986, 1999) defines as 'outsiders within', that is not truly ever fitting in or being accepted. However, on the flipside, they also experience becoming disconnected from themselves, others and their wider community as their educational experiences and journeys begin to socialize them into or closer to the norms and values of elite whiteness. While these experiences and journeys can be painful, they may have some advantages such as becoming an expert in elite whiteness and acquiring different types of resources, encouragement and support – all of which cannot be gained anywhere else and provides benefits when, for example, they enter certain workplace settings.

The experiences of 'being the only one' are contrasted in Chapter 5 when *Nia-Elise* shares what it is like 'being one of many' Black girls or women within PGM educational spaces and places. These educational spaces and places have higher numbers of GM, or, in other words, pupils and students from African, Caribbean, Asian and other racially minoritized backgrounds. I characterize these educational settings as being typically found in inner-city state schools and sixth form/further education colleges, as well as post-1992 universities. *Nia-Elise* illustrates the positives gained from such spaces and places like the appreciation and understanding of self and cultural diversity, as well as strength in numbers which can provide valuable connections, solidarity and affirmation. On the other hand, she reveals how PGM educational settings are still largely controlled by white authority and how Black girls and women are positioned and treated as 'unruly' within them. She also questioned whether PGM educational institutions limit educational opportunities due to the racialized, classed access and the inequality of resources which stunt the growth and exposure of GM students, specifically Black girls and women (Li 2021).

Against this backdrop, in Chapter 6, *Yaa* questions whether educational journeys and experiences culminate in educational 'success' or unnecessary stress. *Yaa* explores how society defines educational 'success' and what it takes to achieve in order to become a Black British woman graduate. She also highlights the unnecessary stresses such as working twice as hard to go half as far that characterize the experiences of many Black girls and women as a requirement of gaining educational 'success'. These reflections lead to Black women graduates considering alternative options with the aim of illustrating the need to redefine educational 'success', especially when it pertains to Black girls and women.

Finally, in Chapter 7, the introduction of *Hamda* and *Hodan* alongside the other composite characters brings them all together in conversation to pay homage to the strength, resilience and power that assisted them to the end of the *educational steeplechase*. The sharing of strategies employed to cultivate strength, resilience and power include having positive but determined mindsets and drawing from their culture, ethnicity, religion and spirituality. The important role of older Black women – their mothers and Black women lecturers and teachers – who can provide vital support, recognition and affirmation on their educational journeys and experiences is discussed. Lastly, they impart the crucial wisdom they learnt from their educational journeys and experiences to their younger selves and future generations of Black girls and women about how they believe the education system could be better navigated and challenged.

Overall, this book has illustrated that the educational journeys and experiences of Black British women graduates are varied and influenced by many different factors but unanimously underpinned by resilience, strength, perseverance and high aspirations to gain the necessary qualifications in order to provide further opportunities for themselves. By critiquing the narrow view of educational 'success', I have highlighted that meritocratic and neoliberal discourses of educational 'success' fail to acknowledge the structural inequalities and the restricted educational investment returns experienced by many 'successful' Black British women graduates. Though my findings illustrate that there are some shared characteristics of the educational journeys of Black British women graduates, the experiences shared are indicative of the participants in my masters and Ph.D. studies and are the basis on which more comments about Black women graduates in general can be made.

Employing my theoretical frameworks and applying these to my analysis of participant narratives has enabled me to identify a systemic social concern that is applicable to a particular heterogenous group. The theoretical frameworks of CRT and BTP are drawn upon and placed within the overarching context of BFE. It is through CRT and BTP that a sociological perspective is provided to articulate specific elements of the Black women's educational experiences and journeys, namely how race, racism, gender and social class are embedded into the institutional structures of the education system. With the incorporation of intersectionality, it weaves through, as well as brings together, the triad of BFE, CRT and BTP, with the recognition of the holistic identities of Black British women. In order to understand the educational journeys and experiences of Black British women graduates, it is imperative that there is a more nuanced understanding of the diversity within the group and how race, culture, ethnicity, gender, religion and social class identities intersect. This emphasizes the unequal power relations embedded within the education system and how for Black African and Black African-Caribbean British girls and women they can operate differently.

Moving forward: learning and healing from the educational experiences and journeys of Black British women graduates

This book highlights the anti-Black, racist, sexist and classist foundations of the education system that bring about the unique struggles and challenges that Black British girls and women will, as a consequence, inevitably encounter as they participate within it. Navigation within the English education system to become Black British women graduates can consist of mentally and psychologically draining processes, requiring additional energy which manifests in internalized pressure, mental health issues and, ultimately, restricted educational investment returns. Therefore, I advocate for **dismantling the education system** – or at least identifying and creating alternative, structural responses that can facilitate the reimagining of an English education system that caters for Black girls and women in an ethical and socially just manner that validates their histories, intersectional identities and experiences in ways that enable them to thrive. However, with the current UK Government, this is unlikely to ever be a priority – especially since the publishing of the Commission on Race and Ethnic Disparities' Sewell report in 2021 which significantly downplayed the role of racism in what they term 'modern British society'. The introduction of Political impartiality in English schools by the Department for Education in 2022 will not aid in honest, critical learning in the pursuit of social justice for children and young people either (Adams, 2022)! Though it must be noted that the UK Government has no mandate for education outside England. So how can we move forward within an increasingly unequal education system (Gillborn et al. 2012; Pennant 2020b; Wallace and Joseph-Salisbury 2022), which by its very nature, will continue to disadvantage Black students, especially Black girls and women?

Firstly, by employing the triad theoretical frameworks of BFE, CRT and BTP, while weaving in intersectionality throughout, I argue that it culminates in the Rastafari Dread talk of Overstanding to see the 'bigger picture' of the education system, as experienced by Black British girls and women. Through Overstanding, alternative, Black-centred knowledge and narratives can be created and shared for collective learning and healing from any educational trauma that may have been encountered from the point of entry to graduation and beyond. With this new Overstanding, it is hoped that the education system can be both navigated easier and challenged. As previously noted, the word 'Overstand' is rooted in Rastafari traditions and Sobers (2016) explains how 'language is and has long been one of the tools that Rastafari use to decolonise and resist'. This resistance in language lends itself to the ways in which the mind can be better equipped to Overstand the anti-Black, gendered racism and classism in the education system, and it is through the research and experiential knowledge shared in this book that the insights and wisdom can help individuals and communities to resist and navigate better. By exploring and reflecting back on the educational stories of Black British women graduates, it is hoped that it will encourage more Overstanding of the education system and lead to dialogue, connections, strategies and (Black) community action to protect future generations of Black youth, particularly girls and women, within the education system.

Secondly, as many of the accounts shared by the Black women participants evoke deep and personal feelings, emotions and insights, they should be viewed and used as invaluable knowledge that provide other ways of knowing and alternatives to 'speak back' to dominant, white educational narratives. Therefore, their knowledge has illustrated significant expertise in the field of GM educational experiences and considerations to build on approaches to widen participation and how to develop culturally relevant curricula and pedagogy. This is one of the central themes in BFE where lived experience and dialogue, the ethics of caring and personal accountability are valued, as well as viewing Black women as agents of knowledge (Collins 2000: 251–69).

More practically, these insights, along with statistical data, can translate to improving equality and diversity policy. For instance, the exploration of this book has demonstrated that in terms of equality and diversity policy, existing institutional understandings of equality and diversity are not sufficient to address the unique challenges experienced by Black British girls and women. This is because this group is subject to historical, intersectional and institutional racism which is rarely acknowledged as a basis from which said policy is developed. Therefore, there is a need for equality and diversity policy to incorporate or strengthen intersectional understandings and approaches to better support this group and others. There is also a need for checks and balances in the system to be implemented to not only identify any issues, as my research has done, but to address them before it is too late. Initiatives like decolonizing the education system, mentoring and funding need to be reviewed and expanded to cover the entire education system to ensure that Black British women students can truly gain the social, gender and racial justice they deserve in the education system. However, these are all longstanding issues which are yet to be sufficiently addressed. The reasons for this can be understood by focusing on Bell's (1980) concept of 'interest convergence' in that, 'the interests of Blacks in achieving racial equality have been accommodated only when they have converged with the interests of powerful whites' (Taylor 1998: 123). Frankly, addressing these issues are not in the interests of 'powerful whites' and it can be argued that they cannot be completed within white institutions. This is because, as Lorde (1984: 112) explains,

> *the master's tools will never dismantle the master's house.* They may allow us temporarily to beat him at his own game, but they will never enable us to bring about genuine change. And this is only threatening to those women who still define the master's house as their only source of support. [emphasis in original]

In other words, while diversifying the curricula, adding more Black girls and women into PW settings and fighting for education policy changes are great starting points – these are all using the 'master's tools' within the 'master's house'.

Thirdly, Black parents, carers and wider Black communities can also learn and take practical steps from the educational journeys and experience of Black British women graduates about the entrenched intersectional barriers many must overcome. Now is the time to seek and provide alternatives. A place to start is the *Babygirl, You've Got This!* Toolkit I have created in the Resources at the end of this book on page 249. Many of the graduates often referred to the significant role and active involvement of parents and wider communities as illustrated in the full study (Pennant 2020a), and particularly mothers, which I centred in Chapter 7.

Lastly, it is important to note that by centring the experiences and journeys of Black British women graduates, their 'existence at the margins presents both constraints and possibilities for all educational reform efforts and overall societal transformation … [to] benefit the whole of society' (Evans-Winters and Esposito 2010: 22). Not *just* Black girls and women.

Final words: speaking to my younger self

It is through my research and the writing of this book that I embarked upon an unintended journey of self-discovery and healing. As I reflected on my own educational journey and experiences alongside my participants, as I comforted some of the women in interviews and analysed the interview data, as I read the literature and previous studies, I realized that many of us, including myself, had experienced some level of trauma. In closing, I say the following words to my younger self as I release my educational trauma and continue along my healing journey.

Babygirl, take off that armour because it's not yours to wear,
Babygirl, take off that armour for it's too heavy to bear.
Always remember that you are
Bless' up,
Bless' up,
So, it is ok to pace yourself –
Res' up,
Res' up.

Babygirl, your work will be an extension of your heart,
Your innate power will give you a head start,
Trust that your focus and drive will pay off, you won't even believe,
Just how far you will go and all the accomplishments you will achieve.

Your light shines so bright, it illuminates the dark,
You will be a source of connection, unifying people, helping them to ignite their spark.
Have no fear for your light will always draw the right people near,
They will support your vision and come to your aid,
Strengthening your work which will leave people feeling empowered and unafraid.

Babygirl, even though you don't know it yet, you have truly got this – yes!
You stand on the shoulders of mighty people who survived all the wickedness,
They paved the way so that you could be you,
They passed down all the tools so that you will always know what to do.
You are and will always be divinely directed.
You are and will always be divinely protected.

So, I ask that you honour your journey and trust where it will take you …
And most importantly, I ask that you honour yourself, yes babygirl,
please do.

Always be kind to yourself,
Always take time with yourself,
Don't ever compromise your integrity or health,
Use your work to contribute to your community's intellectual wealth.

Àṣẹ.

THE END.

Notes

General notes

- Some of the quotes from my research may have been altered to fit with the composite character storylines.
- Use of italics throughout denotes names of TV shows and books, additional sentences, storytelling/narration, pseudonyms or words – some of which are explained in the Glossary.
- Unless stated otherwise, the English education system is the focus of the book as there are differences between the English education system and those across the four nations of the United Kingdom – England, Wales, Northern Ireland, Scotland.
- Black is capitalized throughout the book as it refers to 'Black as a race of people who are connected by a shared history and culture. Through capitalising Black, [I am] taking a political stance against an ever-shifting category of domination and [I] aim to decenter whiteness' (Howell et al. 2019: 20).
- Educational institution categories:
  - **Predominantly White (PW):** predominantly white institutions that have higher proportions of white pupils and students and few students from Global Majority backgrounds. It typically includes institutions located outside inner cities in suburban or rural areas, as well as grammar or private schools and sixth form colleges within those, and elite or pre-1992 universities. This also extends to include certain university subject areas and undergraduate degree courses.
  - **Predominantly Global Majority (PGM):** institutions that have higher proportions of pupils and students from Global Majority backgrounds. Typically includes inner-city, state-funded schools and sixth form/further education colleges, as well as post-1992 universities and certain university courses.
  - **State/state-funded schools:** funded by the UK government, adhere to certain regulations like following the national curriculum and are usually non-academically selective.
  - **Grammar schools:** institutions that are funded by the UK government but are academically selective where an 11+ exam needs to be passed for entrance. It must be noted that there are few English Local Educational Authorities (LEAs) that still have them which represents their exclusivity.

- **Private/independent schools:** institutions that are fee-paying, usually academically selective and independent of finance and regulations from the UK government.
- **Sixth form college/FE college:** dedicated institutions for the study of a wide range of post-16 academic and vocational qualifications such as A-Levels and BTECs.
- **Post-1992 university:** institutions that were given university status in the Further and Higher Education Act (1992) which were (mainly) previously polytechnics. They are also known as new universities and/or modern universities.
- **Pre-1992 university:** the newly created and/or expanded institutions in the 1960s which were called for in the Robbins Report (1963). Beloff (1968) refers to these as 'plate-glass universities' which he used to describe the different building and architectural style that characterized these institutions.
- **Elite university:** the Russell group of universities which are '24 leading UK universities which are committed to maintaining the very best in research, an outstanding teaching and learning experience and unrivalled links with business and the public sector' (Russell Group 2019). They tend to have higher entry tariffs compared to other universities and the prestigious reputations of the institutions open up many opportunities for alumni in the labour market.

- In an effort to decolonize language, 'Global Majority' (GM) has been used to refer to 'people who are Black, Asian, Brown, dual-heritage, indigenous to the global south, and or have been racialized as ethnic minorities. Globally, these groups currently represent approximately eighty per cent (80%) of the world's population' (Campbell-Stevens 2020: 1). It has been used to replace Black, Asian and Minority Ethnic (BAME) or Black and Minority Ethnic (BME) which are problematic and contested terms.
- The following are fictitious but are the intellectual property of the author, April-Louise M. Pennant Ph.D., who retains copyright of them ©:
  - *BBYGRL Nails* ©
  - *educational steeplechase* ©
  - *Babygirls inna, but not of, Babylon* ©
  - *Burnt breadcrumbs* ©
  - *Choppin' & Chattin' Babygirlz* ©

Numbered notes from the text

1. By Black, I mean those with African and/or African-Caribbean, African-North/South American heritage and similar variations, I also extend this to include those with mixed heritage with at least one parent being from the aforementioned categories; though I acknowledge that there are differences in their experiences. This reflects the participants within my study.
2. Considering the variations in educational attainments as illustrated in GCSE statistics where 47.8 per cent of Black British Caribbean girls achieve the average Attainment 8 score compared to 55.9 per cent of Black British African girls (Gov.uk 2022a). Additionally, university demographics show that Black British African girl students are more likely to go to university by the age of nineteen (74.6 per cent) compared to 54.6 per cent of Black British Caribbean girl students (Roberts and Bolton 2020: 5).
3. Despite the focus being on England, it must be noted that rarely are 'Black' and 'English' used in partnership as a form of identification when compared to 'Black British'.
4. Despite the differing histories, race categories, minority experiences and migration patterns in the US and the UK are important areas to bear in mind within research, as with any tools developed elsewhere. Yet, the origins of Black Feminism in the US does not limit its usefulness. I am particularly drawn to it as it was specifically created to centre 'women of African descent who identify as African American women, Afro-Caribbean women, Nigerian American women, Black British women, AfroBrazilian women, and women who claim Blackness in combination with other racial identifications' (Collins 2016: 135).
5. Its origins within the US mean that it needs extra care when transferred and used in Britain. Warmington (2014) points this out and details additional concerns such as its development from Critical Legal Studies and the differences in how Black has been defined and used within British educational research. Another point of contention within the UK is that it is argued that CRT gives insufficient attention to class differences which are seen as equally significant when discussing societal and more specifically educational inequality (Cole 2017). However, there have been numerous Critical Race theorists in the UK that do pay attention to the intersections of class alongside race as its tenet of intersectionality advocates (Gillborn et al. 2012).

6. Bourdieu (1986) defines cultural capital as forms of knowledge, communication and values; social capital as connections and resources which are accrued from membership into certain social networks; and symbolic capital as power and status. Though different from economic capital, these intangible capitals can lead to the gaining of tangible economic capital.
7. There are also some white groups, like Gypsy, Traveller and Roma groups that do not enjoy the same advantages.
8. It must be noted that there are only 163 grammar schools in England, spread unevenly around the country (Danechi 2020: 6).
9. 'Academies are publicly funded but, unlike maintained schools, they are independent of local authorities. They have more freedoms, for example in setting staff pay and conditions and determining their own curriculum. Academy schools are run by academy trusts, which are charitable companies directly funded by, and accountable to, the Department. The Department's underlying objective for academies is that they should improve educational standards in schools' (House of Commons Committee of Public Accounts 2018: 4).
10. See in bibliography: Which? University Guide (n.d.) *The complete guide to A-level, BTEC and International Baccalaureate choices*.
11. The declaration of faith (shahada), prayer (salah), alms-giving (zakat), fasting (sawm) and pilgrimage (hajj) (Islamic Relief Worldwide Relief, Inc 2023).
12. The chakra belief system originated in India, particularly Hinduism and Buddhism, though energy healing is also practised in Africa and China.
13. 'The phrase InI appeals to this broader sense of solidarity within not only us members of the Rastafari faith, but also to "goodwill" people of whatever creed or religion, as there is the belief that people fundamentally want to be, and see, good, and it is Babylon that corrupts' (Sobers 2016).
14. While Ph.D. can take around three years to complete in England, this is different to places like the USA where a Ph.D. can take up to six years or more to complete.

Methodological Appendix

Black Feminist epistemology tenets

As defined by Collins (2000: 251–69; emphasis added), the main tenets of BFE are:

1. *Lived experience as a criterion of meaning* – the idea that knowledge claims made by Black women who have first-hand encounters about what they share and can also cite examples increases credibility.
2. *The use of dialogue in assessing knowledge claims* – the belief that the creation of new knowledge by Black women is hardly created in a vacuum, rather it is the product of dialogue between individuals and members of the community which acts to validate the new knowledge.
3. *The ethics of caring* – the importance of invoking 'personal expressiveness, emotions and empathy' (263) to validate knowledge.
4. *The ethics of personal accountability* – the notion that knowledge claims cannot just be made, there also needs to be consideration of the individual's values, ethics and character to assess them.
5. *Black women as agents of knowledge* – facilitating Black women in the creation of their own knowledge to both speak to/for and self-define themselves.

Critical Race Theory principles

This research is guided by the following CRT principles, specifically within educational research as outlined by Solórzano and Delgado Bernal (2001: 312–14; emphasis added):

1. *Centrality of Race and Racism* – All CRT research within education must centralize race and racism, including intersections with other forms of subordination such as gender, class and citizenship.
2. *Challenging the Dominant Perspective* – CRT research works to challenge the dominant narratives and re-centre marginalized perspectives.
3. *Commitment to Social Justice* – CRT research must always be motivated by a social justice agenda.
4. *Valuing Experiential Knowledge* – CRT builds on the oral traditions of many indigenous Communities of Colour around the world. CRT

research centres the narratives of People of Colour when attempting to understand social inequality.

5. *Being Interdisciplinary* – CRT scholars believe that the world is multi-dimensional, and similarly research about the world should reflect multiple perspectives.

Semi-structured interviewing

One-to-one semi-structured, in-depth interviews with a set of open questions (See Pennant 2020 for Ph.D. interview guide) conducted by April-Louise were used to collect the data. Each interview was approximately 1 hour 30 minutes, and with participant consent, they were audio-recorded and transcribed verbatim. Interview transcriptions were uploaded onto qualitative computer software NVivo where data analysis took place using a thematic approach.

Ethics

Ethical approval was successfully granted before both my masters and Ph.D. research began. All participants were given information sheets and consent forms before the start of the interviews, as well as hard copies of both the information sheet and a signed copy of the consent form. Confidentiality was upheld through pseudonyms in place of names, places and any other identifying information. When upholding anonymity, this proved to be somewhat of a challenge as it meant that I had to alter parts of the in-depth accounts that participants shared in their interviews. Anonymity was achieved through making slight changes to participant stories but every effort was made to keep its authenticity.

Sample

A mixture of snowball and purposive sampling was used to recruit participants as I was looking for a specific sample of Black British women who were or had been studying at English educational institutions, from primary school until (undergraduate) university.

The participants self-defined as Black and more specifically within 'African Diasporic Blackness' (Andrews 2016: 2063), comprising of Black British women with African or Caribbean heritage born and/or residing in England. There were also two participants who were mixed-heritage with one Black parent. As this research reflects a principle of self-definition (Tate 2005), I did not exclude the mixed-heritage participants but embraced their experiences of Black girl/womanhood along their educational journeys.

Masters research participants

Below is participant information from my masters research. Participants were all studying at the same predominately white, elite university, *University of Webb*, at the time of the interviews in 2016.

Table 1 Masters research participants

Pseudonym	Age	Year of study	Degree course	Ethnic/cultural background
Azaria	21	3	Law	Black African
Bola	20	2	Medical Science	Black African
Cassandra	21	3	Drama & Theatre Arts	Black African & Caribbean
Dionne	19	1	History	Black African
Emani	20	2	English	Black Caribbean
Faith	21	2	Anthropology and Archaeology	Mixed – white British & Black Caribbean
Gabrielle	20	2	Policy, Politics and Economics	Black African
Hanna	19	1	Theology and Religion	Black Caribbean
Isioma	20	2	Law	Black African
Jazara	21	3	Psychology	Black African
Kiarna	19	1	Civil Engineering	Black African & Caribbean
Leomie	21	3	Medical Science	Black Caribbean
Mabel	20	2	Psychology	Black African
Nya	20	3	Political Science and Philosophy	Black African & Caribbean
Olivia	20	2	Law	Black Caribbean
Precious	20	2	Social Policy	Black African
Renee	20	2	Pharmacy	Black African

Ph.D. research participants

Below is participant information from my Ph.D. research. Participants came from a diverse range of backgrounds, educational institutions and pathways.

Table 2 Ph.D. research participants

Pseudonym	Age	Ethnic/ cultural background	Social class*	Type of educational institutions attended**	Type of university attended*** and degree course
Grace	24	Nigerian-British	Lower-middle class	*Primary school*: Roman Catholic, State *PW Secondary school:* State co-educational, boarding *PW Post-16 education:* continued on in secondary school	Pre-1992 university Psychology
Camille	21	African – Angolan	Working class	*PW Primary school*: State *PW Secondary school:* State, co-educational *PGM Post-16 education:* State co-educational Sixth form college	Post-1992 university Performing Arts
Kemi	24	Nigerian-British	Working class	*PGM Primary school*: Roman Catholic, State *PGM Secondary school:* Roman Catholic, State, co-educational *PW Post-16 education:* Sixth form at a Roman Catholic, Grammar school	Pre-1992 university Politics and International Relations
Adeola	26	Nigerian	Lower-middle class	*PGM Primary school*: Church of England, State *PW Secondary school:* Private, all girls' *PW Post-16 education:* Sixth form at a co-educational Grammar school	Pre-1992 university Medicine and Physiology

Pseudonym	Age	Ethnic/ cultural background	Social class*	Type of educational institutions attended**	Type of university attended*** and degree course
La'Shay	26	Black British Jamaican	Middle class	*PGM Primary school:* State *PW Secondary school:* Grammar, all girls' *PW Post-16 education:* State co-educational Sixth form college	Pre-1992 university Physiology and Pharmacy
Deja	23	Black British Caribbean	Working class	*PGM Primary school:* Seventh-day Adventist, Private *PW Secondary school:* Grammar, all girls' *PW Post-16 education:* continued on in secondary school	Pre-1992 university International Business and Spanish
Dionne	34	Black Caribbean	Working class	*PGM Primary school:* Church of England, State *PGM Secondary school:* State co-educational *PGM Post-16 education:* Further education, co-educational college	Post-1992 university Psychology with Criminology
Joy	23	British Ghanaian	Middle class	*PW Primary school:* Church of England, State *PW Secondary school:* Grammar, co-educational *PW Post-16 education:* continued on in secondary school	Elite university Business and Economy of Contemporary China
Rachel	23	Mixed – African-American and Ashkenazi Jewish	Middle class	*PW Primary school:* State *PW Secondary school:* State *PGM Post-16 education:* State co-educational Sixth form college	Pre-1992 university Anthropology

Pseudonym	Age	Ethnic/ cultural background	Social class*	Type of educational institutions attended**	Type of university attended*** and degree course
Jumoke	23	Black British of Nigerian heritage	Middle class	*PW Primary school:* Private *PW Secondary school:* Grammar, all girls' secondary school *PW Post-16 education:* continued on in secondary school	Pre-1992 university Law
Takara	23	African Caribbean	Lower-middle class	*PGM Primary school:* State *PGM Secondary school:* State co-educational *PGM Post-16 education:* State co-educational Sixth form college	Pre-1992 university Psychology with Sociology
Chanel	24	Black British	Working class	*PGM Primary school:* Church of England, State *PGM Secondary school:* State, all girls' *PGM Post-16 education:* State co-educational Sixth form college	Pre-1992 university Criminology and Sociology
Yasmin	24	Black Caribbean	Lower-middle class	*PW Primary school:* State *PGM Secondary school:* Church of England, State, co-educational *PGM Post-16 education:* State co-educational Sixth form college	Pre-1992 university Psychology
Afua	24	Ghanaian	Working class	*PGM Primary school:* Church of England, State *PGM Secondary school:* Church of England, State, co-educational *PGM Post-16 education:* State co-educational Sixth form college	Pre-1992 university Criminology and Sociology

Pseudonym	Age	Ethnic/ cultural background	Social class*	Type of educational institutions attended**	Type of university attended*** and degree course
Rochelle	25	Black British	Working class	*PW Primary school:* State *PW Secondary school:* State co-educational *PGM Post-16 education:* Further education, co-educational college	Post-1992 university International Business with Spanish
Beverley	24	Nigerian and Black	Working class	*PGM Primary school:* Roman Catholic, State *PGM Secondary school:* Roman Catholic, State, co-educational *PGM Post-16 education:* Apprenticeship in workplace	Pre-1992 university Business Finance Higher National Diploma with an extra year to get a Business degree.
Claudia	24	Ghanaian British or British Ghanaian	Working class	*PGM Primary school:* Roman Catholic, State *PW Secondary school:* Private, all girls' *PW Post-16 education:* continued on in secondary school	Elite Religion & Theology
Makeda	24	Black Caribbean	Lower-middle class	*PGM Primary school:* Roman Catholic, State *PGM Secondary school:* Roman Catholic, State *PGM Post-16 education:* Further education, co-educational college	Pre-1992 university Law
Sophia	25	Black British or Afro-Caribbean	Working class	*PGM Primary school:* State *PGM Secondary school:* State co-educational *PGM Post-16 education:* continued on in secondary school	Pre-1992 university Politics and International Relations

Pseudonym	Age	Ethnic/ cultural background	Social class*	Type of educational institutions attended**	Type of university attended*** and degree course
Ebony	25	British with Jamaican and Guyanese heritage	Lower-middle class	*PGM Primary school:* State *PW Secondary school:* Private, all girls' *PGM Post-16 education:* State co-educational, Sixth form college	Elite university Sociology and Criminology
Halima	21	Black African	Working class	*PW Primary school:* State *PW Secondary school:* State co-educational *PGM Post-16 education:* State co-educational Sixth form college	Elite university Sociology
Shakirah	23	British Jamaican	Working class	*PGM Primary school:* Roman Catholic *PGM Secondary school:* State co-educational *PGM Post-16 education:* Further education, co-educational college	Post-1992 university Fashion
Simone	21	Caribbean British	Working class	*PGM Primary school:* State *PGM Secondary school:* State co-educational *PGM Post-16 education:* continued on in secondary school	Elite university Mechanical Engineering
Estelle	23	African Caribbean, half Jamaican, half Ghanaian	Middle class	*PW Primary school:* Roman Catholic, State *PW Secondary school:* Grammar, all girls' *PW Post-16 education:* continued on in secondary school	Elite university English

Pseudonym	Age	Ethnic/ cultural background	Social class*	Type of educational institutions attended**	Type of university attended*** and degree course
Janaya	22	Caribbean	Working class	*PGM Primary school:* State *PGM Secondary school:* State co-educational *PGM Post-16 education:* State co-educational Sixth form college	Post-1992 university English

* These are based on subjective categorizations of social class as explained in Chapter 2.

** Types of educational institutions explained in Notes.

*** Types of universities explained in Notes.

The composite characters of *Shamari*, *Eve*, *Nia-Elise*, *Chika*, *Yaa*, *Hodan* and *Hamda* were created based on the forty-two participants detailed above.

Resources

Babygirl, You've Got This! Playlist

Below are the details of all the songs featured throughout the book in order of their appearance.

Song title	Artist
'Letter To My siStars'	Misha B
'Beautiful Flower'	India Arie
'Warrior'	Ray BLK
'Peng Black Girls Remix'	ENNY ft. Jorja Smith
'Point And Kill'	Little Simz ft. Obongjayar
'BROWN'	OSHUN
'Don't Touch My Hair'	Solange ft. Sampha
'I Owe You Nothing'	Seinabo Sey
'Reality Check'	Noname ft. Eryn Allen Kane and Akenya
'Babygirl'	Chlöe x Halle
'I Made It'	Fantasia ft. Tye Tribbett

Babygirl, You've Got This! Toolkit

I have compiled the following list of resources for additional support, enjoyment and learning based on the themes, insights and findings of this book. Some are specifically for Black girls and women, others are for a broader understanding about the experiences of being Black in England (and beyond). I recommend many of these resources as they have been useful parts of my own experiences and journey as sources of inspiration, solace, joy, laughs and deeper understanding. *This list is not exhaustive* but I hope it provides alternative narratives, safe spaces and continuation to Overstand the system/society we navigate as well as amplifying the work of others doing great work to improve the lives and experiences of Black girls and women, as well as the wider community.

Name/Title	Type of resource
Taking Up Space: The Black Girl's Manifesto for Change (2019) by Chelsea Kwakye and Ore Ogunbiyi	Book
Grown: The Black Girls' Guide to Glowing Up (2021) by Melissa Cummings-Quarry and Natalie A. Carter	Book
A Fly Girl's Guide to University: Being a Woman of Colour at Cambridge and Other Institutions of Elitism and Power (2019) by Lola Olufemi, Odelia Younge, Waithera Sebatindira and Suhaiymah Manzoor-Khan	Book
Slay in Your Lane: The Black Girl Bible (2018) by Elizabeth Uviebinené and Yomi Adegoke	Book
A Quick Ting on the Black Girl Afro (2022) by Zainab Kwaw-Swanzy	Book
Don't Touch My Hair (2019) by Emma Dabiri	Book
Take Care: The Black Women's Guide to Wellness (2023) by Chloe Pierre	Book
Black Joy (2021) by Charlie Brinkhurst-Cuff	Book
Our Own Selves (2022) by Nadine Ijewere	Book
Token Black Girl: A Memoir (2022) by Danielle Prescod	Book
Black Girls Take World: The Travel Bible for Black Women with Boundless Wanderlust (Girls Guide to the World) (2021) by Georgina Lawton	Book
The Culture Trap: Ethnic Expectations and Unequal Schooling for Black Youth (2023) by Derron Wallace	Book
Sisters of the Yam: Black Women and Self-Recovery (1993) by bell hooks	Book
Practice Makes Perfect (2022) by Rosa-Johan Uddoh	Book
GIRL: Essays on Black Womanhood (2021) by Kenya Hunt	Book
Cocoa Girl	Magazine
Black Beauty and Hair Magazine	Magazine
SEASON zine issue 09 (2021): Black Joy by Felicia Pennant	Magazine
Black Ballad	Black cultural/ lifestyle platform for black girls and women
Unbothered UK	Black cultural/ lifestyle platform
Rock (2020) dir. by Sarah Gavron	Feature Film

Name/Title	Type of resource
Broken Ceiling (2018) dir. by Adam Davis	Feature Film
Dolapo is Fine (2020) dir. by Ethosheia Hylton	Short Film
A Response To Your Message (2020) by Somalia Nonyé Seaton	Short Film
Judi Love: Black, Female and Invisible (2022) dir. by Antoine Fuqua	Documentary
Hair Power: My Afro and Me (2020) by Emma Dabiri	Documentary
Subnormal: A British Scandal (2021) dir. by Lyttanya Shannon	Documentary
Will Britain ever have a Black Prime Minister? (2016) dir. by Steve Grandison	Documentary
'Small Axe: Education' (2020) dir. by Steve McQueen	TV episode
Jojo and Gran Gran (2020–present)	TV show
Become a Good Ancestor	Podcast
Therapy for Black Girls Podcast	Podcast
Your Favourite Aunties Podcast	Podcast
No Filter Podcast	Podcast
Dope Black Women	Podcast
The Homecoming Podcast with Dr. Thema	Podcast
Black British (2023) by V V Brown	Song
The Race Report from *The Independent* by Nadine White	Mailing list/ newsletter
BRITISHBLACKSTUDIES JISCMAIL	Mailing list/ newsletter
Black History Studies	Community and educational organization
Black History Talks	Community and educational organization
Harambee Organisation of Black Unity	Community and educational organization
The African Caribbean Education Network (ACEN)	Educational organization
The National Association of Black Supplementary schools	Educational organization
Leading Routes	Educational organization

Name/Title	Type of resource
The Black Curriculum	Educational Organization
Communities Empowerment Network (CEN)	Educational Organization
The Ubele Initiative	Community organization
The Black Child Agenda	Community organization
Black Equity Organisation (BEO)	Community organization
Glitch	Charity
Women in the City Afro-Caribbean Network (WCAN)	Personal and professional development for Black women
She Leads for Legacy	Personal and professional development for Black women
Milk 'n' Honey Bees	Personal and professional development for Black girls and women
Girls Like Us	Personal and professional development for Black girls and women
The Catalyst Collective	Personal and professional development for Black girls and women
WE ARE SOUL	Personal and professional development for Black women
KINSIS	Personal and professional development for Black women

Name/Title	Type of resource
You Make It	Personal and professional development for Black women
The Akoma Institute	Personal and professional development for Black women and girls
Black Girl Fest	Black arts and culture festival for Black girls and women
AFROPUNK	Black arts and culture festival for those seeking 'the other black experience'
Everyday People	Black arts and culture event
Afro Hair & Beauty LIVE	Hair, beauty and culture event for Black girls and women
Return to Your Roots Festival	Hair, beauty and culture event for Black girls and women
Misemi	Black woman-run Fashion Brand

Bibliography

Abbas, T. (2007) 'British South Asians and pathways into selective schooling: social class, culture and ethnicity', *British Educational Research Journal*, 33(1), pp. 75–90.

Abdulaahi, S. (2019) *Here's why some Black Muslims feel uncomfortable with Islamic societies at university*. Available online: https://www.amaliah.com/post/34830/heres-why-some-black-muslims-feel-uncomfortable-with-islamic-societies-at-universities (accessed 17 January 2023).

Abrahams, J. (2018) 'Option blocks that block options: exploring inequalities in GCSE and A Level options in England', *British Journal of Sociology of Education*, 39(8), pp. 1143–59.

Adams, R. (2022) *Guidance on political impartiality in English classrooms 'confusing' say teachers' unions*. Available online: https://www.theguardian.com/education/2022/feb/17/guidance-on-political-impartiality-in-english-classrooms-confusing-say-teachers-unions (accessed 8 September 2023).

Adams, R. (2023) *Elite UK schools' financial links to slavery revealed*. Available online: https://www.theguardian.com/world/2023/may/03/elite-uk-schools-financial-links-to-slavery-revealed#:~:text=The%20study%20by%20academics%20at,the%20schools%20identified%20are%20private (accessed 15 May 2023).

Adegoke, Y. and Uviebinene, E. (2020) *Loud Black Girls: 20 Black Women Writers Ask: What's Next?* London: Fourth Estate.

Adewumi, B. (2020) 'Bridging the gap: using Bourdieu and Critical Race Theory to understand the importance of black middle-class parents' educational aspirations for their children', in Stahl, G., Wallace, D., Burke, C. and Threadgold, S. (eds.), *International Perspectives on Theorizing Aspirations: Applying Bourdieu's Tools. Social Theory and Methodology in Education Research*. London: Bloomsbury, pp. 177–94.

Adjogatseand, K. and Miedema, E. (2022) 'What to do with "white working-class" underachievement? Framing "white working-class" underachievement in post-Brexit Referendum England', *Whiteness and Education*, 7(2), pp. 123–42.

AdvanceHE (2018) *Equality in higher education: student statistical report 2018*. Available online: https://www.advance-he.ac.uk/knowledge-hub/equality-higher-education-statistical-report-2018 (accessed 17 January 2023).

AdvanceHE (2019) *Equality in higher education: student statistical report 2019*. Available online: https://www.advance-he.ac.uk/knowledge-hub/equality-higher-education-statistical-report-2019 (accessed 17 January 2023).

AdvanceHE (2020) *Equality in higher education: student statistical report 2020*. Available online: https://www.advance-he.ac.uk/knowledge-hub/equality-higher-education-statistical-report-2020 (accessed 17 January 2023).

AdvanceHE (2021) *Equality in higher education: student statistical report 2021*. Available online: https://www.advance-he.ac.uk/knowledge-hub/equality-higher-education-statistical-report-2021 (accessed 17 January 2023).

Advancing Access (2022) *24 leading universities working together with schools and colleges*. Available online: https://www.advancingaccess.ac.uk/ (accessed 18 January 2023).

Agenda Alliance (2022) *Serious concerns about racial disparity among girls 'kicked out' of school*. Available online: https://www.agendaalliance.org/news/serious-concerns-about-racial-disparity-among-girls-kicked-out-of-school/#:~:text=New%20figures%20obtained%20by%20the,for%20white%20British%20female%20pupils (accessed 17 January 2023).

Ajegbo, K., Kiwan, D., and Sharma, S. (2007) *Diversity and Citizenship Curriculum Review*. Available online: https://education-uk.org/documents/pdfs/2007-ajegbo-report-citizenship.pdf (accessed 13 January 2023).

Alexander, C. (1996) *The Art of Being Black: The Creation of Black British Youth Identities*. Oxford: Clarendon Press.

Allen, T. (1992) *The Invention of the White Race*. London: Verso.

Almeida, T., Brodnock, E. and Lordan, G. (2021) *Black women are missing in the UK's top 1%. LSE Business Review. Blog Entry*. Available online: https://blogs.lse.ac.uk/businessreview/2021/03/03/black-women-are-missing-in-the-uks-top-1/ (accessed 17 January 2023).

Anderson, E. (2022) *Black in White Space: The Enduring Impact of Color in Everyday Life*. Chicago: University of Chicago Press.

Anderson, K. (2016) 'Bourdieu's distinction between rules and strategies and secondary principal practice: a review of selected literature', *Educational Management*, 44(4), pp. 688–705.

Andrews, K. (2013) *Resisting Racism: Race, Inequality, and the Black Supplementary School Movement*. London: Trentham Books.

Andrews, K. (2016) 'The problem of political blackness: lessons from the Black Supplementary School movement', *Ethnic and Racial Studies*, 39(11), pp. 2060–78.

Ansley, F. L. (1997) 'White supremacy (and what we should do about it)', in Delgado, R. and Stefancic, J. (eds.), *Critical White Studies: Looking Behind the Mirror*. Philadelphia: Temple University Press, pp. 592–5.

Arbouin, A. (2018) *Black British Graduates: Untold Stories*. London: Trentham Books and UCL IOE Press.

Archer, L. and Hutchings, M. (2000) "Bettering yourself'? Discourses of risk, cost and benefit in ethnically diverse, young working-class non-participants' constructions of higher education', *British Journal of Sociology of Education*, 21(4), pp. 555–74.

Archer, L., Halsall, A. and Hollingworth, S. (2007) 'Inner-city femininities and education: 'race', class, gender and schooling in young women's lives', *Gender and Education*, 19(5), pp. 549–68.

Arya (2012) 'Black feminism in the academy', *Equality, Diversity and Inclusion: An International Journal*, 31(5/6), pp. 556–72.

Au, W. (2013) 'Hiding behind high-stakes testing: Meritocracy, objectivity and inequality in U.S. education', *The International Education Journal: Comparative Perspectives*, 12(2), pp. 7–19.

Aubrey, E. (2020) *Sugababes' Keisha Buchanan says 'traumatic' racism she experienced left her needing therapy*. Available online: https://www.nme.com/news/music/keisha-buchanan-traumatic-racism-sugababes-left-her-needing-therapy-sugababes-2686091 (accessed 17 January 2023).

Ayling, P. (2021) 'International education and the pursuit of 'Western' capitals: middle-class Nigerian fathers' strategies of class reproduction', *British Journal of Sociology of Education*, 42(4), pp. 460–74.

Bachan, R. (2014) 'Students' expectations of debt in UK higher education', *Studies in Higher Education*, 39(5), pp. 848–73.

Bagley, C. (1996) 'Black and white unite or flight? The racialised dimension of schooling and parental choice', *British Educational Research Journal*, 22(5), pp. 569–80.

Bailey, M. (2021) *Misogynoir nearly killed Meghan Markle*. Available online: https://www.bitchmedia.org/article/meghan-markle-oprah-winfrey-misogynoir (accessed 30 May 2023).

Bailey, M. (2021) *Misogynoir Transformed: Black Women's Digital Resistance – Intersections*. New York: NYU Press.

Bailey, M. and Miller, S. J. (2015) 'When margins become centered: Black queer women in front and outside of the classroom', *Feminist Formations*, 27(3), pp. 168–88.

Bailey, M. and Trudy (2018) 'On misogynoir: citation, erasure, and plagiarism', *Feminist Media Studies*, 18(4), pp. 762–8.

Ball, S. J. (1993) 'Education markets, choice and social class: the market as a class strategy in the UK and the USA', *British Journal of Sociology of Education*, 14(1), pp. 3–19.

Ball, S. J. (2003) *Class Strategies of the Education Market: The Middle Classes and Social Advantage*. London: RoutledgeFalmer.

Ball, S. J. and Vincent, C. (1998) "I heard it on the grapevine': 'hot' knowledge and school choice', *British Journal of Sociology of Education*, 19(3), pp. 377–400.

Barndt, J. (1991) *Dismantling Racism: The Continuing Challenge to White America*. Minneapolis, MN: Augsburg Books.

Bathmaker, A. M., Ingram, N., Abrahams, J., Hoare, A., Waller, R. and Bradley, H. (2016) *Higher Education, Social Class and Social Mobility: The Degree Generation*. London: Palgrave Macmillan.

Bathmaker, A. M., Ingram, N. and Waller, R. (2013) 'Higher education, social class and the mobilisation of capitals: recognising and playing the game', *British Journal of Sociology of Education*, 34(5–6), pp. 723–43.

BBC (2020) *X Factor's Misha B claims show pushed 'angry black girl narrative' on her*. Available online: https://www.bbc.co.uk/news/newsbeat-53049458s (accessed 17 January 2023).

BBC (2022) *Bibaa Henry and Nicole Smallman: Met apologises on anniversary of murders*. Available online: https://www.bbc.co.uk/news/uk-england-london-61721721 (accessed 18 January 2023).

BBC Bitesize (n.d.) *Millennials, baby boomers or Gen Z: Which one are you and what does it mean?*. Available online: https://www.bbc.co.uk/bitesize/articles/zf8j92p (accessed 16 August 2023).

Behrendt, M. and Franklin, T. (2013) 'A review of research on school field trips and their value in education', *International Journal of Environmental & Science Education*, 9, pp. 235–45.

Bell, D. A. (1980) 'Brown v. Board of Education and the interest-convergence dilemma', *Harvard Law Review*, 93(3), pp. 518–33.

Beloff, M. (1968) *The Plateglass Universities*. London: Secker & Warburg.

Berger, M. T. and Guidroz, K. (2010) *The Intersectional Approach: Transforming the Academy Through Race, Class, and Gender*. North Carolina: University of North Carolina Press.

Bernstein, B. (1970) 'Education cannot compensate for society', *New Society*, 15, pp. 344–7.

Berthoud, R. (2000) 'Ethnic employment penalties in Britain', *Journal of Ethnic and Migration Studies*, 26(3), pp. 389–416.

BESA (2021) *Key UK education statistics*. Available online: https://www.besa.org.uk/key-uk-education-statistics/#:~:text=There%20are%20currently%2032%2C163%20schools,pupil%20referral%20units%20 (PRUs) (accessed 18 January 2023).

Bhopal, B. (2020) 'Gender, ethnicity and career progression in UK higher education: a case study analysis', *Research Papers in Education*, 35(6), pp. 706–21.

Bhopal, K. (2011) "What about us?' Gypsies, travellers and 'white racism' in secondary schools in England', *International Studies in Sociology of Education*, 21(4), pp. 315–29.

Bhopal, K. and Chapman, T. K. (2019) 'International minority ethnic academics at predominantly white institutions', *British Journal of Sociology of Education*, 40(1), pp. 98–113.

Bhopal, K. and Pitkin, C. (2020) 'Same old story, just a different policy': race and policy making in higher education in the UK', *Race Ethnicity and Education*, 23(4), pp. 530–47.

Binsardi, A. and Ekwulugo, F. (2003) 'International marketing of British education: research on the students' perception and the UK market penetration', *Marketing Intelligence & Planning*, 21(5), pp. 318–27.

Black Ballad (2021) *Remembering The Black Women Victims Who Are So Easily Forgotten*. Available online: https://blackballad.co.uk/views-voices/remembering-the-black-women-victims-who-are-so-easily-forgotten?listIds=590867cea8c0bab2039c3ac5 (accessed 18 January 2023).

Black Equity Organisation (BEO) (2022) *Who are we*. Available online: https://blackequityorg.com/who-we-are/ (accessed 17 January 2023).

Blankenship, B. T. and Stewart, A. J. (2017) 'Intersectional identities, identity dimensions, and academic contingencies of self-worth', *Identity: An International Journal of Theory and Research*, 17(3), pp. 109–24.

Boliver, V. (2015) 'Are there distinctive clusters of higher and lower status universities in the UK?', *Oxford Review of Education*, 41(5), pp. 608–27.

Boliver, V. (2016) 'Exploring ethnic inequalities in admission to Russell Group universities', *Sociology*, 50(2), pp. 247–66.

Boulton, C. (2016) 'Black identities inside advertising: race inequality, code switching, and stereotype threat', *Howard Journal of Communications*, 27(2), pp. 130–44.

Bourdieu, P. (1977) 'Cultural reproduction and social reproduction', in Karabel, J. and Halsey, A. H. (eds.), *Power and Ideology in Education*. New York: Oxford University Press, pp. 487–511.

Bourdieu, P. (1984) *Distinction: A Social Critique of the Judgement of Taste*. London: Routledge & Kegan Paul.

Bourdieu, P. (1986) 'The forms of capital', in Richardson, J.G. (ed.), *Handbook of Theory and Research for the Sociology of Education*. New York: Greenwood, pp. 241–58.

Bourdieu, P. (1990a) *In Other Words*. Cambridge: Polity Press.

Bourdieu, P. (1990b) *The Logic of Practice*. Cambridge: Polity Press.

Bourdieu, P. (1996) *The State Nobility: Elite Schools in the Field of Power*. Cambridge: Polity Press.

Bourdieu, P. (1998) *Practical Reason*. Cambridge: Polity Press.

Bourdieu, P. (1999) *The Weight of the World: Social Suffering in Contemporary Society*. Stanford, CA: Stanford University Press.

Bourdieu, P. and Passeron, J. C. (1979) *The Inheritors: French Students and Their Relation to Culture*. Chicago: University of Chicago Press.

Bourdieu, P. and Passeron, J. C. (1990) *Reproduction in Education, Society and Culture*. London and Beverly Hills: Sage Publications.

Bourdieu, P. and Wacquant, L. (2004) 'Symbolic violence', in Scheper-Hughes, N. and Bourgois, P. (eds.), *Violence in War and Peace: An Anthology*, 1st edn. Oxford: Blackwell Publishing, pp. 272–342.

Bourdieu, P. and Wacquant, L. J. D. (1992) *An Invitation to Reflexive Sociology*. Cambridge: Polity Press.

Bowl, M. (2001) 'Experiencing the barriers: non-traditional students entering higher education', *Research Papers in Education*, 16(2), pp. 141–60.

Bowl, M. (2018) 'Diversity and differentiation, equity and equality in a marketised higher education system', in Bowl, M., McCraig, C. and Hughes, J. (eds.), *Equality and Differentiation in Marketised Higher Education: A New Level Playing Field?*. London: Palgrave Macmillan, pp. 1–19.

Boylorn, R. M. (2008) 'As seen on TV: an autoethnographic reflection on race and reality television', *Critical Studies in Media Communication*, 25(4), pp. 413–33.

Boylorn, R. M. (2016) 'On being at home with myself: Blackgirl autoethnography as research praxis', *International Review of Qualitative Research*, 9(1), pp. 44–58.

Breach, A., Fawcett Society and Li, Y. (2017) *Gender pay gap by ethnicity in Britain – Briefing*. Available online: https://www.fawcettsociety.org.uk/gender-pay-by-ethnicity-britain (accessed 17 January 2023).

Breen, R. and Goldthorpe, J. H. (2001) 'Class, mobility and merit: the experience of two British birth cohorts', *European Sociological Review*, 17(2), pp. 81–101.

Bridgstock, R. (2009) 'The graduate attributes we've overlooked: enhancing graduate employability through career management skills', *Higher Education Research and Development*, 28(1), pp. 31–44.

Bright, S. (2020) *Exams algorithm scandal brutally exposes the sham of conservative 'meritocracy'*. Available online: https://bylinetimes.com/2020/08/14/exams-algorithm-scandal-brutally-exposes-the-sham-of-conservative-meritocracy/ (accessed 18 January 2023).

British Medical Association (2015) *The right mix: how the medical profession is diversifying its workforce*. Available online: https://questionnaires.bma.org.uk/news/therightmix/index.html (accessed 17 January 2023).

British Sociological Association (BSA) (2022) *What is sociology?* Available online: https://www.britsoc.co.uk/what-is-sociology/#:~:text=Sociology%20is%20the%20study%20of,and%20how%20we%20experience%20life (accessed 17 January 2023).

Brooker, L. (2002) *Starting School: Young Children Learning Cultures*. Buckingham: Open University Press.

Brosnan, C. (2010) 'Making sense of differences between medical schools through Bourdieu's concept of "field"', *Medical Education*, 44(7), pp. 645–53.

Brown, F. (2023) *Home Secretary Suella Braverman threatened with legal action for refusing to implement all Windrush reforms*. Available online: https://news.sky.com/story/home-secretary-suella-braverman-threatened-with-legal-action-for-refusing-to-implement-all-windrush-reforms-12850923 (accessed 12 May 2023).

Brown, P. (2000) 'The globalisation of positional competition?', *Sociology*, 34(4), pp. 633–53.

Brown, P. (2013) 'Education, opportunity and the prospects for social mobility', *British Journal of Sociology of Education*, 34(5–6), pp. 678–700.

Brown, P. and Scase, R. (1994) *Higher Education and Corporate Realities: Class, Culture and the Decline of Graduate Careers*. London: Routledge.

Brown, P., Hesketh, A. and Williams, S. (2003) 'Employability in a knowledge-driven economy', *Journal of Education and Work*, 16(2), pp. 107–26.

Bruce-Golding, J. (2020) 'Black female leaders in education, role, reflections, and experiences', in Peters, M. (eds.), *Encyclopedia of Teacher Education*. Springer, Singapore, pp. 1–6.

Brynin, M. and Güveli, A. (2012) 'Understanding the ethnic pay gap in Britain', *Work, Employment and Society*, 26(4), pp. 574–87.

Burgess, S. and Wilson, D. (2005) 'Ethnic segregation in England's schools', *Transactions of the Institute of British Geographers New Series*, 30(1), pp. 20–36.

Burgess, S., Wilson, D. and Lupton, R. (2005) 'Parallel lives? Ethnic segregation in schools and neighbourhoods', *Urban Studies*, 42(7), pp. 1027–56.

Butler and Grace (2021) *How colour therapy can lift your mood and promote healing*. Available online: https://butlerandgrace.co/blogs/news/how-colour-therapy-can-lift-your-mood-and-promote-healing (accessed 17 January 2023).

Butler, J. (1988) 'Performance acts and gender constitution: an essay in phenomenology and feminist criticism', *Theatre Journal*, 40(4), pp. 519–31.

Butler, J. (1990) *Gender Trouble: Feminism and the Subversion of Identity*. New York: Routledge.

Butler, J. (1993) *Bodies That Matter: On the Discursive Limits of 'Sex'*. New York: Routledge.

Butler, T., Hamnett, C. and Ramsden, M. J. (2013) 'Gentrification, education and exclusionary displacement in East London', *International Journal of Urban and Regional Research*, 37(2), pp. 556–75.

Byfield, C. (2008) 'The impact of religion on the educational achievement of Black boys: A UK and USA study', *British Journal of Sociology of Education*, 29(2), pp. 189–99.

Byng, R. (2017) *Failure is not an option: the pressure Black women feel to succeed*. Available online: https://www.forbes.com/sites/rhoneshabyng/2017/08/31/failure-is-not-an-option-the-pressure-black-women-feel-to-succeed/ (accessed 18 January 2023).

Cage, E., Jones, E., Ryan, G., Hughes, G. and Spanner, L. (2021) 'Student mental health and transitions into, through and out of university: student and staff perspectives', *Journal of Further and Higher Education*, 45(8), pp. 1076–89.

Callender, C. and Mason, G. (2017) 'Does student loan debt deter higher education participation? New evidence from England', *The Annals of the American Academy of Political and Social Science*, 671(1), 20–48.

Campbell-Stephens, R. (2020) *Global majority; Decolonising the language and reframing the conversation about race*. Available online: https://www.leedsbeckett.ac.uk/-/media/files/schools/school-of-education/final-leeds-beckett-1102-global-majority.pdf (accessed 19 January 2023).

Cantle, T. (2009) *Building community cohesion in Britain*. Available online: http://www.tedcantle.co.uk/publications/044%20Lessons%20from%20the%20Local%20Reviews%20iCoCo%202009.pdf (accessed 13 January 2023).

Carmichael, F. and Woods, R. (2000) 'Ethnic penalties in unemployment and occupational attainment: evidence for Britain', *International Review of Applied Economics*, 14(1), pp. 71–99.

Carter, D. J. (2007) 'Why the Black kids sit together at the stairs: the role of identity affirming counter-spaces in a predominantly white high school', *Journal of Negro Education*, 76(4), pp. 542–54.

Carter, D. J. (2008) 'Achievement as resistance: the development of a critical race achievement ideology among Black achievers', *Harvard Educational Review*, 78(3), pp. 466–97.

Carter, P. L. (2003) '"Black" cultural capital, status positioning, and schooling conflicts for low-income African American youth', *Social Problems*, 50(1), pp. 136–55.

Casey, K. (1993) *I Answer With My Life: Life Histories of Women Teachers Working for Social Change*. New York: Routledge.

Castells, M. (1994) 'The university system: engine of development in the new world economy', in Salmi, J. and Verspoor, A. M. (eds.), *Revitalising Higher Education*. Oxford: Pergamon, pp. 14–40.

Chadderton, C. (2013) 'Towards a research framework for race in education: critical race theory and Judith Butler', *International Journal of Qualitative Studies in Education*, 26(1), pp. 39–55.

Chapman, T. K. and Bhopal, K. (2013) 'Countering common-sense understandings of "good parenting": women of color advocating for their children', *Race Ethnicity and Education*, 16(4), pp. 562–86.

Chapman, T. K. and Bhopal, K. (2019) 'The perils of integration: exploring the experiences of African American and black Caribbean students in predominately white secondary schools', *Ethnic and Racial Studies*, 42(7), pp. 1–20.

Chavous, T. and Cogburn, C. (2007) 'Superinvisible women: Black girls and women in education', *Black Women, Gender + Families*, 1(2), pp. 24–51.

Cherid, M. I. (2021) '"Ain't got enough money to pay me respect": blackfishing, cultural appropriation, and the commodification of Blackness', *Cultural Studies ↔ Critical Methodologies*, 21(5), pp. 359–64.

Chetty, D. (2016) '"You can't say that! Stories have to be about white people"', in Shukla, N. (ed.), *The Good Immigrant*. London: Unbound, pp. 96–107.

Child Safeguarding Commissioner (2022) *Local child safeguarding practice review Child Q*. Available online: https://chscp.org.uk/wp-content/uploads/2022/03/Child-Q-PUBLISHED-14-March-22.pdf (accessed 17 January 2023).

Chitty, C. (2007) *Eugenics, Race and Intelligence in Education*. London: Bloomsbury Publishing.

Christofides, L. N., Polycarpou, A. and Vrachimis, K. (2010) *Gender wage gaps, 'sticky floors' and 'glass ceilings' of the European Union*. Available online: https://www.sciencedirect.com/science/article/abs/pii/S0927537113000122 (accessed 17 January 2023).

Chua, A. (2011) *Battle Hymns of the Tiger Mother*. New York: The Penguin Press.

City of London & Hackney Safeguarding Children Partnership (2022) *Local child safeguarding practice review: Child Q*. Available online: https://chscp.org.uk/wp-content/uploads/2022/03/Child-Q-PUBLISHED-14-March-22.pdf (accessed 13 January 2023).

Civil Service (2022) *Devolution: factsheet*. Available online: https://assets.publishing.service.gov.uk/government/uploads/system/uploads/attachment_data/file/770709/DevolutionFactsheet.pdf (accessed 17 January 2023).

Civil, D. and Himsworth, J. J. (2020) 'Introduction: meritocracy in perspective. The rise of the meritocracy 60 years on', *The Political Quarterly*, 91(2), pp. 373–8.

Claessens, L. C. A., van Tartwijk, J., van der Want, A. C., Pennings, H. J. M., Verloop, N., Brok, P. J. D. and Wubbels, T. (2017) 'Positive teacher–student relationships go beyond the classroom, problematic ones stay inside', *The Journal of Educational Research*, 110(5), pp. 478–93.

Clammer, J. (2015) 'Performing ethnicity: performance, gender, body and belief in the construction and signalling of identity', *Ethnic and Racial Studies*, 38(13), pp. 2159–66.

Clarke, J. H. (1984) 'African Warrior Queens', in Sertima, I. V. (ed.), *Black Women in Antiquity, Journal of African Civilizations*, 6(1), pp. 123–34.

Clennon, O. (2013) *What's the problem with Black masculinities?* Available online: https://mediadiversified.org/2013/11/18/whats-the-problem-with-black-masculinities/ (accessed 18 January 2023).

Coard, B. (1971) 'How the West Indian child is made educationally subnormal in the British school system: the scandal of the Black child in schools in Britain', in Richardson, B. (ed.), *Tell It Like It Is: How Our Schools Fail Black Children*, London: Trentham Books, pp. 27–59.

Coldron, J., Cripps, C. and Shipton, L. (2010) 'Why are English secondary schools socially segregated?', *Journal of Education Policy*, 25(1), pp. 19–35.

Cole, M. (2017) 'Critical Race Theory: a Marxist critique', in Peters, M. A. (ed.), *Encyclopedia of Educational Philosophy and Theory*, vol 1. Singapore: Springer, pp. 301–8.

Coleman, N. M., Butler, E. O., Long, A. M. and Fisher, F. D. (2016) 'In and out of love with hip-hop: saliency of sexual scripts for young adult African American women in hip-hop and Black-oriented television', *Culture, Health & Sexuality*, 18(10), pp. 1165–79.

Collins, P. (1990) *Black Feminist Thought: Knowledge, Consciousness, and the Politics of Empowerment. Perspectives on Gender*, vol. 2. New York: HarperCollins Academic.

Collins, P. H. (1986) 'Learning from the Outsider Within: the sociological significance of Black Feminist thought', *Social Problems*, 33(6), pp. S14–S32.

Collins, P. H. (1999) 'Reflections on the Outsider Within', *Journal of Career Development*, 26(1), pp. 85–8.

Collins, P. H. (2000) *Black Feminist Thought: Knowledge, Consciousness and the Politics of Empowerment*, 2nd ed. New York: Routledge.

Collins, P. H. (2016) 'Black Feminist thought as oppositional knowledge', *Departures in Critical Qualitative Research*, 5(3), pp. 133–44.

Commission on Young Lives (2022) *All together now. Inclusion not exclusion: supporting all young people to succeed in school*. Available online: https://thecommissiononyounglives.co.uk/wp-content/uploads/2022/04/COYL-Education-report-FINAL-APR-29-2022.pdf (accessed 13 January 2023).

Congress.Gov (2021) *H.R.1280 – George Floyd Justice in Policing Act of 2021*. Available online: https://www.congress.gov/bill/117th-congress/house-bill/1280#:~:text=The%20bill%20creates%20a%20national,e.g.%2C%20stops%20and%20searches) (accessed 17 January 2023).

Conlon, G. (2005) 'The determinants of undertaking academic and vocational qualifications in the United Kingdom', *Education Economics*, 13(3), pp. 299–313.

Cook, A. D. and Williams, T. (2015) 'Expanding intersectionality: fictive kinship networks as supports for the educational aspirations of Black women', *Western Journal of Black Studies*, 39(2), pp. 157–66.

Cook, D. A. and Bryan, M. (2021) 'Blurring boundaries: the creation of composite characters in critical race storytelling' in Lynn, M. and Dixson, A. D. (eds.), *Handbook of Critical Race Theory in Education*. New York, Routledge, pp. 251–68.

Cook, D. A. and Dixson, A. D. (2013) 'Writing critical race theory and method: a composite counterstory on the experiences of black teachers in New Orleans post-Katrina', *International Journal of Qualitative Studies in Education*, 26(10), pp. 1238–58.

Corbett (2021) *Black women's equal pay day equals an extra 214 days of work*. Available online: https://www.forbes.com/sites/hollycorbett/2021/07/31/black-womens-equal-pay-day-equals-an-extra-214-days-of-work/ (accessed 17 January 2023).

Coughlan, S. (2012) *UK schools 'most socially segregated'*. Available online: https://www.bbc.co.uk/news/education-19548597 (accessed 13 January 2023).

Coultas, V. (1989) 'Black girls and self-esteem', *Gender and Education*, 1(3), pp. 283–94.

Council of Europe (2021) *Combating Afrophobia, or anti-Black racism, in Europe*. Available online: https://assembly.coe.int/LifeRay/EGA/Pdf/Press/2021/20210316-Afrophobie-prov-EN.pdf (accessed 17 January 2023).

Crawford, K. (2010) 'Schooling, citizenship and the myth of meritocracy', *Citizenship, Social and Economics Education*, 9(1), pp. 3–13.

Crenshaw, K. (1989) 'Demarginalizing the intersection of race and sex: A Black feminist critique of antidiscrimination doctrine, feminist theory and antiracist politics', *University of Chicago Legal Forum*, pp. 139–68.

Crenshaw, K. (1991) 'Mapping the margins: intersectionality, identity politics, and violence against women of color', *Stanford Law Review*, pp. 1241–300.

Crenshaw, K., Ocen, P. and Nanda, J. (2015) *Black Girls Matter: Pushed out, Overpoliced and Underprotected*. New York: Center for Intersectionality and Social Policy Studies and African American Policy Forum.

Croxford, L. and Raffe, D. (2013) 'Differentiation and social segregation of UK higher education, 1996–2010', *Oxford Review of Education*, 39(2), pp. 172–92.

Crozier, G. (2005) '"There's a war against our children": black educational underachievement revisited', *British Journal of Sociology of Education*, 26(5), pp. 585–98.

Crozier, G. (2015) 'Black and minority ethnic students on the margins: self-segregation or enforced exclusion?', in Alexander, C., Weekes-Bernard, D. and Arday, J. (eds.), *The Runnymede School Report Race, Education and Inequality in Contemporary Britain*, pp. 36–9. Available online: https://assets.website-files.com/61488f992b58e687f1108c7c/617bccd5f0b573ea69b0b3f3_The%20School%20Report.pdf (accessed 13 January 2023).

Crozier, G. (2018) 'Race and education: meritocracy as white middle class privilege', *British Journal of Sociology of Education*, 39(8), pp. 1239–46.

Dabiri, E. (2013) *Who stole all the Black women from Britain?* Available online: https://mediadiversified.org/2013/11/05/who-stole-all-the-black-women-from-britain/ (accessed 17 January 2023).

Dahlgreen, W. (2014) *The British Empire is 'something to be proud of*. Available online: https://yougov.co.uk/topics/politics/articles-reports/2014/07/26/britain-proud-its-empire (accessed 19 January 2023).

Danechi, S. (2020) *Grammar school statistics.* Available online: https://researchbriefings.files.parliament.uk/documents/SN01398/SN01398.pdf (accessed 19 January 2023).

Daniel, G (2018) *Will The "Black British" Identity Bring An End To The Diaspora Wars?* Available at: "WillThe"BlackBritish"IdentityBringAnEndToTheDiasporaWars?|Black Ballad" (accessed 24 October 2023).

Dash, P. (2006) 'Black hair culture, politics and change', *International Journal of Inclusive Education*, 10(1), pp. 27–37.

Davis, J. (2022) *Adultification bias within child protection and safeguarding.* Available online: https://www.justiceinspectorates.gov.uk/hmiprobation/wp-content/uploads/sites/5/2022/06/Academic-Insights-Adultification-bias-within-child-protection-and-safeguarding.pdf (accessed 17 January 2023).

Davis-Yuval, N. (2015) 'Situated intersectionality and social inequality', *Raisons Politiques*, 2(58), pp. 91–100.

DeCuir, J. T. and Dixson, A. D. (2004) '"So when it comes out, they aren't that surprised that it is there": using critical race theory as a tool of analysis of race and racism in education', *Educational Researcher*, 33(5), pp. 26–31.

Dei, C., Karumancherry, L. L. and Karumanchery-Luik, N. (2004) *Playing the Race Card: Exposing White Power and Privilege.* New York: Peter Lang Publishing.

Delamont, S. (1989) *Knowledgeable Women: Structuralism and the Reproduction of Elites.* London: Routledge.

Delgado, R. (1989) 'Storytelling for oppositionists and others: a plea for narrative', *Michigan Law Review*, 87(8), pp. 2411–41.

Delgado, R. (1993) 'On telling stories in school: a reply to Farber and Sherry', *Vanderbilt Law Review*, 46(3), pp. 665–76.

Delgado, R. and Stefancic, J. (2001) *Critical Race Theory: The Cutting Edge*, 2nd ed. Philadelphia: Temple University Press.

Demie, F. (2021) *The educational achievement of Black African children in England.* Available online: https://dro.dur.ac.uk/34954/ (accessed 17 January 2023).

Demie, F. and Lewis, K. (2010) 'Raising the achievement of Portuguese pupils in British schools: a case study of good practice', *Educational Studies*, 36(1), pp. 95–109.

Demie, F. and Lewis, K. (2011) 'White working class achievement: an ethnographic study of barriers to learning in schools', *Educational Studies*, 37(3), pp. 245–64.

Demie, F. and McLean, C. (2007) 'The achievement of African heritage pupils: a case study of good practice in British school', *Educational Studies*, 33(4), pp. 415–34.

Demos Integration hub (2015) *61% of ethnic minority kids in England – and 90% in London – begin Year 1 in schools where ethnic minorities are the majority of the student body*. Available online: https://www.wired-gov.net/wg/news.nsf/articles/DEMOS+61+of+ethnic+minority+kids+in+England+and+90+in+London+begin+Year+1+in+schools+where+ethnic+minorities+are+the+majority+of+the+student+body+07072015133500?open (accessed 13 January 2023).

Department for Business, Innovation and Skills (2014) *Getting the job done: the Government's reform plan for vocational qualifications*. Available online: https://assets.publishing.service.gov.uk/government/uploads/system/uploads/attachment_data/file/286749/bis-14-577-vocational-qualification-reform-plan.pdf (accessed 17 January 2023).

Department for Education (2014) *The national curriculum in England. Framework document*. Available online: https://assets.publishing.service.gov.uk/government/uploads/system/uploads/attachment_data/file/425601/PRIMARY_national_curriculum.pdf (accessed 17 January 2023).

Department for Education (2023) *The Education Hub: How we are putting apprenticeships on an equal footing with degrees*. Available online: https://educationhub.blog.gov.uk/2023/07/10/how-we-are-putting-apprenticeships-on-an-equal-footing-with-degrees/ (accessed 8 September 2023).

Department for Levelling Up, Housing and Communities (2022) *Levelling up the United Kingdom*. Available online: https://www.gov.uk/government/publications/levelling-up-the-united-kingdom (accessed 18 January 2023).

Devaney, S. and Roberts, D. (2012) 'Who gets the jobs? Factors influencing the employability of property and construction graduates in the UK', *Construction Management and Economics*, 30(3), pp. 233–46.

Diaz, T. (2019) *The complex relationship between Latinas, race, & braids*. Available online: https://www.refinery29.com/en-gb/2019/10/8552306/latinas-black-hair-styles-braids-cultural-appropriation (accessed 18 January 2023).

Dinesen, P. T. (2011) 'Me and Jasmina down by the schoolyard: An analysis of the impact of ethnic diversity in school on the trust of schoolchildren', *Social Science Research*, 40(2), pp. 572–85.

Diop, C. A. (1974) *The African Origin of Civilization: Myth or Reality?*. New York: L. Hill.

Dirshe, S. (2020) *Respect our roots: a brief history of our braids*. Available online: https://www.essence.com/hair/respect-our-roots-brief-history-our-braids-cultural-appropriation/ (accessed 18 January 2023).

Doharty, N. (2018) '"I FELT DEAD": applying a racial microaggressions framework to black students' experiences of Black History Month and Black History', *Race Ethnicity and Education*, 22(1), pp. 1–20.

Dottolo, A. L. and Kaschak, E. (2015) 'Whiteness and white privilege', *Women & Therapy*, 8(3–4), pp. 179–84.

DuBois, W. E. B. (1989) *The Souls of Black Folk*. New York: Penguin.

Dumais, S. A. (2002) 'Cultural capital, gender, and school success: the role of habitus', *Sociology of Education*, 75(1), pp. 44–68.

Dumangane, C. Jr. (2017) 'The significance of faith for Black men's educational aspirations', *British Educational Research Journal*, 43(5), pp. 875–903.

Dumas, M. J. (2014) '"Losing an arm": schooling as a site of black suffering', *Race Ethnicity and Education*, 17(1), pp. 1–29.

Dumas, M. J. (2016) 'Against the dark: antiblackness in education policy and discourse', *Theory Into Practice*, 55(1), pp. 11–19.

Dumas, M. J., and Ross, K. M. (2016) '"Be real black for me": imagining BlackCrit in education', *Urban Education*, 51(4), pp. 415–42.

Education Reform Act (1988) Available online: https://www.legislation.gov.uk/ukpga/1988/40/contents (accessed 17 January 2023).

Eide, E. (2016) 'Strategic essentialism', *The Wiley Blackwell Encyclopedia of Gender and Sexuality Studies*. Available online: https://onlinelibrary.wiley.com/doi/abs/10.1002/9781118786352.wbieg1170 (accessed 17 January 2023).

Elevation Networks Trust (2012) *Race to the Top: the experience of Black students in higher education*. Available online: https://www.equalityanddiversity.net/docs/race-to-the-top.pdf (accessed 17 January 2023).

ENAR (2021) *Afrophobia*. Available online: https://www.enar-eu.org/about/afrophobia/ (accessed17 January 2023).

Essence (2022) *About*. Available online: https://www.essence.com/about/ (accessed 18 January 2022).

Etienne, M. and Jichi, F. (2022) *Coroner concludes death of Blessing Olusegun was accidental with no way of ruling out third-party involvement*. Available online: https://www.gardencourtchambers.co.uk/news/coroner-concludes-death-of-blessing-olusegun-was-accidental-with-no-way-of-ruling-out-third-party-involvement (accessed 18 January 2023).

European Network Against Racism (ENAR) (2014) *Specific forms of racism*. Available online: https://www.enar-eu.org/specific-forms-of-racism-2/ (accessed 17 January 2023).

Evans, C. and Donnelly, M. (2018) 'Deterred by debt? Young people, schools and the escalating cost of UK higher education', *Journal of Youth Studies*, 21(9), pp. 1267–82.

Evans, L. and Moore, W. L. (2015) 'Impossible burdens: white institutions, emotional labor, and micro-resistance', *Social Problems*, 62(3), pp. 439–53.

Evans-Winters, V. E. (2016) 'Schooling at the liminal: Black girls and special education', *Wisconsin English Journa*l, 58(2), pp. 140–53.

Evans-Winters, V. E. and Esposito, J. (2010) 'Other people's daughters: Critical Race Feminism and Black girls' education', *Educational Foundations*, 24(1), pp. 11–24.

Exley, S. (2013) 'Making working-class parents think more like middle-class parents: choice advisers in English education', *Journal of Education Policy*, 28(1), pp. 77–94.

Fairbain, C. (2019) *Charitable status and independent schools*. Available online: https://researchbriefings.files.parliament.uk/documents/SN05222/SN05222.pdf (accessed 18 January 2023).

Fergus, E. (2017) 'The integration project among white teachers and racial/ethnic minority youth: understanding bias in school practice', *Theory Into Practice*, 56(3), pp. 169–77.

Foley, B. and Brinkley, I. (2015) *Unemployed and overqualified? Graduates in the UK labour market*. Available online: https://www.voced.edu.au/content/ngv%3A71656 (accessed 13 January 2023).

Ford, T. (2020) *Dressed in Dreams: A Black Girl's Love Letter to the Power of Fashion*. New York: St. Martin's Press.

Fordham, S. (1988) 'Racelessness as a factor in Black students' school success: pragmatic strategy or pyrrhic victory?', *Harvard Educational Review*, 58(1), pp. 54–84.

Fordham, S. (1991) 'Racelessness in private schools: should we deconstruct the racial and cultural identity of African-American adolescents?' *Teachers College Record*, 92(3), pp. 470–84.

Fordham, S. (1993) '"Those loud Black girls": (Black) women, silence and gender "passing" in the academy', *Anthropology & Education Quarterly*, 24(1), pp. 3–32.

Fordham, S. (1996) *Blacked-Out: Dilemmas of Race, Identity and Success at Capital High*. Chicago: University of Chicago Press.

Fordham, S. (2016) *Downed by Friendly Fire Black Girls, White Girls, and Suburban Schooling*. Minneapolis: University of Minnesota Press.

Francis, D. V. (2012) 'Sugar and spice and everything nice? Teacher perceptions of Black girls in the classroom', *The Review of Black Political Economy*, 39(3), pp. 311–20.

François, M. (2019) *It's not just Cambridge University – all of Britain benefited from slavery*. Available online: https://www.theguardian.com/commentisfree/2019/may/07/cambridge-university-britain-slavery (accessed 15 May 2023).

Freire, P. (1973) *Education for Critical Consciousness*, vol. 1. Continuum. New York: Seabury.

Freire, P. (2008) 'The "banking" concept of education', in Bartholomae, D. and Petrosky, A., *Ways of Reading*, 8th ed. Boston: Bedford-St. Martin's, pp. 242–54.

Fuller, M. (1980) 'Black girls in a London comprehensive school', in Deem, R. (ed.), *Schooling for Women's Work*. London: Routledge and Kegan Paul, pp. 52–61.

Fuller, M. (1982) 'Young, female and black', in Cashmore, B. and Troyna, B. (ed.), *Black Youth in Crisis*. London: George Allen and Unwin, pp. 87–100.

Fuller, M. (1983) 'Qualified criticism, critical qualifications', in Barton, L. and Walker, S. (eds.), *Race Class and Education*. London: Croom Helm, pp. 166–90.

Furlong, V. J. (1984) 'Interaction sets in the classroom: towards a study of pupil knowledge', in Hammersley, M. and Woods, P. (eds.), *Life in School: The Sociology of Pupil Culture*. London: Routledge, pp. 145–61.

Gamsu, S. and Donnelly, M. (2017) *Diverse places of learning: Home neighbourhood ethnic diversity and the ethnic composition of universities*, Institute for Policy Research, University of Bath. Available online: http://www.bath.ac.uk/publications/diverse-places-of-learning-home-neighbourhood-ethnic-diversity-ethnic-composition-of-universities/attachments/Diverse-places-of-learning.pdf (accessed 18 January 2023).

Gentleman, A. and Campbell, L. (2020) *Windrush campaigner Paulette Wilson dies aged 64*. Available online: https://www.theguardian.com/uk-news/2020/jul/23/windrush-campaigner-paulette-wilson-dies-aged-64 (accessed 17 January 2023).

George, R. (2007) 'Urban girls' 'race' friendship and school choice: changing schools, changing friendships', *Race Ethnicity and Education*, 10(2), pp. 115–29.

Geronimus, A. T. (1992) 'The weathering hypothesis and the health of African-American women and infants: evidence and speculations, *Ethnicity & Disease*, 2(3), pp. 207–21.

Geronimus, A. T. (2023) *Weathering: The extraordinary stress of Ordinary life on the body in an unjust society*. London: Hachette UK.

Geronimus, A. T., Hicken, M., Keene, D. and Bound, J. (2006) '"Weathering" and age patterns of allostatic load scores among blacks and whites in the United States', *American Jornal of Public Health*, 96(5), pp. 826–33.

Gershenson, S., Holt, S. B. and Papageorge, N. W. (2016) 'Who believes in me? The effect of student–teacher demographic match on teacher expectations', *Economics of Education Review*, 52, pp. 209–24.

Gharavi, T. (2023) *'Queen Cleopatra' director speaks out: 'what bothers you so much about a Black Cleopatra?'* Available online: https://variety.com/2023/tv/global/queen-cleopatra-black-netflix-egypt-1235590708/ (accessed 12 May 2023).

Gillborn, D. (1997) 'Young, black and failed by school: the market, education reform and black students', *International Journal of Inclusive Education*, 1(1), pp. 65–87.

Gillborn, D. (2005) 'Education policy as an act of white supremacy: whiteness, critical race theory and education reform', *Journal of Education Policy*, 20(4), pp. 485–506.

Gillborn, D. (2008) *Racism and Education: Coincidence or Conspiracy?* Abingdon: Routledge.

Gillborn, D. (2010) 'The white working class, racism and respectability: victims, degenerates and interest-convergence', *British Journal of Educational Studies*, 58(1), pp. 3–25.

Gillborn, D. (2013) 'Interest-divergence and the colour of cutbacks: race, recession and the undeclared war on Black children', *Discourse*, 34(4), pp. 477–91.

Gillborn, D. (2014) 'Racism as policy: a critical race analysis of education reforms in the United States and England', *The Educational Forum*, 78(1), pp. 26–41.

Gillborn, D. (2018) 'Heads I win, tails you lose: anti-Black racism as fluid, relentless, individual and systemic', *Peabody Journal of Education*, 93(1), pp. 66–77.

Gillborn, D. and Youdell, D. (2000) *Rationing Education: Policy, Practice, Reform and Equity*. Buckingham: Open University Press.

Gillborn, D., Demack, S., Rollock, N. and Warmington, P. (2017) 'Moving the goalposts: education policy and 25 years of the Black/White achievement gap', *British Educational Research Journal (BERJ)*, 43(5), pp. 848–74.

Gillborn, G., Rollock, N., Vincent, C. and Ball, S. J. (2012) "You got a pass, so what more do you want?': race, class and gender intersections in the educational experiences of the Black middle class', *Race Ethnicity and Education*, 15(1), pp. 121–39.

Gilroy, P. (1993) *The Black Atlantic: Modernity and Double Consciousness*. London and New York: Verso.

Gin (2016) *The Apprentice*, series 12, episode 10. [TV Programme]. Available from: BBC iPlayer. [Viewed: 8 November 2023].

Givens, J. R. (2016) 'A grammar for black education beyond borders: exploring technologies of schooling in the African Diaspora', *Race, Ethnicity and Education*, 19(6), pp. 1288–302.

Glascock, J. and Preston-Schreck, C. (2018) 'Verbal aggression, race, and sex on reality TV: is this really the way it is?' *Journal of Broadcasting & Electronic Media*, 62(3), pp. 427–44.

Go, J. (2013) 'Decolonizing Bourdieu: colonial and postcolonial theory in Pierre Bourdieu's early work', *Sociological Theory*, 31(1), pp. 49–74.

Godfrey, R. (2018) *Being Black and Muslim in London*. Available online: https://qmulstudyabroad.blog/2018/02/09/being-black-and-muslim-in-london-rachel-godfrey/ (accessed 17 January 2023).

Goffman, E. (1981). *Forms of Talk*. Philadelphia: University of Pennsylvania Press.

Goodkind, S., Brinkman, B. G. and Elliott, K. (2020) 'Redefining resilience and reframing resistance: empowerment programming with Black girls to address societal inequities', *Behavioral Medicine*, 46(3–4), pp. 317–29.

Gordon-Chipembere, N. (ed.) (2011) *Representation and Black Womanhood: The Legacy of Sarah Baartman*. New York: Palgrave Macmillan.

Gorski, P. C. (2019) 'Racial battle fatigue and activist burnout in racial justice activists of color at predominantly white colleges and universities', *Education*, 22(1), pp. 1–20.

Gov.uk (2017) *Common mental disorders*. Available online: https://www.ethnicity-facts-figures.service.gov.uk/health/mental-health/adults-experiencing-common-mental-disorders/latest (accessed 17 January 2023).

Gov.uk (2020) *School teacher workforce*. Available online: https://www.ethnicity-facts-figures.service.gov.uk/workforce-and-business/workforce-diversity/school-teacher-workforce/latest (accessed 13 January 2023).

Gov.uk (2022a) *GCSE results (Attainment 8)*. Available online: https://www.ethnicity-facts-figures.service.gov.uk/education-skills-and-training/11-to-16-years-old/gcse-results-attainment-8-for-children-aged-14-to-16-key-stage-4/latest (accessed 17 January 2023).

Gov.uk (2022b) *Household income.* Available online https://www.ethnicity-facts-figures.service.gov.uk/work-pay-and-benefits/pay-and-income/household-income/latest#:~:text=2021%2C%20on%20average%3A-,45%25%20of%20households%20in%20the%20UK%20had%20a%20weekly%20income,of%20less%20than%20%C2%A3600 (accessed 17 January 2023).

Gov.uk (2022c) *Permanent exclusions and suspensions in England.* Available online: https://explore-education-statistics.service.gov.uk/find-statistics/permanent-and-fixed-period-exclusions-in-england (accessed 17 January 2023).

Gov.uk (2022d) *Regional ethnic diversity.* Available online: https://www.ethnicity-facts-figures.service.gov.uk/uk-population-by-ethnicity/national-and-regional-populations/regional-ethnic-diversity/latest (accessed 17 January 2023).

Gov.uk (2022e) *Types of school.* Available online: https://www.gov.uk/types-of-school/free-schools (accessed 17 January 2023).

Green Park Business Leaders Index 2021 (2021) *Green Park's annual business leaders index records no Black chairs, CEOs or CFOs at FTSE 100 Companies.* Available online: https://www.green-park.co.uk/insight-reports/green-park-business-leaders-index-britain-s-top-firms-failing-black-leaders/s228945/ (accessed 17 January 2023).

Greyerbiehl, L. and Mitchell, D. (2014) 'An intersectional social capital analysis of the influence of historically Black sororities on African American women's college experiences at a predominantly white institution', *Journal of Diversity in Higher Education*, 7(4), pp. 282–94.

Griffin, R. A. (2012) 'I am an angry Black woman: Black feminist autoethnography, voice, and resistance', *Women's Studies in Communication*, 35(2), pp. 138–57.

Guglielmo, J. and Salerno, S. (2003) *Are Italians White?: How Race is Made in America.* New York: Routledge.

Guinier, L. (2004) 'From racial liberalism to racial literacy: Brown v. Board of Education and the interest-divergence dilemma', *The Journal of American History*, 91(1), pp. 92–118.

Gumperz, J. (1982) *Discourse Strategies.* Cambridge: Cambridge University Press.

Guo, K. (2013) 'Ideals and realities in Chinese immigrant parenting: tiger mother versus others', *Journal of Family Studies*, 19(1), pp. 44–52.

Hall, S. (1992) 'What is this "Black" in Black popular culture?', *Social Justice*, 20(1–2), pp. 104–14.

Hamilton, D. G. (2018) 'Too hot to handle: African Caribbean pupils and students as toxic consumers and commodities in the educational market', *Race Ethnicity and Education*, 21(5), pp. 573–92.

Hancock, S. D., Showunmi, V. and Lewis, C. (2020) 'Teaching while Black and female: navigating mental, curricular, and professional aggression', *Theory Into Practice*, 59(4), pp. 409–18.

Harker, R. (1990) 'Bourdieu, education and reproduction', in Harker, R., Mahar, C. and Wilkes, C. (eds.), *An Introduction to the Work of Pierre Bourdieu: The Practice of Theory*. New York: St Martin's Press, pp. 86–108.

Harvey, L., Geall, V., and Moon, S. (1997) 'Graduates' work: implications of organizational change for the development of student attributes', *Industry and Higher Education*, 11(5), pp. 287–96.

Heath, A. and Cheung, S. Y. (2006) *Ethnic penalties in the labour market: employers and discrimination*. Available online: https://www.researchgate.net/publication/265248323_Ethnic_Penalties_in_the_Labour_Market_Employers_and_Discrimination (accessed 18 January 2023).

Heath, A. and Cheung, S. Y. (eds.) (2007) *Unequal Chances: Ethnic Minorities in Western Labour Markets*. Oxford: Oxford University Press for the British Academy.

Heath, S. B. (1983) *Ways with Words: Language, Life and Work in Communities and Classrooms*. Cambridge: Cambridge University Press.

Henry, W. L. (2012) 'Reggae, Rasta and the role of the deejay in the Black British experience', *Contemporary British History*, 26(3), pp. 355–73.

Herelle, T. I. (2022) 'To protect and to prepare: Black mothers' school selection decision-making', *Race Ethnicity and Education*, pp. 1–19.

Hills, J., Cunliffe, J., Obolenskaya, P. and Karagiannaki, E. (2015) *Falling Behind, Getting Ahead: The Changing Structure of Inequality in the UK, 2007–2013*. Available online: http://sticerd.lse.ac.uk/dps/case/spcc/rr05.pdf (accessed 17 January 2023).

Hilpern, K. (2008) *Does a degree guarantee you a good job?* Available online: https://www.independent.co.uk/student/career-planning/getting-job/does-a-degree-guarantee-you-a-good-job-795996.html (accessed 17 January 2023).

Hinchliffe, G. W. and Jolly, A. (2011) 'Graduate identity and employability', *British Educational Research Journal*, 37(4), 563–84.

Hirsch, A. (2018) *Brit(ish): On Race, Identity and Belonging*. London: Penguin Books.

Hirsh, D. (2007) *Experiences of poverty and educational disadvantage*. Available online: https://www.jrf.org.uk/report/experiences-poverty-and-educational-disadvantage (accessed 14 August 2023).

Hollingworth, S. (2015) 'Performances of social class, race and gender through youth subculture: putting structure back into youth subcultural studies', *Journal of Youth Studies*, 18(10), pp. 1–20.

hooks, b. (1989) *Talking Back: Thinking Feminist. Thinking Black*. Boston, MA: South End Press.

hooks, b. (1990) *Yearning: Race, Gender and Cultural Politics*. Boston, MA: South End Press.

hooks, b. (1994) *Teaching to Transgress: Education as the Practice of Freedom*. New York: Routledge.

Horgan, G. (2007) *The impact of poverty on young children's experience of school*. Available online: https://www.jrf.org.uk/report/impact-poverty-young-childrens-experience-school (accessed 13 January 2023).

House of Commons Committee of Public Accounts (2018) *Converting schools to academies*. Available online: https://publications.parliament.uk/pa/cm201719/cmselect/cmpubacc/697/697.pdf (accessed 19 January 2023).

Howell, D., Norris, A. and Williams, K. L. (2019) 'Towards Black gaze theory: how Black female teachers make Black students visible', *Urban Education Research & Policy Annuals*, 6(1), pp. 20–30.

Hua, A. (2013) 'Black diaspora feminism and writing: memories, storytelling, and the narrative world as sites of resistance', *African and Black Diaspora: An International*, 6(1), pp. 30–42.

Huang, S., Hou, J., Sun, L., Dou, D., Liu, X. and Zhang, H. (2017) 'The effects of objective and subjective socioeconomic status on subjective well-being among rural-to-urban migrants in China: the moderating role of subjective social mobility', *Frontiers in Psychology*, 8, 819.

Hyland, N. E. (2005) 'Being a good teacher of Black students? White teachers and unintentional racism', *Curriculum Inquiry*, 35(4), pp. 429–59.

Hylton, C. L. A (2003) 'African-Caribbean group activities, individual and collective consciousness, and enforced "leisure"', *Community, Work & Family*, 6(1), pp. 103–13.

Ignatiev, N. (2009) *How the Irish Became White*. New York: Routledge.

Independent Schools Council (ISC) (2021) *ISC Census and Annual Report 2021*. Available online: https://www.isc.co.uk/media/7496/isc_census_2021_final.pdf (accessed 17 January 2023).

Ingram, N. and Allen, K. (2019) '"Talent-spotting" or "social magic"? Inequality, cultural sorting and constructions of the ideal graduate in elite professions', *The Sociological Review*, 67(3), pp. 723–40.

Islamic Relief Worldwide Relief, Inc (2023) *Five Pillars of Islam*. Available online: https://www.islamic-relief.org.uk/resources/knowledge-base/five-pillars-of-islam/ (accessed 19 January 2023).

James, D. (2017) 'Knowing your place? The urban as an educational resource', *Second International Handbook of Urban Education*, pp. 1041–58.

James, L., Guile, D. and Unwin, L. (2013) 'Learning and innovation in the knowledge based economy: beyond clusters and qualifications', *Journal of Education and Work*, 26(3), pp. 243–66.

Johnson, A. (2018) 'Centring Black Muslim women in Britain: a Black feminist project', *Gender, Place & Culture*, 25(11), pp. 1676–80.

Johnson, A. (2019) 'Throwing our bodies against the white background of academia', *Ethics in/of Geographical Research*, 52(1), pp. 89–96.

Johnson, A. (2020) 'Refuting "how the other half lives": I am a woman's rights', *Area*, 52(4), pp. 801–5.

Johnston, R., Burgess, S., Wilson, D. and Richard, H. (2006) 'School and residential ethnic segregation: an analysis of variations across England's local education authorities', *Regional Studies*, 40(9), pp. 973–91.

Johnston, R., Wilson, D. and Burgess, S. (2004) 'School segregation in multiethnic England', *Ethnicities*, 4(2), pp. 237–65.

Jones, C. (2006) 'Falling between the cracks: what diversity means for black women in higher education', *Policy Futures in Education*, 4(2), pp. 145–59.

Jones, O. (2012) *Chavs: The Demonization of the Working Class*. London: Verso Books.

Jones, T. and Norwood, K. J. (2017) 'Aggressive encounters & white fragility: deconstructing the trope of the angry Black woman', *Iowa Law Review*, 102(5), pp. 2017–70.

Joseph-Salisbury, R. (2019) 'Institutionalised whiteness, racial microaggressions and black bodies out of place in Higher Education', *Whiteness and Education*, 4(1), pp. 1–17.

Joseph-Salisbury, R. (2020) *Race and racism in English secondary schools*. UK: Runnymede Trust. Available online: https://www.runnymedetrust.org/publications/race-and-racism-in-secondary-schools (accessed 18 January 2023).

Joseph-Salisbury, R. and Connelly, L. (2018) '"If your hair is relaxed, white people are relaxed. If your hair is nappy, they're not happy": Black hair as a site of 'post-racial' social control in English schools', *Social Sciences*, 7(11), 219.

Joseph-Salisbury, R., Connelly, L. and Wangari-Jones, P. (2020) '"The UK is not innocent": Black Lives Matter, policing and abolition in the UK', *Equality, Diversity and Inclusion: An International Journal*, 40(1), pp. 21–8.

Joseph-Salisbury, R. (2021) *Afro hair: How pupils are tackling discriminatory uniform policies*. Available online: https://theconversation.com/afro-hair-how-pupils-are-tackling-discriminatory-uniform-policies-159290#:~:text=They%20found%20that%20one%20in,school%20policies%20penalising%20afro%20hair (accessed 17 January 2023).

Jung, E. and Zhang, Y. (2016) 'Parental involvement, children's aspirations, and achievement in new immigrant families', *The Journal of Educational Research*, 109(4), pp. 333–50.

Katz, H. T. and Acquah, E. O. (2022) 'Places of freedom or entrapment? Black adolescent girls' school experiences', *International Journal of Qualitative Studies in Education*, pp. 1–16.

Kenway, J. and McLeod, J. (2004) 'Bourdieu's reflexive sociology and "spaces of points of view": whose reflexivity, which perspective', *British Journal of Sociology of Education*, 25(4), pp. 525–44.

Khan, O. (2019) *Ethnic minority pupils get worse degrees and jobs, even if they have better A-levels*. Available online: https://www.newstatesman.com/politics/the-staggers/2019/02/ethnic-minority-pupils-get-worse-degrees-and-jobs-even-if-they-have (accessed 17 January 2023).

Khan, S. (2012) *Privilege: The Making of an Adolescent Elite at St. Paul's School*. Princeton and Oxford: Princeton University Press.

Khanna, N. (2010) '"IF YOU'RE HALF BLACK, YOU'RE JUST BLACK": Reflected appraisals and the persistence of the one-drop rule', *The Sociological Quarterly*, 51(1), pp. 96–121.

Kia, K. (2020) *The reason why nonBlack people should not wear black hairstyles is actually very simple*. Available online: https://www.popsugar.co.uk/beauty/

black-hairstyles-and-cultural-appropriation-history-47646199 (accessed 18 January 2023).

Knowles, E. D. and Lowery, B. S. (2012) 'Meritocracy, self-concerns, and whites' denial of racial inequity', *Self and Identity*, 11(2), pp. 202–22.

Kohl, E. and McCutcheon, P. (2015) 'Kitchen table reflexivity: negotiating positionality through everyday talk', *Gender, Place & Culture*, 22(6), pp. 747–63.

Kohli, R. and Solózano, D. G. (2012) 'Teachers, please learn our names!: racial microaggression and the K-12 classroom', *Race Ethnicity and Education*, 15(4), pp. 441–62.

Kupchik, A. (2009) 'Things are tough all over: race, ethnicity, class and school discipline', *Punishment & Society*, 11(3), pp. 291–317.

Kwakye, C. and Ogunbiyi, O. (2019) *Taking Up Space: The Black Girl's Manifesto for Change*. London: Penguin/Merky Books.

Kynard, C. (2010) 'From candy girls to cyber sista-cipher: narrating Black females' color-consciousness and counterstories in and out of school', *Harvard Educational Review*, 80(1), pp. 30–141.

Ladson-Billings, G. (1998) 'Just what is critical race theory and what's it doing in a nice field like education?', *International Journal of Qualitative Studies in Education*, 11(1), pp. 7–24.

Ladson-Billings, G. (2009) '"Who you callin' nappy-headed?" A critical race theory look at the construction of Black women', *Race Ethnicity and Education*, 12(1), pp. 87–99.

Lam, V. and Smith, G. (2009) 'African and Caribbean adolescents in Britain: ethnic identity and Britishness', *Ethnic and Racial Studies*, 32(7), pp. 1248–70.

Lane, M. (2018) '"For real love": how Black girls benefit from a politicized ethic of care', *International Journal of Educational Reform*, 27(3), pp. 269–90.

Lareau, A. (2002) 'Invisible inequality: social class and childrearing in Black families and white families', *American Sociological Review*, 67(5), pp. 747–76.

Lareau, A. (2003) *Unequal Childhoods: Class, Race, and Family Life*. Berkeley, CA: University of California Press.

Lareau, A. (2009) 'Watching, waiting, and deciding when to intervene: race, class, and the transmission of advantage', in Weis, L. (ed.), *The Way Class Works*. New York: Routledge, pp. 135–51.

Lareau, A. (2011) *Unequal Childhoods: Class, Race, and Family Life*. California: University of California Press.

Lawler, S. (2012) 'White like them: whiteness and anachronistic space in representations of the English white working class', *Ethnicities*, 12(4), pp. 409–26.

Leath, S. and Mims, L. (2021) 'A qualitative exploration of Black women's familial socialization on controlling images of Black womanhood and the internalization of respectability politics', *Journal of Family Studies*, pp. 1–18.

Leathwood, C. and O'Connell, P. (2003) '"It's a struggle": the construction of the "new student" in higher education', *Journal of Education Policy*, 18(6), pp. 597–615.

Leonardo, Z. (2005) 'Through the multicultural glass: Althusser, ideology and race relations in post-civil rights America', *Policy Futures in Education*, 3(4), pp. 400–12.

Leonardo, Z. (2009) *Race, Whiteness and Education*. Abingdon: Routledge.

Li, Y. (2018) 'Unequal returns: higher education and access to the salariat by ethnic groups in the UK', in Arday, J. and Mirza, H. S. (eds.), *Dismantling Race in Higher Education: Racism, Whiteness and Decolonising the Academy*. London: Springer Nature, pp. 103–24.

Li, Y. (2021) 'Entrenched inequalities? Class, gender and ethnic differences in educational and occupational attainment in England', *Frontiers in Sociology*, 5, pp. 1–17.

Li, Y. and Heath, A. (2010) 'Struggling onto the ladder, climbing the rungs: employment status and class position by minority ethnic groups in Britain (1972–2005)', in Stillwell, J., Norman, P., Thomas, C. and Surridge, P. (eds.), *Population, Employment, Health and Well-Being*. London: Springer, pp. 83–97.

Li, Y. and Heath, A. (2020) 'Persisting disadvantages: a study of labour market dynamics of ethnic unemployment and earnings in the UK (2009–2015)', *Journal of Ethnic and Migration Studies*, 46(5), pp. 857–78.

Lloyd, G. and McCluskey, G. (2008) 'Education and Gypsies/Travellers: "contradictions and significant silences"', *International Journal of Inclusive Education*, 12(4), pp. 331–45.

London Economics (2021) *The costs and benefits of international higher education students to the UK economy. Summary Report for the Higher Education Policy Institute and Universities UK International*. Available online: https://www.hepi.ac.uk/wp-content/uploads/2021/09/Summary-Report.pdf (accessed 13 January 2023).

Long, R. and Danechi, S. (2019) *Faith Schools in England: FAQs*. Available online: https://researchbriefings.files.parliament.uk/documents/SN06972/SN06972.pdf (accessed 17 January 2023).

Lorde, A. (1984) *Sister Outsider*. New York: Ten Speed Press.

Lorde, A. (1988) *A Burst of Light: And Other Essays*. New York: Dover Publications Inc.

Lorde, A. (2009) 'Poet as teacher—Human as poet—Teacher as human', in Byrd, R. P., Cole, J. B. and Guy-Sheftall, B. (eds.), *I am Your Sister: Collected and unpublished writings of Audre Lorde*. London: Oxford University Press, pp. 182–3.

Love, B. J. (2004) 'Brown plus 50 counter-storytelling: a critical race theory analysis of the "majoritarian achievement gap" story', *Equity and Excellence in Education*, 37(3), pp. 227–46.

Love, B. J. (2006) 'Issues and problems in the retention of Black students in predominantly white institutions of higher education', *Equity & Excellence in Education*, 26(1), pp. 27–36.

Lundman, R. J. (2003) 'The newsworthiness and selection bias in news about murder: comparative and relative effects of novelty and race and gender typifications on newspaper coverage of homicide', *Sociological Forum*, 18(3), pp. 357–86.

Lutes, A. (2013) *How The Spice Girls Got Their Nicknames*. Available online: https://www.bustle.com/articles/6890-how-the-spice-girls-really-got-their-nicknames (accessed 17 January 2023).

Luthar, S. S. (2003) *Resilience and Vulnerability: Adaptation in the Context of Childhood Adversities*. New York: Cambridge University Press.

Mac An Ghaill, M. (1988) *Young, Gifted and Black*. London: Open University Press.

Macaskill, A. (2013) 'The mental health of university students in the United Kingdom', *British Journal of Guidance & Counselling*, 41(4), pp. 426–41.

Mahar, C., Harker, R. and Wilkes, C. (1990) 'The basic theoretical position', in Harker, R., Mahar, C. and Wilkes, C. (eds.), *An Introduction to the Work of Pierre Bourdieu: The Practice of Theory*. London: The Macmillan Press, pp. 1–25.

Malisa, M. and Missedja, T. Q. (2019) 'Schooled for servitude: the education of African children in British colonies, 1910–1990', *Genealogy*, 3(40), pp. 1–12.

Mangan, L. (2006) *What it really means to be British*. Available online: https://www.theguardian.com/uk/2006/may/16/britishidentity (accessed 17 January 2023).

Marchant, E., Todd, C., Cooksey, R., Dredge, S., Jones, H., Reynolds, D., Stratton, G., Dwyer, R., Lyons, R. and Brophy, S. (2019) 'Curriculum-based outdoor learning for children aged 9–11: A qualitative analysis of pupils' and teachers' views', *PLoS ONE*, 14(5), pp. 1–24.

Marley Natural (2022) *PEACE, LOVE AND OVERSTANDING*. Available online: https://www.marleynatural.com/blog/overstand-rastafarian-speech (accessed 17 January 2023).

Marsh, K. (2013) '"Staying Black": the demonstration of racial identity and womanhood among a group of young high-achieving Black women', *International Journal of Qualitative Studies in Education*, 26(10), pp. 1213–37.

Martin, M. (2020a) *16 key events in the history of anti-Black racism in the UK*. Available online: https://www.huffingtonpost.co.uk/entry/anti-black-racism-uk_uk_5ed64992c5b6ce87e4781570 (accessed 15 August 2023).

Martin, M. (2020b) *British South Asians speak out about anti-Black racism within their communities*. Available online: https://www.huffingtonpost.co.uk/entry/south-asians-anti-black-racism_uk_5f466f3cc5b697186e2f7742 (accessed 15 August 2023).

Martin, S. (2022) *We Need To Talk About Chicken Shop Date*. Available online: https://www.refinery29.com/en-gb/chicken-shop-date-youtube-backlash-twitter (accessed 17 January 2023).

Maton, K. (2003) 'Pierre Bourdieu and the epistemic conditions of social scientific knowledge', *Space & Culture*, 6(1), pp. 52–65.

Matthews, D. L. and Reddy-Best, K. L. (2021) 'Dressed in dreams: a Black girl's love letter to the power of fashion', *Dress*, 47(1), pp. 99–102.

May, T. (2016) *Britain, the great meritocracy: Prime Minister's speech*. Delivered on 9 September 2016, British Academy, London. Available online: https://

www.gov.uk/government/speeches/britain-the-great-meritocracy-prime-ministers-speech#:~:text=In%20a%20country%20that%20works,to%20be%20a%20great%20meritocracy (accessed 18 January 2023).

MBRACE-UK (2021) *Saving lives, improving mothers' care. Lessons learned to inform maternity care from the UK and Ireland Confidential Enquiries into Maternal Deaths and Morbidity 2017–19*. Available online: https://www.npeu.ox.ac.uk/assets/downloads/mbrrace-uk/reports/maternal-report-2021/MBRRACE-UK_Maternal_Report_2021_-_FINAL_-_WEB_VERSION.pdf (accessed 17 January 2023).

McCall, L. (1992) 'Does gender fit? Bourdieu, feminism, and conceptions of social order', *Theory and Society*, 21(6), pp. 837–67.

McCracken, M., Currie, D. and Harrison, J. (2016) 'Understanding graduate recruitment, development and retention for the enhancement of talent management: sharpening "the edge" of graduate talent', *The International Journal of Human Resource Management*, 27(22), pp. 2727–52.

McRobbie, A. (2009) *The Aftermath of Feminism: Gender, Culture and Social Change*. London: Sage.

Meeting of the Minds (2020) *The Double Glazed Glass Ceiling: Being a Black Woman in the UK Workplace*. Available online: https://meetingofmindsuk.uk/my2cents/the-double-glazed-glass-ceiling-being-a-black-woman-in-the-uk-workplace/ (accessed 17 January 2023).

Meghji, A. (2017) 'Positionings of the black middle-classes: understanding identity construction beyond strategic assimilation', *Ethnic and Racial Studies*, 40(6), pp. 1007–25.

Meroe, A. S. (2014) 'Democracy, meritocracy and the uses of education', *The Journal of Negro Education*, 83, pp. 485–98.

Migration Policy Institute (2019) *Sub-Saharan African Immigrants in the United States*. Available online: https://www.migrationpolicy.org/article/sub-saharan-african-immigrants-united-states-2019 (accessed 17 January 2023).

Mijs, J. J. B. (2016) 'The unfulfillable promise of meritocracy: three lessons and their implications for justice in education', *Social Justice Research*, 29, pp. 14–34.

Mills, C. W. (1997) *The Racial Contract*. Ithaca: Cornell University Press.

Mirza, H. and Reay, D. (2000a) 'Spaces and places of Black educational desire: rethinking Black supplementary schools as a new social movement', *Sociology*, 34, pp. 521–44.

Mirza, H. S. and Reay, D. (2000b) 'Redefining citizenship: black women educators and "the third space"', in Arnot, M. and Dillabough, J. (eds.), *Challenging Democracy: International Perspectives on Gender*. London: Routledge Falmer, pp. 58–72.

Mirza, H. S. (1992) *Young, Female and Black*. London: Routledge.

Mirza, H. S. (ed.) (1997a) *Black British Feminism*. London: Routledge

Mirza, H. S. (1997b) 'Black women in education: a collective movement for social change', in Mirza, H. S. (ed.), *Black British Feminism: A Reader*. London: Routledge, pp. 269–78.

Mirza, H. S. (2006a) '"Race", gender and educational desire', *Race Ethnicity and Education*, 9(2), pp. 137–58.

Mirza, H. S. (2006b) 'Transcendence over diversity: Black women in the academy', *Policy Futures in Education*, 4(2), pp. 101–3.

Mirza, H. S. (2008) *Race, Gender and Educational Desire: Why Black Women Succeed and Fail*. London: Routledge.

Mirza, H. and Reay, D. (2000) 'Spaces and places of Black educational desire: rethinking Black supplementary schools as a new social movement', *Sociology*, 34, pp. 521–44.

Mirza, H. S. and Warwick, R. (2022) *Race and ethnicity*. Available online: https://ifs.org.uk/inequality/race-and-ethnicity-chapter/ (accessed 17 January 2023).

Mitchell, K. (2013) 'Race, difference, meritocracy, and English: majoritarian stories in the education of secondary multilingual learners', *Race Ethnicity and Education*, 16(3), pp. 339–64.

Mitchell, P. M. (2022) 'Measuring ethnic school segregation within local educational markets in England', *Cambridge Journal of Education*, pp. 1–24.

Modood, T. (2004) 'Capitals, ethnic identity and educational qualifications', *Cultural Trends*, 13(2), pp. 87–105.

Mohdin, A. (2021) *Black Caribbean girls in England 'twice as likely to be excluded from schools as white girls'*. Available online: https://www.theguardian.com/education/2021/sep/23/black-girls-in-england-twice-as-likely-to-be-excluded-from-schools-as-white-girls (accessed 17 January 2023).

Mohdin, A. and Thomas, T. (2022) *White applicants to civil service scheme accepted at far higher rate, figures show*. Available online: https://www.theguardian.com/world/2022/jan/23/white-applicants-acceptance-rate-uk-civil-service-scheme#:~:text=People%20from%20black%20African%20or,77%20to%20join%20the%20scheme (accessed 17 January 2023).

Monteith, K., Quinn, E., Joseph-Salisbury, R., Dennis, A., Kane, E., Addo, F. and McGourlay, C. (2022) *Racial Bias and the Bench: A Response to the Judicial Diversity and Inclusion Strategy (2020–2025)*. University of Manchester. Available online: https://documents.manchester.ac.uk/display.aspx?DocID=64125 (accessed 14 August 2023)

Morkot, R. G. (2000) *The Black Pharoahs: Egypt's Nubian Rulers*. London: The Rubicon Press.

Morris, E. W. (2007) '"Ladies" or "loudies?" Perceptions and experiences of Black girls in classrooms', *Youth & Society*, 38(4), pp. 490–515.

Morris, M. (2015) *Supporting ethnic minority young people from education into work*. York: Joseph Rowntree Foundation.

Muhammad, G. E. and MacArthur, S. A. (2015) '"Styled by their perceptions": Black adolescent girls interpret representations of Black females in popular culture', *Multicultural Perspectives*, 17(3), pp. 133–40.

Nadar, S. (2014) '"Stories are data with soul" – lessons from black feminist epistemology', *Agenda*, 28(1), pp. 18–28.

Nandi, A. and Platt, L. (2010) *Ethnic minority women's poverty and economic wellbeing*. Available online: https://www.gov.uk/government/publications/ethnic-minority-womens-poverty-and-economic-well-being (accessed 17 January 2023).

NASUWT and Runnymede Trust (2017) *Visible Minorities, Invisible Teachers: BME Teachers in the Education System in England*. London: NASUWT/Runnymede Trust.

Nationality and Borders Act (2022) Available online: https://www.legislation.gov.uk/ukpga/2022/36/contents/enacted (accessed 17 January 2023).

National Today (2022) *National Black Women's Equal Pay Day – September 21, 2023*. Available online: https://nationaltoday.com/national-black-womens-equal-pay-day/ (accessed 17 January 2023).

Nayak, A. (2007) 'Critical whiteness studies', *Sociology Compass*, 1/2, pp. 737–55.

Niaah, J. A. H. (2020) 'The end of Afropessimism and their-story: Rastafari as ethos, inter-Asia', *Cultural Studies*, 21(4), pp. 587–99.

Nouroumby, M. A. (2021) *The Strong Black Daughter*. Available online: https://man-ange.medium.com/the-strong-black-daughter-da2dac19b65f (accessed 11 August 2023).

Nunn, N. M. (2018) 'Super-Girl: strength and sadness in Black girlhood', *Gender and Education*, 30(2), pp. 239–58.

O'Donoghue, M. (2013) 'Putting working-class mothers in their place: social stratification, the field of education, and Pierre Bourdieu's theory of practice', *British Journal of Sociology of Education*, 3(2), pp. 190–207.

OECD (2012) *Public and Private Schools: How Management and Funding Relate to their Socio-economic Profile*, PISA, OECD Publishing, Paris. Available online: https://doi.org/10.1787/9789264175006-en (accessed 18 January 2023).

OECD (2018) *Programme for International Student Assessment (PISA) results from PISA 2018*. Available online: https://www.oecd.org/pisa/publications/pisa-2018-results.htm (accessed 13 January 2023).

OECD (2019) *Education at a glance 2019*. Available online: https://www.oecd.org/education/education-at-a-glance/EAG2019_CN_GBR.pdf (accessed on 4 September 2023).

Office for National Statistics (2017) The National Statistics Socio-economic Classification (NS-SEC) Available online: https://www.ons.gov.uk/methodology/classificationsandstandards/otherclassifications/thenationalstatisticssocioeconomicclassificationnssecrebasedonsoc2010 (accessed 18 January 2023).

Office for National Statistics (2019) *Ethnicity pay gaps in Great Britain: 2018*. Available online: https://www.ons.gov.uk/employmentandlabourmarket/peopleinwork/earningsandworkinghours/articles/ethnicitypaygapsingreatbritain/2018/pdf (accessed 17 January 2023).

Office for National Statistics (2020) *Child poverty and education outcomes by ethnicity*. Available online: https://www.ons.gov.uk/economy/nationalaccounts/uksectoraccounts/compendium/economicreview/

february2020/childpovertyandeducationoutcomesbyethnicity (accessed 14 August 2023).

Office for National Statistics (2022) *Ethnic group, England and Wales: Census 2021*. Available online: https://www.ons.gov.uk/peoplepopulationandcommunity/culturalidentity/ethnicity/bulletins/ethnicgroupenglandandwales/census2021 (accessed 17 January 2023).

Okwonga, M. (2014) *The nod: A subtle lowering of the head you give to another Black person in an overwhelmingly white place*. Available online: https://medium.com/matter/the-nod-a-subtle-lowering-of-the-head-to-another-black-person-in-an-overwhelmingly-white-place-e12bfa0f833f (accessed 18 January 2023).

Olufemi, L., Younge, O., Sebatindira, W. and Mazoor-Khan, S. (2019) *A FLY Girl's Guide to University: Being a Woman of Colour at Cambridge and Other Institutions of Power and Elitism*. Birmingham: Verve Poetry Press.

O Neill, B. (2021) *UK's first Black royal Emma Thynn says she was 'naïve' to think she lived in 'post-racial society'*. Available online: https://evoke.ie/2021/03/07/royal/uks-first-black-royal-emma-thynn (accessed 30 May 2023).

ONS (2020) *Child poverty and education outcomes by ethnicity*. Available online: https://www.ons.gov.uk/economy/nationalaccounts/uksectoraccounts/compendium/economicreview/february2020/childpovertyandeducationoutcomesbyethnicity (accessed 13 January 2023).

ONS (2021) *Coronavirus and first year higher education students, England: 4 October to 11 October 2021*. Available online: https://www.ons.gov.uk/peoplepopulationandcommunity/healthandsocialcare/healthandwellbeing/bulletins/coronavirusandfirstyearhighereducationstudentsengland/4octoberto11october2021 (accessed 17 January 2023).

Operario, D. and Fiske, S. T. (1998) 'Racism equals power plus prejudice: a social psychological equation for racial oppression', in Eberhardt, J. L. and Fiske, S. T. (eds.), *Confronting Racism: The Problem and the Response*. London: Sage Publications, Inc, pp. 33–53.

Osei, K. (2019) 'Fashioning my garden of solace: a Black feminist autoethnography', *Fashion Theory*, 23(6), pp. 733–46.

Owusu-Kwarteng, L. (2019) '"Educated and Educating as a Black woman" – an auto/biographical reflection on my grandmother's influence on my academic and professional outcomes', *Gender and Education*, 33(1), pp. 1–17.

Oyedemi, T. (2016) 'Beauty as violence: "beautiful" hair and the cultural violence of identity erasure', *Social Identities*, 22(5), pp. 537–53.

Palmer, L. A. (2020a) 'Diane Abbott, misogynoir and the politics of Black British feminism's anticolonial imperatives: "In Britain too, it's as if we don't exist"', *The Sociological Review*, 68(3), pp. 508–23.

Palmer, L. A. (2020b) '"Each one teach one" visualising black intellectual life in Handsworth beyond the epistemology of "white sociology"', *Identities*, 27(1), pp. 91–113.

Paper Whispers (2023) *Black Women Professors*. Available online: https://www.paperwhispers.com/ (accessed 15 May 2023).

Parliamentary Labour Party (2021) *Code of Conduct: Labour's Afrophobia and Anti-Black Racism Policy*. Available online: https://labour.org.uk/members/my-welfare/rules-and-codes-of-conduct/labours-afrophobia-policy/#:~:text=It%20includes%20every%20day%20and,detrimental%20to%20the%20Labour%20Party (accessed 17 January 2023).

Parsons, C. (2019) 'Social justice, race and class in education in England: competing perspectives', *Cambridge Journal of Education*, 49(3), pp. 309–27.

Paschel, T. S. (2017) 'From Colombia to the U.S. Black lives have always mattered', *NACLA Report on the Americas*, 49(1), pp. 27–9.

Pásztor, A. and Wakeling, P. B. J. (2018) 'All Ph.D.s are equal but … Institutional and social stratification in access to the doctorate', *British Journal of Sociology of Education*, 39(7), pp. 982–97.

Payton, L. T. (2021) *Colorism is the key ingredient in the Meghan Markle debate*. Available online: https://www.bitchmedia.org/article/meghan-markle-colorism-debate (accessed 30 May 2023).

Pearce, S. (2005) *You Wouldn't Understand: White Teachers in Multiethnic Classrooms*. London: Trentham Books.

Pennant, A.-L. (2020a) '"Look, I have gone through the education system and I have tried damn hard to get to where I am, so no one is gonna stop me!": The educational journeys and experiences of Black British women graduates', [Unpublished Ph.D. thesis]. University of Birmingham.

Pennant, A.-L. (2020b) 'My journey into the "heart of whiteness" whilst remaining my authentic (Black) self', *Educational Philosophy and Theory*, 53(3), pp. 245–56.

Pennant, A.-L. (2022) 'Who's checkin' for Black girls and women in the "pandemic within a pandemic"? COVID-19, Black Lives Matter and educational implications', *Educational Review*, 74(3), pp. 534–57.

Pennant, A.-L. (2023) 'Rebuking the "Work twice as hard for half as much" mentality among Black girls and women', in Lessard-Phillips, L. et al. (eds.), *Migration, Displacement and Diversity: The IRiS Anthology*. Oxford Publishing Services, pp. 138–43.

Pennant, F. (2022) *In Conversation: Aindrea Emelife and Ayana V. Jackson: Art historian and curator Aindrea Emelife and contemporary artist Ayana V. Jackson discuss the shift in how Black women present themselves*. Available online: https://www.matchesfashion.com/stories/2022/09/people-in-conversation-black-venus-aw22 (accessed 30 May 2023).

Persad, S. (2020) *You can't say Black Lives Matter if you're still appropriating Black culture*. Available online: https://www.cosmopolitan.com/politics/a33470990/black-lives-matter-cultural-appropriation/ (accessed 18 January 2023).

Peters, A. L. and Nash, A. M. (2021) 'I'm every woman: advancing the intersectional leadership of black women school leaders as anti-racist praxis', *Journal of School Leadership*, 31(1–2), pp. 7–28.

Phillips, A. (2004) 'Defending equality of outcome', *Journal of Political Philosophy*, 12(1), pp. 1–19.

Phillips, D. (ed.) (2000) *The Education Systems of the United Kingdom*. Oxford Studies in Comparative Education.

Phoenix, A. (2009) 'De-colonising practices: negotiating narratives from racialised and gendered experiences of education', *Race Ethnicity and Education*, 12(1), pp. 101–14.

Pickens, T. A. (2015) 'Shoving aside the politics of respectability: black women, reality TV, and the ratchet performance', *Women & Performance: A Journal of Feminist Theory*, 25(1), pp. 41–58.

Pitts, J. (2021) *Students lose when Black women aren't supported*. Available online: https://www.learningforjustice.org/magazine/students-lose-when-black-women-arent-supported (accessed 17 January 2023).

Platt, L. (2005a) *Migration and social mobility: the life chances of Britain's minority ethnic communities*. UK: Joseph Rowntree Foundation (JRF). Available online: https://www.jrf.org.uk/report/migration-and-social-mobility-life-chances-britain%E2%80%99s-minority-ethnic-communities (accessed 18 January 2023).

Platt, L. (2005b) 'New destinations? Assessing the post-migration social mobility of minority ethnic groups in England and Wales', *Social Policy and Administration*, 39(6), pp. 697–721.

Platt, L. (2007) 'Making education count: the effects of ethnicity and qualifications on intergenerational social class mobility', *The Sociological Review*, 55(3), pp. 485–508.

Pollard, V. (1979) 'Dread talk: the speech of the Rastafarians of Jamaica intervention', *Conference on Theoretical Orientations in Creole Studies*, St. Thomas, Virgin Islands, 1–10; *Caribbean Quarterly*, 26(4), 198.

Pollard, V. (1982) 'The social history of Dread Talk', *Caribbean Quarterly*, 28(4), pp. 17–40.

Powell, T. and Coles, J. A. (2021) '"We still here": Black mothers' personal narratives of sense making and resisting antiblackness and the suspensions of their Black children', *Race Ethnicity and Education*, 24(1), pp. 76–95.

Power, S., Taylor, C., Rees, G. and Jones, K. (2009) 'Out-of-school learning: variations in provision and participation in secondary schools', *Research Papers in Education*, 24(4), pp. 439–60.

Pratt, M. L. (1991) 'Arts of the contact zone', *Profession*, pp. 33–40.

Proweller, A. (1998) *Constructing Female Identities: Meaning Making in an Upper Middle Class Youth Culture*. New York: State University of New York Press.

Pugsley, L. (2004) *The University Challenge: Higher Education Markets and Social Stratification*. London: Routledge.

Purcell, K., Elias, P. and Atfield, G. (2009) *Analysing the relationship between higher education participation and educational and career development patterns and outcomes. A new classification of higher education institutions.* Available online: https://warwick.ac.uk/fac/soc/ier/futuretrack/findings/ft3.1_wp1_access_tariff_classification.pdf (accessed 13 January 2023).

Puwar, N. (2004) *Space Invaders: Race, Gender and Bodies Out of Place*. Oxford: Berg Publishers.

Race Relations Act (1965) Available online: https://www.parliament.uk/about/living-heritage/transformingsociety/private-lives/relationships/collections1/race-relations-act-1965/race-relations-act-1965/ (accessed 17 January 2023).

Race Relations Act (1968) Available online: https://www.legislation.gov.uk/ukpga/1968/71/enacted#:~:text=1968%20CHAPTER%2071,people%20of%20different%20racial%20origins (accessed 17 January 2023).

Race Relations Act (1976) Available online: https://www.legislation.gov.uk/ukpga/1976/74/pdfs/ukpga_19760074_en.pdf (accessed 17 January 2023).

Race Relations (Amendment) Act (2000) Available online: https://www.legislation.gov.uk/ukpga/2000/34/notes/division/3#:~:text=place%20a%20duty%20on%20specified,discrimination%20by%20police%20officers%3B%20and (accessed 17 January 2023).

Raffe, D., Brannen, K., Croxford, L. and Martin, C. (1999) 'Comparing England, Scotland, Wales and Northern Ireland: the case for "home internationals" in comparative research', *Comparative Education*, 35(1), pp. 9–25.

Ramdin, R. (2017) *The Making of the Black Working Class in Britain*. London: Verso Books.

Ramesh, R. (2010) *More black people jailed in England and Wales proportionally than in US*. Available online: https://www.theguardian.com/society/2010/oct/11/black-prison-population-increase-england (accessed 14 August 2023).

Ramirez, J. J., Garcia, G. A. and Hudson, L. T. (2020) 'Mothers' influences on Latino collegians: understanding Latinx mother-son pedagogies', *International Journal of Qualitative Studies in Education*, 33(10), pp. 1022–41.

Rampersad, R. (2014) '"Racialised facilitative capital" and the paving of differential paths to achievement of Afro-Trinidadian boys', *British Journal of Sociology of Education*, 35(1), pp. 73–93.

Reay, D. (1998) 'Surviving in dangerous places: working-class women, women's studies and higher education', *Women's Studies International Forum*, 21(1), pp. 11–19.

Reay, D. (2012) 'What would a socially just education system look like?: saving the minnows from the pike', *Journal of Education Policy*, 27(5), pp. 587–99.

Reay, D., Crozier, G., and Clayton, J. (2009) '"Strangers in paradise"?: working-class students in elite universities', *Sociology*, 43(6), pp. 1103–21.

Reay, D., Crozier, G. and Clayton, J. (2010) '"Fitting in" or "standing out": working-class students in UK higher education', *British Educational Research Journal*, 36(1), pp. 107–24.

Reay, D., David M. E., and Ball, S. J. (2006) *Degrees of Choice: Social Class, Race and Gender in Higher Education*. Stoke on Trent: Trentham Books.

Reay, D., Hollingworth, S., Williams, K., Crozier, G., Jamieson, F., James, D. and Beedell, P. (2007) '"A darker shade of pale?" Whiteness, the middle classes and multi-ethnic inner city schooling', *Sociology*, 41(6), pp. 1041–60.

Reid, E. (1989) 'Black girls talking', *Gender and Education*, 1(3), pp. 295–300.

Reynolds, T. (1997) '(Mis)representing the black (super)woman', in Mirza, H. (ed.), *Black British Feminism: A Reader*. London: Routledge, pp. 97–113.

Reynolds, T. (2002) 'Rethinking a black feminist standpoint', *Ethnic and Racial Studies*, 25(4), pp. 591–606.

Reynolds, T. (2020) 'Studies of the maternal: Black mothering 10 years on', *Studies in the Maternal*, 13(1), pp. 1–11.

Rhamie, J. (2012) 'Achievement and underachievement: the experiences of African Caribbeans', *Race Ethnicity and Education*, 15(5), pp. 683–704.

Rhiney, D. (2021) *Where is the coverage of missing black women? Attack survivor Dr Diahanne Rhiney argues that Black disappearances or murders are not considered as newsworthy*. Available online: https://www.voice-online.co.uk/opinion/comment/2021/10/08/where-is-the-coverage-of-missing-black-women/ (accessed 14 August 2023).

Ricks, S. A. (2014) 'Falling through the cracks: Black girls and education', *Interdisciplinary Journal of Teaching and Learning*, 4(1), pp. 10–21.

Ringrose, J. (2007) 'Successful girls? Complicating post-feminist, neoliberal discourses of educational achievement and gender equality', *Gender and Education*, 19(4), pp. 471–89.

Roberts, N. and Bolton, P. (2020) *Educational outcomes of Black pupils and students*. Available online: https://commonslibrary.parliament.uk/research-briefings/cbp-9023/ (accessed 17 January 2023).

Robinson, C. L. (2011) 'Hair as race: why "good hair" may be bad for Black females', *Howard Journal of Communications*, 22(4), pp. 358–76.

Roediger, D. R. (2018) *Working Toward Whiteness: How America's Immigrants Became White: The Strange Journey from Ellis Island to the Suburbs*. New York: Basic Books.

Rokicka, M. (2014) *The impact of students' part-time work on educational outcomes*, ISER Working Paper Series, No. 2014-42, University of Essex, Institute for Social and Economic Research (ISER), Colchester. Available online: https://www.econstor.eu/bitstream/10419/126485/1/812470478.pdf (accessed 17 January 2023).

Rollock, N. (2007) 'Legitimizing Black academic failure: deconstructing staff discourses on academic success, appearance and behaviour', *International Studies in Sociology of Education*, 17(3), pp. 275–87.

Rollock, N. (2014) 'Race, class and "the harmony of dispositions"', *Sociology*, 48(3), pp. 445–51.

Rollock, N. (2019) *Staying Power. The career experiences and strategies of UK Black female professors*. Available online: https://www.ucu.org.uk/media/10075/Staying-Power/pdf/UCU_Rollock_February_2019.pdf (accessed 17 January 2023).

Rollock, N. (2021) '"I would have become wallpaper had racism had its way": Black female professors, racial battle fatigue, and strategies for surviving higher education', *Peabody Journal of Education*, 96(2), pp. 206–17.

Rollock, N., Gillborn, D., Vincent, C. and Ball, S. J. (2015) *The Colour of Class: The Educational Strategies of the Black Middle Classes*. London: Routledge.

Rollock, N., Vincent, C., Gillborn, D., and Ball, S. J. (2013) '"Middle class by profession": Class status and identification amongst the Black middle classes', *Ethnicities*, 13(3), pp. 253–75.

Roscigno, V. J. and Ainsworth-Darnell, J. W. (1999) 'Race, cultural capital, and educational resources: persistent inequalities and achievement', *Sociology of Education*, 72(3), pp. 158–78.

Rose, D. and Pevalin, D. (ed.) (2003) *A Researcher's Guide to the National Statistics Socio-economic Classification*. London: SAGE Publications.

Rottenberg, C. (2018) *Neoliberal Meritocracy, Cultural Studies*. Abingdon: Routledge.

Rousseau, C. K. (2006) 'Keeping it real: race and education in Memphis', in Dixson, A. D. and Rosseau, C. K. (eds.), *Critical Race Theory in Education: All God's Children Got a Song*. London: Routledge, pp. 113–29.

Rowe, M. (1977) 'The Saturn's Rings phenomenon', in *Conference on Women's Leadership and Authority in the Health Professions*. Santa Cruz, CA.

Russell Group (2019) Available online: https://russellgroup.ac.uk (accessed 11 August 2023).

Russell Group (2022) *About*. Available online: https://russellgroup.ac.uk/about/ (accessed 17 January 2023).

Sabelli, S. (2011) '"Dubbing di diaspora": gender and reggae music inna Babylon', *Social Identities*, 17(1), pp. 137–52.

Salih, S. (2002) *Judith Butler*. London: Routledge.

Sandeen, D. (2022) *What to Know About Dreadlocks: A Guide*. Available online: https://www.byrdie.com/locs-or-locks-400267 (accessed 15 May 2023).

Savage, M. (2015) *Social Class in the 21st Century*. London: Pelican Books.

Sawyer, M. Q. (2008) 'DuBois's double consciousness versus Latin American exceptionalism: Joe Arroyo, Salsa, and Négritude', in Marable, M. and Agard-Jones, V. (eds.), *Transnational Blackness: Navigating the Global Color Line*. London: Palgrave MacMillan, pp. 135–48.

Sayyid, S. (2017) 'Post-racial paradoxes: rethinking European racism and anti-racism', *Patterns of Prejudice*, 51(1), pp. 9–25.

Schultz, T. W. (1961) *Investment in Human Capital*. Chicago: University of Chicago Press.

Schwarz, O. (2016) 'The symbolic economy of authenticity as a form of symbolic violence: the case of middle-class ethnic minorities', *Distinktion: Journal of Social Theory*, 17(1), pp. 2–19.

Sewell, T. (2021) *Commission on Race and Ethnic Disparities: The Report*. Available online: https://www.gov.uk/government/publications/the-report-of-the-commission-on-race-and-ethnic-disparities (accessed 17 January 2023).

Shackle, S. (2019) *'The way universities are run is making us ill': inside the student mental health crisis*. Available online: https://www.theguardian.com/society/2019/sep/27/anxiety-mental-breakdowns-depression-uk-students (accessed 17 January 2023).

Shelton, J. (2022) *Yale creates Pennington Fellowship for New Haven students to attend HBCUs*. Available online: https://news.yale.edu/2022/12/12/yale-creates-pennington-fellowship-new-haven-students-attend-hbcus (accessed 15 May 2023).

Sherine, A. (2022) *The innocent insidiousness of "Where are you from?": People of colour are all too familiar with Lady Hussey's question to Ngozi Fulani*. Available online: https://www.newstatesman.com/quickfire/2022/12/ngozi-fulani-where-are-you-from-lady-hussey-royal-family (accessed 30 May 2023).

Showumni, V. (2017) *Suffering in silence: Black British young women and their wellbeing*. Available online: https://www.academia.edu/16100459/Suffering_in_silence_Black_British_Young_Women_and_their_Well_Being (accessed 17 January 2023).

Sibieta, L. (2021) *The growing gap between state school and private school spending*, The IFS. Available online: https://ifs.org.uk/articles/growing-gap-between-state-school-and-private-school-spending (accessed 14 August 2023).

Smith, N. and Middleton, S. (2007) *A Review of Poverty Dynamics Research in the UK*. York: Joseph Rowntree Foundation.

Smith, W. A., Yosso, T. J., and Solórzano, D. G. (2011) 'Challenging racial battle fatigue on historically white campuses: a critical race examination of race-related stress', in Coates, R. D. (ed.), *Covert Racism*. Leiden, the Netherlands: Brill, pp. 211–37.

Smith, W. A., Hung, M. and Franklin, J. D. (2011) 'Racial battle fatigue and the miseducation of Black men: racial microaggressions, societal problems, and environmental stress', *The Journal of Negro Education*, 80(1), pp. 63–82.

Sobande, F. and Wells, J. R. (2021) 'The poetic identity work and sisterhood of Black women becoming academics', *Gender, Work and Organization*, 30(2), pp. 469–84.

Sobers, S. (2016) Language and resistance: memories of slavery and Rastafari language. Available online: https://www.opendemocracy.net/en/beyond-trafficking-and-slavery/language-and-resistance-memories-of-slavery-and-rastafari-langua/ (accessed 17 January 2023).

Social Market Foundation (2021) *Black graduates get worse degrees and earn less than white peers*. Available online: https://www.smf.co.uk/black-graduates-get-worse-degrees-and-earn-less-than-white-peers/ (accessed 17 January 2023).

Solórzano, D. G., and Delgado B. D. (2001) 'Examining transformational resistance through a critical race and LatCrit framework: Chicana and Chicano students in an urban context', *Urban Education*, 36(3), pp. 308–42.

Solorzano, D. G. and Yosso, T. J. (2001) 'Critical race and LatCrit theory and method: counter-storytelling', *International Journal of Qualitative Studies in Education*, 14(4), pp. 471–95.

Solórzano, D. G., and Yosso, T. J. (2002) 'Critical race methodology: counter-storytelling as an analytical framework for education research', *Qualitative Inquiry*, 8(1), pp. 23–44.

Souto-Otero, M. (2010) 'Education, meritocracy, redistribution', *Journal of Education Policy*, 25(3), pp. 397–413.
Spivak, G. (1988) 'Can the subaltern speak?', in Grossberg, L. and Nelson, C. (eds.), *Marxism and the Interpretation of Culture*. Houndmills: Macmillan, pp. 66–111.
Spivak, G. (1996) 'Subaltern studies: deconstructing historiography?', in Landry, D. and MacLean, G. (eds.), *The Spivak Reader*, London: Routledge, pp. 203–37.
Spohrer, K.(2016) 'Negotiating and contesting "success": discourses of aspiration in a UK secondary school', *Discourse: Studies in the Cultural Politics of Education*, 37(3), pp. 411–25.
Stamp, C. (2020) *Post-university depression: feeling lost after graduating university and getting found (again)*. Available online: https://plexuss.com/news/article/post-university-depression-post-graduation-blues (accessed 17 January 2023).
Statista (2022) *Estimated number of podcast listeners in the United Kingdom (UK) from 2017 to 2026*. Available online: https://www.statista.com/forecasts/1147560/podcast-reach-uk (accessed 17 January 2023).
Steele, C. M. (1997) 'A threat in the air: how stereotypes shape intellectual identity and performance', *American Psychologist*, 52(6), pp. 613–29.
Stephens, N. and Delamont, S. (2010) '"They start to get malicia"': teaching tacit and technical knowledge', *British Journal of Sociology of Education*, 30(5), pp. 537–48.
Stevenson, J. (2018) *Muslim students in UK higher education: issues of inequality and inequity*. Available online: https://www.azizfoundation.org.uk/wp-content/uploads/2021/01/Bridge-Higher-Education-report-2.pdf (accessed 17 January 2023).
Strand, S. (2010) 'Do some schools narrow the gap? Differential school effectiveness by ethnicity, gender and poverty, and prior achievement', *School Effectiveness and School Improvement*, 21(3), pp. 280–314.
Strand, S. (2014a) 'Ethnicity, gender, social class and achievement gaps at age 16: intersectionality and "getting it" for the white working class', *Research Papers in Education*, 29(2), pp. 131–71.
Strand, S. (2014b) 'School effects and ethnic, gender and socio-economic gaps in educational achievement at age 11', *Oxford Review of Education*, 40(2), pp. 223–45.
Sue, D. W. (2003) *Overcoming our Racism: The Journey to Liberation*. San Francisco, CA: Wiley.
Sue, D. W., Capodilupo, C. M., Torino, C., Bucceri, J., Holder, A. M. B, Nadal, K. L. and Esquilin, M. (2007) 'Racial microagressions in everyday life: implications for clinical practice', *American Psychologist*, 62(4), pp. 271–86.
Sveinsson, K. (2009) *Who cares about the white working class?* The Runnymede Trust Report. Available online: https://www.runnymedetrust.org/publications/who-cares-about-the-white-working-class (accessed 18 January 2023).

Sylvester, R. (2021) *British education system 'only average' in international league table.* Available online: https://www.thetimes.co.uk/article/british-education-system-only-average-in-international-league-table-xlk5mx7sx#:~:text=The%20UK%20has%20slipped%20back,lowest%20levels%20of%20life%20satisfaction&text=The%20UK's%20education%20system,Estonia%2C%20Switzerland%20and%20the%20Netherlands (accessed 18 January 2023).

Tackey, N. D., Barnes, H. and Khambhaita, P. (2011) *Poverty, ethnicity and education.* Available online: https://www.jrf.org.uk/sites/default/files/jrf/migrated/files/poverty-ethnicity-education-full.pdf (accessed 13 January 2023).

Tan, J. A. (2017) *For women of color, the glass ceiling is actually made of concrete.* Available online: https://www.huffpost.com/entry/for-women-of-color-thegl_b_9728056?guccounter=1 (accessed 17 January 2023).

Tapper, T. and Palfreyman, D. (2009) 'Oxbridge sustaining the international reputation', in Palfreyman, T. and Tapper, T. (eds.), *Structuring Mass Higher Education: The Role of Elite Institutions.* New York: Routledge, pp. 312–28.

Tate, S. (2007) 'Black beauty: shade, hair and anti-racist aesthetics', *Ethnic and Racial Studies*, 30(2), pp. 300–19.

Tate, S. A. (2005) *Black Skins, Black Masks: Hybridity, Dialogism, Performativity.* London: Ashgate Publishing.

Tate, S. A. (2014) 'Performativity and "raced" bodies', in Murji. K. and Solomos, J. (eds.), *Theories of Race and Ethnicity: Contemporary Debates and Perspectives.* Cambridge: Cambridge University Press, pp. 180–97.

Tatum, B. D. (1999) *Why Are All the Black Kids Sitting Together in the Cafeteria?* New York: Basic Books.

Taylor, C., Rees, G. and Davies, R. (2013) 'Devolution and geographies of education: the use of the Millennium Cohort Study for "home international" comparisons across the UK', *Comparative Education*, 49 (3), pp. 290–316.

Taylor, E. (1998) 'A primer on critical race theory', *The Journal of Blacks in Higher Education*, 19, pp. 122–4.

Taylor, E. (2009) 'The foundations of Critical Race Theory in education: an introduction', in Taylor, E., Gillborn, D. and Ladson-Billings, G. (eds.), *Foundations of Critical Race Theory in Education.* London: Routledge, pp. 1–17.

Teixeira, F., Alvarez-Figueroa, F., Nelson, L. and Alhalafi, S. (2021) *Breaking the glass: understanding the barriers faced by Black professional women in career progression.* Available online: https://documents.manchester.ac.uk/display.aspx?DocID=57553 (accessed 17 January 2023).

Tereshchenko, A., Mills, A. and Bradbury, A. (2020) *Making progress? Employment and retention of BAME teachers in England.* Available online: https://discovery.ucl.ac.uk/id/eprint/10117331/1/IOE_Report_BAME_Teachers.pdf (accessed 13 January 2023).

Terzi, L. (2014) 'Reframing inclusive education: educational equality as capability equality', *Cambridge Journal of Education*, 44(4), pp. 479–93.

Tett, L. (2010) '"I'm working class and proud of it"—gendered experiences of nontraditional participants in higher education', *Gender and Education*, 12(2), pp. 183–94.

The African American Policy Forum and Center for Intersectionality and Social Policy Studies (2014) *#SAYHERNAME: African American Policy Forum: Black women are killed by police too*. Available online: https://www.aapf.org/sayhername (accessed 18 January 2023).

The Challenge, School Dash and the iCoCo foundation (2017) *Understanding School segregation in England: 2011 to 2016*. Available online: https://tedcantle.co.uk/wp-content/uploads/2013/03/Understanding-School-Segregation-in-England-2011-2016-Final.pdf (accessed 13 January 2023).

The Commission on Young Lives (2022) *All together now inclusion not exclusion: supporting all young people to succeed in school.* Available online: https://thecommissiononyounglives.co.uk/wp-content/uploads/2022/04/COYL-Education-report-FINAL-APR22.pdf (accessed 14 August 2023).

The Fawcett Society and The Runnymede Trust (2022) *Broken Ladders: The myth of meritocracy for women of colour in the workplace*. Available online: https://www.fawcettsociety.org.uk/broken-ladders (accessed 17 January 2023).

The Financial Times (2020) *What makes Nigerians in diaspora so successful.* Available online: https://www.ft.com/content/ca39b445-442a-4845-a07c-0f5dae5f3460 (accessed 17 January 2023).

The Home Office (2019) *Windrush lessons learned review by Wendy Williams.* Available online: https://www.gov.uk/government/publications/windrush-lessons-learned-review (accessed 17 January 2023).

The Sutton Trust (2008) *Social selectivity of state schools and the impact of grammars.* Available online: https://www.suttontrust.com/wp-content/uploads/2019/12/GrammarsReviewSummary-1.pdf (accessed 17 January 2023).

The Sutton Trust and the Social Mobility Commission (2019) *Elitist Britain 2019. The educational backgrounds of Britain's leading people*. Available online: https://www.suttontrust.com/wp-content/uploads/2020/01/Elitist-Britain-2019-Summary-Report.pdf (accessed 17 January 2023).

The United Nations (2023) *UK: Discrimination against people of African descent is structural, institutional, and systemic, say UN experts*. Available at: UK: Discrimination against people of African descent is structural, institutional and systemic, say UN experts | OHCHR (accessed 15 August 2023).

Themelis, S. (2008) 'Meritocracy through education and social mobility in post-war Britain: a critical examination', *British Journal of Sociology of Education*, 29(5), pp. 427–38.

Thomas, T. (2021) *Black youth unemployment rate of 40% similar to time of Brixton riots, data shows*. Available online: https://www.theguardian.com/society/2021/apr/11/black-youth-unemployment-rate-brixton-riots-covid (accessed 14 August 2023).

Thomas, K. M., Johnson-Bailey, J., Phelps, R. E., Tran, N. M., and Johnson, L. (2013) 'Moving from pet to threat: narratives of professional Black women', in Comas-Diaz, L. and Green, B. (eds.), *The Psychological Health of Women of Color: Intersections, Challenges, and Opportunities*. Westport, CT: Praeger, pp. 275–86.

Thompson, C. (2009) 'Black women, beauty, and hair as a matter of being', *Women's Studies*, 38(8), pp. 831–56.

Thompson, W. (2018a) *Black Girls from the hood are the real trendsetters*. Available: https://medium.com/@WannasWorld/black-girls-from-the-hood-are-the-real-trendsetters-a2c1490d1897 (accessed 18 January 2023).

Thompson, W. (2018b) *How white women on instagram are profiting off Black women*. Available: https://www.papermag.com/white-women-blackfishing-instagram (accessed 18 January 2023).

Tichavakunda, A. A. (2019) 'An overdue theoretical discourse: Pierre Bourdieu's theory of practice and Critical Race Theory in education', *Educational Studies*, 55(6), pp. 651–66.

Tierney, W. G. and Venegas, K. M. (2006) 'Fictive kin and social capital: the role of peer groups in applying and paying for college', *American Behavioral Scientist*, 49(12), pp. 1687–702.

Tobitt, C. (2021) *Survey finds growing UK journalism workforce of nearly 100,000 still lack ethnic diversity*. Available online: https://pressgazette.co.uk/news/nctj-diversity-journalism-number-journalists/ (accessed 30 May 2023).

Tomlin, C., Wright, C. and Mocombe, P. (2014) 'A structural approach to understanding Black British Caribbean academic underachievement in the United Kingdom', *Journal ofSocial Science for Policy Implications*, 2(2), pp. 37–58.

Tomlinson, M. (2008) '"The degree is not enough": students' perceptions of the role of higher education credentials for graduate work and employability', *British Journal of Sociology of Education*, 29(1), pp. 49–61.

Tomlinson, S. (1981) *Educational Subnormality: A Study in Decision-Making*. London: Routledge & Kegan Paul.

Trueland, J. (2021) *A shared struggle*. Available online: https://www.bma.org.uk/news-and-opinion/a-shared-struggle (accessed 17 January 2023).

Tso, D. T. (2018) *Nail salon brawls & boycotts: unpacking the Black-Asian conflict in America*. Available online: https://www.refinery29.com/en-gb/2018/08/207993/red-apple-nails-brawl-black-asian-conflict (accessed 17 January 2023).

TUC (2006) *Black women and employment*. Available online: https://www.tuc.org.uk/research-analysis/reports/black-women-and-employment (accessed 17 January 2023).

TUC (2016a) *Black workers with degrees earn a quarter less than white counterparts, finds TUC*. Available online: https://www.tuc.org.uk/news/black-workers-degrees-earn-quarter-less-white-counterparts-finds-tuc#:~:text=About%20unions-,Black%20workers%20with%20degrees%20earn%20a,than%20white%20counterparts%2C%20finds%20TUC&text=Black%20workers%20with%20degrees%20earn%2023.1%25%20less%20on%20average%20than,analysis%20published%20by%20the%20TUC (accessed 17 January 2023).

TUC (2016b) *Black, qualified and unemployed*. Available online: https://www.tuc.org.uk/research-analysis/reports/black-qualified-and-unemployed (accessed 17 January 2023).

TUC (2016c) *Insecure work and ethnicity*. Available online: https://www.tuc.org.uk/sites/default/files/Insecure%20work%20and%20ethnicity_0.pd (accessed 17 January 2023).

UK Parliament Education Committee (2021) *'Forgotten' white working-class pupils let down by decades of neglect, MPs say*. Available online: https://committees.parliament.uk/committee/203/education-committee/news/156024/forgotten-white-workingclass-pupils-let-down-by-decades-of-neglect-mps-say/ (accessed 13 January 2023).

Unghar, M., Ghazinour, M., and Richter, J.(2013) 'Annual research review: what is resilience within the social ecology of human development?', *Journal of Child Psychology and Psychiatry*, 54(4), pp. 348–66.

University of Glasgow (2023) *Historical Slavery Initiative*. Available online: https://www.gla.ac.uk/explore/historicalslaveryinitiative/#:~:text=This%20world%2Dleading%20initiative%20has,voices%20previously%20marginalised%20by%20history (accessed 15 May 2023).

van Dijk, H., Kooij, D., Karanika-Murray, M., De Vos, A., and Meyer, B. (2020) 'Meritocracy a myth? A multilevel perspective of how social inequality accumulates through work', *Organizational Psychology Review*, 10(3–4), pp. 240–69.

Vaughan-Bonas, D. (2019) 'The oppression in appropriation', *Footnotes*, 12, pp. 1–5.

Vincent, C., Rollock, N., Ball, S., and Gillborn, D. (2012a) 'Being strategic, being watchful, being determined: Black middle-class parents and schooling', *British Journal of Sociology of Education*, 33(3), pp. 337–54.

Vincent, C., Rollock, N., Ball, S. and Gillborn, D. (2012b) 'Raising middle-class Black children: parenting priorities, actions and strategies', *Sociology*, 47(3), pp. 427–42.

Vincent, C., Ball, S., Rollock, N. and Gillborn, D. (2013) 'Three generations of racism: Black middle-class children and schooling', *British Journal of Sociology of Education*, 34 (5–6), pp. 929–46.

Virk, K. (2020) *Ruby Williams: No child with afro hair should suffer like me*. Available online: https://www.bbc.co.uk/news/newsbeat-45521094 (accessed 17 January 2023).

Wallace, D. (2017) 'Reading "race" in Bourdieu? Examining Black cultural capital among Black Caribbean youth in South London', *Sociology*, 51(5), pp. 907–23.

Wallace, D. (2018) 'Cultural capital as whiteness? Examining logics of ethno-racial representation and resistance', *British Journal of Sociology of Education*, 39(4), pp. 466–82.

Wallace, D. and Joseph-Salisbury, R. (2022) 'How, still, is the Black Caribbean child made educationally subnormal in the English school system?', *Ethnic and Racial Studies*, 45(8), pp. 1426–52.

Wallis, J. (2020) *Blackfishing is a huge problem, but the White silence about it may be even worse*. Available online: https://fashionjournal.com.au/beauty/blackfishing-is-a-huge-problem-but-the-white-silence-about-it-may-be-even-worse (accessed 18 January 2023).

Ward, J. (1996) 'Raising resisters: the role of truth telling in the psychological development of African-American girls', in Leadbetter, B. and Way, N. (eds.), *Urban girls: resisting stereotypes, creating identities*. New York: New York University Press, pp. 85–99.

Ward, M. R. M. (2015) *From Labouring to Learning Working-Class Masculinities, Education and De-Industrialization*. London: Palgrave Macmillan.

Warikoo, N. (2018) 'What meritocracy means to its winners: admissions, race, and inequality at elite universities in the United States and Britain', *Social Sciences*, 7(8), p. 131.

Warmington, P. (2012) '"A tradition in ceaseless motion": critical race theory and black British intellectual spaces', *Race Ethnicity and Education*, 15(1), pp. 5–21.

Warmington, P. (2014) *Black British Intellectuals and Education: Multiculturalism's Hidden History*. London: Routledge.

Warmington, P. (2020) 'Critical race theory in England: impact and opposition', *Identities*, 27(1), pp. 20–37.

Warren, C. A. and Coles, J. A. (2020) 'Trading spaces: antiBlackness and reflections on Black education futures', *Equity & Excellence in Education*, 53(3), pp. 382–98.

Watson, J. (2013) 'Profitable portfolios: capital that counts in higher education', *British Journal of Sociology of Education*, 34(3), pp. 412–30.

Watson, W. (2018) 'We got soul: exploring contemporary Black women educators' praxis of politicized care', *Equity & Excellence in Education*, 51(3–4), pp. 362–77.

Weekes, D. (2003) 'Keeping it in the community: creating safe spaces for black girlhood', *Community, Work & Family*, 6(1), pp. 47–61.

Weekes-Bernard, D. (2007) *School choice and ethnic segregation – educational decision-making among Black and minority ethnic parents*. Available online: https://www.bl.uk/collection-items/school-choice-and-ethnic-segregation-educational-decision-making-among-black-and-minority-ethnic-parents (accessed 13 January 2023).

Weekes-Bernard, D. (2017) *Poverty and ethnicity in the labour market*. Available online: https://www.jrf.org.uk/report/poverty-ethnicity-labour-market (accessed 17 January 2023).

West, A. and Wolfe, D. (2018) *Academies, the school system in England and a vision for the future*. Available online: http://eprints.lse.ac.uk/88240/1/Academies%20Vision%20Report%202%20JUNE.pdf (accessed 13 January 2023).

West, L. M., Donovan, R. A. and Daniel, A. R. (2016) 'The price of strength: Black college women's perspectives on the strong Black woman stereotype', *Women & Therapy*, 39(3/4), pp. 390–413.

Which? University Guide (n.d.) *The complete guide to A-level, BTEC and International Baccalaureate choices*. Available online: https://www.stjohnplessington.com/_site/data/files/sixth%20form/939C60F5582C8F448740FD19E6294F72.pdf (accessed 5 September 2023).

White, N. (2019) *What is it like to be a young Black journalist in the UK?* Available online: https://www.britishcouncil.org/voices-magazine/what-is-it-like-to-be-new-journalist-uk (accessed 30 May 2023).

White, N. (2023) *Black schoolgirl 'left unable to eat' after 'racially motivated' attack*. Available online: https://www.independent.co.uk/news/uk/crime/black-schoolgirl-thomas-knyvett-college-b2279929.html (accessed 30 May 2023).

Williams, O. (2016) *British journalism is 94% white and 55% male, survey reveals*. Available online: https://www.theguardian.com/media-network/2016/mar/24/british-journalism-diversity-white-female-male-survey (accessed 30 May 2023).

Williams, P., Bath, S., Arday, J. and Lewis, C. (2019) *The broken pipeline: barriers to Black Ph.D. students accessing research council funding*. Available online: https://leadingroutes.org/the-broken-pipeline (accessed 17 January 2023).

Willis, P. (1977) *Learning to Labour: How Working Class Kids Get Working Class Jobs*. Westmead, Farnborough: Saxon House.

Wilson (2016) *The meaning of #BlackGirlMagic, and how you can get some of it*. Available online: https://www.huffingtonpost.co.uk/entry/what-is-black-girl-magic-video_n_5694dad4e4b086bc1cd517f4 (accessed 18 January 2023).

Witherspoon, N. and Taylor, D. L. (2010) 'Spiritual weapons: Black female principals and religio-spirituality', *Journal of Educational Administration and History*, 42(2), pp. 133–58.

Wong, B. (2015) 'A blessing with a curse: model minority ethnic students and the construction of educational success', *Oxford Review of Education*, 41(6), pp. 730–46.

Wright, C., Weekes, D., McGlaughlin A. and Webb, D. (1998) 'Masculinised discourses within education and the construction of Black male identities amongst African Caribbean youth', *British Journal of Sociology of Education*, 19(1), pp. 75–87.

Wright, C., McGlaughin, A. and Webb, D. (1999) 'Gender-blind racism in the experience of schooling and identity formation', *International Journal of Inclusive Education*, 19(1), pp. 293–307.

Wun, C. (2018) 'Angered: Black and non-Black girls of color at the intersections of violence and school discipline in the United States', *Race, Ethnicity and Education*, 21(4), pp. 423–37.

Yancy, G. (2000) 'Feminism and the subtext of whiteness: Black women's experiences as a site of identity formation and contestation of whiteness', *The Western Journal of Black Studies*, 24(3), pp. 156–66.

Yosso, T. J. (2005) 'Whose culture has capital? A critical race theory discussion of community cultural wealth', *Race Ethnicity and Education*, 8(1), pp. 69–91.

Youdell, D. (2003) 'Identity traps or how Black [1] students fail: the interactions between the biographical, sub-cultural, and learner identities', *British Journal of Sociology of Education*, 24(1), pp. 3–20.

Young, I. M. (1994) 'Punishment, treatment, empowerment: three approaches to policy for pregnant addicts', *Feminist Studies*, 20, pp. 33–57.

Young, M. (1958) *The Rise of the Meritocracy 1870–2033: An Essay on Education and Society*. London: Thames and Hudson.

Zwysen, W. and Demireva, N. (2020) 'Ethnic and migrant penalties in job quality in the UK: the role of residential concentration and occupational clustering', *Journal of Ethnic and Migration Studies*, 46(1), pp. 200–21.

Zwysen, W. and Longhi, S. (2016) 'Labour market disadvantage of ethnic minority British graduates: university choice, parental background or neighbourhood?'. Available online: https://www.iser.essex.ac.uk/wp-content/uploads/files/working-papers/iser/2016-02.pdf (accessed 17 January 2023).

Zwysen, W. and Longhi, S. (2018) 'Employment and earning differences in the early career of ethnic minority British graduates: the importance of university career, parental background and area characteristics', *Journal of Ethnic and Migration Studies*, 44(1), pp. 154–72.

Zwysen, W., Stasio, V. D. and Heath, A. (2021) 'Ethnic penalties and hiring discrimination: comparing results from observational studies with field experiments in the UK', *Sociology*, 55(2), pp. 263–82.

Index